AGHORA III

THE LAW OF KARMA

AGHORA III

THE LAW OF KARMA

ROBERT E. SVOBODA

BROTHERHOOD OF LIFE PUBLISHING / SADHANA PUBLICATIONS

©1997 Robert E. Svoboda
First published in 1998

Published by
Brotherhood of Life, Inc.
110 Dartmouth SE
Albuquerque, NM 87106
ISBN 0-914732-37-4
                &
Sadhana Publications
PO Box 365
Floresville, TX 78114
ISBN 0-9656208-1-6

Cover art: from a photograph by Stuart Haman
(The Preakness, 1996, Pimlico Park, Maryland)

03 02 01 99 98 97
10 9 8 7 6 5 4 3 2 1

༄

PRINTED IN THE UNITED STATES OF AMERICA

CONTENTS

ACKNOWLEDGEMENTS

I appreciate all the advice, intentional and inadvertent, that I received from everyone who read this manuscript in its various stages of completion, including Pamela Barinoff, Hart de Fouw, Gulrukh Irani, Margaret Mahan, Roshni Panday, John Pilskog, Lynda Raby, Dr. Fred Smith, Bill Vincent, and Claudia Welch. I thank the machines, including especially my computer, that have made it so easy for me to rewrite this work so many times. I bow down to Vimalananda's Guru Maharaj, whose blessings transcend time and space to continue to preserve and protect me. Most of all, I esteem those players without whom there would have been no story: the stouthearted foals and yearlings, fillies and colts, geldings, stallions and mares that raced in Western India during my tenure there. Finally, I salute the man who moment by moment enlivened this story for me as he created it: the peerless Vimalananda.

INTRODUCTION

It is always better to live with reality, because otherwise, without fail, reality will come to live with you. —The Aghori Vimalananda

IF TO BE RELIGIOUS, in the truest sense of that much misunderstood word, is to thirst for water from reality's fountain, then to walk the spiritual path is to turn your compass toward its ever-flowing well. The organized religions, which have set up camps downstream from that spring, all provide sketchy maps that trace a single trail to the source. The one map illuminating all the tracks leading spiritwards through the diverse terrains of existence is accessible only through the world's sole dogma-free spiritual trekking agency: *Aghora*. Aghora, which literally means "unagitated," teaches *aghoris* (its practitioners) to focus and intensify their craving for reality until they learn how to transcend all that galls (the *ghora*) in life. Then no internal or external stimulus, however ordinarily 'agitating,' will be able to interrupt or interfere with their one-pointed guzzling of the nectar of being.

I obtained my orientation toward reality from my mentor, the Aghori Vimalananda, who showed little regard for organized systems of belief:

> "I have never believed in religion. Religions are all limited because they concentrate only on one aspect of truth. That is why they are always fighting amongst one another, because they all think they are in sole possession of the truth. But I say there is no end to knowledge, so there is no use in trying to confine it to one scripture or one holy book or one experience. This is why I say, when people ask what religion I follow, 'I don't believe in Sampradaya (sect), I believe in Sampradaha (incineration).' Burn down everything which is getting in the way of your perception of truth."
>
> (Robert E. Svoboda, *Aghora, At the Left Hand of God*, Brotherhood of Life, Albuquerque, 1986, p.167)

Aghoris, who do their damnedest to stand up to reality without having to lean on any reassuring doctrine or creed, strive always to do exactly what must be done at the moment when it becomes necessary. They learn what they need to know in the *smashan*, the cremation ground, worshipping death that they may die to their restrictions and be reborn into purity of perception. They accept with love everything that comes their way, knowing that whatever reality serves up is after all the meal that their karmas have created for them.

The Law of Karma, which is one of the most profound and fiendishly perplexing of reality's axioms, is the Law of Cause and Effect, the law of "as you sow, so shall you reap." The oldest of the Upanishads expresses it this way: "Truly, one becomes good by good action and bad by bad action." (*Brihadaranyaka Upanishad* III.2.13). This law is better known to most of us as Newton's Third Law of Motion: For every action there is an equal and opposite reaction. The mandate of this succinctly complex law regulates the potentially limitless implications of every small act performed by every actor within the manifested universe, meteor and microorganism alike. Everyone lives within the precincts of the ubiquitous Law of Karma, whether or not they accept its reality. Ignorance of this Law is no defense in the Court of Cause and Effect. As Lord Krishna declared in the *Shrimad Bhagavata*, "Karma is the guru; nay, it is the Supreme Lord."

Every physical or mental action you perform and with which you identify yourself as the doer becomes a karma for you and produces a reaction which you will eventually have to experience. Like everyone else, aghori or atheist, you consume at each moment of your life that portion of your karmic grain that has finally matured. Likewise, each of your self-identified actions or reactions today shapes your future by seeding yet further reactions. Every individual being is a karmic slate of coming attractions and repulsions. Though we all physically share the same Earth-space and Earth-time, our individual causative schemata create for us individual universes of experience. There are as many universes as there are beings, each locating the environment—war or peace, wealth or penury, misery or ecstasy—that each assortment of karmas requires. Since limitations of time and space prevent everything from happening in our world all at once, the Law of Karma schedules its events to occur just in time, every time, in each cosmos large and small. Every interaction between two different universes of experience creates its own karma which duly propagates its own reaction. The more strongly you identify with your karmas, the more closely your experience will conform to the reaction they promise.

Though very few people ever graduate from quotidian religion to authentic Aghora, everyone is free to make use of the truths that the world's aghoris have sucked from reality's teat. Arguably the most fundamental of these realizations is this: the essence of living with reality is to continually surrender to what is. You have already created your own personal universe with your karmas and now you must live in it. Everyone who has sown the wind will eventually reap the whirlwind. However, most people try to ride out their karmic storms by barricading themselves inside psychological houses no building however weatherproof can withstand every tornado, earthquake, flood and conflagration. Almost everyone accordingly finds himself or herself existentially homeless one day or another. Religions make good ideational roadhouses: you are free to shelter yourself under these roofs for as long as you like—or at least until a tempest blows in and causes that shelter to collapse.

A good aghori recognizes the innate flimsiness of all doctrinal thatch and knows there is no security of any kind to be had in life except the surety that each of us is going to die. Many aghoris forestall future personal derangement by emigrating to the *smashan* where they can live their lives with nothing more substantial above their heads than God's never-failing umbrella. Vimalananda, who could be one of the most sophisticated of philosophers when the mood struck him, never mistook philosophy for reality. Time and again during the more than eight years that I was with him, the faith he displayed in Nature's ultimate beneficence brought home to me the value of capitulating to what is. Time and again I was wowed when I saw how his submission to reality solved his problems. It was that awe that inspired me to write this book.

The Law of Karma, the unimaginable complexity of which has cowed the greatest of scholars, loses some of its ability to dismay when viewed through the prism of surrender. If having decided to surrender you are willing to keep surrendering, and then you surrender some more, you will simplify your personal choreography to the more managable—if still convoluted—process of resolving how, when, and what to yield. But though this simplification, properly applied, makes karma easier to work through it in no way neutralizes the Law of Karma's power to mystify and consternate. Nor does it render karma's logic any more linear, as the Mughal Emperor Akbar discovered in the following, possibly apocryphal tale:

WHATEVER GOD DOES IS FOR THE BEST

The Emperor Akbar once developed a chronic non-healing sore on his left pinky finger. It became so severe that his physicians eventually decided the whole finger would have to be amputated. The idea of losing a part of his body so upset the emperor that he sought a second opinion from his dear friend, confidant and advisor Raja Birbal. Birbal told his liege, "If the doctors say it has to come off, then it has to come off."

Akbar told Birbal, "Here I am a very religious man, who makes all the proper donations at the proper times, and still God is taking away part of my body? What have I done wrong?"

Birbal replied, "Your majesty, whatever God does is for the best."

This remark irritated Akbar to no end. He grudgingly agreed to the operation, but decided simultaneously to teach Birbal a lesson. His opportunity came some weeks later when the two of them, out hunting with a few retainers, came across a dry well. Akbar promptly commanded his men to deposit the astonished Birbal into it. When the emperor rode over on his charger and bent over the well's rim Birbal shouted up at him, "Why are you doing this?" Akbar shouted down to his friend, "Birbal, whatever God does is for the best!" Then, to let Birbal stew for a bit, he rode off alone to a different part of the forest, thinking, "Now we will see what good God can do for him there!" Birbal meanwhile sat in the well, cursing his fate and wondering what was going to happen to him next.

All at once Akbar was surrounded by a band of ruffians. This particular pack of thieves selected only rich people as their victims, first robbing them and then offering them as human sacrifices. The highwaymen accordingly stripped Akbar of all his clothes and jewelry, and the bandit chief told him, "Prepare yourself for death!"

Seeing his end approaching, Akbar began to feel Birbal's absence severely. For, Birbal had always been able to extract the emperor from otherwise hopeless situations. The gangleader meanwhile busily inspected Akbar, as he did all his prospective victims, to make sure that they carried no untoward sign. When he got down to Akbar's missing pinky he shouted in dismay, "Egad! You are not whole! You are not fit to be offered to my Goddess!" Disappointed, the thug ordered Akbar to don his clothes and ornaments quickly, and to depart thence.

Being told that he was unfit to be offered hurt Akbar's feelings and infuriated his ruler's ego. He maintained his presence of mind, though, and as he dressed he thought to himself, "Birbal was right: had I not lost my little finger I would have been dead today." He mounted his horse and rode directly back to the dry well and immediately ordered his waiting men to raise Birbal who now was wondering why the emperor had changed his mind. Akbar began by apologizing to Birbal, and then told him, "I was so upset with you I was actually considering leaving you here to die, but did I ever learn my lesson! In truth, everything God does is for best!" The emperor then narrated the whole adventure to his amazed audience.

Suddenly Akbar furrowed his brow and asked his friend, "But now tell me, Birbal, if 'whatever God does is for the best,' what good came of your being in the well?"

Birbal told him, "Isn't it obvious, Refuge of the World? If I had not been in the well I would have been captured with you, and after the bandit had rejected you I would have been next in line for sacrifice. And since I am not missing any parts of my body he would have sacrificed me!"

"The Lord is truly marvellous!" repeated Akbar distractedly, stroking his beard in wonder as they rode to the palace.

LESSONS IN SIMPLICITY

Vimalananda made "whatever God does is for the best" the refrain for many of his adventures. For, early in life reality had shown him, as it had shown to Akbar and Birbal, how wise it is to cooperate with the universal flow. Vimalananda rarely tried to force his will on the world; when he did he usually lived to regret it. He openly declared his failings as warnings to others, and openly identified in others similar foibles when he felt that such pinpointing could teach valuable lessons. For, the teaching of lessons was one of his great interests in life. So concerned was he that his listeners not misinterpret his message that he often pared his expressions down to their least common denominators. He often observed that "unnecessary detail enmeshes people in maya. The mind loves to learn; in fact, the Sanskrit word for mind is *manas*, that which measures or compares. And the power by which manas measures is *maya*." In his opinion, when you try too hard to pin down a thing's detail all you end up pinning down is its shadow, the illusion that is its maya.

Vimalananda's penchant for reduction to fundamentals has led some people to complain that he willingly distilled karma's daunting intricacy into a relatively unsophisticated theory of brute retribution. Though there is of course more to the Law of Karma that the simple formulation, "If you killed Michael last time, Michael will kill you next time," this criticism seems to me to be unjustified. Though Vimalananda did not waste his time debating karma's theoretical minutiae, he was well acquainted with them and he would speak in karmic technicalities whenever he had an audience who could appreciate them. However, he did expect that most people would misunderstand karma's precepts. I have seen little to suggest he was wrong to do so. The sad truth is that today the poor Law of Karma, which has long been centerstage in India's theater of thought, has reached its conceptual nadir in the world of post-industrial civilization. We of the late twentieth century have mutated it into a mammoth fad, a causative catchword, a universal excuse. Modern people speak glibly of those with whom they "have karma," and of it being "their karma" to get this promotion or buy that new trinket. Our philosophical carpetbaggers have even pressed it into the service of Californian used-car dealer propaganda!

Unfortunately, many Indian thinkers and systems of thought are just as guilty of willfully perverting karma's basic nature without the excuse of ignorance that our hedonistic Western lotus-eaters might plead. Reality crouches perpetually before you in India, gazing steadfastly into your face, cuffing you purposefully about the head whenever you dare to turn away from it. Indian reality's very inexorability has given innumerable seers and thinkers no alternative to devoting their lives to the contemplation of its chief cause, the Law of Karma. Indian thinkers began in early antiquity to develop and test sophisticated hypotheses of karma, inspired by the revelations that India's *rishis* (seers) gathered with their inner sight as they performed intense *sadhanas* (spiritual practices). While certain of these ancient philosophies are still vigorous, others have lost their vitality and have been mummified into systems or fossilized into dogmas by heavy-thinking hair-splitters. Some Indian texts even apply shameless, self-congratulatory sophistry to "prove" the validity of their competing versions of the Law of Karma with "one-size-fits-all" explanations.

KARMIC THEORY

The pervasive temptation to oversimplify the Law of Karma rises from the collision of the irresistible force of humanity's innate need to comprehend cause and effect with the immovable object of karma's extreme reluctance to divulge itself to humans. *Gahana karmano gatih* ("karma runs indescribably deep"): The simple Law of Cause and Effect sets into motion such a near-infinity of past, present, and future ramifications for each purposely performed act that it effectively precludes a complete description of the entire karmic slate of even one living being. When it comes to comprehending the sum of the karmas of every living being we can go nowhere at all without the systematizing help of a theoretical model.

There is no lack of competing explanations of causation, for any cogent explanation of cause and effect, including those of physics, chemistry and biology, can function as a theory of karma. We could even elucidate into a theory of karma some psychological conjecture which details how specific events in the past influence an individual's present and may shape his or her future. But scientific causation notions are crimped by their materialism, which limits cause and effect observations to the physical reactions which arise from physical actions. Psychological theories are similarly defective to the extent that they restrict themselves to the limited domain of the psyche. A truly efficacious model of karma represents a system of causation relevant to all conceivable states of existence, to anything that can be named.

Karma being so intricate, decent theories of karma are as difficult to objectively "prove" or "disprove" as is the theory of quantum mechanics. One practical difficulty with testing either theory is that cause and effect is only rarely linear. One cause sometimes produce one effect, but far more commonly a number of cooperating, concomitant causes are needed to produce a single effect. And a distinct cause quickly spirals into a cascade of interconnected effects. Also, while neither sort of theory is inherently unprovable, neither can be observed by an external observer in the manner approved by scientific materialism. Both karma theory and quantum mechanics refuse to accept that observers can exist independent of the systems they observe. Spiritual science goes so far as to take the observer's own internal universe and its states as its experimental field. For it is within that field that karma is produced and stored.

Fortunately, it is not my task to attempt to prove or disprove anything other than that my mentor, the Aghori Vimalananda, possessed his own unique vision of the Law of Karma which he tried at all times to remain aware of and act in accordance with. Though many of his favorite spiritual processes are preached by certain 'recognized' lineages of Aghoris, Vimalananda refused to denominate himself. Instead he shopped the metaphysical mall, donning and doffing assumptions until he found one that resonated with his experience, which he would then wear so long as it continued to fit. Over time he tailored for himself the philosophical garment which he wore while I knew him, apparel which was basically Tantric in design. This makes the *darshana* (philosophical vision) that underlies Tantra is a good vantage from which to survey Vimalananda's world view.

TANTRA

Among the beliefs that Vimalananda shared with orthodox Tantrics are:

♦ that the One Reality creates, underlies, and weaves together (the word tantra derives from a root meaning "to weave") the multiplicity of matter;

♦ that the Oneness of Reality is clearly perceived only when all the many varieties of personal obstructions have been removed;

♦ that these obstructions can be removed by manipulating the matter of which they are formed;

♦ that there is no substitute for a personal guru who shows you your path by gifting you a spark of living knowledge. (There is no Tantra without a guru.)

The "matter" from which we and our obstructions are created includes both the dense physical material from which our bodies are built and the thoughts, attitudes and emotions that make up our minds. Tantric practice is karmic engineering within this field of name and form, orchestration of substance and action into result. First you direct new causes against previous effects to nullify adverse influences on your awareness, then you unleash yet further actions to negate the influence of the nullifying actions.

While all Tantras—Buddhist, Jain, or Veda-inspired (like most "Hindus" Vimalananda hated the word "Hindu")—play current karmas against pre-existing karmas, the various Tantric systems disagree over the question of how cause and effect mutually relate. While the Buddhists, and certain Vedics like the *Mimamsakas*, assert that cause and effect are separate from one another, other "Hindu" traditions aver that cause and effect are implicit in one another, even though they do not simultaneously exist in our world. According to this latter evolutionary interpretation, effect is nothing but cause seen in a different state. A seed causes the effect of tree which produces seed that produces more trees; the totality of "tree" is a sum of all its states, all of which are equally real. Vimalananda espoused this second category of karmic theory, which is known in Sanskrit as *Satkaryavada*; he expressed the essence of Satkaryavada as, "Cause is effect concealed, and effect is cause revealed."

Satkaryavada has two variants: the *Sankhya* school sees occurrences in the world as actual transformations (*parinama*), while the school of Shankaracharya and his version of *Advaita Vedanta* (there are five major forms of Advaita Vedanta) sees worldly activity as nothing more than the appearance of transformation (*vivarta*). Sankhya is the philosophical foundation of much of *Ayurveda* (Indian medicine) and *Jyotish* (Indian astrology), and of most *Puranas* (compendia of spiritual traditions) and Tantras. Vimalananda followed Sankhya in asserting that the world of duality in which karma exists is as real as the condition of absolute nonduality which is the Ultimate Reality of the universe, and that each is implicit in the other: All-in-One, One-in-All.

SANKHYA

Sankhya sees the universe as a continuous evolution from a "Big Bang" event during which a sense of separateness develops within a portion of the Singularity that is the One Reality in unmanifested form. That portion of the One which sees itself as separate is known as *Prakriti* ("Nature"), and the remainder, which remembers that All is One, is referred to as *Purusha*. The Law of Karma comes into effect at the instant Prakriti separates from Purusha, the first act from which all other acts develop; it is an act motivated, it is said, by a spontaneously-arising desire within Purusha to produce individuals who might perceive and know It. Each atom of the cosmos contains within it a fragment of that Singular Consciousness Who desired to experience. Consciousness continually evolves by projecting itself into physical vehicles. Though it is minimal in "inert" matter and maximal in humans, a smidgen of consciousness and its resulting *soupçon* of self-awareness appears in even the densest matter. Human activity is valuable in the Sankhya system only to the extent that it makes us more aware of that undifferentiated Consciousness.

Prakriti forms, limits, and finitizes. After projecting from Oneness She evolves into undifferentiated transcendent intelligence (*mahat*), which partitions itself into individual parcels of *ahamkara*, the force which produces "I-ness" in an organism. Ahamkara (literally, the "I-creator"), which gives living beings that sense of individual existence without which no further differentiation could occur, possesses three *gunas*, or attributes: *sattva* (equilibrium), *rajas* (activity) and *tamas* (inertia).

Sattva is the internalizing "I," the subjective consciousness which resides within a being, revealing its environment. From *sattva*, the innate nature of the thinking mind, develop the ten senses: the five senses of perception— hearing, touch, sight, taste and smell—through which we take in from the world, and the five senses of action, though which we put out into the world:

speech (which represents all forms of communication), hands (creative action), feet (locomotion), genitals (reproduction) and anus (elimination).

Sattva is the most conscious of ahamkara's three qualities. Rajas is the externalizing "I," the active "I" always on the move, searching for something with which to self-identify. Tamas is the objectifying "I," the expression of unconscious individuality which veils consciousness as it evolves into the five objects of the senses: sound, touch, form, taste and odor. These in turn produce the Five Great Elements (*pancha mahabhutas*)—Space, Air, Fire, Water and Earth—which are the building blocks for everything that exists in the manifested universe, including the physical bodies of living beings.

The Sankhya philosophy maintains that embodied life is the functioning together as one unit in one place at one time of the Five Great Elements, the ten senses, the thinking mind, *ahamkara*, and the intellect, all enlivened by the individual soul, which is a reflection within the field of matter of the cosmic Purusha. Of these only the Purusha Itself is wholly and forever outside the field of the Law of Karma. Everything else that exists within the entirety of the aggregate of all possible universes is a form of matter, which makes it subject to action and reaction. Purusha is pure, passive, present consciousness which no more interacts with the events it perceives than a movie screen interacts with the pictures projected upon it. All forms of action, including all mental functions, are orchestrations of matter within the closed cause-and-effect system that is the Prakriti-field. All secondary distinctions (male/female, body/mind, rationality/intuition) are significant only within Prakriti and have not the least effect on Purusha-Consciousness Itself.

Sankhya is in a sense a species of materialist philosophy in that it teaches that even the most inconsiderable thought is as material as the doornail, and that all thinking, however hasty and offhand, is action which must create reaction. Even awareness itself is a karma-producing activity when your ahamkara, the force which self-identifies, identifies with it. Inaccurate perceptions encourage tighter bondage; proper perception promotes freedom.

As *ahamkara* solidifies your individual identity it also solidifies your attachments to your previous karmas and your current actions. All the actions you have performed and with which your ego self-identified act as seeds for karmic reactions, each of which will take its own time to mature and bear fruit. *Ahamkara* plants its seeds in the ethereal nursery known as the *karana sharira* (causal body). The karmic seeds which have collected in the causal body lie quiescent until it is time for them to sprout. Once they sprout their course becomes predestined. As they mature they produce fruit which filters down into your *sukshma sharira* (astral body). Each karma induces your astral body (which is composed of your conscious, subconscious, and unconscious minds) to induce your *sthula sharira* (physical body) to put yourself into the proper place and time to enjoy the pleasant or unpleasant results of your past actions. In general, then, your physical body reflects the effects of your past actions while your astral body mirrors your present-day existence. Your causal body is your future; it determines how and where you will continue your evolution.

FOUR KARMIC CATEGORIES

Although the cause-and-effect relationship is essentially an indivisible whole we can for easier comprehension partition it into four categories: *Sanchita, Prarabdha, Kriyamana,* and *Agama. Sanchita* ("heaped together") *Karma* is the sum of all past actions, known and unknown, that appear in your causal body nursery; it is Sanchita Karma that prompts some Indians to claim that the ways of karma are unfathomable. "Unknown" actions include those performed in past lives. *Prarabdha* ("set in motion") *Karma* is that portion of Sanchita Karma which is ready to be experienced by an individual during this lifetime, the fruits which have ripened and are ready to be consumed.

Sanchita and Prarabdha Karmas are in a sense "destined," or "fated" as the product of past actions that have matured. However, they are truly inevitable only to the extent that they are not modified by *Kriyamana* ("being made") *Karma* or *Agami* ("coming, arriving") *Karma.* Agami Karma is our capacity to envision future actions, while Kriyamana Karma is what we do at any moment with our capacity to will and to create. You cannot destroy your past, but neither need you permit your past to manipulate you like a puppet, since you can alter your future by acting in your present. Kriyamana Karma can also include Agami Karma, and Kriyamana Karma and Agami Karma can together be termed *Vartamana* ("current, living") Karma. Each of these types can be *arabdha* ("begun, undertaken") or *anarabdha* ("not commenced, dormant"). A famous agricultural analogy to this system of karmic classification equates karma with rice. This makes Sanchita Karma the already grown rice that has been harvested and stored in the granary. Prarabdha Karma is the small portion of that stored rice that has been removed from storage, husked, and readied for cooking and eating. Kriyamana Karma is the rice that is now being planted in the field to produce a future crop.

THREE KARMIC INTENSITIES

Though some texts use the Sanskrit words *karma* and *daiva* (fate) inter-changeably, fate and karma are not synonymous. The human condition always arises from the dynamic coalition of fate and free will, not by either on its own. No one is ruled only by fate, as some Indians insist, and no one's life is wholly malleable by free will, as some New Agers claim. How much Agama and Kriya-mana effort you will need to modify your fate will depend on how intense is the Prarabdha Karma in that area of your life and (to a reduced extent) in the lives of all those other beings with whom you share collective karma: your family, extended family, friends, neighbors, fellow countrypersons, nation and planet.

Tradition distinguishes three degrees of intensity in Prarabdha Karma. These may apply to one, many, or all areas of your life: *dridha, dridha-adridha,* and *adridha. Dridha* ("fixed") *Karmas* are so intense they are non-changeable. They create those seemingly "fated" events, pleasurable and painful, that either occur despite all our efforts to avoid them or fail to take place despite all our efforts to create them. The good or bad results produced by *Dridha-Adridha* ("fixed-unfixed") *Karmas* can be changed by anyone who is willing to apply the concentrated creative will needed to change them; in the absence of any sustained effort their predicted results will appear. *Adridha* ("unfixed") *Karmas* are so easily altered that you may do more or less what you please (within reason) in these areas of your life.

This current life of yours is fundamentally a swim across the river of your Prarabdha Karma. If your Prarabdha current is dridha, it is likely to over-power you and sweep you away, even if you are a strong swimmer. If you and your current are of roughly equal strength, you will face a dridha-adridha sit-uation, and will probably make it across your river if you swim like the devil. When the current is weak your karmas are adridha, and you are unlikely to be imperiled even if you swim poorly. Free will operates here as elsewhere with each of your decisions: where and when to enter the river, how fast to set your pace, what stroke to use. Each act of free will adds to your eventual fate. If you use up your free will early on—if you exhaust yourself just before you reach the rapids—you may find that you have nothing remaining at that cru-cial moment when you need your reserves to try to "cheat" your fate.

In the world of finance, non-callable investments pay back their principal and fixed-term debt instruments require repayment at term only, not before. Until you invest, your money is as fluid and free as your will, but at the mo-ment you invest you lock yourself into a result that has become "fated." Banks may fail, technologies may innovate, interest rates may skyrocket, markets may crash, but your eventual payoff or payment is locked in. The result is now effectively "destined" unless you can use your free will to do something with these investments or loans during their terms. You will alter your fiscal destiny if you can sell your investments or create derivatives from them, or if you can pay off your higher-interest loan with one bearing a lower rate of interest. Whether or not you will be able to make such alterations will depend on the inherent value of the investment or debt, prevailing market and general economic conditions, and related factors. How possible or impossible it is for you to make such changes, i.e. how fixed or unfixed your monetary destiny is, is an expression of the degree of karmic intensity in your life in the pecuniary sphere.

Similar degrees of karmic intensity apply to every realm of your existence. Adridha health karmas, for instance, produce diseases which run their course and disappear on their own (unless you use your free will to do things to reinforce them). Dridha-adridha health karmas may produce chronic illnesses which can usually be controlled with the help of intensive therapies, but will continue to worsen if neglected. Dridha karmas in the health realm tend to produce conditions which refuse to respond even to the most heroic treatments.

Probably the most important of the karmic intensity factors is self-awareness, the force that allows you to self-identify with your actions. The more you are self-aware, the more effectively individual you can be. Humans, who appear to possess more self-awareness than do most other lifeforms, are better able to self-identify with their actions, consciously, intently, and passionately. This allows us to sow and reap more than other sentient beings can.

REINCARNATION

The karmas that you perform in dizzying number—think of all the things you accomplish in the space of an hour—grow and mature at different rates, making one lifetime insufficient for you to experience all their effects (unless you happen to be immortal). Karmic theory therefore proposes that beings die and are again reborn—reincarnated—to continue working out pending reactions. What transmigrates, of course, is Prakriti and the principles which devolve from Her. Purusha, Who is eternally free, is never bound to or released from a body. Purusha's sole pastime is to silently observe as the mass of karmas that have accumulated in your causal body steers you from life to life, permitting you to re-interact with those who helped you to create the karmic bed in which you lie. Each time you are ready to be reborn your Prarabdha Karmas forge for you a mind and body and a milieu in which they will live. Your progress in each life is fertilized and watered by the karmic reactions that support you and is interfered with by karmas that act against your interests. Finally your terminating karmas catch up with you and kill you. The thought you think at the moment of death—a thought which will reflect either the force of the strongest karmas you performed during that lifetime, or your state of mind as you lie dying, or the force of your habits, or whatever reaction has just matured to join your karmic queue—sets you up for your next birth.

Reincarnation is so handy a concept that it has been an integral part of almost all Indian philosophies since ancient times. Implied in the Vedas themselves, its earliest clear formulations appear in the *Brihadaranyaka*, *Chandogya* and *Svetasvatara Upanishads*. By the time of the *Bhagavad Gita* reincarnation has become one of Indian thought's central concepts. The stories in the *Jataka Tales*, for example, are Gautama Buddha's experiences in previous existences which he used to teach his disciples.

Reincarnation was used in Ayurveda to explain incurable diseases, congenital deficiencies, and other inborn physical, economic and social handicaps. Ayurveda generally tried to put a positive spin on the experience by advising sufferers (advice is a karma) to be of good cheer and use their free will to try to improve their health now in expectation of an improved physique next time around. Ancient India's hegemonistic priests used this same doctrine of karma as a negative model to try to keep the majority of the common people in subordinate social positions. The priests advised the peasants that their future living conditions would improve if they would avoid rocking the karmic boat in the present, and promised the lower castes a happier future for themselves if they would pay priests to perform purifying rituals on their behalf.

Venal priests and their willingness to sell karmic indulgences were one reason that Vimalananda hated organized religions. Another reason was their tendency to confuse karma with sin. While sin is a violation of the rules of your society, religion or affinity group, karma is an innate property of the universe. If your religion enjoins you to, say, slaughter an infidel, then failing to do so will be a karma (to refuse to act is also an action) that may be a sin. By doing so you are likely to escape sin and will gain some good karma for living up to your cultural responsibilities, but you will also incur the probably bad karma involved in taking a life. The Vedas and Tantras, which teach that black magic is dangerous, unwise and productive of evil karma, also indicate that you may resort to it when you find yourself in that condition of extremity when it alone may save you or those who depend on you. Your distress will not exempt you from the karma involved, but it will at least ensure that you performed it for a worthy cause.

DHARMA

Evil karma is evil for you because it sets you up today for a fall tomorrow. As one Tamil woman put it, karma means that "we are punished not *for* our actions, but *by* our actions." (quoted in O'Flaherty, p. 37) A predator in one birth needs to return as prey, to earn both the points of view needed to round out the whole experience. But evil karma did not become sin until the lawgivers made it into sin. Until then it was *adharma* ("against dharma"), a state which encompasses all acts that impede or pervert the current of your existence. *Dharma*, which some people mistranslate as "duty," others as "religion," and yet others as "vocation," is really "doing what you are born to do." "Conforming to your dharma" means following that path through life and performing those actions that best agree with you as an individual in the context of the environment in which you exist. Dharma is the universal law which makes a thing what it is. The dharma of the moon to shine, of volcanoes to erupt, of boats to float, and of hyenas to laugh. Horses run, whinny, and toss their manes because it is their dharma to do so, not because they feel any moral obligation in that direction. Adharma is neither "sin" nor "evil"; it is simply a "non-conformity" with the nature of things, a crime against harmony.

Plants, animals, minerals, and the things constructed for them possess unambiguous dharmas to the extent that they exist independent of human society. Human dharma is more equivocal. It involves aligning the dharma of an individual's personal Prarabdha Karmas with the consensus dharma constructed by the society into which he or she was hatched. To effectively follow your dharma as a individual human you need to know how much you must conform to the demands of your community. Between the two poles of human adharma—an all-consuming sociopathic disregard for human association and a fanatical subsuming of self into group—lies a catwalk of dharma above a swamp of adharmic dissonance. One false step in either direction from this "straight and narrow path" and you plop into adharmic muck, either by violating the tenets of your personal consonance or by transgressing the "rules" of rapport that someone else has set.

Everyone's road to reality is personalized, for one person's dharma is another person's adharma. Dharma precedes karma. For, actions which conform to your dharma are as likely to give you good reactions as actions which disagree with your dharma are likely to yield disgreeable results. Humans are social animals: most people find their paths to dharma within the context of a society. However, there are a few whose dharma it is to live apart. The dharma of such "renunciates" is to be dead to the world. Any "renunciate" who gets involved in politics (some do in India) thus commits a crime against dharma. While it is against almost everyone's dharma to live in the smashan, Aghoris find it agreeable to do so because it is their dharma to live there. A good aghori is always fanatically intent on trying to act in harmony with his personal dharma.

The concept of "natural" dharma prevailed in India until the day the law-givers decided to equate dharma with religion. Dharma now shifted from an innate nature—knowable by the introspective—to an external, moralistic, socialized construct maintained by lawgivers. The early lawgivers were probably looking to simplify life for their outer-directed flock by creating rules of dharma to follow. For, it is impractical for most individuals to know cause and effect in detail. But these rules deteriorated into dogma, and sin came to be defined as violations of these rules.

The *Manu Smriti*, a famous *Dharmasastra* (treatise on dharma in its incarnation as Hindu religious law), speaks of karma but focuses on sin when it assumes rebirth to be necessary to complete the results of many actions. The text, which sees reincarnation as an action's first and most important karmic consequence, also advises the prompt performance of penance in hope of modifying the results of these sins. It details several sorts of rebirths, expected for specific crimes or states of being, according to five different karmic payback systems and a number of miscellaneous rules. Thieves are for example reborn as a variety of animals, and those who fail in their specific caste duties descend into the wombs of the hungry ghosts (*pretas*). Theft from a Brahmana (member of the priestly caste) is punishable by many years in terrible hells, after which the opportunity to take a degraded incarnation will finally arise. The ungrateful wife returns as a jackal (there is no mention of any punishment for a husband's lack of gratitude).

Though many people today are cheerily convinced that once you become human you will always return to earth as a human, most authorities in ancient India concluded with Manu that you may well descend the evolutionary path before you again ascend it. The Buddha Himself offered this discouraging analogy: A blind turtle who lives at the bottom of a vast ocean surfaces only once each century. On the surface of that ocean sits a storm-tossed ring of wood. You are as likely to be reborn as a human as the turtle is likely to stick his head precisely through that ring of wood when he rises next.

KARMA'S MECHANISM

The Dharmasastras are so ardent to present their retaliatory systems that they pay little attention to another pressing question, viz. the technique by which karma is stored and rebirth occurs. Patanjali's Yoga system teaches that each intentional act creates a karmic residue (*karmashaya*) which will conform either to dharma or adharma. Each residue has various *samskaras* ("dispositional traces") which produce numerous results, including two types of *vasanas* ("residual impressions"). While one sort of vasana stores the memory of the act, the other produces *kleshas* ("afflictions"). These usually-erroneous conceptions cause people to remain in bondage to their karmas by spurring them to create yet further karmic residues. Even the memory of a partial incarnation can fasten you more firmly to error if you cannot digest the experiences you had therein—which is why Nature ordinarily will not permit you to remember your past lives until you are in no danger of being overwhelmed by them.

When a person dies her *jiva* (the sum of her unactivated karmic residues and their attached samskaras and vasanas, gathered together within her awareness field) prepares for rebirth. The residues determine *jati* (the kind of body, e.g. tiger or human), *ayus* (lifespan), and the varieties of *bhoga* (pleasure or pain) that that new body will enjoy during its life as each residue matures (*vipaka*) to give its fruit. The nature of our karmic fruit depends substantially on how we use ahamkara to identify with our actions, which depends in turn on the relative balance of the Three Gunas in our personalities.

Until a human can completely self-identify with the Absolute Purusha, his or her human's awareness is itself a substance, a form of matter that possesses gunas. This matter interacts with other forms of matter either to bind pure consciousness more firmly to inaccurate perception or to release it somewhat, that it may shine freely forth by prying apart those bindings. When sattva predominates a person performs karmas without becoming attached to their results. People who act from passion, blinded by desires, evince a predominance of rajas, while tamas predominates in those who act without thinking. Only those whose minds are fixed solely on the Absolute remain untouched by the Three Gunas. In the words of that greatest of Puranas, the *Shrimad Bhagavata*, "The *shastra* (text) that one studies, the water one uses, the people one consorts with, the place where one is habitually found, the time of day that one favors, the karma one performs, the sacrament that one receives, the object of one's contemplation, the mantra that one is initiated into, the kind of purification that one practices—these influence one's gunas."

The images among which we exist are formed when guna pattern gets multiplied by vasana-produced memories and their associated conceptions, erroneous or otherwise. Images can be weak or strong, spiritual or mundane, altruistic or selfish, creative or destructive, intellectual or emotional, sensual or chaste. Each of us continually spawns thought forms as we attract the thought forms of others. Images of similar nature resonate with and reinforce one another according to the universal law of attraction. Like continues increasing like until the force of an image becomes so strong that its pressure on the mind can no longer be withstood. When it projects, the image's owner acts out the image in the "real" world. People can be possessed by their own images, by those of their families (fortified by shared genetics), by those that assemble in the psychic atmosphere of an individual's familial, local, and national environments, or by combinations of all the above. Images can become so strong that they propagate themselves from generation to generation; indeed, we see this daily in locales like the Balkans and the Middle East.

Once an image is created it cannot be destroyed; its physical representations will disintegrate, its energy can dissipate or bleed away, but its name and form will not pass away until the universe passes away. Though most modern people think of material things as real, even though they can be destroyed in a matter of moments, it is imagination, memory, and the other creations of the mind that are really real. Everything that has ever been thought, imagined, or done has left its mark on the cosmos, and can be recalled to awareness by anyone who knows how to recall it. Previous incarnations are also subject to recall, although there is no guarantee that what you may recall is what "really" happened to you. Your "remembered" incarnations might equally well be images from your imagination, images from someone else's imagination, images from the "lives" of archetypal beings, or experiences of an ancestor's incarnations.

A superb example of the mysterious relationship between self-identification and incarnation appears in the compendium known as the *Yoga Vasistha*. A certain spiritual aspirant had by dint of meditation so purified his mind that he gained the power to materialize his thoughts. One day when he was tired of meditating he imagined himself to be an illiterate fellow—which he instantly became. This "dream-being," who felt he had the name of Jivata, wandered about in his dream world until one day he got drunk and slept. While sleeping Jivata dreamt he was a Brahmana, who dreamt he was a king, who dreamt he was an emperor, who dreamt of being an *apsaras* (celestial dancing damsel), who dreamt of being a deer, who dreamt of being a creeper, who envisioned itself as a bee, who began to drink the nectar from the creeper's own flowers. The bee saw an elephant on which it contemplated, becoming thereby an elephant, which was captured by a king. When the elephant saw a hive of bees it remembered its past birth and became a bee, which became a creeper, which became a swan. While the seeker was meditating on the swan, death collected him, and his consciousness entered the swan's body. When that swan beheld *Rudra* (the god of death and transformation) it thought, "I am Rudra," and became Rudra, who went to the abode of Rudra, and recognized what had occurred.

Rudra proceeded to where the aspirant's body lay and revived him, at which point the seeker saw that he was in fact Rudra and remembered all that had happened. When the pair revived Jivata they all three realized that they were in reality one only. When they awakened the Brahmana and the king and the swan, and all the others, they all grasped the truth that they were all the same, and were all Rudra. Then the Rudra, Who knew fully that He was Rudra, sent the rest of them all back to the world to play out their parts in the grand drama of maya until they returned to Him at the end of their apparently individual existence.

RNANUBANDHANA

One persistent question about reincarnation's grand design is, "How exactly does that jiva get into the body of the plant, animal or human through whose womb it will be reborn?" Probably the most ancient explicit explanation of transmigration from the Vedic period appears as the "five-fire doctrine" (*panchagnividya*). According to this scheme, the properly propitiated souls of the dead proceed to the sphere of the moon where they eventually become *soma* (lunar nectar). They then fall to earth as rain, which produces food, which when eaten by humans produces semen, which finally becomes another human being. This scenario is rather hazy, however, on how one's bad and good actions influence the process and its results and how the jiva locates the right raindrop that will land on the proper plant that will enter the appropriate parent for it. Presumably it has something to do with the universal law of attraction.

Vimalananda, who was not concerned about which raindrop you may have boarded on your journey here, did believe that jivas find their parents via the law of attraction. Karmas are not performed in a vacuum; performed action always has an object, however obscure. Energy (*shakti*) of all kinds flows only when it has some destination to flow to, just as electrical energy flows only when a circuit is created. Your action creates a relationship with its object, be it of dense or subtle matter. Even something so seemingly insubstantial as a thought can act as an action's object. Vimalananda called the relationship thus created *rnanubandhana* ("binding karmic debt"). The energy flux that your action initiates creates a debt (*rna*) that is payable to you if you sent energy to your object, and that you must pay if you extracted something from that object. Every action creates another "tie that binds," another band that will draw you back toward that object so that you can square up your karmic account when that residue matures.

Blessings and curses bind you to whatever you have blessed or cursed; if they are strong enough they will take on lives of their own, and pursue you. Thought rnanubandhanas, which create obsessions when they draw their creators to them, are equally adhesive. Throughout your life you will be drawn to the people, places and things with whom you have rnanubandhanas, and when you are ready to be reborn you will be drawn "automatically," as it were, to those parents with whom you have some karmic affinity, with whom sufficient rna-bonds have accumulated.

If karmas were numerical quanities that could be added and subtracted, life would become easy and predictable. All you would need to square up a karmic account would be to total the outstanding karmic credits and debits and then pay them off or be paid off accordingly all at once. But this it is not feasible since each significant residue among the astronomical numbers of karmas that we set in motion and then quickly forget about must be settled separately. The fate that is built into your rnanubandhanas will continue to draw you into those situations in which your karmic residues can work themselves out, and you will still be able to use your free will to try to alter or negate the vasanas that they create. These transactions will continue indefinitely, birth after birth, until you exhaust your casual body's stock of karmic residues.

KARMIC TRANSFERS

While there seems to be no theoretical limit to an individual's capacity to self-identify with new substances, actions, and situations, the question of transferring the karmic residues of already self-identified action from one being to another is a little muddier. Some texts refuse to accept that one person might experience the results of another person's actions, while other texts insist that this must be so. Vimalananda's position was that both situations can occur. Since no one can become so subsumed into communal reality that all individuality is irrevocably lost, no one in our world becomes wholly independent until he or she is freed of all need to consume all nourishment from the environment. What makes it impossible to completely dissect an individual's karma from that of his or her community is the fact that each person exists in a fluid continuum between two opposing poles:

community benefit — individual benefit
transactional life — philosophical life
this world — other world
householder — renouncer
creation — dissolution
pravritti — *nivritti*
dharma — *moksha*

The Vedas placed great weight on genetics and community; they assumed outright that the members of a family or clan share with one another both their individually-performed karmas and those performed in concert. Some later texts, however, taught that an individual's karma is separate and unsharable; they therefore prohibit karmic transfer: "A man reaps that at that age, whether infancy, youth or old age, at which he had sowed it in his previous birth.... A man gets in life what he is fated to get, and even a god cannot make it otherwise." (*Garuda Purana*, p. 68).

Early Buddhism took an individualist approach: "Each being must be an island unto himself, working out his own salvation.... Meritorious action well laid up is a treasure 'not shared with others.'" (McDermott, p. 190). Mahayana Buddhism, though, returns to a community-based view of karma with its *Bodhisattva ideal*. A Bodhisattva resolves to take on the burden of all suffering and to offer his store of merit to others. Those who have the ability naturally produce and donate good karma; those who need it receive and enjoy it. Later Hindu traditions, particularly those of the *bhakti* (devotion) sects, also swung back from rugged karmic individualism towards shared karmic experience.

Renouncers and householders both have their place in the world. Renouncers cannot exist without householders to feed, clothe and shelter them. However, a culture becomes totally and unattractively materialistic if it is composed wholly of householders. Back and forth, to and fro, Indian philosophers have argued the advantages and disadvantages of sharing your karma with others. Living in a community requires attention to its dharma as well as your own; it requires interactions with other community members in which you will be exposed to the karmic residues of others, and vice versa.

Food and sex are two salient ways through which karma can be shared. The *Manu Smriti* (6.58) mentions that even a *jivanmukta* (someone who has been liberated while still alive from the need for rebirth) can become "bound with the fetters of the *samsara* (the universe of manifested existence)" by accepting food from the wrong hand. A wife's sexual loyalty is said to be integral to her husband's karma. But while a chaste wife can compensate for her husband's sins, a man can also be destroyed by his wife's concupiscence.

Consanguineous ties are of immense significance. One rule of thumb in Jyotish states that from birth until age seven a child mainly experiences the results of her mother's karmas, and from age seven to fourteen, her father's karmas. Only after age fourteen (and puberty) does she come into her own, karmically. Transfer of merit within families appears in many Vedic rituals, including the *pinda* offering, which is made to appease potentially angry or harmful ancestors. Karmas can also be resssigned in the opposite direction; the *Kausitaki Upanishad* (II.15) describes how a son inherits his dying father's karma.

PRAVRITTI AND NIVRITTI

All these swaps promote *pravritti* (further development of worldly entanglements and future reincarnation) if the exchangers identify themselves with their exchanges. Minimizing swaps and/or failing to identify with them promotes *nivritti* (withdrawal from the world of action). Vimalananda preferred nivritti, but not at the expense of neglecting to pay off any residual rnanubandhanas. Though there is a general perception that Indians as a people are otherworldly (this slant is noisily preached now in certain Indian spiritual circles), it was not always thus. The disdain for the world of matter, regularly preached by followers of Shankaracharya's impersonal Vedanta, is even today less predominant a world view among Indians than is belief in the efficacy of worshipping a loving, personal god who can help us both in the here and now and in the hereafter.

Pravritti and nivritti both date from the Vedas, which advise the performance of all manner of sacrifices for the achievement of all manner of specific ends both in this world and the next. For many centuries, however, most of those who sought to follow the path toward nivritti which culminates in *moksha* (cessation of the necessity for rebirth) have tried to isolate themselves from mundane community and the karmic transactions community inevitably arouses. By renouncing the world such people become *sannyasins*. *Sannyas* literally means "coma," so a *sannyasin* is (or should be) literally "comatose" to the world. Sannyasins try to minimize the actions of their many bodily and mental functions as they retreat from their worldly obligations. Until they become enlightened, however, the "spiritually comatose" retain their individual causal bodies and karmic slates. Moreover, they continue to share karmas with their fellow sect members, to the extent that they imbibe ascetic power and spiritual energy (*tapas* and *tejas*) from their gurus and enjoy the aid and comfort of their fellow disciples.

Clear-thinking people may be disheartened and disgusted by the implications of the karmas we perform for self-preservation, including our dogged rape of Nature. These karmas stretch from the destruction of the wilderness to the swindling of our domesticated plants and animals to work for us for slave wages under savage conditions. We breed and propagate these species only to gobble them down with very little benefit to them or to the Nature Who is their Mother. These karmas teach us humans in turn to gull one another: "Fraud was at the basis of our present-day agricultural and stock-farming industries. Among humans exchange took the form of mutual deceit—the start of which was buying and selling. Therefore, the basis of trade is fraud, trickery and deceit. . . . There is no profit without a type of fraud. A totally fair exchange leaves you with a profit of zero." (Engler and Hayashi, p. 124-5)

Running away from a duplicitous human society is however rarely an effective strategy. The demoralized usually act dispiritedly, and usually collect dispirited results. The renunciation that is of value happens automatically, whenever the karmas that detain you in your world have become depleted. As Vimalananda iterated and reiterated, "If you have to think about renouncing the world you are not ready to do so. When your interest in worldly activities drops away by itself you will automatically move onto the path of nivritti, and only then will you be successful in following that path. Until then there will be no end to karma in this lifetime."

HUMAN SACRIFICE

Diligent research into the nature of cause and effect permitted the seers of the Vedas, who well understood the necessity of action in life, to evolve methods through which they could achieve specific ends through the willful performance of specific karmas. These methods, called *yaga* or *yajna* in Sanskrit and referred to in English as "sacrifices," feed and satisfy deities and other ethereal beings with *prana* (life force) transported to them via the fragrance of the smoke from the burnt offerings of consecrated plants or animals. Sacrifice is a prominent feature in many ancient religions, including Judaism, and continue to be performed in India today (all but a few of these are however highly simplified versions overseen by priests who no longer understand what they are doing). Sincere sacrificers avoid fraud by ensuring that the beings they sacrifice receive some benefits as well. When a Vedic ritual is properly performed, the evil karma that Vedic sacrificer incurs by killing his victims is negated by the good karma for all that the ritual engenders.

While goats, horses, bulls, alcoholic beverages, and the juice of the *soma* plant have all been used in Vedic sacrificial ritual, the archetypal victim is a human. At the beginning of its explanation of the Agnichayana sacrifice, for example, the Vedic text known as the *Shatapatha Brahmana* states clearly that a human is the best sacrifice of all. Another text provides a mantra to be used when you accept a severed human head. No one knows how often humans were offered in Vedic sacrificial rituals—or whether they ever were—but there is little doubt that human sacrifice did occur in ancient India. We find evidence in works like the *Mahabharata*, which relates the story of King Somaka, who was so worried that his only son might die that he had the boy sacrificed in order that all one hundred of his wives might conceive. The Jataka Tale called "The Folly of Garrulity" describes a human sacrifice performed to protect a city gate. In the *Simhasana Dvatrimshati* ("Thirty-Two Tales of the Lion Throne") the semi-mythical King Vikramaditya barely escapes becoming a victim himself. In historical times the Thugs made human sacrifice their religion and isolated cases continue to come to light in India even now.

SELF-SACRIFICE

Though Vedic sacrificers have not used human victims for many centuries, sacrificial symbolism continues to pervade much of Hindu ritual. The coconut, for example, is a particularly auspicious fruit because it so well represents the human head, with its three eyes in a hard skull-like shell which contains a brain-like flesh and a quantity of liquid that represents the blood, hormones, cerebro-spinal fluid and other "juices" contained in a human head. Today's people offer coconuts in lieu of severed heads on occasions such as the full moon during August, when the citizens of Bombay go down to the sea with their coconuts to attempt to appease the rain gods and calm the monsoon's frenzy.

The head has long been regarded in India as the most important part of the body. In it concentrates the power that is the excellence of existence, the essence of the universe. The head is the seat of the personality and therefore karma; before the body can act to perform the karma the head must direct it to act. It is by the head that we know the body. The essence of a sacrifice is in its "head," the means by which the karma of recreating harmony in both the internal and external universes is performed. The more symbolic our sacrifice becomes, the less karma we need to perform; we can take the head, the chief, essential, important element, and leave the rest. To emphasize the literal in sacrifice is to maximize its karma, which limits its potential benefits. Some modern people are beginning to suggest that it is generally appropriate to worship God or the Goddess with sex, alcohol, and meat, and that blood sacrifices should be performed because they are effective means of achieving our desires. Though such rituals can indeed be effective they are rarely skillful means since for they are karmically expensive and commonly lead to intoxication and addiction instead of worship. The astral aura they generate is also likely to strengthen the will of people like the pedophiles and pushers who are already greedily consuming the flesh of the throwaway children whom they "sacrifice."

It is true that Aghoris worship with sex, alcohol, meat, and sometimes human sacrifice, but solely for the purpose of working off their leftover rnanubandhanas, not for creating new ones. They do so with full awareness of what can happen to them if they fall into self-identifications with these actions. While the Law of Karma may be temporarily transcended it can no more be nullified than the law of gravity can be negated. An airplane continues to fly in violation of gravity for only so long as its engines continue to whir. Aghoris who complete their flights successfully can get from place to place very quickly and get much of their rnanubandhana work done, but if their engines should stop in mid-air down they will drop. If they do crash they know they have themselves alone to blame.

Aghoris prefer to offer their own blood in sacrifice; they ask themselves, "If my Beloved requires prana, why should it not be mine?" In this they follow the lead of the Veda's themselves. One of the world's handful of remaining Vedacharyas is Agnihotram Ramanujan Tatacharya whose mastery of Vedic ritual and text is truly dazzling. When last we met he reported to me that there is a passage in the Taittiriya Samhita of the Yajur Veda which states that originally all sacrifice was of the sacrificer's own flesh. These first sacrificers did not expect other animals or humans to contribute on their behalf; only after they lost their own grit did they begin to settle for substitutes. A good Aghori even today accepts no substitutes.

Blood's chief task is the transport of prana, and the offering of blood to a deity is fundamentally the offering of that being's prana. Vimalananda, who always valued refinement over crudity, generally preferred to use sacrificial techniques that were subtler, and less messy, than the literal spilling of gore. This is the sort of penance the Tantras intend when they speak of *antaryaga* ("internal sacrificial rites"). The *Kaushitaki Upanishad* provides an example of antaryaga in its description of "inner *agnihotra*." Agnihotra usually refers to worship of an external sacred fire, but the inner *agnihotra* involves the of-fering of breath (another transporter of prana) as an oblation in speech when you speak, and the offering of speech as an oblation in breath when you fall silent. In this way you can offer oblations continually as long as you continue to breathe, using your body as your sacrificial altar and your life itself as your sacrifice.

A good aghori masters the art of self-sacrifice. Good aghoris fiercely love to consummate that action within themselves and refuse to forgo it even for a moment. Instead they take the smashan with them wherever they go, even to the racecourse, that their oblations need never be interrupted. What is our world, after all, but one big smashan in which each of us is already burning? For a sincere Aghori life in the "internal smashan" is no metaphor; sincere Aghoris make the smashan real for them. This is a subjective, internal reality, a reality that is more real to them than is the maya outside themselves. Agho-ris know that all that is not pure, unalloyed Consciousness is filth. Because they do not discriminate between one variety of filth and another, they liter-ally come to see no reason to discriminate between feces and fruit! Instead they ignore everything except their own pertinacity to bring themselves again and again to the melting point, willingly consuming their own filth when need be, the dung becoming ambrosial when it is transmuted in the furnaces of their longing.

Emotional muck, which is usually worse than the physical variety, deserves thorough immolation. The nineteenth verse of the *Karpuradi Stotra*, a hymn to Kali, states that the Goddess delights in receiving in sacrifice the flesh of goat, buffalo, cat, sheep, camel and man. Though the greedy for meat use this and similar textual references to sanction animal slaughter, what an aspirant really needs to sacrifice is his lust (the goat), anger (buffalo), greed (cat), stu-pefaction due to delusion (sheep), envy (camel), and pride and infatuation with worldly things (man). These thick cords that yoked us to the world must be severed if we are to become truly independent (*sva-tantra*). Until these limitations are sacrificed the seeker is himself no better than an animal—which is why the Tantras call such people *pashus* (animals).

OFF WITH YOUR HEAD!

You can butcher all your emotional attachments in one fell swoop if you are willing to part with your head, which will be for you more of a cesspit of toxins than a reservoir of excellent essence so long as it is polluted with your personal limitations. Severing your head can help you cast off your attachment to your individual, finite self, for at the moment you perform the karma of this surrender you sacrifice a bit of your imagined control over your life and offer some of your prana to the divine. This allows divinity access into you; "sacrifice," after all, literally means "to make sacred." The Maharashtrian poet-saint Tukaram said it right:

> If we want to enjoy God, we should lop off our head from our body and hold it in our hands.
> When the body has been sacrificed to god, says Tuka, all worship has been accomplished.
> (*Tukaaraama Gaathaa* 3414, 3171)

Tukaram speaks here of dissevering one's awareness (the head) from all distortions provoked by any kind of physical, mental, or other material limitations (the body). Though the ideal head offering would extinguish all limitations at once, for most of us a single donation will not suffice. Most of us are so attached to our self-definitions that we need to chop off and offer our heads daily, internally. The force of self-identification is called *ahamkara* so long as it self-identifies with the actions of the body and mind into which it was born, a self-identification which monopolizes a great deal of energy. When ahamkara begins to release its self-identification with the limited, temporary personality that portion of energy which is freed is called *Kundalini*. The only difference between ahamkara and *Kundalini* is the object with which they self-identify. Until Kundalini is completely awakened ahamkara will continue to act in large part as if it were the self, and whatever you do will continue to be motivated by your own self-importance and attachment to your sense of difference from the rest of the world. As you chop your awareness and prana free of ahamkara's grasp, you free them to identify with something new.

When you act you make use of your free will; to react is to conform to your "fated" karmas. If you really want to transform yourself you will have to take charge of your reactions and learn how, when, and where to act. Free will is the ability to choose to remember that we sent our trains of karma in motion and that we can by dint of repeated action eventually change the direction of that train. Your current karmas can be negated at any moment, but only if your present force of intention is equal to the force you used to create those karmas. The key to creating and solidifying new samskaras that will negate your old ones is to repeat your new actions so often and so intently that nothing can stand in their way.

If anything that you do in total selflessness tends to move you in the direction of nivritti, every karma you perform with a desire for a result is likely to lead you further into pravritti. There is no real advantage in renouncing participation in the world to which you belong until you are ready to give up self-identifying with your actions. Until ahamkara has been transformed into Kundalini you will just continue creating new rnanubandhanas wherever you go. Even the desire to make karmic amends may be fraught with peril, for fighting against your residues tends to create yet more residues, and a conscious effort to repay all your rnas may make you run amok. If you find the thought of rebirth distasteful you will do well to learn how to act appropriately, according to your dharma, in a state of *karmasamya* ("active balance") and refuse to self-identify with the performance of your duties. By reflecting on the transitory nature of existence, you can live in your family and society unfettered, like a chance guest, and forsake your attraction to the sense objects that make up your world. All bondage disappears as soon as you relinquish the idea of "me" and "mine" in all things: "Realize, then, that smell and taste have to be given up! They are nothing but a steady flow of craving and desires! How, thus liberated, could you ever think of the fishmonger's shop as stinking?" (Kohn, p. 241)

TYAGA

All Vedic rituals contain three basic elements: *dravya*, the material that is offered; *devata*, the deity to whom it is offered; and *tyaga*, the renunciation of the fruits of the ritual in favor of the deity. Tyaga is the essence of sacrifice—in Vimalananda's formula, "the *marma* (core or nucleus) of dharma is tyaga." In the *Bhagavad Gita* Krishna describes tyaga, which He defines as the renouncing of the fruits of all one's activity, as life's ultimate goal. He advises Arjuna to waive his attachment to all potential results of every karma and to focus on Him and Him only: "Abandon all other duties, and come to me alone for refuge. Be not sorrowful, for I shall give you liberation from all sins." (*Bhagavad Gita* XVIII.66) Though there is no escape from karma in this world, you can free yourself from all other karmas by assigning the fruits of all your actions to Him. When you dedicate your actions to the Lord they produce well-being in all fields of activity, just as watering the roots of a tree nourishes each of its branches. Your offering creates the rna that gives Him the power to help you, to grant you His grace in return. In Vimalananda's words, "A fair exchange is no robbery."

Daily sacrifice of your self-importance provides daily sustenance to your deity, who after "laundering" it of your vasanas returns it to you with interest. Your sole ritual becomes a quest to see and worship Him in all beings in all places (including the race track, if your karmas take you there), with every exertion of body, mind and speech. Jesus would have you follow the same path. He made Himself the Passover lamb, the sacrificial "first fruits" of the harvest, that whoever opened themselves to Him might escape the burden of their karmas. When you contract to surrender your all to Jesus, or Krishna, or another deity, or your guru, you are in danger only if you fail to perfect your gift. A single unsurrendered karma in the causal flowerbed is sufficient to seed a new forest of karmas and another string of rebirths. This hazard is easily surmounted if you are willing to extend to your devotion that commitment that Zen Buddhist abbot Harada Sekkei Roshi advocates when he advises his student to "crave dharma like a fish that is out of water, and work as you would if your hair were on fire." (Roshi, p. 77)

This was the sort of commitment that the *gopis* (milkmaids) of Vrindavana showed to Lord Krishna. Krishna said of them, "They want Me with all the force of their minds; they look on Me as the life of their life; for My sake they have abjured all the ties of the flesh. And I cherish and sustain those who sacrifice for Me all the joys of this world and the next, and the Dharma of which they are the fruit." (*Shrimad Bhagavata* X:46:3) In time, when the intensity and repetition of the gopis' whole-hearted devotion to Krishna had completely destroyed their vasanas, they attained Krishna, and freedom.

Krishna similarly saved King Parikshit. The *Shrimad Bhagavata* is the story of how Parikshit extricates himself from the constraints of his vasanas and samskaras. His intensity is stimulated by the curse that he would die within seven days; the repetition is provided by the story. The first half of the book uses genealogies and lineages to awaken and release Parikshit's Kundalini from its ancestral, archetypal, and transmigrational memories; the second half provides new objects for his Kundalini to attach herself to, in the form of Vishnu's *avataras* (divine incarnations). By Book Ten, which tells the tales of

Lord Krishna's transcendent pastimes, Parikshit is ready to listen, and to surrender.

Whoever constantly contemplates Krishna merges completely with Him. But though He is Perfection Personified (*Purnatmaka Purushottama*), Krishna is but one of the countless deity-images to whom one can surrender. Vimalananda liked to speak of submission to Krishna when he spoke of surrender because of his love for Krishna and for the *Shrimad Bhagavata*. Tantric sadhanas can also lead to union with one's deity, but Tantric texts rarely emphasize bhakti (Vimalananda claimed that this is because by and large they were written by ambitious, unperfected disciples). While the texts of Tantra tend to concern themselves with karmic transactions and the achievement of results, texts on Krishna, in particular the *Shrimad Bhagavata*, pursue the goal of unbounded bhakti. Those who can bring their karmas to equilibrium (*karmasamya*) on their own should do so; those who cannot should permit Krishna, or Shiva, or Ma, or another Beloved to do it for them.

Vimalananda, who was always rebelling against something or other, loved both the Tantras and the bhakti movement for their refusal to kowtow to petrified social conventions. While the Tantras use heterodoxy as a means to their end of extracting themselves from society's conditioning, devotees of Krishna simply have no time to think of orthodoxy: "To dedicate an action to Me is to purify it. What is right may in certain circumstances be wrong; what is wrong may…become right. The rules that declare what is right and what is wrong thus show only that the distinction is based on no intrinsic difference…. Whatever a man gives up, that he is freed from. The observance of this law puts an end to sorrow, fear, and delusion and delivers men from bondage." (*Shrimad Bhagavata* XI:21:14-18)

VIMALANANDA

To Vimalananda, who yearned above all else to be free from every form of bondage, the worst sort of thralldom was entanglement in the ossified ideological pabulum of calculated spirituality. Brahmanical Hinduism has throughout its history sought to control potential troublemakers by defining them into harmlessness. All too often this drive has led Indian culture to expropriate its saints. After a saint is safely dead and seemingly gone his well-meaning devotees usurp his reputation and readjust his image and message to fit their understanding of what he was trying to teach. Most of Ramakrishna

Paramahamsa's disciples followed this game plan when they confiscated his memory and tailored it to suit Victorian Bengali culture, emphasizing the Vedantic aspects of his teachings while downplaying its Tantrism.

Vimalananda, who loved his freedom, worked hard not to be appropriated either by neo-puritans or neo-epicureans. While he sometimes actively sought to outrage, his normal daily life was usually outrage enough. I am sure that this book will give the people in the West who have already accused him of practicing black magic (Beware the Dark Side!) new ammunition with which to attack his memory (Horse races! Gambling! We are shocked, *shocked*!).

But what else should we expect from those prigs and bluenoses who are after all simply reacting, conforming to their karmas? What can someone who is bedevilled by concern for external purity and piety understand of someone to whom the external is merely a detail? "He who lies down on the ground cannot fall," says the *Shrimad Bhagavata* (XI:21:17), and there is no ground further down than that of the smashan. Every act that Vimalananda performed was a calculated excuse, a ploy to maneuver himself into a position from which he could square up some rnanubandhana or other. Inspired perhaps by the example of Lord Krishna, Who certain bhakti texts describe as a "sweet thug" because He would dupe people into doing what their karmic debts required them to do. Vimalananda never failed to stoop to crookery when he required it to take care of a rna. He thus fit right in at the racecourse, where everyone is crafty. You cannot speak your mind candidly to all and sundry at the racecourse and hope to win any races. This makes you crooked—but it need not make you a cheat.

Life at the races is an apt allegory for life in general. On the track or in the home or office, the best way to deal with the karmic reactions that have come due is by *kala* (stratagem, finesse), not *bala* (brute force). Never to try to force the issue, but negotiate patiently as you slip and slide your way toward extrication. Vimalananda, who characteristically preferred tact to coercion as he navigated the ship of his life through the sea of his world, illustrated this point on one occasion with the following story:

> There was once a man who owned an old pair of sandals which had been patched so many times that they had no spot left unpatched. The man then decided that it was time to get rid of these sandals, so the next time he went to the temple for worship he removed them and left them outside. When he came out he deliberately neglected to pick them up, thinking that some poor person would come along and take them. But some busybody ran after him, handed them to him, and said, "You've forgotten your sandals! Don't you have any better sense?"

The man walked back home, where he concluded that the best way to get rid of the sandals was simply to throw them away and let anyone pick them up. So he went directly to his window and threw them out, but they happened to land on a small child who was passing at that moment beneath his window. The child and its mother screamed so loudly that a crowd gathered. When they heard what had happened the crowd abused the man for injuring such a dear, helpless child, and the child's mother beat the man soundly with his own sandals.

Once the commotion had died down the man sat to think the situation over. He reflected to himself, "All I wanted to do was to get rid of these old sandals, and as a result I get both insults and a good beating. What can I do now?"

Suddenly the sandals started to talk. They said, "Why are you causing such a fuss? All right, I know that I have been resoled so many times that nothing but patches remain. But all you have to do is remove all the patches and attach some good leather, and then attach a new sole, and I'll be just as good as new." And that is what the man did.

A WORLD OF STORIES

Vimalananda, who patched and resoled his personality whenever he wished to become "good as new," made his whole life into a teaching tale. Rarely would he hesitate to hyperbolize to drive a point home; he did, after all, sometimes describe himself as *Bandal-e-aftaab* ("the sun among exaggerators"). His overstated displeasure with figures like Adi Shankaracharya and Mahatma Gandhi does not imply a lack of appreciation for their real achievements. It suggests instead an acute awareness of their imperfections, enhanced that I might not mistake the lessons they carried. He sometimes exceeded his own limits for similar purposes, and as you read his excuses for such questionable behavior remember the many ways in which we each use self-justification to our advantage. The human brain has been compared to an attorney who will argue whatever side of a case it has been hired to argue regardless of its merits. Once Vimalananda had divined a course of action it was child's play for him to construct a rationale for it.

Though he never succeeded in winning me over to certain of his more outlandish positions, I was always at least willing to consider being convinced by Vimalananda's arguments. Doing so facilitated free communication in the same way that rambunctiousness on my part would have obstructed it, and most of the time Vimalananda's conclusions were themselves self-evident to me. But perhaps the main reason that I would sometimes accept the possibility of truth in an assertion so wild that coming from anyone else I would have instantly discounted it was his transparent sincerity. In Aghora, lack of heart is very dangerous, and Vimalananda was a child at heart until his dying day. His love for everyone around him was so genuine and childlike that many people took mean advantage of him, which eventually made him wary enough of humans that a certain external trickiness came to seem to him prudent.

What seems to me prudent is to accept his stories for what they are and allow the heart to extract from them their vital essence. A good tale is such a useful tool because even if it suggests nothing to you when you first hear it, it can mature within your consciousness into a form that in due time may begin to communicate with you. Like many other teachers of traditional Indian wisdom, Vimalananda preferred to teach in stories, some of which speak to the deepest levels of human awareness. There were times when Vimalananda would be trying to explain to me something exceptionally esoteric—like the relationship between the causal body, the chromosome pattern and the *Jnanendriya-Karmendriya Nyaya* ("the Law of the Sense Organs of Cognition and Those of Action"), and how the Jnanendriya-Karmendriya Nyaya controls fertilization and impregnation—that everything would begin to go far over my head. Then he would suddenly shift his discourse into a story instead. Though at the time he delivered it the story often seemed to have little connection with the topic at hand, the truth of their connectedness would indeed gradually begin to arise within me as it all sank in.

Even with time, of course, some myth-packed narratives never reveal themselves fully, even when they seem most nailed-down. When you read in Chapter One the story of Prithviraj Chauhan, for instance, please remember that there was a time when it was common practice in India at the start of a construction project to drive a nail or stake into the head of *Shesha Naga*, the gargantuan serpent who supports the world. The structure's cornerstone would be laid above the snake's head, thus placing it at the exact center of the world. Mircea Eliade has traced this tradition to the "primordial gesture" of Indra when he "struck the Snake in his lair" (*Rig Veda* IV:17:9), when his lightning bolt "cut off its head" (*Rig Veda* I:52:10). To transfix or behead the snake is to pass from the virtual and amorphous to the formed and organized, to concretize a potential karma's causation stream in time and space. Properly fastened karmas churn out well-tempered, benefic effects.

Shesha means in Sanskrit "that which remains," not in the sense of someone's leavings but rather a background or setting, a matrix which so complements an item that without it that item would be incomplete. When you dig a well on your property, you may value the well for its water, but the condition of the ground that forms the remainder of your property will govern how valuable that well will be to you. Your well draws its water from your property's *shesha*; change those surroundings and you change the well. Like a wisely-dug well, a story whose stake stretches down into Shesha Naga's head taps into its own *shesha*, the inexhaustible waters of living myth which will continue to stream into it so long as that stake remains in place.

Vimalananda rarely met a story he didn't like, and he freely adapted many of them for his purposes. In this he was but following tradition, for recycling legend is an ancient and respected practice in India. In Vimalananda's world no story was a good one unless it possessed at least seven layers of meaning, and he would tinker with his stories until they did. You can if you like compare Vimalananda's version of the story of Sudama with that of the *Shrimad Bhagavata* (Book X, Chapters 80 & 81), and find in the Sanskrit text known as the *Panchatantra* versions of at least two tales that Vimalananda ascribed to Akbar-Birbal (that of the unlucky one-eyed washerman and that of the man who claims to be able to go to heaven by getting his "old" body burned). Vimalananda, who had done an M.A. in Mughal history, was particularly fond of tales of Akbar and Birbal, many of which continue to be told for fun and profit all over North India. He added some of the better-known of these to his repertoire, and possessed others that seemed to be known only to him. These may have been gleaned from some obscure oral tradition, or he may have deliberately created them as teaching tools; if so, he would not have been the first to do so.

This book, which I crafted with the same sort of heedfulness that we used to craft our winners at the track, is an episode in the personal saga of the Aghori Vimalananda. This introduction represents a slice of the book's shesha. As you turn now to the narrative, please release any need you might have to perfectly understand the literal meanings of its words and sometimes eccentric reasoning. Open yourself, rather, to the words. Let them course through you in their own way and they will surely deliver to you their message.

REFERENCES

Dutt, Manmatha ed. *The Garuda Purana*. Calcutta: Society for the Resuscitation of Indian Literature, 1908, in *The Pocket World Bible*, ed. Robert O. Ballou, London: Routledge and Kegan Paul, Ltd. 1948.

Engler, Robert and Hayashi, Yuriko *The Way of No Thinking: The Prophecies of Japan's Kunihiro Yamate*. Tulsa: Council Oak Books, 1995.

Kohn, Livia ed. *The Taoist Experience: An Anthology*. Albany: SUNY Press, 1993.

McDermott, James P. "Karma and Rebirth in Early Buddhism," in *Karma and Rebirth in Classical Indian Traditions*, ed. Wendy Doniger O'Flaherty. Delhi: Motilal Banarsidas, 1983.

O'Flaherty, Wendy Doniger "Karma and Rebirth in the Vedas and Puranas," in *Karma and Rebirth in Classical Indian Traditions*, ed. Wendy Doniger O'Flaherty. Delhi: Motilal Banarsidas, 1983.

Svoboda, Robert E. *Aghora, At the Left Hand of God*. Albuquerque: Brotherhood of Life, 1986.

Everyday Mind: Dharma Talks by Harada Sekkei Roshi. Bangalore: Buddha Vachana Trust, 1991.

NOTE

Aside from known historical figures like Akbar, General Sleeman and Seth Sagal Shah and known mythological figures like Smashan Tara and Gorakh Nath, the following actual people appear within under their own names: Robby (the author), Roshni, Ranu, Faram, Chotu, Vaidya B. P. Nanal, Dr. Vasant Lad, Dr. Shantilal Mehta, Dr. Gomes, Dr. Durandar, R. D. Shah, Dinkar, Damle, Chabbu Ranbuke, Begum Akhtar, Chandramohan, Taat Maharaj, Sevadasji & Chunilal, Balam Bhat, Madhavbaba Patil, Shankargiriji Maharaj, Hambir Baba, Baba Chandal Das, K. Narayana Baba, Dada Maharaj, Das Bapa, Chaitanyananda, George McGrath, Sir Lester Piggott, Mr. Williams, Sir Cusrow N. Wadia, Admiral Eric Shipton, the Chief of Jat, and the Maharajas of Bikaner, Gwalior and Mudhol. "Lizoo" was really the dog's nickname (her registered name was Lady Elizabeth), and "Prof. Joker the Guru" really was that tipster's nickname. Black Dog really is a blend of premium Scotch, and Kersasp Kolah really does produce a savory Spicy Carrot

Pickle. The horses Potooooooooo, Waxy, Eclipse, Kincsem and Mount Everest actually raced under those monikers. Everyone else, horse and human alike, has had his or her name changed, to protect the innocent, the guilty, and those who aren't sure. Stoney's photo on Vimalananda's wall showed her winning a race other than the Mother Lode Cup. Although Colonel Pratap Singh of Jodhpur was a real person, the Big Race that Redstone won was named for another nobleman.

Every event in which I am involved that I recount in this book actually occurred—insofar as things actually 'occur' here in the physical universe.

chapter one
STONEY

"WHY DO YOU THINK I own horses and come to the race track?"

Vimalananda and I sat, in March 1977, on his usual bench in the First Enclosure of the Bombay Racecourse. We had reached there well in advance of the first race, and while we awaited the arrival of his colleagues, the friendly gamblers with whom he would wrangle, wager and roar, the man who was my mentor sprang this question on me.

"I know you wonder about this all the time," he went on, "because your orthodox friends in Poona have taught you that good Hindus don't gamble. Do you have any idea at all why I come here?"

"No," I responded truthfully, "none at all."

He was right: gambling was anathema to my acquaintances among the orthodox of Poona, the city 100 miles southeast of Bombay where I was a student in a college of *Ayurveda*, India's traditional medical system.

"Sometimes I come here to gamble," he went on, "and at other times I come just to watch the races. But whatever my other reasons I always come to study the karmas of the people who are here with me."

"Their karmas."

"Yes. Do you know Newton's Third Law of Motion?"

"Er, yes: For every action there is an equal and opposite reaction."

"Yes. Newton's Third Law of Motion is the Law of Karma. We can also call it the Law of Cause and Effect, the law of 'as you sow, so shall you reap.' Any time you self-identify with an action—any time you act and think of yourself as the doer of that action—that action becomes a *karma* for you. All your self-identified actions, good and bad, act as causes which eventually produce effects, good and bad, which you will have to experience. The race track happens to be a great place to gain practice in knowing other people's karmic accounts."

"You mean, to know who karmically owes what to whom?"

"Right. We call that *rnanubandhana*, the bondage of karmic debt. Let me give you a little illustration of my point so that you will know exactly what I mean. Suppose you want to predict the results of a horse race, like the race Stoney is running this afternoon." Stoney was his nickname for Stone Ice, who was his favorite mare. Today was to be the last race of her career.

"To know who will win a horse race you need to know about the luck— which means the sum of the karmas and rnanubandhanas—of many different beings. First, and foremost, the horse: Is he or she destined to win? Next, the horse's *syce* (groom) and the *jemadar* (head groom): Are they destined to collect bonuses from the owner, which he awards them when his horse wins? Then, the trainer: Is he destined to obtain his share of the stakes for saddling a winning horse? As for the jockey: Is he destined for both a share of stake money and a big tip from the owner for winning? And what about the owner: Do the horse and the club owe him the stake money for the horse's victory? Is his horse meant to enhance his fame by a victory, or weaken his prestige by flopping miserably?

"Next to last comes the bookie: Is he karmically meant to pay you, or to collect from you? Only now do we finally come to you, the gambler: Are you meant to win or lose money on that horse?"

"I can see that it is not so simple."

"My God! I should think not! If it were simple someone would have figured out a foolproof system to predict winners by now, and would be getting rich. Actually, it *is* fairly simple for the public. Most of the people who come to the track are debtors; they owe money either to the bookies or to the Club. They are the cannon fodder that provides the cash that pays those few people who are the horses' creditors, who are the only people destined to make money on the horses. These karmic debts get settled up on race days, when the public comes to play its favorites. The horses do the work, the creditors win, and the debtors lose. The horses themselves are mainly debtors: they work hard so that the others can make money. At best, if they win, they get some extra carrots and some sweet words; at worst, if they lose race after race—well, the worst can be pretty gruesome.

"I go to the race track to finish up a large number of rnanubandhanas all at once. I always race my animals to win. Knowing what I do about the Law of Karma, how can I do otherwise? I want to die with a clean karmic balance sheet. Every time my horse wins I pay off hundreds or thousands of bettors. The horse owes them the money, no doubt, but because I own the horse and am supporting him it is really me that is paying them off. Neat, isn't it?"

"It is for you," I responded, "but what about everyone else? Are all the other people who own horses automatically paying off their rnanubandhanas too?"

"They are if they are not creating some substantial new karmas in the process of paying off their previous ones."

"Oh."

"Clear?"

"For now."

"Look at it from this angle: when an owner races a horse to win and doesn't interfere in any way with how that horse runs the main effect of the race is to pay off existing rnanubandhanas. So far, so good. But things don't always work this way. Sometimes an owner, in cahoots with a trainer or a jockey, will try to do something to make sure that his horse wins or loses. That effort is a karma, which will either create a new rnanubandhana or perpetuate one that already exists.

"These consequences are not limited to the actions of owners, of course. Sometimes the trainer will be in cahoots with the jockey, and they keep the owner in the dark about it. Sometimes the bookies and the jockeys are in cahoots and leave everyone else in the dark. This sort of thing is unfortunate, but it happens all the time; the lure of easy money is too much for many people, and they become greedy.

"Many bookies get involved in conspiring with the jockeys to make extra money by fixing up races. When he can arrange for a favorite horse to lose a bookie can swallow all the money the public had bet on the favorite." As in Great Britain, licensed bookies operate legally at Indian racetracks.

"They can swallow the money, but will they be able to digest it?" I contributed sardonically.

"That is precisely my point," he responded with some vehemence. "Here is the creation of a new karma: the mare does her job for her creditors by trying to win, but the jockey and the bookie pocket the money when they stop her from winning. The members of the public who were the horse's creditors have still not been paid, so they now become creditors of the bookies and jockeys; the debts are transferred. The bookies and jockeys, who think they are getting something for nothing, are merely borrowing money which they will have to pay back later, with interest. Moreover, the jockeys will also have to be reborn so that the horses that they whip into exhaustion now will have an opportunity to work them to death in return. If these people ever realized how many millions of lives it will take to pay off all these debts they would never play dirty.

"But they don't realize it, and they do play dirty. In fact, we're about to have a practical demonstration of this kind of treachery right now."

The horses were now leaving the Paddock to tramp toward the starting gate. "Did you hear what that no-account excuse for a rider Jhendu Kumar said to me yesterday at the stables?"

"No." Jhendu Kumar was Stoney's jockey that day. After a moment of puzzlement I suddenly realized that Vimalananda fully expected Stoney to lose. Sickened by that thought I turned to watch her and the other horses walk and canter away from us, roused into friskiness by the impending race.

"When I told this fellow that this would be Stoney's last race and that I was confident she would win it he told me, 'Don't count your chickens before they hatch.'"

"Which means that he is not too confident."

"Yes, but why shouldn't he be? I have watched Stoney work, and I can tell you that she is absolutely at the top of her form. Jhendu Kumar himself has been working her over the past few weeks, and he has also won atop her before. So he has to know that in her present form she is unbeatable today—she is a class above the other horses in this race. Isn't it natural that I become suspicious?"

"You're suspicious of him?"

"I am very suspicious of his intentions. I *could* take what he said as an omen, but it just doesn't add up to one when I consider Stoney's condition, her track record, and the weakness of the rest of the field. Also, I have to consider *how* he said what he said—he seemed to boast when he spoke those words, as if he alone knew what was going to happen. When I add this boasting to his own previous track record—he has been in trouble for hooking horses before—and his own current precarious financial condition, it makes me think that he may hook her today."

"By 'hooking her' you mean prevent her from winning?"

"Exactly."

"But won't anyone notice that he has hooked her?"

"Anyone who has eyes in his head instead of samosas probably will notice, but so what?" I suppressed a snicker as the vision of a Jhendu Kumar with those savory Indian snacks for eyes trotted into my head. "There are so many ways to hook horses that look so much like ordinary misfortunes that the Stewards of the Club, even if they suspect foul play, can often do nothing about it."

"But what about the patrol camera, and the instant replay?"

"Horses are not machines, you know; you can't ever tell what might put them off. Sometimes the tempo of the race won't agree with the horse. Sometimes the *way* the race is run will set the horse off; some horses like to be shut in, and others prefer to see daylight in front of them. Sometimes when a horse visits some other racing venue he may become homesick, or decide that he doesn't like the taste of the food or water there." I remembered Kincsem, the famous Hungarian mare who would never travel anywhere without her cat.

"But those are all legitimate excuses. Hooking is different. One way a jockey can hook a horse is to hesitate for a split second so that he fails to leave the starting gate with the other runners. Then, if he settles in at the rear of the pack he can let himself get hemmed in on the rail at the turn and cross the winning post well behind the leaders. Or, the jockey can craftily send the horse wide and then suddenly veer out into the flat by shortening one rein with a sharp turn of his wrist and swiftly kicking the horse in the ribs with his opposite foot. Or, a jockey who knows that his mount needs to be whipped to win can 'accidentally' drop his whip. A jockey who is desperate to lose may even fall off in mid-race—but that takes guts, as it is a very dangerous stunt.

"The trainer has more ways to make a horse lose. He can 'stuff' the horse, by substituting normal racing feed (mainly hay and bran) with a full meal of grain on the night before and the morning of the race. Have you ever tried to run a race on a full stomach? Or you can give the horse extra salt to eat and then plenty of water to drink, to make it temporarily gain lots of water weight. It is also easy to overtrain the horse, to gallop it too frequently so that it passes its peak before race day. There was one trainer named Udgith who used to tie up the horse in its stall so that it couldn't get any rest, or even move, the night before the race. That would certainly mar the horse's performance for the next day, but how cruel it was to the horse! Udgith was a cruel man.

"Given these words from my jockey and the peculiar omen that I happened to see on our way to the track today, I didn't bet very much on Stoney, despite being so convinced that she is the best horse in this field."

"Which omen?" No reply. I tried again: "If you think she is going to lose why bet anything at all?"

"It's an owner's bet, an expression of confidence in my mare; it's like saying, 'I still love you, and even if that bastard hooks you I'm going to put money on you because I know that you would run an honest race if only you were permitted to do so. Besides, she might win; who can say? Fixed races also unfix themselves sometimes."

"How?"

"What if a gang of owners decides that my horse is going to win, but the jockeys conspire together to make your mare succeed? I've seen it happen before. The jockeys who are in on the plot will select a rank outsider, a horse who will be available at long odds because no one expects him to win. He has to be a horse being ridden by an apprentice jockey, or maybe by a broken-down old rider who is not a member of their clique. The plotters have their accomplices bet heavily on that horse just before the race begins, at the very last moment. That way no one else has an opportunity to get in on the deal. After the start of the race the conspirators guide the apprentice along without his knowing it, bunching him in and moving him up. At just the right moment they give him an opening. Out in front he goes, with the others swinging their whips furiously behind him pretending they are trying their damnedest to catch up. *Voila!* The kid thinks he's a champion for booting home a horse who had no chance to win, and the pirates who arranged for him to win enjoy a handsome payday. If it is done properly no one will suspect a thing."

He was convincing. "If you are so sure about Jhendu Kumar, why didn't you just replace him? Wasn't there still time yesterday?"

"There was, but what would I have gained by doing that? I have no proof that he is going to hook her. If I make unsubstantiated allegations against him it will only look bad for me. It might even make all the other jockeys hook all my runners from now on, to teach me a lesson. Jockeys are jockeys, after all; they show solidarity with others of their breed. Besides, why should I be worried? If Stoney still owes me money she'll have to give it to me later somehow, maybe via one of her foals, even if Jhendu Kumar hinders her from giving it to me now. So I can afford to relax and watch the show unfold. It's just that it would be so nice for her to go out on a winning note. She's a horse with so much heart! She deserves to win so that she can enjoy the crowd's adulation again this one last time."

"The horses have reached the starting gate," came the announcer's voice over the public address system. We lifted our binoculars to watch the race. It was a clean start, and I quickly located Vimalananda's racing colors—pink with red chevrons—amidst the pack. Stoney looked good coming out of the gate and looked good coming round the bend. But in the stretch she didn't rise to the challenge of the horse who came on strong from the outside; she finished the race a close second to him. Even though I was just a tyro of a race watcher in those days it didn't seem to me that Jhendu Kumar had done much to encourage Stoney to win. He had standing orders not to whip her, but nothing precluded him from riding her out with his feet and hands, or from showing her the whalebone (whips were once made of that material). But he had done neither of these things. Instead, he had made a histrionic exhibition of effort by ineffectually slapping the reins up and down around her neck. I suppose that he brazenly thought that this would somehow impress us, but as I dropped my binoculars for a sidelong glance at Vimalananda I could see that he too was convinced of Jhendu's guilt.

Vimalananda said nothing more about the matter until that evening, when we were back at home and he had a glass of Scotch at his right hand. He spoke with calm firmness: "Since my mother died two years back life no longer interests me much. I've done a lot in my life, much more than most people. I have endured the heights of pleasure and the depths of misery. I've gained a lot, and lost a lot, and thanks to my beloved Smashan Tara I have achieved almost everything that I set out to achieve." *Smashan Tara* ("The Saviouress of the Cemetery," "She Who Transports You to the Other Side of Existence") is the second of the group of Tantric goddesses known as the Ten Mahavidyas. She is the deity that introduced Vimalananda to his spiritual path.

"There is very little in the world that can keep my attention now. I am still interested, though, in my spiritual 'children,' in my little dog, Lizoo," who lifted her head from his lap expectantly when she heard her name, "and in horseflesh.

"For me horse racing is splendid sport because I find something wonderful in the whole process of preparing a horse to race. This is why I keep my horses with lesser-known trainers. The famous trainers like Ardeshir Rustomjee who probably do a better training job than the smaller fry won't let you interfere with their plans for the horse. If you make too many suggestions they just tell you, 'Get out!' because they know they can get more horses at any time. But a small trainer who never knows where he'll be able to find another owner has no alternative; he has to put up with interfering owners like me who interest themselves in the nuts and bolts of training.

"You begin by sifting through the pedigrees of the foals that come into the auction until you find one that you can afford that you think can win, and you bid on it. If you are able to purchase it you then direct its training program until it is ready to see the track. Meanwhile you pore over the racing calendar to find appropriate races in which it might run. As the months pass you check regularly on the progress of your colt or filly by watching her do her morning work and by visiting her at the stables in the evening. You worry over her when she is sick. You pamper her more than you would your own child, feeding her supplements to improve her health and to give her that extra vigor that she will need to best the field.

"Eventually you enter her in a race. When the list of entries is published you study each runner, closely comparing their current handicaps with their previous race records. Finally, on those occasions when everything seems to come together you start to get a feeling that yes, in this particular race, your filly can do it! She can trounce the opposition! Then you go to the track and put your money where your mouth is, and she comes and runs her heart out and wins! When you walk out onto the grass near the finish line to lead her in, amidst cheers of adulation from the crowd—well, it's a unique feeling, I tell you, unique!

"Now, what if, after all this expenditure of time and energy you've invested in your mare, she had every chance to win the last race of her life and then at the last moment a scoundrel appeared on the scene, a human scum who spoiled everything. How would you feel? I doubt that it would make you very happy." He sipped his Scotch sternly. "Don't get me wrong; I'm glad she's going to retire. She'll have a chance to relax and be well fed in a peaceful paddock. She'll enjoy some nice sex with a well-hung stallion and learn what it means to be a mother. No, I don't feel bad about her leaving racing at all; I just feel bad about the way she left."

"According to you," I ventured, "because Stoney was destined to win both her syce and the jemadar were destined to receive winning bonuses from your hand, and her trainer Mr. Lafange was destined for his share of the stake money, and you were destined for both stake money and prestige enhancement. Jhendu Kumar, who was destined only to get stake money and a tip, elected instead to conspire with a bookie who was karmically meant to pay you. The bookie collected from you and Stoney's other creditors the bets that you all were supposed to have won money on and gave some of that money to Jhendu Kumar. This makes the two of them the new debtors for all the rest of you."

"Absolutely correct."

"What about the debtors who owed money to the club and the bookies?"

"They were going to lose anyway, and they lost; those debts are cleared."

"Mustn't it also have been your karma, or Stoney's karma, that involved Jhendu Kumar in the first place?"

"Indeed it was, but however much it has been my karma or Stoney's to be involved with such a cheat it is even more a result of Mamrabahen's karma." (Mamrabahen was a woman to whom Vimalananda had long been a father figure.) "Mamrabahen dragged me back into racing, after a gap of nearly thirty years. I had no need for it, but she thought she did. She wanted to be able to parade around at the racecourse in fancy saris, and show off her connection to my horses. I cooperated because I wanted to try to satisfy these desires of hers so that she could get beyond them and drop them. And what was the result? Her new-found 'affluence' went to her head. She acts as if she herself is the owner, which makes everyone think that she is my mistress. Meanwhile she has been running around with all the jockeys, flirting with them and doing God knows what else in order to get hot tips on which horses are going to win.

"By permitting myself to get involved with Mamrabahen and her schemes I opened myself to being influenced by her karmas, almost all of which are bad—if they had been good something good would have have happened to her by now."

"If her karmas are so evil why would you want to expose yourself to their influence?"

"Well, it is a complicated situation. For one thing, I have been part of her life ever since she was small. How can a mother ever give up on her child? For another, she is part of my karmic family—part of the group of people that I have an obligation to relate to during this lifetime whether I like it or not."

"Since you are so karmically connected to her why can't your influence, which I have seen help so many others, help her overcome the bad influences in her life so that she can make some progress too?"

"It is not an easy thing to explain, Robby, but it has to do with her *causal body*. Do you remember the difference between the causal body and the *astral body*?"

"The causal body is the storehouse of all the memories of all your rnanubandhanas. Karmas when ripe and ready to be experienced project from the causal body into the subtle or astral body, which is the mind, where they cause us to act in conformity with the karmas we have to experience."

"Correct. The problem is that in Mamrabahen's causal body there are so many negative karmas that it will be almost impossible for her to get rid of them all in the space of one short lifetime."

"You mean that if Mamrabahen's causal body were a shirt it would be so coated with the greasy dirt of her nasty karmas that no matter how many times you wash it and bleach it it will still be absolutey filthy?"

"Yes," replied Vimalananda with cold sobriety as he continued to sip, "that's the idea. Her karmas are so bad that she has steadfastly continued down the road to ruin no matter how many times I have tried to change her course. I have had to save her dozens of times from all sorts of unpleasant circumstances. Once she had even been sold into slavery and was about to be sent to the Persian Gulf! We only caught up with her the day before she was to depart and extricated her with great difficulty.

"I forced this girl to do her M.A.; I have found jobs for her; I have tried to find her a husband. I have spent thousands and thousands of rupees on her, but has she appreciated anything that I have done for her? Not a thing; she even says to my face, 'What have you ever done for me?' She's wretchedly spiteful and thankless, yet I still continue to try to save her. Why? Because it's my karma to do so. You see, I once ordered her to be killed."

"You ordered her to be killed?" I asked, incredulous.

"Yes, in a previous lifetime, as the result of a pre-existing curse. Most of what we call karma is made up of the effects of curses and blessings. As a matter of fact I would say that 75%, or maybe even 90%, of all karma is either *abhishapa* (curse) or *ashirwada* (blessing)."

"When you say 'curse' you don't mean vulgarity—what we call 'cuss words' in Texas—do you? You must mean some kind of hex like the gypsies use, which makes it sound like almost all karma results from people throwing whammies on one another?"

"Not exactly. There are still a few people who know how to consciously deliver real curses and blessings, but very few. Most curses and blessings are not deliberate. If you do something really nice for someone, if you help him out when he really needs help his heart will melt, if he is any kind of human at all, and a wave of gratitude will flow from him towards you. This is a blessing. A curse is the same sort of thing: if you afflict someone terribly then at some point, often at the moment of death, he in his misery will cry out from his heart. That cry will act on you like a curse; its vibrations will follow you around and interfere with your life. A *sadhu* (Hindu religious mendicant) can only bless or curse when he is overwhelmed with emotion; only then does the real *shakti* (power, energy) flow. When he is overcome with anger out comes a curse; when it is joy that overflows it comes out in a blessing.

"I'll explain to you just exactly how this works—eventually. All you need to know right now that the curse that binds Mamrabahen and me together is a true curse, delivered on purpose by someone who was very powerful—which is why we are still being affected by it. The force of a real curse lasts for seven births. In our case those seven are still not complete. I have already killed her more than once, and she has been taunting me for years that she will force me to kill her in this incarnation also. This is not her speaking, really; it is the curse speaking through her. If she succeeds at inciting me and I kill her that progression will continue and I will kill her in a total of seven births. After that she will gain the right to kill me in seven incarnations."

"Huh???"

"It's nothing but the Law of Karma, Robby, Newton's Third Law of Motion, the Law of Action and Reaction: If I kill her she gets to kill me in return."

"That's all there is to it?"

"Basically, that's all there is to it. But does that sound like nothing to you? The Law of Karma may sound simple, but understanding all its ramifications is truly a hell of a job. There was once a disciple who claimed that his guru never taught him anything. Disciples are always like this; it is part of God's *lila*, His Cosmic Play. We humans perform *krida*, which is unconscious play, play which we do not know how to control. Only the play of the gods, and of our ancient *Rishis* (Seers), is *lila*: cosmic pastimes which are always under their control.

"Anyway, this disciple pestered his guru for knowledge for so long that the guru finally decided to force the boy to learn something. The next day when they were out walking together they saw a cobra being gobbled up by thousands of ants. No matter how the cobra twised and turned he couldn't escape

a horrible death. The disciple asked, 'Guruji, what has the cobra done to suffer like this?' The guru replied, 'Keep quiet! Come on!'

"Further along the road they came to a fishing village. One fisherman had
just returned to shore after hauling in a big catch. He was resting, obviously
enjoying himself, smoking a good pipe.

" 'Do you understand?' asked the guru.

" 'No,' replied the boy.

" 'That cobra we saw will become a fisherman, and those ants will become
fish. This man was once a cobra who was eaten by ants, and that is why he has
a right to torture and destroy these fish who were once ants.'"

"Oh," I said, in a tone of hush. "I see. If you slay Mamrabahen again she
will eventually get to slay you, one way or another."

"Yes, and if I break this cycle right now I will never have to kill her again and
she will never get the right to kill me. That will end this peculiar karmic dance,
which is what I want. There are times that the force of that curse on her mind
makes her provoke me so much that the force of the curse on my mind makes
me decide to wring her neck—but then I calm down and remember my plan."

"And this will continue until the entire energy of the curse is expended?"

"Exactly, for that long and not one moment longer. But who knows how
much power remains behind the curse? There is no limit of time. It's difficult
to know such things, but I have seen no change in her behavior thus far. This
makes me think that I still have a long way to go to pay off this particular *rna*
(karmic debt). Once the rna is paid the rnanubandhana ends. In the meanwhile I help to moderate the curse's force by sharing in her karmas. Because
she is destined to suffer I have to suffer, and I have really suffered due to
Mamrabahen, on so many accounts. After involving myself with her some of
her evil karmas have affected me directly—my recent heart attack was partly
due to her making me furious, partly to my taking on some other karmas
that I don't want to talk about right now. Some of her evil karmas have also
affected me through others. Currently one portion of her karmas is affecting
me through the person of Jhendu Kumar. She has latched onto him thinking
that together they will collaborate with the bookies, hook lots of horses, and
make quick money. Quick money, that is all she can think of; 'long-range
planning' is not in her vocabulary.

"Now, just because Jhendu Kumar had the ability and the opportunity to
hook Stoney doesn't mean that he was forced to do so. He had the free will to
say 'no,' and to go ahead and win. If he had won he would have obtained a little less money this time, but he would have maintained good relations with
me. That would have helped him out in the long run. But he followed a policy of short-term gains, for which he will have to pay."

"Eventually."

"Eventually, and also very soon, since I will never give him a mount again. I will also tell of my experience to my owner friends, who are unlikely to give him any mounts either. And then where will he be? He could have seen this coming, but his own evil karmas, coupled with all the booze that he drinks, have clouded his mind. To refrain from taking easy money when it is offered to you on a platter takes backbone, and you can't really expect many jockeys to show much of that. A few do have character, I know, but most jockeys are taught to be crooks from an early age. They are tutored in crime by the trainers and the bookies.

"Today's debacle was partly my own fault. One of my previous trainers, old Maneckjee, always warned me about giving a jockey a winning mount more than twice. 'Let him win twice, you moron-molester,' he would say, 'and then give the mount to someone else. A jockey will try hard to win the first two times, but after two victories he will start to think that you can't do without him, that he can do as he pleases and you won't dare to do anything about it. Remember what I say, you sister-screwer!' Maneckjee was a true Parsi—he couldn't speak a single sentence without at least one vulgarity in it. One of the reasons that I love Parsis is their colorful way of speaking."

The ancestors of today's Parsis emigrated to India from Persia more than 1300 years ago. The Parsis, who worship fire, follow the religion of Zarathustra (Zoroaster) who 2500 years ago or more preached a dualistic faith in which good and evil continuously battle for control of the universe. About half of the world's one hundred thousand Zoroastrians live in Bombay.

"When I call Jhendu Kumar a bastard, by the way, I'm not just talking out of my wits. He *is* a bastard; no one knows his pedigree. He grew up in an orphanage. You know how important pedigree is to racehorses; do you think it is any less important to humans? Oh no—it is tremendously important. And even more important than your physical heredity is your mental heredity, the lineage of karmas and *samskaras* (personality characteristics) that you carry with you from birth to birth. How can I expect Jhendu Kumar to be honest when he doesn't seem either to have inherited any good samskaras from his parents or brought over into this lifetime any good karmas from his previous incarnations? Some people leave the orphanage and go on to live decent lives, but not this fellow. In fact, he was tossed out of the orphanage for misconduct. Now he is misbehaving with me. It is his fate to be a cheat, and there is nothing I can do about it, unless I want to get myself filthy cleaning out the cesspool of his karmas. But why bother? My job is to complete my rnanubandhana with him. Then I can go my own way, and he can go on experiencing the results of his own karmas, which is his fate.

"What is fate, after all, but the sum of all your past karmas? And what are karmas except debts to be paid? You act, and your action sows the seeds of a reaction that you will have to endure, like it or not. I can't try to prevent everyone from enduring their fate. People go on and on arguing about fate *versus* free will, but they're all fools. Everyone has free will. You are free to decide either to live your life cooperating with Nature or to try to go off on your own. But even if you go off on your own you will still end up having to walk the path that Nature (which means the Law of Karma) has set for you. If you cooperate with Nature from the beginning you will waste less time and energy, and suffer less misery. Isn't it more sensible and rational to choose the path of least resistance that entails the least pain? It is always better to live with reality, Robby, because otherwise, you can be sure of it, reality will come to live with you."

"So we can be absolutely sure that reality will eventually come to live with Jhendu Kumar?"

"As sure as you and I are sitting here. Nature's wheels grind slowly, but they grind very, very thoroughly, and nothing escapes them. Do you know who Vidhata is?"

"I do not."

"*Vidhata* is Fate personified, an ethereal being who manages the conversion of past karmas into present results. Vidhata exerts his influence on us through his representatives, the ethereal beings who create the circumstances in which he can work. In *Jyotish* (Indian astrology) we recognize nine such representatives, which we call the Nine Planets. Each planet influences different aspects of an individual's life. The Sun, for instance, represents the soul. The Moon represents the mind, especially its intuitive and emotional aspects. The position of the Moon in the horoscope thus shows a good astrologer exactly how an individual's emotions are innately arranged, and how those emotions will change as the planets transit the skies.

"The most important of the Nine Planets is Saturn, the planet in charge of experience (*anubhava*). We call Saturn the 'son of the Sun' in Jyotish because all experience occurs due to the presence of the soul, who is the true 'experiencer' in a living being. It is Saturn who is responsible for your fate, who forces you to experience your karmas whether you want to or not."

"Good karmas and bad."

"Good karmas and bad. Saturn causes dramatic changes, both good and bad, in everyone's life. Saturn can cause you to reach the heights of fame or riches or whatever, or can make you sink into the depths of misery, all according to the credit or debit balance in your karmic account. Some people are naturally lucky; you see it everywhere, and there is no accounting for it except by invoking the Law of Karma. In one and the same family one man may have to slog all day long just to keep bread on his family's table, while his brother may unexpectedly receive some windfall that allows him to live a luxurious, carefree life. 'Bad luck' is the state in which your karmic account consists mainly of bad karmas, which causes Saturn to dish out mostly miseries for you to endure. 'Good luck' means that you have plenty of good karmas to enjoy. To have a positive karmic credit balance means that you are the creditor of a large number of rnanubandhanas, that you will have many things to collect from other beings. A person with a negative credit balance owes lots of things to other beings; he is the debtor of a large number of rnanubandhanas.

"Saturn causes you to experience pleasure or pain by affecting your innate 'nature' (*svabhava, prakriti*), which is the thing that determines how you relate to your surroundings. Some people have an angry, irritable nature; others are naturally calm and complacent; still others are by nature fearful and timid. This nature is inborn in each of us; it is present in our genes and chromosomes, and controls how we experience the world. The 'nature' of Ma, the Great Goddess, is Nature itself, the force which causes the creation, preservation, and destruction of the universes."

"Doesn't environment count for anything?" Roughly speaking *prakriti* represents the root and *svabhava* the fruit of human awareness.

"It counts for a tremendous amount. If you are given proper samskaras when you are young enough you can go a long way off. But beneath all your samskaras is still your nature.

"In the limited human sense your *prakriti* is your 'first action' (*pra + kriti*), the choice of action which you naturally, instinctively make when you are confronted by some situation. Except in a few rare cases this choice is purely instinctive in animals, whose conscious minds are very limited. And even if you teach an animal to restrain itself you can rely on it only so far. After a certain point the temptation to return to its original temperament will prove too great for its training. After all, the nature of Nature is automatic and instinctual behavior. The consciousness of human beings is supposed to be more advanced than that of animals, but how much more advanced is it? Your human consciousness has plenty of limitations which can cause you in critical situations to forget all the good things you have learned. These influences include your food, your air, and the company you keep, but without a doubt the most important of the limitations on your consciousness is the hereditary characteristics that you have inherited from your family and your past births.

"Until you have conquered this innate nature, either through long, hard penances or by creating overwhelming affection and love for your deity, Saturn can still affect you. Directed by Fate, Saturn searches out the weaknesses in your personality and exposes them to full view. This forces you to experience the many limitations of your nature. In life you ultimately have to depend on your own inner knowledge, which is all you'd be able to save in a shipwreck. How well you can tap into your inner knowledge depends on how strong an influence Saturn exerts on your mind. This in turn is determined by *ahamkara* (ego). Ahamkara is called *Kundalini Shakti* when it begins to awaken from its 'sleep' of self-delusion. Until that time ahamkara creates and reinforces your limited human personality by self-identifying with your physical and mental attributes. So long as your awareness remains trapped in your body you will be at Saturn's mercy, for you will be unable to control your own nature. Only when you have completely overcome 'what comes naturally' to you can Saturn no longer have any effect on you.

"This is why we say in Sanskrit, *Svabhavo vijayati iti shauryam*—'the true heroism is to conquer your own nature.' But it's not so easy to permanently conquer your own nature! Not at least until you become immortal. Fate can affect an immortal being only if he or she again willfully accepts subjection to time, space and causation. I emphasize all this just so you will know that to make any kind of fundamental change in your nature—which means to alter your fate—you must be able to change the chemical patterns in your brain, patterns which are controlled by your genes and chromosomes."

"So there is no hope for Jhendu Kumar?"

"There is hope for everyone; everyone will eventually realize God. But eventually is a long way off for Jhendu Kumar. Given the karmas he came in with and the ones he has been creating there is very little likelihood that he is going to make any sort of desirable progress during this birth. Translate this Sanskrit phrase for me: *Purva datteshu vidya, purva datteshu bharya, purva datteshu dhanam, purva datteshu maranam.*"

"Well . . . 'previously given knowledge, previously given wife, previously given money, previously given demise.' Is that close?"

"It is. What it means is that whatever knowledge or skills, spouse, wealth and property, and death you enjoyed in previous lives you will also enjoy in this one. Good karmas and bad, curses and blessings, all your rnanubandhanas continue with you from life to life for at least seven births in a row. Saturn is the planet who by swaying your mind forces you into the situations which will fulfill the conditions set out in the karmic debts that you have contracted. Suppose because of your rnanubandhanas you are destined to marry a certain girl. When you meet her you will probably fall into some *love-aria* which will cause you to jump into matrimony. The stage is then set for the two of you to square up your karmic accounts."

" 'Love-aria'??"

"Love-aria is just like malaria except that it is caused by romance instead of by a physical parasite. Most of the time a sufferer from love-aria remains normal, sane, and rational, but during an attack of the fever of love he falls into delirium. Like malaria love-aria usually won't kill you, and like malaria it is very difficult to cure."

"Huh." I paused for thought before I asked, "If you get your exact same spouse back in a new form will you get your exact same knowledge back?"

"The form of all these things may change but the essence will remain the same. A butcher may be reborn as a surgeon, perhaps, but both live by cleaving flesh. In fact, whenever you see an expert surgeon, like my son, you should know that he must have been a butcher in a previous birth. Otherwise he would not have such a love for his job. Sometimes my son will tell me, 'Papa, whenever I go in to operate I feel such a thrill!' That love for cutting is characteristic of a flesh-cleaver. When I hear these words come out of my son's mouth I say to myself: 'Purva datteshu vidya!'

"A person who can play a part well can do so because of the traits of previous lives which he retains within him. If I can convincingly play a king I was very likely a ruler in a previous life. If I can perfectly self-identify with merchants, villains or prostitutes then I must have been a merchant or a villain or a prostitute in the past. And so on."

"Does this mean that Akbar likes to come to you because you play the king well, which you do because you were a ruler in some previous life?" Vimalananda was fond of opening himself to possession by the spirits of deities and saints, a process known in Sanskrit as *avishkara*, and he would frequently host the shade of the Mughal Emperor Mohammed Jalal-ud-Din Akbar.

"Yes, I was a ruler, more than once, and if I have achieved something in this life it is because I have some pedigree, both from my past lives and from my parents. Jhendu Kumar might hope to make something of himself in this lifetime if he had some foundation to build on, some 'previous knowledge.' But he has nothing to build on. And what can he do well? Nothing! He is no great shakes as a jockey, and he is useless as a crook. He is a nobody."

"He can cook."

"He can cook—adequately. Are you prepared to call him a chef?"

"By no means."

"And even in the food he cooks he continues to create future limitations for himself."

"How?"

"By cooking meat. Unless you are a Tantric adept or an *Aghori* (a practitioner of *Aghora*, the 'super-Tantra' in which all sense of limitation is removed), meat-eating creates a powerful negative influence on your mind by causing your ego to self-identify with the animals that you eat. You'll notice that most Indians who eat meat eat goats, chicken, and fish—and have you noticed all the chicken and goat and fish mentality in people nowadays? And this effect is not even limited to the animals that we kill for food. With the big rat eradication program that's going on now in our country rat qualities will appear more and more. You will see it. Do you know the character of a rat? You get along fine with the fellow until one day he gives you a good bite!" He laughed.

"Like Jhendu Kumar bit you."

He laughed again. "Precisely. Every animal, even an insect, which is willfully killed by a human gains thereby the right to be eventually reborn as a human. Whenever I see a line of animals being led to the slaughterhouse I want to say to them, 'Quick! Quick! Quick work! Just a little pain, and then you are in the queue to come back and be reborn as a human.' That is its right, and why shouldn't it be? It's the Law of Karma. Even insects have this privilege. Fortunately for us, though, insects and other non-mammals are not adapted to live as mammals. They can't thrive as mammals, and they don't enjoy it either. They each get their chance, but they die very young. This is why we don't see more cockroach, ant, fly, or mosquito humans. Can you imagine how terrible a bedbug human or a tsetsefly human would be?"

"Oh my God!"

"We are fortunate that insects and other animals which are killed accidentally don't have this privilege. They don't have it because you didn't intend for them to die. You don't kill them intentionally; they die thanks to their own karmas. But vermin that are deliberately killed get a chance to be human, if even temporarily. This is bad enough for those who kill vermin for a living, because it establishes a rnanubandhana with the vermin they kill. But that's not the end of it. Most of those vermin will be human only temporarily; this is why the number of abortions increases with the number of vermin exterminated. Even so, some vermin—most likely those that have already been mammals in some birth or other—will probably develop into humans, if even briefly. Suppose those vermin-humans then perform some evil karmas during their human rebirth. It is likely that they will; mayhem comes natural to vermin. If they do, won't the exterminator be at least partially responsible for that mayhem, since he enabled them, violently, to become human in the first place? He must be!"

"But if we don't kill off cockroaches, rats and other vermin how can we keep them under control?"

"Well, there are better ways. In Rajasthan there is a famous temple of Karni Mata. Thousands of white mice live in it. If you sit inside the temple long enough they will begin to climb all over you, which is an eerie feeling. The Maharaja of Bikaner allots to the temple a certain amount of grain, which is distributed to these mice. And in the surrounding area, for miles around, very little if any of the grain in the fields is ever eaten by rodents. Nature likes it when we try to work with Her, and She loses Her temper when we don't.

"But at least when you kill vermin they can't remain human for too long. Most of the higher mammals that we murder, though, can adapt fairly well to the human body. Most Westerners are fond of beef and pork, and when I have visited the West I have not been surprised to find large numbers of pig-humans and cow-humans there; pigs and cows who have been temporarily reborn as humans. They gravitate to the flesh of the animal they used to be because it feels so familiar to them. But even those people who were recently other animals show a perverse sort of fondness for beef or pork. Why perverse? Well, for one thing neither of those meats is fit for human consumption. From the point of view of your health a regular diet of either beef or pork will make you more prone to degenerative diseases like arthritis, rheumatism and gout.

"But the worst effects of beef and pork are on the mind. One of the words for cow in Sanskrit is *go*, which also means sense organ. This suggests that anyone who eats the flesh of the cow becomes more animalistic, more physical, more attached to the world of the senses and their objects. Those who eat beef will find it very difficult to control their senses and soar into the astral regions, which is what you must do if you want to make real spiritual progress. And pork! If you want to know what pork can do to you just look at the sow. She will have sex with any boar she likes whenever she likes, even if she is pregnant. And if she is hungry after delivery she will eat her own piglets."

I knew this to be true.

"If you think carefully about this whole meat business you will realize that the more violence you use to obtain your food the more violence you will use and experience in your everyday life. Violent food will cause you to tend to attract violence to yourself, and will make you more interested in inflicting violence on others. For example, it is because meat eaters are so intent upon cutting flesh that both they and the doctors that treat them usually prefer surgical medicine."

"The Law of Karma; curses and blessings."

"Exactly. You know, once all the goats who had been slaughtered by humans, in ritual sacrifices and for food, held a congress. After they compared notes with one another regarding the various miseries they had suffered at the hands of priests and butchers they decided that they should perform some rituals themselves. So the goats organized a *Maha Vidweshan Prayoga* (a great ritual for causing hatred and discord), and dedicated the fruits of this ritual to the human race so that men would slaughter one another just as they slaughter goats."

"The goats seem to have done a pretty good job of spreading strife with their *prayoga* (ritual)."

"Yes they have. And I'll tell you this too: until people stop eating meat the population of the world will not go down no matter what the governments try to do. Animals love to procreate, you know, and when they become humans they retain many of the impressions of their animal lives, including especially the desire for sex. No matter how much the authorities push birth control it won't help. And abortion is not the answer either! Sometimes abortion may be necessary, of course, and when it is necessary it is not so bad if it is done before the fourth month. Before the fourth month the *jiva* (individual soul) is not so firmly connected to the fetus that the baby has started to move. The karma for an abortion which is done later, though, after the heart begins to beat, is the same as for murder."

"Hitler was a vegetarian."

"Yes, I know that. Meat-eating is just one of the factors which causes war—but it is a significant one."

"Some people insist that the earliest humans were hunter-gatherers whose diet consisted almost entirely of meat."

"There is considerable doubt among modern scientists that ancient men were strict carnivores. I personally believe that primitive man in India never ate meat. Instead he ate only tubers, roots and fruits, and when he realized what he was doing he began to live only on air. Some of those early men and women who were super-dupers went beyond air also. However, it would not astound me if in most other countries people became more and more primitive instead of more and more refined as time passed, and started to kill and eat animals.

"And don't think that this belief of mine makes me some sort of namby-pamby pacifist. I have killed men when I was in the army. I also used to enjoy hunting, until the day I went out with Mr. Williams of Stanvac, the company that later became Esso. He was an American, and I wasn't much impressed with him; he would get tired after a few miles and then go back to the tent and drink beer.

"Anyway, on this trip I happened to shoot a *gaur* (Indian bison). I dropped him with a clean shot. As I stepped up to finish him off, if need be, I looked into his eyes. The look he gave me made me stop dead in my tracks. It said, 'The only reason you killed me is that I am so much better than you. You couldn't appreciate me for being stronger and more handsome than you are; in your weakness your only way to gain power over me was to kill me.' He was right. I pulled my earlobes and I have never hunted since that day."

Like many people in India Vimalananda would pull his earlobes when admitting to being at fault. Though convinced of his sincerity on this subject one thing still bothered me: "You yourself still eat meat occasionally," I noted.

"Yes I do, but only when I am convinced that doing so is the best to settle a specific rnanubandhana. Besides, I know how to eat that meat so that it will not pollute my mind. Nor I have not forgotten the Law of Karma, for after I eat meat I always repay my debt to the animal by making sure that it will be promptly reborn in a higher womb. Do we think that Jhendu Kumar knows anything at all about such things, or that he would bother to think about them even if he did? Any meat eater who can't take care of the animal he eats is asking for big trouble."

"Which is a big reason that you have told me never to eat meat." I had actually become vegetarian a year and a half before being introduced to Vimalananda.

"Correct. If I told you to eat meat either I would have to take responsibility for that animal's welfare, even if it was your gullet that its body went down, or I would have to teach you how to repay your debt to the animal, which I am not yet ready to do. There may be some times, though, that I will advise you to eat a specific piece of meat in order to settle a specific rnanubandhana. In those cases I will take personal responsibility for the animal and will do something for it. And for you, too, if your mental digestion is not yet strong enough to handle its meat."

During our years together Vimalananda enjoined me to eat meat on three separate occasions.

"It is because killing the animal is far worse than just enjoying its meat that the Buddhists have the Three-Hand Law. They say that three hands participate in preparing of meat for the table: the hands of the slaughterer, the butcher, and the cook. Each of these people takes up part of the meat's karma, leaving the eater of the meat with much less karma to take on than if he had killed, dressed and prepared the flesh himself. This is why I tell those of my 'children' who eat meat that they should never select a living animal and instruct a butcher to kill it for them. That action of identifying yourself with the karma—that intention that 'this animal should die for me'—magnifies its effects tremendously. I always advise people to go to the cold storage shop and see what is available. If nothing is there, well, your rnanubandhanas are with other animals than those whose bodies lie there, and you will have to wait until later to eat meat. As it is everyone who goes to a butcher can only obtain meat from those animals with which they have some rnanubandhana. Furthermore, they can only buy those body parts which that animal owes to them. If no animal that day has any rnanubandhana with them, then even if they want to buy the meat they will not be able to do so: they will run out of money, or will suddenly have to leave, or will change their minds at the last minute, or whatever."

"The butcher is also ruled by rnanubandhana. He has a right to slaughter animals because he himself was slaughtered in so many births. He can kill as many as killed him in times past; only that number and no more. When he runs out of animals to kill he will automatically retire, or change his business, or develop arthritis in his hands so he can no longer hold his knife, or something like that. Nature really knows Her job best.

"Remember this: Any time you have an opportunity to deliberately slay an animal it is nothing but payback for a time in the past when the animal slew you. This is the only reason that you get the chance to kill it now. If you decide to go ahead and settle your score your new action will guarantee that animal the opportunity to hunt you down later and kill you yet again—unless you know how to avoid it. Butchers could also, if they liked, refuse to exercise their right to slaughter. If they did their personal karmic cycles of killing and being killed would then cease—but the weight of their accumulated karmas is so heavy that only a handful of butchers have ever even considered such a thing.

"One who did was a poor fellow who eked out a meager living for himself and his family by slaughtering and butchering one goat each day. It so happened that one night a guest arrived at his place after the family had already eaten. The law of hospitality clearly states that a guest must be fed, but there was no food left in the house. The butcher could slaughter the next day's goat, but the meat that was not eaten that night would spoil by the next day, for there was nothing like refrigeration then. Such a loss would ruin him.

"The butcher went out into the pen and looked morosely at the goat, which was a mature billy-goat. Suddenly he had an idea: If he only castrated the goat instead of killing it he would be able to get just enough meat from the testicles to feed the guest. The goat would continue to live, albeit in agony, until the next morning, when he could be dispatched.

"Pleased with this plan the butcher had begun to sharpen his knife when he heard a strange noise coming from the goat. When he removed the knife from the grindstone and listened more attentively he found that the goat was simultaneously crying and laughing. A more intellectual man would have been astonished that he could understand goat language, but the butcher simply went over and asked the goat what he was doing. Calming somewhat the goat replied, 'I am crying because I am thinking of the torture I will suffer tonight after you cut me, but I am laughing because that torture will last only until morning. Then I will die, which will free me from my misery, and after I am reborn I will be able to seek you out and take my revenge!'

"The butcher dropped his knife and stood stock still for a moment. Then he left the goat, left his family, left the guest in the house, and went straight to the jungle without saying anything to anyone. Eventually he became a saint."

"He was lucky."

"He *was* lucky—which means that he was destined for it. His good karmas had matured to the point that he was able to hear the goat, and to understand what the goat told him. Most beings, though, never realize what they are doing, and remain bound tightly to the wheel of karma. A dead mink, who was still weeping bitterly from the pain of having been flayed alive, was once ushered into the presence of God. God's heart was so touched that He told the mink, 'Ask whatever you want and I will give it to you.'

"Sobbing between its words, the little mink said, 'O Lord, now I have no skin to keep me warm. What I want is a human skin coat, so the humans who tormented me will know what it means to have your skin torn from your living body.'

"God replied softly but firmly, 'If you understood the Law of Karma you would know why you had to be flayed alive and such words would never emerge from your mouth.'"

"But according to the Law of Karma the mink will eventually get a chance to flay its flayer alive, right?"

"Yes indeed—but how will that help? It will just keep the whole process in motion. Forget about revenge; that is God's job. The Old Testament says, 'Vengeance is mine, saith the Lord.' Jesus went even further; He said, 'Turn the other cheek.' An ordinary person has no patience. He wants immediate revenge when he is wronged; he always strikes back when injured. But that is not the way to do things. That way ties you even more firmly to the wheel of action and reaction. So often when someone plays dirty with me I want to retaliate. But then I remember, *kshamam virasya bhushanam* ('forbearance is the ornament of a hero'). If you can be patient Nature will arrange your life for you in such a way that you will eventually gain what you desire; about this there is no doubt. Doubt exists only in how long it will take for your desired result to come to pass."

"Is this what you are talking about when you talk about cooperating with Nature?"

"Yes. When you get to the point where you can manipulate your karmas on your own, or you find someone who is willing to manipulate them for you, then you may be able to fine-tune your destiny to some extent. Otherwise, your fate in the form of your karmas is going to determine your path for you. Then your job will be to walk that path in the most graceful way possible. There is nothing graceful about revenge because it is so very difficult to know precisely how much retribution your previous karmas entitle you to. Do you remember Shylock from the *Merchant of Venice*? He was entitled to a pound of flesh but to none of the blood therein. Any compensation beyond the amount to which you are entitled creates a rnanubandhana, a new karmic account that you will eventually have to square up.

"Moreover, the world of rnanubandhana is such that if I owe you cash I will have to pay you back in cash even if I want to pay you back in kind. And I will pay you as much as I owe you even if I don't want to. Everything depends on the size of the debt. If I reach into my pocket to give a ten-paise coin to a beggar and I pull out a fifty-paise coin, I owed him more than I thought I did. And what if I offer a beggar a ten-paise coin and he gets wild and refuses to accept it, saying, 'Why are you trying to give me this when I want a rupee?' The reason I cannot pay him is because I don't owe him anything. If you know about debt you can know how to repay."

All I could say at this point was, "This is all very complex."

"Let us take a practical example," responded Vimalananda with increasing enthusiasm, "so that you will understand exactly what I mean. Mohammed Jalal-ud-din Akbar, the greatest of the Great Mughals, was every inch a ruler. Although he grew up among the cruelest of the cruel, and although he himself was very hard about certain things, Akbar was never overcome by blood-lust. At thirteen he won his father's empire back from the Hindu usurper Hemu. When Akbar's adviser and boyhood mentor Bairam Khan dragged the defeated Hemu in front of Akbar he told the boy, 'Cut his throat personally, my lord, and become *ghazi* (the title applied to a Muslim who has killed an infidel).' But Akbar told Bairam Khan, 'I am not a butcher to kill an unarmed captive. Let my butchers do it.' The 99.9% of rulers who lack true nobility destroy themselves; only the rare ones, like Akbar, have any idea of what is really going on. Akbar was a true king, and the life he lived is the type of life one calls *shahi* (regal, majestic). Even though at that tender age Akbar probably knew nothing of the Law of Karma, he seemed to have a natural understanding of right actions and wrong actions.

"True kingliness has always been rare among rulers, all throughout history, and we do not see it at all among today's rulers. So ask yourself now how we could see it in Akbar? On one side of his family he was descended from Genghis Khan and on the other side from Tamerlane, both extremely cruel, bloodthirsty conquerors. Why did he not show their traits of barbarism in his own life when he showed that he had inherited their expertise in strategy and in battle? The answer is not too difficult. In his previous life Akbar had been Prithviraj Chauhan, the Hindu emperor of Northwest India. Prithviraj was a *Rajput*, a warrior from Western India, who exhibited all the noble traits that he had inherited from the Rajput rulers who came before him. Akbar inherited these traits from his previous incarnation, and they were strong enough to overshadow the viciousness that he inherited from his immediate forebears.

"Prithviraj's story is very educational. Like Akbar Prithviraj was a great king with great associates, and yet he was defeated in battle, blinded, and forced to commit mutual suicide with his best friend. Prithviraj was a fearless and able warrior whose kingdom was well defended. Even his servants had achieved success with their worship of Ma. The goddess Chamunda, one of Ma's terrifying destructive aspects, appeared to Prithviraj's general Chamunda Rai every day to invigorate and advise him. A different aspect of Ma appeared each day to Chand Barot, Prithviraj's bard, and provided even more shakti to strengthen Prithviraj's authority. With such powerful shaktis at Prithviraj's beck and call what could have gone wrong? How could he have ever been conquered? I'll tell you how: Prithviraj lost his throne, his sight, and his life because of the theft of a woman. He stole his wife Sanyukta from her father's house. This was no doubt a custom of the time, but it was still a karma. Back in the time of the *Mahabharata* the great hero Arjuna stole Lord Krishna's sister Subhadra. It is true that Arjuna did so at Krishna's instigation, but karma is karma. What was the result? Arjuna's enemies conspired to isolate Abhimanyu, Arjuna's son by Subhadra, on the battlefield, and killed him there. To obtain shakti is not so difficult; to retain it is no joke."

The *Mahabharata* is one of India's two great epic poems. "How exactly did all this happen?"

"Sanyukta's father hated Prithviraj. When he arranged a swayamvara for his daughter he made it a point not to invite Prithviraj." In a *swayamvara* ("personal choice" ceremony) a girl chose her own husband from among a number of eligible suitors. "To insult Prithviraj yet further Sanyukta's father ordered a statue of Prithviraj to be made. He installed this statue outside his door and told all his visitors, 'Look, Prithviraj is my doorkeeper; how will he marry my daughter?'

"This was because the law books stated that a lowly doorkeeper was not fit to marry a princess?"

"That's right. But Prithviraj was not to be denied. He came to the swayamvara anyway, in disguise, with Chand Barot and some supporters. Sanyukta, who had been secretly informed of the plot, made a big show of circulating among the assembled princes, trying to choose, when suddenly she garlanded the statue! That sparked off a major fracas which expanded into a brawl when Prithviraj and his men sprang up and ran off with Sanyukta.

They escaped to Prithviraj's kingdom, where they married."

"Hold on—if Sanyukta voluntarily went off with Prithviraj, how can you call it a theft? Was Sanyukta her father's property, like Hebrew girls were their father's property in Biblical days, that he could do with her as he willed?"

"Not at all. If that were the case, where would the question of svayamvara have arisen? But Sanyukta's father *saw* it as a theft, and acted accordingly."

"Wait, wait, wait! If one day I pick something up off the road that is free for the asking, do you mean that you could accuse me of theft just because you happen to *think* you own it?"

"Why not? Remember, almost all of karma is curses and blessings. There is no law that says a curse or a blessing has to be based in clear perception. If people had really clear perception they would never curse each other! Even a misguided blessing or curse can produce some effect if it is strong enough. I could give you plenty of incidents from Indian tradition, but let us take one that you are probably already familiar with. Have you forgotten your own Bible? Don't you remember how Jacob covered himself with fur to trick his father Isaac into giving him the blessing that was really meant for Jacob's brother Esau? Even though it was not what Isaac had intended it happened anyway, and when Esau arrived late Isaac had to tell him, 'I'm sorry, but your brother has taken by guile that which was yours.' Jacob had to pay for his deception—he lost his favorite son Joseph for so many years—but the blessing accrued to him nonetheless. And this is just one instance of misdirected blessings and curses in the Bible. Read it again and you'll find many more!"

I knew there was more to Jacob's story than this, but I also knew that Vimalananda was intent on making a point.

"Don't forget that the size of the blessing or the curse will determine the size of its effects. Isaac's words had extra power because he was a patriarch, and a dedicated worshipper of God. His blessing became extraordinarily powerful because it was a deathbed blessing. In moments of extreme emotion even ordinary people can put powerful shakti behind their words. Right or wrong, if I have some good shakti you are going to feel the effects of my curse when if I curse you, even if it is for taking something that I only think belongs to me. It is true that I will eventually have to suffer for cursing you, but first you will have to suffer. That is the Law of Karma."

"Do I understand this correctly? Even though Prithviraj's elopement was in no way a theft Prithviraj had to suffer just because Sanyukta's father acted as if it were a theft?"

"Yes, the curse had an effect because Sanyukta's father hated Prithviraj passionately for carrying off his daughter. That effect was multiplied because Sanyukta's father was a king, a man of power in the mundane world. You have to be cautious with the mighty. We have a saying in Hindi:

Raja jogi agni jal, kabhi na kijiye prit,
Are prit kiye to nibayie Parashuramji, kyonki un ke ulti rit.

"Lord Dattatreya, who is teaching his disciple Parashurama, says, 'O Para-shurama, you should never befriend a king, a yogi, the fire, or water, but if you do befriend them then tend to that friendship very carefully, because their nature is very contrary.' The king can award you lands and wealth in one breath and sentence you to death in the next. The fire can cook your food, or burn you. Water can wash you or drown you. And a sadhu? If he is pleased with you he'll do anything for you; the sky's the limit. But if you get him angry you'll be finished, totally ruined.

"Sanyukta's father cursed Prithviraj by sending a message to the tyrannical Mohammed Ghori of Afghanistan to invite him to invade India and conquer Prithviraj. He also provided Ghori with many of the defense secrets of the kingdom. This was bad enough. Still, Prithviraj had all the advantages that I just told you about, and he could easily have survived Ghori's attacks had he not made one fatal blunder."

"What was that?"

"Not too long after the wedding Prithviraj's guru, who happened to be an Aghori, came to call. The guru told the king, 'I will take a nail and put it into the head of *Shesha Naga* (the great thousand-headed serpent who supports the earth). Then the Hindu Empire will be firmly established and will remain unassailable for centuries.' Everyone watched solemnly while the guru ceremoniously placed an iron nail into the ground. Then Prithviraj's wife Sanyukta said to her husband, 'What is this naked fellow trying to tell you? "Put the nail in the head of Shesha Naga?" What nonsense! Tell him to prove that the nail has reached Shesha Naga.' It was always foolish to taunt an Aghori and dare him to prove himself, but we can't blame Sanyukta too much because something else was speaking through her mouth."

"Something like the curse of her own father?"

"At least in part. Some other karmas were probably influencing her mind too. Whatever the factors may have been Prithviraj now fell wholly under their influence because of his own karmas. The Aghori told him, 'Great King, do not listen to her!' But Prithviraj insisted that the Aghori do as the queen had bidden him. The guru stared sadly for a moment at his wayward 'child.' Then he sighed, 'Led astray by a woman's words,' and pulled up the nail—which was dripping with blood. Everyone was horrified. Prithviraj begged his guru to return the nail to Shesha Naga's head, but the guru told him, 'It is too late now; the auspicious moment has passed. You were blinded then by love for your wife, but now you will literally be blinded; you cannot escape it.'

"And what happened next? Ten times Mohammed Ghori invaded India, and ten times he was defeated and captured by Prithviraj. Each time that he was brought into Prithviraj's presence Ghori would say, 'I am your cow. A *Kshatriya* (member of the warrior caste) must protect all cows. I put myself at your mercy.' Each time this happened, Prithviraj would release him— *kshamam virasya bhushanam*.

"Prithviraj resisted revenge ten times. The eleventh time his luck—his good karmas—finally ran out, and he was captured by Mohammed Ghori. Ghori then exhibited his own variety of compassion and gratitude by immediately blinding Prithviraj, thus fulfilling the Aghori's prophecy. How low can a man go! Only a bigoted barbarian would dare to touch the person of the man who had forgiven and protected him not once but ten times before. And that's what Ghori was: a filthy, vulgar barbarian, human dregs. He took Prithviraj back with him to Afghanistan as sport for his populace. After parading him around for a while Ghori installed Prithviraj in his palace, along with Chand Barot. Prithviraj now had plenty of time to reflect over his guru's words, and he realized all his follies. He became filled with a terrible resolve and determined that such a brute as Ghori should not continue to live. He and Chand concocted a plan.

"The next day Prithviraj boasted to Ghori: 'You consider yourself a great conqueror, but you are just a vandal. I, on the other hand, am a true warrior. Why, even without eyes I can still hit a target's bull's-eye with an arrow, solely with the help of Chand Barot's guidance. You could not do such a thing even in your dreams.'

"This stung Ghori, so he decided to force Prithviraj to make good his boast. He even invited all the residents of his city to watch Prithviraj make a fool of himself. As Prithviraj stood facing the target, Chand gave him directions not for the target but for the conqueror, who sat nearby on a throne observing the proceedings. Chand being a bard, his directions came out in a couplet:

> *Char bhanj, chaubis gaz, angula ashta praman,*
> *Vahan pe baitho sultan he, mat chuke Chauhan.*

"Four bhanj, twenty-four gaz, eight angulas away,
There is sitting the Sultan, Chauhan, don't dare miss him now."[1]

"These instructions were so accurate that Prithviraj's arrow sped straight to Ghori's chest, pierced his heart, and killed him. Then, to forestall recapture and torture, Prithviraj and Chand swiftly stabbed each other to death."

"Wow."

---

1. An *angula* is approximately 3/4 of an inch, and a *gaz* is about 25 inches. The length of a *bhanj* is uncertain.

"Ghori was a beast, and Prithviraj was a hero. Prithviraj, who had been unable to succeed as emperor, was rewarded for his sufferings by being reborn as Akbar, and as Akbar he reigned as the most glorious of emperors. Chand was reborn as Birbal, Akbar's closest confidant and the originator of much of his policy. See how karma works! Prithviraj was a Kshatriya and Chand was a low-caste bard. Akbar, though Emperor of India, was not a Hindu, and Birbal was born a *Brahmana* (a member of India's priestly caste)!

"Many of Akbar's personality traits were holdovers from his life as Prithviraj. Even when he had the chance to personally kill Hemu he refused to sink to Ghori's level of predation."

"Yes, but he still had him executed."

"True, but in those days if you let a rival live there was every chance that one fine morning you would find a dagger between your shoulder blades. At least Akbar had Hemu executed quickly without torture. That in no way saved Akbar from the karma of Hemu's death, but it was still a form of compassion. It was in fact the form of compassion that was appropriate in this situation. Torture was omnipresent in those days; why, Akbar's own son used to enjoy watching condemned prisoners being flayed alive. For Akbar to have been able to live in the environment of intrigue and assassination into which he was born and still not become a boodthirsty tyrant showed remarkable nobility.

"Akbar could not have learned this sort of nobility in his one lifetime as Prithviraj, of course. It had to be cultivated within him over many, many lives. But Akbar did 'inherit' many of his principal character traits from Prithviraj. Because Prithviraj had been a Hindu Akbar's chief advisers were Hindus and Jodha Bai, his favorite wife, was a Hindu. He loved her dearly, but because Prithviraj had been blinded when he was led astray by Sanyukta, Akbar never allowed himself be ruled by his wife's advice alone. And because a Muslim had betrayed and blinded him he was always wary of his fellow Muslims. Most of the Rajput chiefs realized this, and cooperated with Akbar to build the empire. Man Singh of Jaipur, who was Akbar's commander-in-chief, was a Kshatriya, and Man Singh's sister Jodha Bai, who became Akbar's empress, was the mother of his son Salim, who succeeded Akbar as the Emperor Jehangir."

I have recently learned that Jodha Bai, daughter of Udai Singh of Marwar, was actually Jehangir's wife, mother of the Emperor Shahjehan. Jehangir's mother, daughter of Bhar Mal of Amber and sister of Man Singh, was named Harkha.

"Although Akbar was a Muslim he wore a Vedic sacred thread, worshipped the sun, and put an end to cow slaughter throughout his empire. The secular government of India has not been able to end cow slaughter, but the Muslim Emperor Akbar could! What do you have to say to that?"

"I'd say that it showed substantial compassion for the cows."

"Indeed it did. But what is even more remarkable is that Akbar even started his own religion, which called *Din-e-ilahi* ('the religion of God'). His own religion—can you beat that? Has any other Muslim ever dared to try this? Most Muslims think that Islam is the only true religion, and those Muslims who have strayed even slightly from the path, like Mansur and Shams-i Tabrizi, have been butchered. And here was a Muslim who said, 'No, what we need is a religion of God'!"

"Didn't Akbar have a profound mystical experience during his youth? Perhaps that had something to do with his interest in religion."

"I'm sure that it did. Akbar wanted Din-e-ilahi to be a synthesis of all the religions, just as his Empire was a federation of all the Indian states. He wanted to make people realize that everyone worships the same God and that everyone works toward reaching God at his own rate of speed. This is what I also say: everyone should carve out his own niche. Akbar wanted to stop all the animal sacrifices and other meaningless rituals. He wanted to show people that the way to God leads inwards, not outwards into repetitious rites. This attitude caused many of the clergy from all the religions to hate him, but he was their Emperor, so there was nothing they could do about it. They dared not even wag their tongues lest those tongues be torn out by their roots by Akbar's executioner, Mian Kamruddin. Akbar was very strict about decorum and discipline.

"Akbar was meant by Nature to be Emperor. He was able to bring all of India under his control because it was his destiny to do it. If the English and the Germans believe in 'divide and conquer,' well, I think Akbar was greater. He believed in 'unify and rule,' and he practiced what he preached. Nowadays in India Rana Pratap Singh of Udaipur is regarded as a great hero because he was the sole major Rajput king to resist Akbar. The Hindu fanatics say that this showed his willingness to resist tyranny. But what was the ultimate result of his actions? Thousands of Rajput women commited mass suicide by self-immolation after their husbands had died on the battlefield, and that's about it. When Akbar requested Rana Pratap to enter the federation peacefully he said, 'No, never!' with great bravado. Is that the way to behave with someone who is infinitely stronger than you? A true Kshatriya would think of his subjects and their wives and have compassion for them before starting a futile war.

"You know, I did my M.A. in Mughal history, and I think I know what I am saying when I say that Akbar was one of the greatest rulers ever. His was a truly secular state. Even though he was an illiterate Afghani he patronized the

arts and sciences, and gathered all the top men of music, poetry and adminis-
tration into his court. He built Fatehpur Sikri entirely from scratch as his capital city; even today you can see how architecturally unequaled and amazing
it is. Akbar's rule was really the culmination of the entire age. There were
other kingdoms in the world at that time, but none could rival the splendor,
the power and the glory that was his. He was and until today still is unique,
one of a kind. None of his successors could match him, and after him the decline of independent India began in earnest.

"And even though India is again independent we are in such deep decline
that the wisdom of the world has become *kshamam virasya dushanam*—not
bhushanam (ornament) but *dushanam* (error)."

" 'Forbearance is a hero's stain?' "

"Yes, today children are taught, 'Do unto others before they do unto you';
they are told that only stupid people fail to speedily retaliate. After Stoney lost
I had a good mind to take the whalebone to Jhendu Kumar's hide myself—
but why? I could have Jhendu Kumar maimed or killed in a trice by paying a
few rupees to a thug, or by showing some fake tears to one of my ethereal
friends. But that would make me beholden to them, which would cost me
dearly later on. No thanks! I'd rather bide my time and let Nature deal with
Jhendu Kumar so that I need not soil my hands. I try to live my life cooperating with Nature from the beginning, which is the true path of least resistance.
When I take this sort of long-term look at the situation I remember where I
am headed, and I think of how retaliation would make me detour from my
course. It would be such a pity for a boat to cross a storm-filled ocean and
then sink within sight of the shore."

"So all you have to do is to be patient."

"Do you think that's some kind of joke? The hardest thing in the world is
to bide your time."

chapter two
ELAN

I MET VIMALANANDA first in September 1975 on the day that Elan, one of his most reliable mares, won her first race for him. I first accompanied him to the races on the day of Stoney's last outing. Horse racing began in Bombay in the early decades of the nineteenth century when a race ground emerged in what is now the predominantly Christian district of Byculla. When the time came to search for greener pastures, the Royal Western India Turf Club Limited (R.W.I.T.C. for short) selected a low-lying site near Bombay's famous temple of Mahalakshmi, the goddess of wealth and prosperity. Most members of the Indian racing public mistakenly assume that the Mahalakshmi racecourse, which is among the world's most beautiful wagering venues, was a British production. In truth it was an Indian, Sir Cusrow N. Wadia, the Parsi who was then head of the textile giant Bombay Dyeing, who oversaw the entire project from concept through planning to construction. He gave the club an interest-free loan of Rs. 4 million ($10 million or more in today's dollars) and went himself to Melbourne, Australia to obtain a blueprint. Thanks to his farsightedness there is only one turn for all races up to and including 1600 meters (one mile).

After racing ceases in Bombay in April, when the heat makes the course too hard for horses to safely run upon it, those horses which do not proceed to Hyderabad, Bangalore or some other venue for monsoon racing are moved to the R.W.I.T.C.'s facility in Poona. There they relax during the summer and the first part of the rainy season while torrents inundate the Bombay stables. The course in Poona sits atop land which is rented from the Southern Command of the Indian Army. It is a little jewel box that occupies the southeast corner of the hundreds of acres of military installations that is collectively known as the Poona Cantonment. At the end of the Poona season, which usually lasts less than three months, the horses are again loaded aboard their vans or aboard a special train and return to Bombay, where racing commences in late November or early December after the mud in the stables has thoroughly dried.

Racegoers have a choice of three enclosures inside that eminently tangible allegory for life that is the Bombay racecourse. Inside the Members' Enclosure sit the nobility of the racing world: horse trainers, horse owners, Stewards, and Members of the Club and their guests. Club Membership is an exceptionally exclusive privilege which postulants achieve only after dangling for a decade or more on the waiting list. Many Club Members are also owners. Most of those who weren't were, at least at that time, nouveau riche industrialists, old-monied erstwhile maharajas, nawabs, and other upper-crust cavaliers and their wives. These grandees graced races mainly to see and be seen as they reclined in comfortable chairs sipping and nibbling, hazarding trivial sums on their whims or on favorites whose names were bruited about by those in the know. Each year one or more of these dignified personages would be fatally bitten by the gambling bug and embark upon the road to ruin. Sometimes I would turn my field glasses on the latest reputedly doomed victim and watch him saunter on the grass below the winning post as he sank deeper into economic quicksand with each step of his gallant promenade.

The Second Enclosure is reserved for commoners, those petty tradespeople, underpaid clerks and unemployed slackers who bet only a few rupees but study the racing form with the concentration and scream with the delight or anguish of those who bet thousands. These people, who lack all access to the insider information that is crucial for placing sensible wagers, mostly come to the races to lose money agitatedly. They count among their number a smattering of expert (though rarely formally trained) statisticians, pedigree investigators, hunchmeisters and the like, men and women who occasionally flabbergast both themselves and onlookers with their serendipity.

In between the Member's and the Second is the First Enclosure, on whose wooden benches Vimalananda and I would sit when we came to watch the races. True to its central location it is the home of mostly middle-class bettors who may have some peripheral connections to people at the track and so are often able to stake their money on "good things." If only "good things" could be guaranteed to win! Though he was an owner Vimalananda hated the incestuously cloying atmosphere of the Member's and preferred to breathe the free air of the First Enclosure. His friends there, who were mostly Parsis, included Cama, an upper-echelon civil servant, and Firoz Godrej, the bluff, broad-shouldered transport manager of a local soft-drink bottling firm who was usually squired to the track by his milder son Noshir.

A week after the Stone Ice debacle I again accompanied Vimalananda to the Bombay races in his 1967 Austin Cambridge station wagon, which we protected by promising a few rupees to one of the young boys who loitered in the parking lot posing as attendants. At the entrance we were accosted by the usual gang of avid sellers of race cards (Cole is the most popular brand), desperate tipsters (the most enduring of whom is a devalued coin who styles himself "Prof. Joker, the Guru"), and despairing gamblers seeking inside information. Just past the entrance stands the Ring, the oval enclosure composed of the stalls of the bookmakers licensed by the Club. Around the Ring stand the hardened gamblers, the men and women with eyes of coagulated greed, who ignore everything except the odds that the bookies chalk onto their narrow blackboards. When the odds become unexpectedly favorable at one stall these maniacs elbow and shove their way there en masse to scream out their wagers. Vimalananda, the ex-wrestler, could easily hold his own with the most raptorial of these gamesters when he entered the Ring, but my height gave me a signal advantage when it came to thrusting money into a bookie's hands. Since I could also by then run up and down stairs more fleetly than he, I was often given the task of betting his favorites for him.

Bettors who lack the money or the nerve to wager with the bookies in the Ring utilize the Tote, or Totalizator, which is run by the Club. The minimum Tote risk is five rupees (then about 70 cents). Between the Ring and the Tote swirl the flotsam and jetsam of racecourse society, propelled on waves of avarice toward their rendezvous with an equine-mediated destiny. On that afternoon it was a world still unknown enough to me to be fascinating. Here huddled a group of astrology buffs debating the latest predictive theory; there leaned a man bent on seducing his pretty companion with the promise of a winner at long odds. Before me the clerks in the office sat calculating stipends and logging payments; behind me the racing populace conferred enigmatically in hurried tones. I navigated this corridor with all the care that one would accord a piranha-filled river.

Vimalananda's friends in the stands were invariably happy to see him trudge up the stairs to his usual seat, for he always tried to give them at least one good horse to bet on during a long afternoon of racing. From where we sat we could see to our right, in the east, the chimneys of a few of the more than one hundred textile mills that are strewn about Bombay. To our north we viewed the planetarium, and to our left sat the naked horizon that betokened the sea beneath it. Cama was already in his place that afternoon, and Firoz and Noshir soon joined us, but Vimalananda's mind seemed too preoccupied to participate in their enthusiasms. When he announced that he had come only to watch these runners and not to bet on them, the others quickly retreated to the business of their calculations. Vimalananda then looked at me with the eyebrow equivalent of a wink, and as I looked into his race book I watched him mark with his thumbnail one horse in each of the races. This was the first time I saw a procedure which I and others would see now and again thereafter, with the same results: each horse that he marked thus would always win, and never would he bet on those races.

Eventually it became old hat, but on this first occasion I was frankly astonished that he could pick eight winners in a row and neither bet himself nor let his friends in on his secret. I was also shocked that though Elan was running she was not a "good thing." "You told me," I protested, "that you always race your animals to win."

"And I do," he replied, "provided that they are in fact on the job. When they *are* on the job everyone knows that they are on the job, so that they can all bet and enjoy along with me. It is always best to share your profits with good people; when you spread the karma around by making others your 'partners in karma' your own burden gets significantly reduced. But only the greatest horses can win every race they run in, and while I love Elan she is not unbeatable. I could have just galloped her to make her fit, but this run will act as a gallop. Besides, I will be paid for it; I get a subsidy from the Club each time one of my horses runs. Also, by running and losing she will go down in handicap, which will make it easier for her to win next time. When she *is* on the job everyone will know it, have no fear."

We continued to chat about racing until, after the fourth or fifth race, he began to comment conspiratorially from an astrological standpoint on the day's large number of unlucky-looking attendees. Jyotish regards such characteristics as oddly-shaped bodies and uneven teeth as indications of affliction by malefic planets, which impede the free flow of *prana* (the life force). When such unusual individuals appear at critical moments in one's life they often foretoken negative events, and at first I thought that he had refrained from betting that afternoon from fear of some temporary obstruction to his own luck.

But he picked up on my thought and contradicted it: "Luck is nothing but a matter of karmas, and there is nothing wrong with my luck—not today, at least. Today I am in a different mood. Only a handful of people have ever entered the racecourse and left it again in one piece with their money, character and balance of mind intact. I was an inveterate gambler, uncontrollable, until my Junior Guru Maharaj brought me under control. My gurus cured me of the gambling disease. I gamble now, but I control it; it doesn't control me. Still, gambling is a serious karma; it permanently devastates your mind. In fact, they say that it is one of the three things that cannot ordinarily be atoned for in this lifetime."

"What are the other two?"

"Rape and guru-murder."

"Gambling is that serious?"

"It is very serious, but I have learned how to karmically atone for my gambling, so I'm not worried about that karma. What I *am* worried about is misusing my other talents. I am always happy to bet on my own fancies, on the horses that I have selected as winners on the basis of their pedigrees, records, handicaps and recent track work. But suppose that someone, some ethereal being, comes to me and says, 'Why do all that work? Here are the winners for today's races; go out and enjoy yourself!' I could take his advice and make lots of money that way—but what about the karma? What about the gambling karma, and the karma of taking money that I didn't deserve, and most of all the karma of going under the obligation of that ethereal being? Somewhere along the line he will want me to do something for him, something I may not want to do. How will I be able to refuse him if I am in his debt?

"I used to make money on racing with the help of information from the ethereal world, just to test it—and then I would promptly dispose of my winnings. Sometimes I would pay off my debts or other people's debts with that money. For the longest time I would go down to Crawford Market whenever I had a good day at the races and buy up all the pigeons and doves and other birds waiting there to be slaughtered. Then I would free them, just to watch them fly away and enjoy their freedom. Eventually, though, my mentors made me see what I was getting myself into. Now I just like to sit, and watch, and appreciate the cleverness of my ethereal friends. Besides, if I take everything that I am due from these horses too soon that will be all I'll be able to get from them. Then there will be no fun in coming to the races; if I had no promissory notes to cash in I wouldn't be able to do anything but lose!

"When I owned my dairy in Borivali in North Bombay all the other owners used to complain that while their buffaloes would go dry within nine months after calving mine were still producing even after fourteen or fifteen months. I told them, 'It's simple. You add water to your milk to increase your profit, but I never add water. Each buffalo and calf has an individual rnanubandhana with me, a debt of a specific size that will repay me a specific sum of money. I am content to receive repayment at the rate which Nature feels is appropriate for me. You want your money faster, but because you cannot get more from your buffaloes than they owe you your buffaloes have to go dry sooner. They go dry, in fact, as soon as they pay you back what they owe you, according to their rnanubandhanas with you.'"

"So the only buffaloes that would enter your stable would be those that owe you money?"

"How else would they be able to come to me?"

He interrupted his train of thought so that we could watch the next winner flash past our stands. Then some railbirds haled us into their dispute over likely Derby winners. It was only after the races had ended for the day that he again took up the threads of his argument, as we began our drive home. The sun was just then setting tumescently behind the tomb of Haji Ali like a well-cooked samosa dunked by the Creator into a deep dish of cerulean chutney. Haji Ali was a pious Muslim who gained his title ("Haji") after performing *Haj*, the pilgrimage to Mecca that all pious Muslims are expected to perform once in their lives. After his return to India he came to be regarded as something of a saint, and his sepulcher as something of a shrine after his death. Accessible only at low tide, his mausoleum is frequented mainly by Muslims seeking the Haji's ethereal assistance in mundane matters, including the divination of likely winners. As we veered past Haji Ali's last resting place, which juts out into the Arabian Sea on a small spit of land very near the track's main gate, my mind skidded toward food. I was thankful after a hard day at the races to find Vimalananda driving us to our favorite *pani puri* stand near the temple at Babulnath. We arrived there just in time to watch the last golden rays of the vanished sun settle to the ground between the faded pastels of the apartment buildings that loomed above us.

Pani puri (known in North India as *gol guppa*) consists of silver-dollar-size medallions of wheat dough deep fried to make them swell into hollow balls (*puri*). The stallholder breaks open the ball with his thumb, scoops a few cooked beansprouts or chickpeas into the cavity thus formed, adds a chutney or two, and then fills the ball with at least two types of thin sauces (*pani*): one spicy with chilies and the other sweet and sour, preferably from tamarind and dates. The customer now alertly stuffs the ball into his mouth and when he bites it all the flavors rush together and riot on his tongue. Win or lose we usually stopped for pani puri at the end of a race day.

As we munched Vimalananda waxed oratorical: "How many are the ways to make money, and how few of them are free of karma! And the karmas are often very hard to recognize. I have had to work, and I have had to make money. I had a rock quarry for a while, I was in the textile business, I owned a dairy. I have had practical experience of the many unsuspected repercussions of the karmas you incur when you earn money. I have always believed in treating *Lakshmi* (the goddess of wealth) as a mistress, not a wife; I tell Her, 'Come to me if You want to, but I am married to *Saraswati* (the goddess of learning), and I don't want a charge of bigamy to be laid against me.' That way I do not tie myself down to Her.

"But even with this attitude it is very hard to earn a living without creating a big bunch of karmas in the process. To begin with, certain things like knowledge, food, and women were traditionally forbidden for commercialization. These three were never supposed to become objects of commerce because they embody the Mother, and how can you even conceive of selling your mother? But people today don't seem to be concerned about this. They do a roaring business in all three, and reap horrendous karmas as a result."

We paid and saluted the vendor. As Vimalananda sped onto Marine Drive heading for home I asked him, "Weren't you selling food when you sold the milk from your dairy?"

"Indeed I was, and that is my point: I know of what I speak, because I have been through the grind. I have had practical experience of the truth of this principle. But this is only one of many things for you to consider. Even among the things which are permitted for sale there are variations in the karma involved. For example, to make money from the sale of live animals is better than to earn money from the sale of the corpses of dead animals, but it is still not a good thing. Suppose you own a pet store and you sell an animal to an owner who mistreats his pet. Who will be to blame for that abuse? You will! And that pet will curse you for it, day after day. Dealing in grains and vegetables is better than dealing in meat. Plants will still curse you when you kill them, but a plant's curse is less severe than an animal's curse because plants have less awareness than do animals. Selling live plants is better than selling pieces of dead plants, but what if you sell a tree to someone who mistreats it, or who hangs himself from it? Even when you plant a tree some of the karma will come to you if that tree is somehow mistreated."

"Or if someone chops it down and builds a gallows from it."

"Exactly. Selling fruit is better than selling live plants, and dealing in milk is better even than selling fruit, assuming that the calf drinks its fill first, because there is no killing at all. But you can get yourself into trouble selling milk also, especially if you or your hired hands ill-treat your animals, or if you sell your old dried-up animals to the slaughterhouse, or if you breed the animals and then separate the calf or the kid from its mother. And that also goes for breeding pets for sale and separating pet mothers from their children. Do you think that animal mothers have no feelings? They do, and they and their children can curse you!

"But as bad as they are, these karmas pale before the karmas incurred by the people who sacrifice the millions of animals that are used every year to test and improve medicines and cosmetics. Our ancient Rishis used to test their medicines on themselves; they never asked animals to do their work for them. And their medical system, Ayurveda, has been used safely for thousands of years on millions of patients without requiring any kind of animal experimentation. But in the modern world millions of animals are butchered annually without any thanks for laying down their lives in the service of science. Alexander Fleming was knighted for discovering penicillin and many other scientists have received Nobel Prizes, but has a laboratory monkey, or dog, or cat, rabbit or rat ever received a medal, or had a statue erected in its memory? No! Never.

"Millions of animals are sacrificed each year so that humans can enjoy safe drugs, but what happens to all the violence that is used to perfect the medicines? The Law of Karma tells us that it will not just evaporate; it has to appear somewhere. One day I got the idea that each of these preparations must contain a fraction of the torture that was inflicted on those animals. Some of that hate and pain must be there, and it comes out in the form of the terrible side-effects that many of these drugs produce. I don't think anyone else has ever thought this way, do you?"

"I doubt it."

"And what about modern agriculture? Today we try to prevent the insects, birds and other 'pests' from eating their fair share of the crops. Why should we give them a share? Because then they would also have a share in the karma of digging into Mother Earth's body with plows to produce the food. Jains are forbidden from farming, or even selling milk, for this very reason. This prohibition has made many Jains into moneylenders—which is even worse. Instead of sucking life from the earth a moneylender sucks the prana out of those who borrow from him. Besides, think for a moment about what it means to lend money at interest. Money is the embodiment of Lakshmi Shakti. If you regard all shaktis as mother, could you ever dream of taking your mother to someone else's house and making her work there? And on top of that, demanding her earnings from her at the end of the day? I hope not!

"Jesus said, 'The love of money is the root of all evil,' and He was right; but He should also have gone on to say that money itself is a very filthy thing. It is Lakshmi, but Lakshmi in Her whore form, the form in which She is passed from person to person and used over and over again. Think of all the karmas that pile up on just one piece of money! Do you know what happened to Croesus, the king who invented money? He died by having molten gold poured down his throat. That should give you an idea of the magnitude of the curse he has unleashed upon us. The Rishis never used money, and I personally never keep any on my person unless I simply cannot avoid it. I hate to handle it, which is why I always prefer to give it to you or to Roshni to handle."

"Oh, great."

Roshni was Vimalananda's foster daughter. She and I respected each other sufficiently that we were willing to work together for Vimalananda's benefit despite what was at that time an ongoing foster-sibling rivalry.

"What are you worried about? It is my job to see that this curse doesn't affect you. If I ask you to dig in the slush for me then I have to arrange for you to bathe as well. But not everyone has this advantage; those who don't are affected by these curses."

He swung the car onto our street and parked it. Upstairs Roshni served us drinks. "Do you know the story of gold? Gold itself once told me this story: 'I was resting peacefully in the womb of my mother, Earth, when men came and dug into Her and dragged me from my home. Then they tortured me by burning and melting me and forming me into new shapes. But I have altered their minds so that they do not keep me outside working for them; instead they keep me hidden in dark, cool vaults, very much like my mother's womb. I have cursed them for tormenting me, and now they torment each other over possessing me.'

"Every substance which is stolen from the earth has its own tale to tell. Iron, which is also mined, becomes weapons when men hold it. Just as the earth's skin is punctured in strip mines for iron ore, iron and steel are used to puncture men's skins, in the form of bayonets and shrapnel, razors and knives, needles and scapels. Likewise coal has its tale to tell, and oil. Oil is the earth's blood; by pumping oil from the earth we are sucking Her blood. Doesn't She have a right to suck our blood in return? And She does, via modern medical science; every syringe that draws blood from a human is helping to pay back this debt."

"Particularly if they are plastic syringes; plastic is made from oil."

"How can human beings be so blind as to fail to offer the greatest respect and love for Ma, for our Mother Earth? We spill urine, feces, and toxic wastes onto Her, we walk on Her and spit on Her, but She never objects. We tear Her skin and extract treasures like gold, silver, and precious stones from Her, and She gives them freely. Even though we pump Her own life's blood up from the depths of Her body She still supports us. And when we die She welcomes us into Her lap. Only Ma has such magnanimity. But even She cannot save us from the Law of Karma, because She looks on all Her children—every mineral, plant and animal—with an equal eye. What we do to Her children we have to pay for.

"Gorakh Nath says, 'When you don't ask you get milk; when you ask you get water; when you take you get blood. This is Gorakh's Rule.' He means that if you don't demand things from Nature She will give them to you of Her own free will, just as mothers give milk to their babies out of the exuberance of their joy. If you ask, Nature will give you just what you ask for. Because you cannot know what is best for you it is best not to ask, but if you ask for something you will receive it. Even though water is not so tasty and nutritive as milk it will keep you alive, at least for a while.

"If you grab you get blood. Theft is always a karma, just as theft of an animal's life in order to enjoy its flesh is a karma. According to the Law of Karma the repayment for blood is blood. Blood is also hard to digest and may cause you to get sick if you are not used to drinking it. Milk is a beautiful, sweet drink; pure water is pleasant, but blood tastes good only to vampires. So never take anything; always remain in the lap of the Mother, and let Her feed you from the abundance of Her milk."

"OK, so producing things is out of the question, karmically. What about the professions?"

"What *about* the professions? Are they any better? I would never want to make money from law. That money is tainted with whatever evil karmas your client has performed to get him into the sorry plight that has brought him to you. Then those karmas are multiplied by all the lies you will have to tell if you want to win your case. I have a law degree, but I've never practiced law. My father was trained as a lawyer as well, and he too refused to make money from law. On his first day at work he advised his clients to settle with each other and avoid litigation. His British boss took him aside and said, 'Young man, if this is your attitude you'll never thrive in this profession.' My father told him, 'I'm sorry, I can't do what you are asking me to do,' and he quit.

"As for medicine, well, it is better than law, because you don't need to lie all the time. But Ramakrishna Paramahamsa himself said that a doctor's money is 'all blood and pus.' When you take money for treating someone you still share in that patient's karma, and maybe even create some new karmas. You might as well just take on all the patient's karmas and be done with it; that way he would get well immediately. And whatever you do you are only helping Nature out. What is so heroic in that? If anyone deserves to be paid when a sick person gets well it is God, because it is God that does everything. Of course, for that matter, what beneficial activity is there in the universe that God does *not* do?

"It is true, though, that a doctor who treats people without demanding a fee helps to clean his karmic slate. I have also trained as an *Ayurvedic* physician, but I have never charged any fee for my services and never will."

"What about me? Here I am attending this Ayurvedic medical college."

"*Why* do you keep worrying about yourself? If I told you to go there that makes it my karma, my responsibility. If I tell you to practice medicine, and you do, then there too am I responsible, provided that you practice to the best of your ability. I am doing this for you because of my love for you and my rnanubandhana with you. As for all the other doctors in the world, well, they have their own karmas and rnanubandhanas, and if they are lucky they have someone to take responsibility for them. If they don't that's their problem."

"Their fate, you mean."

"Their fate. Now, if they are clever they can try to alter their fate. They can practice for free, or for donations alone. Or, if their economic circumstances force them to charge a fee, they can sincerely offer some of what they earn to God, and God will appropriate some of their karmas."

"And so will the priest, if the doctor hires a priest to do the worship that offers some of what they earn to God."

"And so will the priest, to some extent."

"But you don't like priests."

"The priests that are good men are the ones I like. The ones I don't like unfortunately form the vast majority of priests. They practice their profession not because they really love God but only because they want to make money. All of the religions of the world have been ruined by those greedy priests who loot the gullible—but I am certain that even most of those priests would never loot the people the way they do if they really understood the Law of Karma. It is a terrible karma to sell spiritual teachings. Even though you may hope to escape from most other karmas you cannot escape the ill effects of collecting money from people as a condition for providing them spiritual advice. I wonder how many of our phony "bhagavans" and "swamis" are aware of this.

"Of all the looting that priests do, that surrounding death is undoubtedly the worst. When a person dies the priests do their rituals and pray their prayers. After collecting plenty of money from the family of the deceased they announce that the soul has reached heaven. But how do they know that? Is it so easy to reach heaven? To get to heaven you pretty much have to die planning to go there, because it is what you are thinking about when you die which determines where you will go after your death: *ante mati sa gatih*. After death people tend to try to insulate themselves from their new reality. They try to remain wherever it is that they find themselves, and tell themselves just as we humans do that they are very happy right there. People must *want* to change before change can occur.

"But no priest today even has an inkling of what happens after death, so of what use are their assurances? The only reason they reassure the family is because they want to be well paid and want to be well fed. Unfortunately for them, the food and the money they receive from these rituals is contaminated by the carnal desires of the dead person. Today's priests are not taught how to digest this food and the money, which means that those desires will pollute them by making them more worldly. This in turn will cause them to enjoy themselves lavishly, in so many ways. Is this not a sort of heaven? By the time they die they will have used up all their good karmas, which gives them no alternative but to go to hell and endure the effects of their bad karmas. Is that not terrible?

"Stealing from God creates similar results. The former trustee of one of our famous Bombay temples was very fond of the horses. He would oversee the counting of the temple's daily collection, and when he needed money for betting he would loudly abuse whoever was doing the counting: 'Hey, you idiot, count properly!' When he heard this agreed-upon signal the counter would let some coins roll under the furniture. Then, when the sweeper came to sweep up he would also be roundly abused by the trustee, and would sweep up and deliver the money; the sweeper also knew the signal.

"To rob God is bad enough, but to gamble with God's money is even worse. Especially when God is your cook; this trustee lived exclusively on food that the temple was providing him. Given these facts you will not be surprised at how this fellow died. He was in such a state that he couldn't eat, or even drink water. Horrible—but that is the Law of Karma.

"Why, the Law of Karma has not even spared God Himself! Look at that temple I regularly visit in the South. Last year gold, silver and jewels worth hundreds of thousands of rupees, including one of the enormous emeralds presented to the temple by Krishnadevaraya of the Vijayanagaram Empire, disappeared into the hands of thieves. Everyone was asking, and rightly so, why such an ancient temple where so much worship has been performed for so many centuries should have to suffer like this. The Brahmanas, of course, are partly to blame; they always are. But here we should look deeper. Where did Krishnadevaraya get that emerald? He was a king, so most likely he stole it from somewhere. Isn't that unrighteous?

"And where did the temple get so much money? Much of it came from the sorts of people who have pots and pots of money nowadays. Those are the people who have stolen, cheated, lied and killed to get rich. When these people realize what they have done they try to purchase deliverance by giving some small fraction of their wealth to some temple. When God tries to eat all this karmically indigestible tainted money shouldn't he also be given a good purge? Shouldn't he also be taught a lesson? And shouldn't the people who come there and try to be clever also be taught a lesson? Like Bhai Kaka from Bombay, who dropped dead of a heart attack in the toilet of the ashram he had built for his guru near that very temple, on the very day of Guru Purnima when gurus are to be worshipped. What a message *that* sent to all concerned!"

"So poor God has to suffer for His devotees' karmas."

"Yes, but He's happy to do so; that's how much He loves them. And how much work is it for Him anyway? But for a human to try to do what God does—well, Namdev (a famous Maharashtrian saint) tried it once. He took over from his beloved deity Lord *Vitthala* ('Vishnu Who Stands on the Brick') for a day, just so he could see what it was like to be worshipped—and what a day he had! He had to stand up straight without even a quiver, so that no one would discover he was there; he had to put up with all the complaints that all the worshippers brought to throw at his feet; and he couldn't eat any of the beautiful food they brought him! Deities eat with their eyes instead of their mouths, but this was beyond Namdev, who had to stay hungry. By the end of the day he was exhausted and fed up. When Lord Vitthala returned to His temple that night Namdev fell at Vitthala's feet and cried, 'Enough, Lord, enough! Forgive me! Take your job back, I can't handle it.'

"It's so easy to bollix things in this business of money that it's hard to believe anyone ever survives the effects of their errors."

"Well, I am very lucky that way, because even when I have made mistakes someone has been there to correct them for me. Once I was in desperate need of money. I was so desperate that I just didn't know what to do, but I was thinking of doing something drastic. Thinking, thinking, thinking I fell into a deep sleep, and had a dream.

"In the dream someone showed me a man with a big fat belly, the kind of belly so many successful businessmen have. I was told his name and his wealth: 'He is worth fifty million rupees.' Then I saw a second man, who was thin absolutely; four times thinner than any man you have ever seen. I was also told his name and, 'This man is worth one hundred million rupees.' Finally I was shown a man who was absolutely rotten, literally eaten up by disease, full of leprosy and eczema. I heard his name and, 'He is worth five hundred million rupees.'

"Then I was asked, 'Now do you want to become wealthy?' I said, 'No, please forget it. All I want is for Nature to take care of me, and whatever She provides for me I will accept with great thanks.' Since that day I have forgotten to try to become rich. I don't need to be rich; Someone is taking care of me."

~

The next day I proceeded to Poona to resume my Ayurvedic classes. A couple of weeks passed before I could escape again on a train bound for Bombay and descend through what is some of the loveliest scenery in India, the range of hills known as the Western Ghats. The Deccan Queen arrived at Victoria Terminus that morning precisely at its scheduled time of 10:35 A.M., and once I reached the egress it took me my usual seven minutes to walk to Vimalananda's digs. He was awaiting me excitedly.

"It truly amazes me," he began, "that so many people who should know better willfully ignore the terrible karmas that are connected with tainted money, and merrily continue to scuttle themselves just for the sake of a few rupees. You can call unimaginable calamities down on your head when you start to play about with life and death. Only a few days after you last left a sadhu came to meet me. He told me, 'Get me half a pound of meat from a black goat and half a pound from an owl and I will work miracles.' I could see that he was willing to do this just to put me under his obligation so that I would have to do some other work for him. No thanks.

"I told him, 'I know what an owl can do; you needn't think you are telling me anything new. But I am not interested; please get out of my house.'"

"Was he upset?"

"Who cares? I don't even want his thoughts in my neighborhood. Do you remember that I told you that the Goddess Lakshmi rides on an owl?"

"Yes."

"I explained to you then that when you become rich your discrimination becomes clouded and works well only at night or when you are otherwise in the dark, literally or figuratively. But that is just one interpretation of this 'myth.' Now I think you should know some more things about owls, things that very few people know.

"Suppose you were to apply to your eyes the collyrium that has been prepared from an owl according to the appropriate ritual. You could then meet the richest man in the world and request a billion-dollar loan and he would give it to you without even batting an eyelid. What is more he would follow you around like a puppy dog and become so fond of you that he'd never be able to leave you. Or you can use it on some movie star. You can marry her and never have to fear that she'll go with another man; how can she leave when she is crazy about you? You can also prepare from an owl a thing which can make you invisible—and there is no need for me to tell you how advantageous it can be to be able to become invisible whenever you please. The owl can be an extremely useful bird, if you know how to use it.

"We can call the process by which you use an owl the *Uluka Sadhana*; *uluka* means owl, and *sadhana*, as you know, means any kind of spiritual procedure that is designed to achieve some specific result. You begin the Uluka Sadhana by taking an owl to the *smashan* (cremation ground) and performing a ritual to call a certain class of spirit to sit in the owl's body. The spirit will start to talk to you through the owl's mouth, and will tell you all about each part of the owl's body and how it can be used.

"Now comes the dangerous part. You must watch the owl closely, and listen to it very vigilantly. As soon as it seems he is about to stop talking you must hit him very hard, with a stick or with your fire tongs. If he gets to the end of what he has to say he will conclude his remarks by saying, 'Now you are ruined!' Coming from an owl this is such a tremendous curse that you will be a destitute, disease-ridden beggar to the end of your days. But even death will not save you; after you die you will become one of the most miserable of spirits for uncountable ages.

"So you have to be alert, and ruthless. You repeat the same procedure of calling the spirit into the owl's body several days in a row until you are satisfied that you have collected all the information that you can safely extract. Then, if you want to save yourself, just as the owl is about to stop speaking on that last day you take a sword or a large knife and cut off its head with a single blow. A moment's hesitation for any reason—and the spirit will do his best to pervert your mind just long enough for him to get his curse in edgewise—and you are doomed. No one on Earth can save you, and even God will not come to your rescue.

"Even if you do succeed in murdering the owl your problems have only begun. First you must see that it is reborn into a higher womb, unless you want it to slaughter you in some succeeding birth, according to the Law of Karma. Also, how do you think the Goddess Lakshmi, who rides on an owl, will feel about you if you kill Her vehicle? I'm sure you can imagine what will happen to your wealth and prosperity, if not immediately then in the future, if She gets angry with you. Never approach these things lightly.

"And anyway, is it right to torture an owl just for the sake of mundane gains? Never! I did this sadhana once, simply because an ethereal being had told me about it and I was determined to see whether or not it worked. Well, it works, but I have never done it again; I really don't think that anyone should ever do it."

"I killed an owl when I was out hunting when I was young; do you think Lakshmi is still angry with me?"

"Well, even though you did it deliberately you didn't know any better, so I suspect that Nature will eventually let you off the hook on this account. At least it was an owl and not a frog. Killing a frog is such a terrible karma that they say it is equal to killing a human, but I would go further. I would go so far as to say that although you may be able to pay off the karma of killing a human during that same lifetime you will not be able to pay off in the same lifetime the karma of deliberately killing a frog. When you kill a frog you will have to be born again to endure being slaughtered by that frog."

Instantly my blood froze, for though I had never killed a frog even in a laboratory I had a few years earlier been involved in a Tantric ritual in which a frog was used. Fortunately it was released alive. I told him about it.

"Thank God it didn't die! That's all I can say. Besides, the whole project wasn't your idea; the fellow conducting the ritual will have to pay for its karma. Does he realize what he has got himself into?"

"But what about the people who kill frogs in laboratories in the name of science, and the people who eat them?"

"Even though 'ignorance of the law is no defence,' the degree of the karma depends a lot on intention. In the context of science the karma is minimal if you are a student and your instructor directs you to kill a frog. But if you design some sort of research project that involves killing frogs then you are responsible for those deaths. Eating them makes you responsible too, of course. You know, when I owned my rock quarry over on Sheva Island I more than once saw my workers break open a rock in which there was a frog. Out it would jump, alive—don't ask me how—and then as the poor thing was trying to hop away they would grab hold of it and eat it on the spot!"

"Didn't they even *wonder* how the frog had stayed alive in there?"

"Not at all. They were being driven by their karmas. Being illiterate and ignorant, all they could do was conform to the nature of their rnanubandhanas. But what of all the educated people who look at a frog and immediately think, 'Frog legs!' How many people ever wonder about the life of frogs? How many people ever look at a little frog and appreciate it for how *beautiful* it is just enjoying its life! The frog is the farmer's friend; when it begins to croak in the summer the farmer knows the rains are about to start. Frogs eat thousands of insects during their lives, so they are a natural form of pest control. And, whenever you see a frog you know there is a snake about, because frogs are the natural food of snakes; life lives off life.

"But instead of being respected frogs are cruelly tortured. Their legs are chopped off while they are still living and conscious, and the torso is tossed aside to die. And those who exterminate them by the hundreds every day, how many hundreds of times must they have been sliced apart to give them the right to slice in turn? And how many times in how many thousands of future lives will they be killed by the frogs they are killing now? It is so difficult to know the Law of Karma."

Hmm. "I did hear that a frog is used to sweep the ground in the area where a Vedic *yajna* (sacrificial ritual) is to be performed, and that there is a Vedic hymn that is used to obtain rain that compares frogs to Brahmanas. Even the scientists say that so far frogs are the only animals they can clone—so all told I suppose frogs must have some unusual shakti."

"They certainly do. For example, you can use frogs to 'enchant' a piece of money. I won't go into the details, but it involves taking a pair of frogs and burying one of them alive. Once the money is enchanted you mark it, so you will be able to recognize it, and then you go spend it on something. Within a few hours it will return to your bag; don't ask me how. You can keep using it, and getting it back, indefinitely. But what about the cost to you? The price is far too high to pay."

"Do you still have to pay the price when you sacrifice an animal to a deity?"

"You will unless you know how to escape it. A certain ruler who was a great devotee of Ma used to offer a number of animal sacrifices to Her daily. After he died he found himself surrounded by thousands of angry animals, and asked Ma what was going on.

"She told him, 'You have taken their lives; shouldn't they get an opportunity to take your life now? This is the Law of Karma.'

"This came as a great shock to the ruler, who begged, 'But Ma, I sacrificed them only from the love of You.'

"Ma smiled and said, 'No, there was some self-interest behind your love and affection for Me. The real reason you sacrificed them was to get Me to benefit you and your family. And besides, did I ever ask you for these sacrifices? No, I never did. If you were really so interested in sacrificing to Me why couldn't you have cut your own flesh and offered Me your own blood? They at least belong to you. If you really loved Me why didn't you give Me the thing you are most fond of: your own life?'

"At last the king realized what he had gotten himself into.

" 'But wait,' Ma went on, 'My grace is there for you. I am here to look after you. Instead of having to be born and then slaughtered thousands of times you will only have to do it ten times. But those ten times you will have to experience what these sacrificial beasts have experienced.'"

"Sacrifice is very big in Judaism; is that one of the reasons that the Jews have been suffering for so long, that they have all those dead animals angry with them?"

"That is a part of the problem, obviously. Another part is that when they invaded Canaan they massacred everyone they could find."

I knew from Sunday school that in a number of places in the Old Testament (e.g. Joshua 9:24) Jehovah exhorts the Israelites to ensure that no Canaanite be left alive. The ensuing carnage amounted to genocide of the Canaanites—was the twentieth-century Holocaust a part of the karmic reaction to that long-ago extermination? I thought at first to ask his opinion but then kept this thought to myself and asked instead, "So Islam, which is big into sacrifice, will not be spared either?"

"The Muslims are already starting to slaughter each other; look at Iran and Iraq."

"Does *everyone* who performs animal sacrifice end up this way?"

"Almost everyone. You should slaughter an animal only if you know your rnanubandhana makes it necessary for you to do it; you must have that sort of karmic debt with the animal. Then, you must properly select the animal you want to slay. The only fit victims are those animals which carry certain signs on their bodies which show they are meant to be sacrificed. If you perform a sacrifice without a fit victim your karma will be much worse.

"But even if you have a fit victim you must also have the power to make the dead body live again. When our Rishis used to sacrifice animals they always brought the animal back to life afterwards by means of a special mantra. That way there is no stain of karma at all, as there is when you murder an animal without being able to revive it. For instance, you can sacrifice a chicken, cook it and offer it to Ma. Then you distribute its flesh as Her *prasada* (blessing), but you must retain at least one small bone. From that bone you reconstruct the chicken and bring it back to life. It will live again, but it must never again be sacrificed. Instead you must either set it free or keep it and feed it well. If you cannot or choose not to do this then you must still bring the animal back to life, but in a different way. You do this by ensuring that the animal gets an immediate, higher rebirth. This is what I do whenever I eat a piece of meat. If you sacrifice an animal without this power you are the biggest fool. Ordinary people kill only for the tongue, which is what causes the karma. They kill and eat now and afterwards they are killed and eaten, birth after birth. The wise slaughter only to redeem.

"And this is only for ordinary sacrifices. The karma for human sacrifice is far, far worse. Human sacrifice—*Nara Bali*—is the most difficult of all sacrifices. To kill a human being is a terrible karma, but to offer a human soul to Ma offers unbelievable benefits, both for the offerer and for the soul. It is a good thing to do Nara Bali, but you can do it safely only if you know exactly what you are doing. For one thing, even though almost everyone today is a *pashu*, an animal, you can't just go out and slaughter whomever you please like the Thugs did."

The *Thugs* ("Deceivers") were a secret society of Indians which offered unsuspecting victims as sacrifices to the goddess *Bhavani*. During their heyday they waylaid and murdered an estimated two million travellers. Their depradations ended when they were suppressed by General Sleeman and the British Army during the last century.

"In the wrong hands these rituals bring nothing but trouble. The reason there are almost no Aghoris left in Girnar today is all because a group of Aghoris once kidnapped a little boy, sacrificed him, and ate him. When his distraught mother came to them to ask about her son they lied to her and said they had not seen him. Then she complained to Guru Dattatreya, the first of all Aghoris in the world, who used his yogic power to discover what had happened. He became wild and personally expelled all but the best Aghoris from Girnar."

"So what they say about Aghoris and human sacrifice is true." Earlier in his life Vimalananda had lived as a naked sadhu at Mount Girnar, a renowned pilgrimage spot in Western India, where he met his Senior Guru Maharaj.

"Aghoris have always been fond of Nara Bali, but no true Aghori kills without being able to resurrect. There is one very hard group of Aghoris which uses Nara Bali if they enter a village and the villagers fail to welcome them properly. These Aghoris perform *homa* (fire worship) and invoke a goddess like *Chandi* (goddess of cholera) or *Shitala* (goddess of smallpox and chickenpox) to ravage the village. While it might seem that this could not help anyone these deaths in fact act as Nara Balis, which makes Ma pleased with the Aghoris. The victims are benefitted because Ma has taken them and they are bound to be saved. And the remaining villagers, who come to their senses after a few deaths, learn proper manners. Everyone gets some benefit, but the process does produce some karma."

"Doesn't it produce a lot of karma? It certainly seems like a lot of ego is involved here, like there was with the Aghoris that Dattatreya threw out of Girnar. I mean, all right, the villagers fail to welcome you properly, but is that a good reason to kill them? Shouldn't you be a little more compassionate if you are a sadhu?"

"Suppose though that you are an Aghori whose worship of Chandi or Shitala has matured and your goddess is with you twenty-four hours a day. Then the villagers are not offending you as much as they are offending your goddess. It is She who loses Her temper, She who performs the homa through you, and She who consumes the sacrifices.

"And besides, if a tiger were to waltz in here right now you would behave toward it with respect, wouldn't you? I should hope so! Similarly, you would be very wise to behave respectfully toward a powerful goddess, in whatever form She might choose to appear to you. It is true that the villagers probably did not ask for the yogis to come to their village, but once they arrived the locals ought to have realized the potential consequences for disregarding them. This is India, after all. There is no lack of precedent for this kind of thing. Remember, don't ever make friends with a king, a yogi, the fire, or the water unless you plan to live up to your friendship!"

He started to laugh.

"My Senior Guru Maharaj, my Bapu, is both a ruler and a yogi, so you have to be extra careful with him. One day he took me to a place where an immense underground treasure lay buried. We passed through stacks and stacks of gold bricks, heaps of jewels and what-have-you, but neither of us stopped for them. We were both interested in an amulet, one small amulet. In order to obtain it, though, a small child would have to be sacrificed. Bapu ordered me to do it, but I refused. Why stain my hands?

" 'All right,' he said, 'I'll make you a deal. I will come to you, in any form. Watch out for me and catch me, and if you can catch me I will see that you get the amulet.' Great!

"Back in Bombay a few days later I was just sending my son Ranu up to bed when suddenly an enormous black cobra appeared. I was on one part of the divided staircase and my friend Dinkar was on the other, with Ranu. The cobra wound itself around Ranu's leg; my Senior Guru Maharaj always did love that boy! Ranu didn't do anything, as if he understood. Then the cobra headed toward me.

"Unfortunately by this time Dinkar, the stupid idiot, had started shouting, 'Snake! Snake!' He grabbed a walking stick and began to beat the cobra before I could stop him. The snake disappeared forthwith and I became furious: 'I told you not to hit that snake Ñ'

"He cut me off: 'Now, Pratap, you don't *know*, those snakes are deadly poisonous. Ranu was here; he might have been bitten.' But, numbskull, if the snake was going to bite Ranu he would have done so while he was curled around the boy's leg. What can you do with such people?

"A few days later I met my Senior Guru Maharaj again. He was wild with rage: 'Look at what you've done! Most of my bones have been battered,' showing me the place on his back where he had been clubbed.

'What could I do, Maharaj?' I asked him. 'I couldn't stop him in time.' And until today neither of us has obtained that amulet."

We both smiled and moved on to other things. The next morning Vimalananda returned to the subject of sacrifice in what seemed an incongruous venue: the R.W.I.T.C. cafe at the racecourse, where we sat over buttered toast and milky tea after witnessing the early morning trackwork. Vimalananda's then trainer Mr. Lafange sat with us for a while, trying to convince us that the mediocre work we had witnessed was something more than mediocre. After he left Vimalananda grimaced briefly as the euphony of the chirruping birds was contaminated by the stridor of two of the stuffier Club members. They were hypothesizing over foreign jockeys: who George McGrath would be riding for this year, and whether Sir Lester Piggott, then the Queen of England's retained rider, would be out for the Derby again.

Vimalananda spoke: "I have always believed in avoiding karma whenever possible. The more you do to try to accomplish your ends the more karma you create for yourself. Whether in human sacrifice or in horse racing, avoiding karma is the sensible way to go. One way to avoid karma in human sacrifice is to follow the example of the Rishis and use a mantra to bring the man back to life after sacrificing him. But even without such a mantra you can still offer as many human sacrifices as you like without ever becoming stained by karma, if your intelligence is subtle enough. Can you guess how?"

"It must have something to do with the victim's prana."

"Right. Ma has no use at all for the bodies of sacrificial victims. She is ethereal, She has use only for the spirit which is separated from the body at death, and the prana which that spirit carries. Knowing this, a clever person can offer a human sacrifice without any danger by taking a spirit and offering it to Ma. You can take any spirit, even one killed on a battlefield; wars kill so many every year. You can give thousands of Nara Balis this way if you so desire; all you have to know is how to do it.

"First you locate a country in which a war is going on. Then you tell Ma, 'Ma, I am going to provide You with a certain number of Nara Balis within two days, if You give me permission to do so.' If She gives you permission you proceed; otherwise not! You collect all the spirits of everyone who has died in the war thus far, soldiers and civilians, innocent victims and guilty warmongers alike. Since they have all died violent deaths they don't know where to go and cannot find their way into a new rebirth.

"After collecting the spirits you bring them to the spot where you will invoke Ma to devour them. Then you perform stambhana ('immobilizing') and kilana ('nailing') to lock them inside a circle from which they will be unable to escape. This is the ethereal equivalent of tethering a sacrificial animal to the sacrificial post by tying a noose around its neck.

"Then you invoke Ma. When Ma arrives She is ready to eat, but because She is ethereal She does not eat with Her mouth. She inhales the spirits— they are ethereal anyway, just like puffs of wind—taking their prana from them and enjoying Her own cosmic intoxication. Have you ever seen a puppy playing with a ball? You throw the ball, he runs after it, catches it, and runs back to you with the ball in his mouth so that you can throw it again. It is the same thing here: Ma has caused all these beings to take birth, to be thrown into the samsara (the universe of manifested existence). You are just restoring them to Her so She can throw them out again.

"She doesn't toss them into some ditch, of course. Because of Her grace, Her aspect of motherhood, they all receive immediate high rebirths. Ma is the mother of all, and what mother refuses to save her children even when they are naughty? So the spirits are bound to be satisfied by this process. Ma is also satisfied, and She rewards the sacrificer. Everyone is happy, and the real beauty of the whole thing is that the karma is very minimal."

"Great! Why aren't more people doing this sort of thing?"

"Because it is very difficult to do, unfortunately. This is why we have yet other ways of offering Nara Bali. One way requires that you find an animal or a human with whom you have the right rnanubandhana. Then you invoke into that person or animal a goddess, or a spirit of a certain class who also has the right rnanubandhana with the prospective victim. The goddess or the spirit then sits inside that victim and drinks up all his blood. The victim gradually loses weight, and wastes away to a skeleton, because his prana is being lost. There is no cure; death comes as soon as Ma wishes, or as soon as the spirit has taken all the blood it is entitled to in that case.

"For instance, you might select *Chinnamasta*, the Great Goddess Who holds Her severed head in Her hand and drinks an unceasing stream of Her own blood. She is the goddess of wasting diseases like leukemia in which the red blood cells decrease and the white blood cells increase. Sometimes ordinary leukemia patients survive, because Ma chooses only to take a part of their prana when She calls on them. But no victim of a Nara Bali can survive unless you botch the ritual.

"Whatever goddess you may select will be happy, because She will get the spirit of the being She wanted without having to bother about all the flesh and other disagreeable offal produced in a physical sacrifice. The victims are made to remember God by their pain, which is nothing but the effects of all the karmas of their millions of previous births. When they die Ma saves them. You get the benefit of giving the souls to Ma while you sit on the sidelines as a spectator, and none of the karma in actually killing the person comes to you.

"In these ways one hundred thousand Nara Balis can be given. The result? Tremendous! You could never do so many physical sacrifices, which is why I always say that physical worship is limited. But if you try to fool about in this way without knowing your rnanubandhana with your victims you are heading for big, big trouble."

"So how to know rnanubandhana?"

"All in due time, my boy," laughed Vimalananda, "all in due time."

TEASERS and STALLIONS

BOMBAY'S SUMMER USUALLY begins near the end of March. With the summer of 1977 summer came the problem of where to send Stoney to brood. Pedigrees of all sorts fascinated Vimalananda; when we watched Wimbledon together he would sigh and say, "If only Jimmy Connors and Chrissy Evert would get together, their child would really be something!!" Now he had the opportunity to select the genes that would mingle with those of his beloved Stoney. He invested more and more of his spare time in pedigree comparisons, to ensure that the ensuing foal would bring glory to its mare's name.

I too would have willingly focused my full attention on these family trees, but my college continued to monopolize the majority of my time. Two separate lives developed for me as my regular daily slog of anatomical structures, symptom complexes, and medicinal substances began to intersect, at seemingly opportune moments, with participation in Vimalananda's unusual world. When we were together I stuck close to him to sponge up whatever knowledge he chose to spill before our parting left me again on my own, mired in an existence that seemed indecently tedious in his absence.

Shortly after Stoney's last race Vimalananda's momentum gathered me up from my Poona purgatory and swept me along with him to inspect a nearby stud farm. At least half a dozen such breeding establishments dot Poona's environs, most snuggled up against fields fecund with sugar cane, chickpeas, sorghum, corn and kohlrabi. As our vehicle passed the largest and most renowned of these studs, the one owned by the two Anklesaria brothers, Vimalananda's eyes narrowed into seriousness: "The Anklesarias do an excellent job of breeding horses, and they know their horseflesh. Darius is something of a blowhard, but Nariman is a real gentleman. I would love to purchase one of their two-year-olds, but they are simply priced too high for my budget.

"One of the things I don't like about their operation, though, is their factory for manufacturing serum from horses and mules. Because their products are used to treat diseases there is some good karma to be had from this business; but what about the bad karma that is their by-product? Slaughtering animals outright is bad enough, but here you are slowly bleeding them to death—leeching their prana from them little by little, but never enough for them to die outright. You keep them just alive enough that you can continue to suck their blood."

"Like a moneylender gives a farmer just enough money to keep him functional so that the farmer can continue to pay the interest on the loan."

"Exactly. And the interest rate is so high that the farmer can never pay back the principal. Some farmers begin by borrowing as little as Rs. 500 (then about $65) and end up paying the moneylender thousands of rupees over decades—and then the farmer's children have to take over the debt. That kind of extortion is bloodsucking, without a doubt. But even that doesn't quite compare to literally having your blood continuously drained from your body."

"So that your tissues always feel starved because they always lack blood— ooh, that's nasty. Never for a moment any feeling of wellbeing. What sort of karma must that be that causes beings to be born as blood-factory animals?"

"A very horrible karma indeed. Some of them may even have been moneylenders in their past lives!"

We laughed over that thought as we turned into the drive to our destination. There sat the owner, an eccentric old Parsi lady, anticipating our arrival on the veranda of her bungalow which by the looks of its architecture had been built for a Britisher some decades previously. "Sahibrao," she called to her servant in desultory Marathi as we walked up to her, "bring these gentlemen some refreshments."

After our snacks we were led down to a paddock where a mare in heat was standing, preparing to be covered. As this was my first visit to a stud farm I had to whisper a question to Vimalananda: "Surely that little pony who is rubbing up against the mare is not the stallion?"

"No, certainly not," replied Vimalananda in a similar whisper which those around us would take for sage deliberation. "He's the teaser; his job is to play with the mare until she is fully in heat, to titillate her until she can't stand it any longer. Then, when she is at her peak they bring out the stallion and send away the teaser. Watch!"

As if on cue the stallion now appeared, tossing his mane like a horse possessed, an enormous erection poised ramrod-straight along his belly. The two handlers brought him into position, helped him to mount, and stood watchfully as he thrust. Within 30 seconds or so it was all over and he and the mare were led, jubilant, back to their respective stalls.

That pageant turned out to be the high water mark of our visit, and as soon as we were again on the road the comments that I had been suppressing swarmed out: "What a difference in karmas between the stallion and the teaser! Both are male horses who are valued for their hard penises. But one gets pampered with the best of food, shelter and care and does nothing but screw all day, while the other gets by on leftovers and never even gets a chance to have an orgasm. Always a groomsman and never a groom; brought to the peak of arousal day after day and never allowed to enjoy release. What a life! What a case of blue balls! Couldn't they at least have one little mare for him to cover, one little pony?"

"Why should they? Then he would feel satiated, which means he would lose the intense sexual craving that he must transmit to the mare he's teasing. Besides, he might get the pony he covered in foal, and who would want that child? Who would feed it?"

"They could use it for another teaser, if it were male."

"Teasers are a dime a dozen. And what if they took your advice, and then sent that foal to the serum factory—how would you like that responsibility?"

"Forget it!"

"*Gahanah karmano gatih*: 'The current of karma is very deep.' Why does one stone go to form an idol which is worshipped and another, perhaps from the same quarry, goes to form a urinal which is insulted? It's all a matter of previous karma. Karma is so peculiar in India because some of the strangest karmas in the world have been performed here. India is a land where you never know what is going to happen next. If you do not know what is going on you had better be very prudent, because you can get into deep trouble here. Take the practice called *Visha Kanya* ('poison damsel'), which was very common in ancient times and may even survive somewhere today. Beginning when she is only a few months old a girl who is to become a Visha Kanya is given gradually increasing doses of many types of poisons. She never gets enough to kill her, just enough make her body immune to them. By the time she reaches her teens she has imbibed a huge amount of poison which has lodged in her tissues forever. Then she is ready to be tested."

"Tested?"

"If she has been well prepared a fly who alights on her skin should immediately die."

"Ooof."

"After she passes her test she is ready to be used; no need to administer anything more. When the king of the country finds someone he wants to get rid of he invites that fellow to a nice feast and then presents this girl to him to enjoy for the night. The moment the man has a nice enjoyment with her he takes in enough of her venom to kill him after a very short time. No one but the king understands what has happened. What do you think happened to Alexander the Great? Part of the tribute he was given after he defeated King Porus was a Visha Kanya. That was sufficient."

"A horrible way to die."

"Yes, but think of the plight of the girl! How could she ever get married? The first time her husband embraced her she would become a widow. The poison of a Visha Kanya is so strong that even if you just kiss her, once only, your fate is sealed. Nothing can save you, though it may take some time for you to die. What kind of karmas must such a girl have performed in her past to be tortured like this? It is very hard to know karma, but we can guess. And what of the fate of someone who dooms a Visha Kanya to an existence of total sexual and emotional frustration? Perhaps such a person ends up a teaser at a stud farm!"

"That does seem appropriate."

"And for that matter, what do you think will happen to the stud farm owner who uses such a teaser? It's not likely to be pleasant. There is really no end to action and reaction in this world of duality in which we live, particularly in this business of sex. It is a terrible karma to disturb two beings who are in a sexual embrace; even the Rishis have not escaped."

"So say the texts," I offered. Indian legend is filled with examples of such karmas. Durvasas Rishi was separated from his wife because he separated *Indra*, the king of the celestial gods known as *devas*, and the *Apsaras* (celestial dancing damsel) Rambha when they were copulating. It was because the planet Jupiter hindered the lovesport of *Kamadeva* (the god of erotic love) with the Apsaras Ghritachi that the Moon abducted Jupiter's wife and fathered a son on her. Gautama Muni interrupted the Moon and Rohini; as a result he was cuckolded, and lost his wife for millennia because of his own curse. And when King Harischandra (whose name was a byword for truthfulness) punished a ploughman who had had an illicit liason by expelling him to wander in a lonely forest, he lost his wife, his son, and his kingdom, and was tormented by the Rishi Vishvamitra.

"Interrupting someone's sexual enjoyment is bad enough," Vimalananda continued, "but the karmic repercussions of sex go far further than that. Let's talk about the billions and trillions of insects in the world, most of whom live for only a few moments and die. Their large numbers are chiefly due to the wastage of semen by human beings. Every sperm is alive; don't the millions who are killed after each ejaculation have the right to be born again to take revenge on the humans who killed them for no reason except momentary pleasure? They have every right to do so. Because this is Kali Yuga, more men waste their semen and more insects are created when *asuric* (demonic) tendencies predominate.

"In English we might call this 'poetic justice.'" *Kali Yuga* is the fourth of the Four Ages through which the world passes again and again. In Kali Yuga, the so-called "Iron Age" which the texts say lasts for 432,000 years, only one-fourth of the normal amount of righteousness remains in society, which makes it very easy for people to be overcome by delusion.

"Here in India we call it 'divine justice,' and it can be really severe. There is no favoritism in the Law of Karma. Even the prophets and *avataras* (incarnations of God) have had to suffer. Think of the doleful life of *Ramachandra*, who was God incarnate. He had to relinquish His kingdom on the day He was anointed king. He roamed about in the forest for fourteen years, and was separated from His beloved wife Sita for most of His life. And His is only one instance. Why did Mahavira die by a nail in the ear? Why did Buddha die after eating the little suckling pig? Why was Zarathustra stabbed? Why was Mohammed poisoned? Why was Jesus crucified? Why did Krishna die with an arrow in His heel? When you set out to play with God you had best be ready for whatever He is going to dish out, no matter who you think you are.

"Never ask for divine justice. If you think about it with a clear head you will realize that you have so many pending karmas that if you ever did get justice you would really have to pay through the nose. You would never be able to take it. Once a sadhu sat in penance for twelve years on the same rock, never leaving it. Eventually God became pleased with his penance. When God appeared to the sadhu and told him to ask for a boon the sadhu replied, 'I want justice.'

"God said to him, 'Look, you fool, you have no idea of what justice is all about. I have come here to help you. You please listen to me and ask for some useful boon.'

"But the sadhu replied, 'No, I insist; I must have justice!'

"God gave the sadhu one last chance, but when he insisted on justice God got tired of arguing with such a dunderhead and said, 'All right, you want justice? Fine. You have sat on this rock for twelve years? Now it is the turn of the rock to sit on your head, for twelve years. That is justice, isn't it? Now enjoy your justice!'"

"Ouch."

"Some of our scriptures discuss the nature of divine justice, and mention penalties for indulging in certain actions. They are not talking about guilt and retribution; they are talking about karmic reaction. Because these scriptures were originally written by seers who could look ahead to today and know what would happen, some of the writings are strangely prophetic. One day a Parsi friend who has read a lot of our scriptures, both Vedas and *Puranas* (classical texts), was discussing karma with me and he asked, 'Why is it that in the *Garuda Purana* they say that a man who enjoys too much sex will be spreadeagled in hell on a red-hot pillar of iron?'

"I replied, 'Well, look at yourself! You have had a lot of sex, through which you have also contracted a venereal disease. For the strictures caused by the VD you were treated by a hot steel rod poked up your urethra. Don't you think there is some kind of connection there?' He couldn't say anything after that."

"So you maintain that there's nothing like guilt in Hinduism?" This was a novel idea.

"The word 'Hindu' is a Persian corruption of the word 'Sindhu,' which is the Sanskrit name for the River Indus. India is also called Hindustan, which makes anyone who lives there a 'Hindu.' This means there is no Hindu religion. There is only the Vedic religion."

"What about Aghora?"

"We can hardly call Aghora a religion when it has no dogma. And if you argue that Aghora is just Tantra taken to the extreme, then what else is Tantra but the Veda expressed in a new way?"

"Hmm."

"Now, in their original form the Vedas had no commandments and no use for apportioning guilt, so they could not bother themselves with sin. They were concerned only with karma, and there is nothing like a moral sense to the Law of Karma; there is only cause and effect. The Law of Karma is a law of physics, a law which cannot be repealed any more than the law of gravity can be repealed. You can temporarily evade the Law of Karma, just like you can temporarily evade the law of gravity, but eventually it always catches up with you. If you jump off the ground you can avoid gravity for a second or two; if you fly high in an airplane, for a few hours. But what goes up will still have to come down."

"And if you fly into space?"

"Even if you head off into space you will still be affected by the gravity of some heavenly body or other. But how likely is it for you to fly into space? Do you have enough good karma for that? How many humans in the history of the world have made it into space?"

"A handful."

"And all of those that have gone and survived thus far have returned to Earth after a few days or weeks at the most. It's all a matter of shakti. You need just a little shakti to jump; you need a moderate amount of shakti to fly in an airplane—you need influence or money to get you a ticket, and influence and money are also types of shakti. But to go into space you need tremendous shakti, and to become permanently free of Earth's gravity while still in your physical body you need more shakti than any human being has been able to accumulate thus far. King Trishanku tried to get to heaven in his physical body, propelled by the force of the Rishi Vishvamitra's austerities, and where is he now? Hanging upside down for all eternity, suspended between the earth and the sky."

"What about the people who know how to go into space with their astral bodies?"

"They remain limited by Earth's astral gravity. To become permanently free of Earth, free even of its astral gravity, is something only the Rishis can do."

I nodded my head contemplatively.

"The Law of Karma is *the* law of the universe; it is the basis of divine justice. Like it or not you have to abide by this law. If you break the Law you will have a penalty to pay, but that penalty is only a reaction; it has very little to do with guilt and retribution. A bad karma is bad mainly because you have to pay a price for performing it. Bad karmas make you and those around you suffer. Once you realize this principle you will try to stop performing bad karmas, if you are sensible, rational human being. As you generate less bad karma your suffering will gradually decrease, which will make your joy increase. It is all very simple and mathematical. 2 + 2 = 4; it can't equal 3 or 5.

"You obtain sin only when you add guilt to bad karma, when you tell people that they are evil and are bound for hell because they have performed bad karmas. There is a tremendous amount of guilt being passed around nowadays by self-proclaimed swamis and babas who chatter on and on about 'sin.' But are they experts in the Law of Karma that they can know who is headed to hell and who to heaven? In different religions the ideas of sin are different and can conflict. What is a sin in one religion, like killing animals in Jainism, may be required in others, such as in Judaism and Islam. The phony swamis are ruining what is left of the Vedic religion by trying to tie it down to their wrong ideas about its dogma. The Vedic religion is the only religion that tells each individual to carve out his own niche; that is why it is eternal. And if our country now has seven hundred million people then there must be seven hundred million gods here, all with their own individual religions.

"Jesus said, 'Hate the sins, not the sinners.' But I ask you, why should anyone even think about sin? If you assume that your followers are going to sin won't that encourage them to do so? This is why there is only one perfect religion: the Veda. It is the Eternal Dharma because there is no question of sin. Show me even a single mention of distinction of sin in the Veda and I will bathe in your urine! In the Upanishads, yes, such things may occur. The Upanishads were written by the junior students of the senior Rishis. Children are bound to make mistakes. Not in the Vedas, though. But then, the Rishis had a totally different perspective on existence than we do. When two Rishis used to meet they would not greet each other with, 'Hey, Rishi!' like people might do today. They would address each other as *Aryaputra* (Son of the Just), or as *Mahanubhava* (Great Experiencer). What grace, to speak of one another as 'Great Experiencers'! What broadness of vision that required!

"But even this broadness of vision creates a problem! When people have no fear of sin many of them unfortunately begin to believe that they can somehow escape the Law of Karma. This tends to make them lazy about maintaining their purity, which lets their bad karmas accumulate. It is a real problem: if you harp on sin like some Christians do you tend to perpetuate it; if you try to ignore it, it tends to increase."

"So what do you do?"

"If you are the head of some religion you have a big problem. But if you are like you and me you worry about your own things, and let God take care of everything else."

A pause ensued, followed by an engaging discussion of potential mates for Stone Ice. When we reached the section of road which skirted a certain ashram Vimalananda expelled a puff of air from his cheeks in disgust and spat, "Just what we need here—one more self-styled *bhagavan* ("God"). You've listened to this infamous bugger talk, haven't you? This 'bhagavan' says that he contradicts himself because of the nature of Reality, or some such thing. Now, the real Bhagavan will speak only in *Para Vani*—in telepathic speech— and in Para Vani it is impossible to contradict yourself. It cannot be done, because Para Vani is *Prasadika Vani*, a direct expression of Reality which does not require the medium of words for its expression. We can only conclude from this claim of this 'bhagavan' that he is irrational."

"Well, he in fact claims to be irrational, because he says the universe is irrational."

"If that is so then I have nothing more to say, because then there is no Law of Karma, no cause and effect, and no meaning to the whole universe. Which may well be—but if that *is* the case then how does a 'bhagavan' arise from the chaos?"

"Well, if the universe is irrational . . ."

"Enough of this bull! He is just an idiot who doesn't know what he is talking. He just goes on jabbering to collect donations from his disciples so that he can eat, drink and be merry with his lady devotees." He paused, then continued calmly. "Enough about this character; why should we pollute our minds by bothering ourselves about him? We have our own things to think about, instead of finding faults with others. Nature knows Her job best. If the Law of Karma does exist this fellow will one day get the lesson of his lifetime.

"Look," he said, pointing his index finger at me, "When I point my finger at someone else I always remember that three fingers are pointed at me and only one finger is pointed at him. Then I know that it is my *ahamkara*, my ego, which is accusing him, and that my accusation makes me fall prey to the law of action and reaction. I may do one finger's worth of damage to him, but three times as much damage will come to me. This helps keep me from becoming aggressive."

"Most of the time."

"If I didn't remember this I might be finishing people off left and right. It's very easy to do, once you have accumulated a certain amount of shakti. This is also one reason that some sadhus scuttle themselves. The more shakti you have the more scrupulous you have to be since the karmic implications for any of your actions become graver and graver. You have to walk through the world like an elephant that is being chased by a yapping dog. The elephant knows that a single tap from his foot will be the end of the dog. But he refrains from squashing the dog because he knows that the dog does not realize the gravity of what it is doing. If you do succeed in enraging an elephant, watch out! You will never escape. When Franklin Roosevelt was informed of the Japanese attack on Pearl Harbor he said simply, 'Does Mikado realize the gravity of what he has done?' And Admiral Yamamoto, who never was in favor of the attack, said, 'I fear that all we have done is to awaken a sleeping giant and fill it with a terrible resolve.' We all know what happened next: Japan was finished, utterly. But look at the Law of Karma! Japan is now headed for the top again, at the expense of the United States."

"Do you think the United States shouldn't have responded to Pearl Harbor?"

"If they hadn't responded you might be speaking Japanese or German today. No, the United States had to respond to end the tyranny of Hitler, Mussolini and Tojo. But even though it was the right thing to do it was still a karma, and karma is karma—full stop. Every action creates a reaction which will inevitably occur. But karma is so very deep that whether a specific karma is going to be good or bad for you in the end is no easy thing to know.

"I rarely even give money to beggars and when I do it is almost always to blind ones. Your eyes are the organs that lead you into projecting your mind outward into the world. All your senses tend to do this, but your eyes are primary. Suppose you are walking down the street behind someone with long, flowing beautiful hair. You start to fantasize about how her face looks. Then 'she' turns around—and you see that 'she' is a boy! Your eyes have led you astray. The blind find it much more difficult than you or I to project their awareness out into the world; the *samsara*, the ever-changing outer world, does not exist for them, practically speaking. The blind deserve alms because their lack of sight makes it more difficult for them to perform karmas.

"But suppose I feel so bad for the blind that I donate my eyes after I die. That is quite a blessing for some sightless individual; it is a very fine thing to get sight after many years of blindness. But look at the result for me! The blind person who gets my eyes will be attracted by so many things since everything is new to him. The sensory attraction will make him want to enjoy those pleasures. He will make efforts to enjoy them and self-identify with his enjoyment. But karma is created every time he self-identifies. And who is responsible for that karma? I am! Why? Because I gave him sight. I enabled him to desire so many things, and to be able to act on those desires. Had I not interfered he would never have had either the idea or the opportunity to want and to experience so many things. It is thus my responsibility and I have to pay for it. The price may not be too heavy so long as he behaves himself. But suppose he sees a beautiful woman and, overcome with his new desires, rapes her—then it is I who am guilty of rape, because I facilitated his crime! Though it may seem very unfair, this is the way things are. And this applies to any organ that is donated: heart, kidney, liver, even the skin used in skin grafts. You have to be very careful of whom you bless and how you do it."

Vimalananda swerved a bit to miss a jaywalker and then asked, "Have you ever heard the Hindi phrase *ankhon ki tara*?"

"Yes—'star of the eyes'; isn't that equivalent to the English phrase, 'apple of my eye'?

"Right. It would be better if that phrase was *ankhon ko tara*."

"Which would mean, um, 'the eyes were saved'?

"Exactly. When your eyes have been 'saved' they are no longer susceptible to being overcome with desires. This is why controlling all your senses is so important. Once there was a king who couldn't sleep. It's not uncommon; kings have so many things to worry about. Most rulers even today will look for a woman, or a drink, or some amusement to divert themselves when they have insomnia. Many of our past rulers, though, had more refined sleep-inducing methods. This one was a poet, so as he strolled sleepless on his terrace he repeated to himself the first line of a poem he was trying to write. It was a poem on the appropriate subject of slumber.

" '*Shete Sukham Kas Tu?*', repeated the king. '*Shete Sukham Kas Tu?*' 'Who is it that sleeps happily?' Without warning, from out of the darkness beneath him, came a rejoinder: '*Samadhi Nishtah*'—'He who is in permanent *samadhi* (spiritual trance).'

" 'Very good,' thought the king, 'and very true. OK, *Shete Sukham Kas Tu? Samadhi Nishtah*—"He sleeps well whose consciousness is ever connected to the Universal Consciousness"; that is the sort of 'sleep' that is truly valuable. Good! Now, *Ko Shatrur Iva? Ko Shatrur Iva?* Who is the enemy?'"

"Did he mean, 'the enemy of sleep?'"

"Yes, and by extension enemies in general; the Great Enemy. He wanted something that would fit both meanings. What is the use of poetry that does not have many layers of meaning?

"The king kept muttering, '*Ko Shatrur Iva?*' until the voice he had heard before volunteered, '*Nijendriyani*'—'one's own sense organs.' They are the enemy of sleep. When you fall in love with a woman will you be able to sleep without her? If you are obsessed with riches they are bound to keep you awake at night. And so it is with all the senses; they are the enemy of sleep, and of samadhi.

" 'Wonderful!' said the king. '*Ko Shatrur Iva? Nijendriyani.* And now, *Mitrani Kani?* Who are my friends?'

" '*Jitendriyani*—the conquered senses,' came the voice, which was right yet again. You don't want to destroy your senses, like some of these yogis claim. You want to bring them under your control and make them work for you.

"When the king heard this last response he called down below to the speaker: 'Please be so kind as to show yourself, great poet!' And who stepped out into the light but his own watchman! 'I never knew of your greatness before,' the king continued. 'You must become my adviser!'

" 'No, your majesty,' came the reply. 'I have been serving as your watchman because I wanted no one to know of my talents, so that I would to be left alone to do my own things. I answered you only because as your servant I felt an obligation to assist you. Now I must leave your service and find a new place where I can live in peace and quiet.' And off he went, in spite of all the baffled king's pleas."

"Just as you continue to escape from the people who discover too much about your talents."

"If you want to preserve your solitude you have to be ready to leave. You won't be able to leave if you are not careful of whom you bless or curse, because that sort of karma can bind you like steel cables. Moreover, what is a blessing for the person you bless may end up being a curse for you. Think for a moment of the Emperor Akbar, who had no sons until he was blessed by the Muslim saint Sheikh Salim Chishti. Even after that blessing it is said that his Queen became pregnant only after the saint's own one-year-old son, Balle Miyan, died. By knowing this we can know something of the kind of blessing that Salim Chisti gave to Akbar. We know that he absorbed some of those of

Akbar's karmas which were preventing him from having a son. These karmas then blocked Salim Chishti from having a son—so his own son died. It was as if he transferred his son to Akbar.

"But because Salim Chishti enabled that boy to be born into Akbar's family the saint became responsible for some of the bad karmas that this boy performed when he became the Crown Prince and later when he ruled as the Emperor Jehangir. And let me assure you, Jehangir was responsible for some very nasty karmas. I doubt that dealing with these karmas was any fun for the poor saint."

"Do you think he was not aware that there would be repercussions from his blessing?"

"Oh, he probably was, but he must have been overcome with emotion. When he saw that the Emperor himself had come to him barefoot to ask for a son he must have said to himself, 'Let whatever happens tomorrow happen; today I will make this man happy!' Only a Muslim saint has enough guts to give such a blessing; not a Hindu. Hindu saints are too cautious; they want to make sure whoever they bless will be able to handle the blessing. It is good to be circumspect, but then the emotion can't freely flow."

"Does that mean that you think Muslims are superior to Hindus in some regards?"

"Of course! It's only the bigoted Muslims that I don't like. And I don't like the bigoted Hindus any better."

"How could Salim Chisti have become overcome with emotion if he was a saint? Shouldn't saints be beyond emotion?"

"Saints are beyond the *Three Gunas* (the three fundamental qualities of physical and mental reality), but only those who follow the path of *jnana* (transcendent, unqualified wisdom) go beyond all emotion. Misery remains in *bhakti* (devotion). But that misery is the misery of separation from the beloved, not the misery of hatred. That misery is so fierce that we call it *mahapida* ('massive affliction')—which is why we call bhakti *asu ka marg* ('the path of tears'). When you become so God-intoxicated that the tears in your eyes blind you to the world you will see nothing but God everywhere you look. And when you see your God standing before you in a pitiable plight, you won't be able to stand it. You will do whatever you can to help that God out, to make Him happy, even if that act makes you more miserable. Don't ever listen to the so-called swamis who tell you that you have to become cold and dead in order to make spiritual progress. They can say such things only because they have forgotten what it means to have a heart."

We had now reached the Poona Cantonment, and shortly thereafter we arrived at our destination: the home of Shernaz, a Zoroastrian who by the time

I met her had already been part of Vimalananda's circle of 'children' for nearly a quarter of a century. As she scurried off to make us some tea Vimalananda looked out the window to a tree he had become friendly with, laughed suddenly, and said, "Always be mindful, Robby, of everything that you do! Once I told Shernaz to feed monkeys every Saturday for ten Saturdays, to reduce an affliction of Saturn in her horoscope. I warned her that not just any monkey would do; they had to be *langurs*, the type of monkey which *Anjaneya* (the monkey-god Hanuman) is reputed to be. Langurs are vegetarian. In spite of being small they are very, very strong. Fortunately for her a troop of langurs lives in the graveyard near here, and they roam through town looking for handouts on Saturdays."

"Just on Saturdays?"

"Yes, they somehow know that Saturday is the day they are likely to be fed. A male—and my God, he was a big one!—led the pack. When someone offered the troop some food he would first approach and check out the terrain to make sure it was safe. Once he was satisfied he would summon the others with a peculiar sort of cry. Only then they would come to eat. Every Saturday this whole process would be repeated at Shernaz's house when she fed them with a prescribed article of food. Unfortunately she then became frivolous and decided that if ten Saturdays would help her eleven Saturdays would do her even more good. So she fed them for an extra Saturday."

"Wouldn't feeding them more normally do more good?"

"Perhaps, but it was more important for her to do as she was told. She was not feeding them because she loved them. She was feeding them for her own benefit, and when she became greedy for more benefit Nature decided that she needed to be taught a lesson. One fine morning during the week following that eleventh Saturday the langur chief swung into her home through an open window. He strutted around the house for a while in a furious mood and then left. Everyone who was inside was scared silly, including Shernaz, Arzoo, and Shernaz's son Sohrab. I happened to come to visit shortly afterwards. While they were telling me all about him, exaggerating his size and ferocity and everything else, he came back. He was really enormous for a langur. He strutted all through the house, growling but not touching anything.

"When he came to where we were all sitting at the dinner table he sat on the table right in front of me. He caught hold of my right wrist, still growling and showing his teeth, and patted me gently on my head. Then he jumped off the table and jumped back out the window. Because I lived so long in jungles I am used to animals, but you should have seen everyone else! I told my quaking friends that this fellow would not live long, and that they should close their outside windows for the next ten days so that he couldn't get back in. He started harassing everyone in the neighborhood from that day. On the tenth day he was jumping from one roof to another when he slipped and grabbed an overhead wire and was electrocuted. The local people, many of whom regard langurs as incarnations of Hanuman, took his body in a big procession and had it cremated. And you know, even the other langurs in the big fellow's troop joined the procession! It was just like they knew exactly what was happening. First they collected somberly around the body—even the babies behaved themselves—and when the body was carried away they marched along with everyone else. And people say that animals have no intelligence and no emotions! I think it is the humans who are deficient!

"Everyone learned a good lesson from this incident. Even Shernaz learned not to try to be so smart about things which humans cannot easily understand, like the relationship between monkeys and Saturn."

"Now wouldn't you say," I said, scratching my head reflectively, "that this Goliath of a monkey effectively died because of her extra feeding? Doesn't this make Shernaz incur at least some of the karma for his death? Not to mention the karma of disturbing the relationship between Saturn and the langurs?"

Just then Shernaz arrived with our tea, and Vimalananda asked her, "You remember the big langur, don't you, Shernaz?"

Shernaz replied, with some satisfaction, "He was a giant!"

"By having Shernaz try to placate Saturn," Vimalananda went on, "I was trying to relieve her of some of the pressure of the karmas she was having to experience. Suppose you are destined to have a rock fall on your head. If the rock is a boulder there will be nothing left of you after it lands, but if it is only a pebble it will bounce right off. This is how it is with karma. Unless someone takes your karmas on himself you cannot escape experiencing their effect. You can diminish their bad effects, however, and enhance the good effects by the skillful use of sadhana. When you fail to do as you are told, though, as this woman did—I am telling you to your face," he said, looking pointedly at Shernaz, "you are bound to get yourself into trouble; then all your efforts may be wasted. And that, too, is an experience provided to you by Saturn."

"Is worshipping Anjaneya the best way to control Saturn?"

"Yes it is, for many reasons, but especially because Anjaneya knows how to manage the Law of Karma. I think you know that at one point during the *Ramayana* Anjaneya flies over the ocean to Lanka where He was to search for Sita."

The *Ramayana*, the other of India's two great epic poems, is the story of the life of King Ramachandra, or Rama, the seventh avatara of *Vishnu*, the Great God Who Preserves The Cosmos. During the fourteen years that Ramachandra resides in the forest His wife Sita is stolen by the Ravana, a *rakshasa* (demonic being) who is king of the island of Lanka. With the help of an army of monkeys and bears Ramachandra invades Lanka and after many tribulations kills Ravana in battle and regains Sita. Before the invasion Ramachandra sends Hanuman over to Lanka to reconnoiter the area and locate Sita.

"Anjaneya leapt into the sky and was flying bravely toward the island when he suddenly felt Himself begin to weaken. When He looked around He saw the reason: the giant demoness Simhika. She said to Him, 'I am very hungry, O son of the wind god, and very glad to see you! It happens to be your destiny to enter my mouth and be eaten by me!'

"When Anjaneya examined His causal body to find out if she was telling Him the truth He got the shock of His lifetime when He saw that, yes, it was His destiny to enter her mouth. But if He allowed Himself to be eaten how would He be able to accomplish the mission that His beloved Lord Ramachandra had sent Him to perform? Anjaneya was not concerned for His own life, but He was concerned for the success of His mission, for He thinks only of Rama. He realized that something needed to be done urgently, because Simhika was drawing His shadow, and so Himself, nearer and nearer to her."

"How was she doing that?"

"Your shadow is a part of you, isn't it? If I can grab hold of your body and pull you toward me why shouldn't I be able to do the same thing with your shadow? Shadows are made up of matter, and even though that matter is very subtle shadows are not that difficult to pull, provided that you know how to grab hold of them.

"Anjaneya, who had been thinking fast, hastily used His *siddhi* (extra-natural ability) of *Mahima* to expand His body into enormous size. Seeing that her meal had become the size of a billowing cloud Simhika opened her mouth equally wide. Then Anjaneya suddenly contracted His body, using His siddhi of *Anima*, and fell into her open mouth with the force of a thunderbolt. When He emerged from her body after tearing her vital parts to pieces with His claws Simhika's hulk fell into the ocean with a gigantic splash. Then Anjaneya was free to continue His flight to find Sita. In this way He complied with the letter of karmic law but escaped its undesirable consequences."

"Does Saturn have no effect at all on Anjaneya?"

"Saturn has to cast his glaze on everyone; there is no exception. He also had to affect Anjaneya, but he couldn't figure out how to do so. In fact, he even asked Anjaneya for help! He said, 'You are *Maha Rudra*; how will I sit on you?'"

"*Rudra* is another name for *Shiva* (the god of death and transformation), fine, but why *Maha* (great)?"

"Anjaneya is the greatest Rudra because he is the Final Rudra, the last of the eleven Rudras, just as *Mahakala* ('Great Time') is the First Rudra, the *Adi*

Rudra. Anjaneya, who is an incarnation of Lord Shiva, is the perfection of Shiva. The Rudras control life and death by controlling memory. Life is just a memory; bitter or sweet, it is nothing but memory."

"You mean that if I can't remember I might as well not even be alive?"

"That too, but without memory life *itself* is not possible. Your exist because of ahamkara, which is your 'I-causing' faculty. Ahamkara continuously self-identifies with every cell of your body and every facet of your limited human personality. Without ahamkara you cannot exist as an individual because it is ahamkara that integrates the many many parts of you into *you*. Mahakala, the Rudra who separates you from your life, causes you to die by causing your ahamkara to remember that She is the Kundalini Shakti. When Kundalini sees Mahakala She is so overwhelmed with love for Him that She can think only of Him, and cannot continue to remember your mediocre human personality for even an instant longer.

"But death is not the end; oh no, not by a long shot. So long as your causal body continues to exist you must be reborn after you die, so that you can self-identify with a new body and personality. Only when you can completely forget yourself—when you have nothing with which to identify because your karmic warehouse has been emptied of all unpaid karmic debts—can you completely cease to exist. Only when you get into the causal body can you go beyond it. And then, finished! You have gone beyond attribution into *Nirvikalpa Samadhi* (pure non-dualistic consciousness, unstained by even a shred of ego)."

"But until then you are stuck."

"So long as you have a causal body filled with rnanubandhanas that remain to be worked out Saturn can keep you under his thumb, subject to fate and to the Law of Karma. Thought waves are continuously being projected into your mind—your astral body—from the karmas collected in your causal body. Most people forget that these thoughts are simply temporary manifestations. They try to cling to them or avoid them, and that creates yet more karma.

"There *are* ways to lose your causal body other than Nirvikalpa Samadhi, but most of them are not so easy to come by. You know, even if you live in India for lifetimes on end, there are some things going on that you would never suspect. You would never even dream about them unless you are meant to see them. For instance, there is a place in India where every day three or four chosen people bring a fresh corpse. They remove its clothing, wash it, and prepare it in certain other ways. Then they take it to a giant luminous figure with long black matted locks and fixed, staring eyes which never blink. He takes the corpse's head and cracks it open and eats part of the brain. Sometimes, depending on his intentions, he may eat other parts of the body as well. By his consumption of the brain the dead person's causal body gets completely eradicated, which means that he or she never has to be born again. This being has to have one corpse every day, and where he gets them from is a mystery. To see it is truly horrifying, but I saw it, and survived."

"My goodness! But this doesn't mean that anyone who eats brain is destroying that corpse's causal body, does it?"

"If that were true then all the cannibals in New Guinea would have merged by now! No, it is no easy thing to destroy your causal body, and so long as you have a causal body you will continue to be subject to the Law of Karma, and to fate. So long as you have karmas you will have memories and experiences, which is where Saturn comes in. Saturn stands for experience, good or bad, and your memory is the sum of your experiences. The Rudras cause forgetfulness, which is the only way in which old life can cease and new life can begin. The Rudras can do this because They self-identify so little with Their own 'bodies.' Mahakala, for example, has no single form; He takes whatever form He needs to perform His task. Anjaneya may be *Mahavira*—the 'Greatest of Heroes'—but He is also *Dasanudasa*—the 'Servant of Servants.' He self-identifies with Rama so much that He rarely remembers His own body. Because of this detachment Saturn cannot affect the Rudras—much.

"When it came time for Saturn to afflict Anjaneya he couldn't figure out how to do so. So he asked Anjaneya, 'How can I sit on you?'

"Anjaneya told him, 'Sit on my tail.' When Saturn did, Anjaneya's tail flipped him over and pinned him. Then Saturn could not even move, much less throw his gaze on Anjaneya. Anjaneya's mace controls all the planets except Saturn, who is controlled by His tail.

"In spite of being pinned, though, Saturn still eventually exerted his effect. When Anjaneya went to Lanka and was captured there Ravana caused His tail to be set afire—the same tail that had pinned Saturn. Thereafter Anjaneya heroically set fire to the entire city of Lanka. Sita's prayers protected Him from being scorched, but even so the tip of His tail was slightly burned in the process.

"Moreover, due to the exuberance of his heroic nature Anjaneya lost control of Himself just for a moment. As He soared through the sky He was so full of shakti that just for a moment some of this shakti overflowed into His sweat. He caught Himself in the next moment and retracted most of that shakti back into Himself, but a tiny amount of that shakti escaped His body in a drop of sweat. That drop of sweat happened to drop from His body into the open mouth of a female crocodile who lay just below Him. She conceived immediately, and shortly after gave birth to the sage *Makaradhwaja* ('The Crocodile-Bannered One').

"Anjaneya, the perfect celibate, thus had to experience loss of His *ojas* (subtle essence of semen), however slight, which caused Him to father a son, just as an ordinary householder does. Anjaneya had to experience that aspect of life thanks to the effect of Saturn, the planet of experience. In certain things no one is spared by Nature."

"I have never seen Anjaneya's name mentioned in the Vedic lists of the eleven Rudras."

"Anjaneya does not appear anywhere in the Vedas; He has nothing to do with the Vedas. He is strictly Rama's heart. Do you know the story of His birth?"

"Not entirely."

"The story of Anjaneya begins with a Rishi who was named *Rishya Shringa* ('Antelope Horn') because he had a horn on his head. King Dasharatha had wanted for long years to father a child, and although his guru Vasistha Rishi had tried various methods he had failed to produce any offspring for the king. Vasistha therefore requested Rishya Shringa to perform a sacrifice known as the *Putra Kameshti Yajna* for this purpose. After the sacrifice Rishya Shringa distributed its *prasada* (consecrated offerings) to the king's three wives. As Kaikeyi, the king's third wife, was trying to decide whether or not to eat it a hawk, of the kind we call a kite, came along and snatched the prasada from her grasp. The kite flew straight to where a certain female langur named Anjani sat, and dropped the prasada into her hands. Anjanii ate it and became pregnant with Anjaneya.

"Back at the sacrifice the remaining prasada had to be divided so that Kaikeyi could have some. All three queens ate the prasada, and became pregnant with Rama and his three brothers as a result. All four of these brothers were filled with divinity, but their divinity was limited, because the prasada had been subdivided. Only Anjaneya's mother Anjani got a full piece, which is why Anjaneya's power is unlimited.

"Besides, Anjaneya was born because of the intervention of two Rishis, Angiras and Rishya Shringa, whereas Rama and His brothers were blessed by Rishya Shringa alone. The blessing of a single Rishi is enough to create a god, but when you are blessed by two, well, that is something else. That's one of the reasons why I love Anjaneya so much."

"Where does Angiras come into the picture?"

"Before Anjani was a monkey she was one of Indra's celestial dancers. One day Angiras Rishi was sitting in Indra's court deep in meditation, watching her dance. When she finished her dance she mocked him, saying, 'Look here, you old man, didn't you enjoy my dance? If you did you should tell me so.'

"Angiras replied, 'My dear, I was admiring not your artistry but the artistry of the One who made you and Who made you want to dance.'

"She became annoyed, and told him, 'What do you know about dance, anyway? You are bereft of artistry.'

"It is never wise to insult a Rishi. Angiras replied, 'Oh, is that so? Would you like to see my artistry? All right then: become a female monkey!' Then Anjani realized what she had done. But it was too late; a Rishi's curse must always come true. All she could do then was beg for forgiveness. Angiras, after his heart had been softened by her wretched pleas, modified his curse: 'You will become the mother of a monkey god who will be immortal and whose fame will endure as long as the sun and the moon endure.'

"A Rishi's curse is always a blessing in disguise. It will change you for the better, no doubt about it, just as it changed Anjani. Without the curse she would never have become the mother of such a great being. Anjani was born on the earth as a female monkey, but with the memory of her previous existence. Before she fell to earth Angiras had given her precise instructions on how to worship Lord Shiva. When the kite flew by and dropped the prasada from the Putra Kameshti Yajna into her hands she had no idea of what it was or where it had come from, but she took it to be Shiva's prasada and ate it. This is what faith can do for you."

"Faith, and following instructions," I said, mischievously, with a quick glance at Shernaz, and we all laughed.

More obedient than Shernaz, and more fortunate than she, was a Bomaby couple in financial distress who invited Vimalananda to their home. While there he observed, "It is a good thing that you have a well in front of your house. Burn a little incense there every day and wait. If I am correct a monkey will come. Offer him a wheat *chappati* (unleavened bread) and a lump of *gud* (crude cane sugar). If he eats any of it you are made." Four days after this conversation a monkey appeared, took one bite of the chappati, and vanished. Within a month this fellow sold some property for a fabulous profit and quickly parlayed that money into more than a million rupees. All this happened in the middle of Bombay city, in an area where there are no monkeys for miles around.

If Vimalananda had been willing to use even one of his various "knacks" for his own benefit he could easily have made for himself the millions that he "made" for others. Instead, he was perennially short on ready cash. This severely limited his stud choices for Stoney, for mares continue to eat even after they cease to race, and stallions charge covering fees for impregnating those mares. Many were the stud farms that Vimalananda surveyed, and many were the stallions, both Indian and foreign born, whose racing and breeding prowess we discussed over many a cup of tea, but the choice finally came down to the best deal rather than the best stallion.

The best deal he could strike in 1977 was with Vitu Karve, a trainer who was the son of the well-known jockey Ramu Karve, whom Vimalananda had first known thirty years before during his first foray into the world of racing. Vitu, who had recently opened a small stud farm, needed mares and was willing to make contingency deals. He was willing to pay for Stoney's upkeep himself and to give over to Vimalananda her first live foal, after which Stoney would belong to Vitu. It was an all-round gamble: Vimalananda was wagering that her first live foal would be a humdinger while Vitu was betting that Stoney would throw some additional good foals after that first one. Vimalananda's enthusiasm for this bargain was minimal, for Vitu's stallion would pass on merely adequate genes to Stoney's child, but without cash there was then no alternative that would have paid Stoney's way other than selling her outright, an idea which Vimalananda detested.

On the day Stoney left for stud Vimalananda sat in Bombay with me and Roshni, staring long and hard at the wall on which hung one of his favorite photos: a shot of him and his then-trainer Maneckjee leading Stoney back to the Paddock after she had won the Mother Lode Cup. Vimalananda looked in the photo to be on the brink of kicking up his heels with pleasure as he escorted in the prancing Stoney.

As the three of us sat together thinking our private thoughts we chewed *paan*, that popular Indian chaw that is composed of betel nut, betel leaf, *khatta* paste, slaked lime, and sundry other additives. Vimalananda always enjoyed a good paan, not least because he had fond memories of his mother and aunts feeding it to him when he was young. I was learning the art of paan preparation, which is a ritual in itself, from Roshni, who had recently started making paan for Vimalananda. First you select the leaf, which must have no brown spots of deterioration on it. As Vimalananda loved to remind us, "Three things must always be kept turning: betel leaves, rotis, and horses." If you don't turn betel leaves regularly they will rot; an unflipped *roti* (tortilla-like flatbread) will burn; and a horse who does not keep walking or running will likely to die of acute colic. Once you have selected a worthy leaf you deftly slice out its central rib, then coat the leaf with the lime and khatta, whose mixture creates the red color that paan chewers are always spitting out. Atop this sanguine spread go the other ingredients, and then the whole mixture is folded into a triangle, square or cone.

Roshni had added a little tobacco to Vimalananda's paan—she wanted it to have none and he insisted that it have some—and as he spat out its remains he began to tell me the secret of his prize mare's racing success: "Just after Stoney had come to me I asked my son, 'What do you want for your birthday?' That fellow knows me too well, so he replied, 'First promise me that you'll give it to me.' I promised, and then he told me, 'I want Stoney to win a race.' Now I was stuck. What if she wasn't destined to win, or I was not destined to make money from her? But I had promised, and I had to go through with it. I sat and did *homa* on Stoney's behalf, and she won a race as a result. Then I warned my son: 'Don't you ever try to trap me like this again or you've had it, whether or not you are my son.'

"Stoney won six races altogether. I knew that she had it in her to win, but I wanted to make it sure. So one day I went to my Junior Guru Maharaj to get some insurance. I pleaded, I pestered, and I coaxed. I told him all sorts of things, and even accused him of not caring for me. I also hinted that maybe it was beyond his capabilities. Finally he lost his temper and said, 'You don't think I can do it, do you? Well, I will show you just how I can do it. I will sit on that mare myself and win five races for you. First, I will come from the back. Then, I will go start to finish. Then . . .'

"The old man described in detail exactly how each race would be run. And you can believe it or not, but those five races were run just as he had predicted and she won each one. Am I right, Roshni?" Roshni nodded her assent. "He must have done just as he had predicted he would do; he must have possessed the bodies of the jockeys at race time, and forced them to do as he wanted them to do."

"Which made him responsible for the karma involved in arranging things so that she would win."

"Naturally; why else would I bother my mentor with such trifles? To deal with such karmas is child's play for him, but it is better for him to have to deal with it as a favor he has done for me than it is for me to deal with it as something I did for myself. And it's not like I expected something for nothing; I did something nice for him in return for this favor. After all, a fair exchange is no robbery."

"So why should he have refused at first to grant your request?"

"Well, why should he grant it? Should he indulge me in every request that I make? Besides, even if such karmas are child's play for him they are still karmas. I am asking him to soil his hands for me. Guru Maharaj has the power to make my mare win a hundred or a thousand races, if he wants to. But each race that he manipulates adds to the load of karmic filth that he has to wash off. Why should he bother?

"You know, most people go to saints to ask them for money, or to punish their enemies, or to get their children married, or whatever, but they are all stupid. When a saint has given up everything worldly how will he be able to help you with your worldly problems? I was equally stupid at first. My Junior Guru Maharaj asked me at least ten times if I preferred to have money or devotion to God, and I always said, 'Money,' because I thought that if I had money I could purchase anything I needed.

"One day when I was with him he asked me the same question. When I gave him the same answer he got so angry that he gave me a good slap. That slap somehow changed my way of thinking, and from that day on when anyone asks me what I want I always say, 'Bhakti, because if I have true devotion God will provide me with whatever I need.'"

I opened my mouth to speak but he intercepted my riposte.

"I know what you are thinking; you need not speak. You are thinking: 'If now you want nothing but bhakti, why did you ask Guru Maharaj to make Stoney win?' Don't worry, I am already prepared for that question. I have plenty of reasons ready for you. First, my rnanubandhana with Stoney, which I want to be completed in the best way possible. And whether anyone likes it or not this time around she is a racehorse, and racing is her lot in life. The more she wins the more she'll be respected and the better she'll be treated, both in the racing stables and now at stud. Second, it's a sort of competition between me and Guru Maharaj: I am testing him to see how much he is willing to soil his hands while doing things for me, and he is testing me in much the same way. Third, what about my rnanubandhanas with my poor friends at the racecourse? When one of my horses wins and they make money they bless me, and there is value in such blessings."

"And in curses too, I guess."

"O my God, there is tremendous power in curses! When I say that most of these jockeys and bookies are going to be finished I am not talking through my hat. Some years back there was a horse named Mount Everest. What a horse he was, Robby—a real mountain! He won race after race, and the punters at the track all knew that they could bet him fearlessly.

"Derby Day came around, and Mount Everest instantaneously became the 'on money' favorite. Everyone backed him down to 1 to 10 'on money'— meaning that for a bet of 10 rupees you'd get only 11 back: your bet of 10, plus 1. For most horses this is terrible odds, but not for Mount Everest. Everyone knew he was going to win, so it was just like getting 10% interest on your money for leaving it in the bank for half an hour.

"The bookies also knew he was going to win and decided to do something about it to save themselves from certain ruin. They got to the jockey and offered him an immense sum. The jockey refused, hesitated, wavered, and then agreed. Derby Day arrived, and everyone who was anyone went to the track to watch Mount Everest win in convincing fashion. And what happened? Mount Everest's jockey tried frantically to hook him by making his pre-planned errors. But the horse was so much better than his rivals that the best the jockey could do was to cross the finish line neck and neck with another horse in a photo finish. Like everyone else at the track I was watching very carefully, and I was sure that Mount Everest had won. But the bookies had prepared for this too; in a few moments word came that the photo finish camera had failed. Failed! This was the only time in the world, up to that moment, that a photo finish camera had failed. The company that made the camera was so concerned to protect their reputation that they checked the camera later—and found nothing wrong with it. But that was later; on the day of the race there was no photo, which meant no review, which meant that the unbeatable Mount Everest had been pipped at the post."

"These things happen."

"Of course they do; unbeatable horses do get beat. It is also true that winning a photo finish is often just a matter of luck. When a horse gallops he thrusts his head first forward and then back with each of his strides. Suppose that at the finish line two horses are nose and nose, and one's head is pushing forward when the other is pulling back. Then the first one's nose will cross the finish line before the second one's will, even if the second one's body is in front of the first one's body. That nose will make all the difference between first and second place.

"But Mount Everest was not supposed to have been in a photo finish in the first place. He should have trounced his rivals, and when he did not there was silence at the racecourse. Total silence—everyone was so shocked. Everyone knew what had happened, it was so obvious. Mount Everest himself made the conniving even more obvious when he won his next race, the R.W.I.T.C. Invitational Cup, convincingly—by streets! In fact, the Derby was the only race he ever lost. There was an enquiry and everything, but nothing could be proved, so the culprits went scot-free.

"Or so they thought, until the morning after the race when *The Times of India* carried the tragic news of the death of an entire family that had drowned in the Arabian Sea. A few days later a suicide note surfaced and the truth came out. It seems that the father of the family had been skimming money from where he had worked to feed his gambling habit. He had lost steadily, as ordinary racegoers always do, until he was about to be found out. Then he recklessly took an enormous sum from the office on Friday. He planned to wager it all on Mount Everest, recover his arrears, and replace it before anyone would come to know. After the unthinkable occurred and Mount Everest lost the race, he realized that he would be going to jail, and

117

that as the family's only breadwinner his wife and children would starve. He took what he thought was the only honorable course of action left to him. At least this way they would still be together as a family and would see what fate had in store for them next time around.

"Can you imagine what his last thoughts must have been as he choked to death under the water? Like everyone else at the racecourse he knew that Mount Everest had been hooked. Don't you think he must have been thinking of the jockey and the bookies, the people who had caused him to kill himself? And what about the last thoughts of his family? This kind of curse, one that is delivered with all the force of someone's last breath, possesses a terrible power. So I would not want to be in that jockey's shoes, not even if you offered me tens of millions of rupees. He's going to be regretting his action for a long, long time."

"And the bookies will surely regret as well."

"Yes, the bookies too; where will they go? They cannot escape."

"If the curses of poor people are so powerful, what about all the curses that Mamrabahen has been spewing at me?" Mamrabahen hated me ever since she asked Vimalananda whether he loved me or her more and he had told her that he loved me more because I did not double-cross him. Mamrabahen thereupon began to repeatedly threaten to kill me, or at the very least to disfigure my face with acid, and amused herself thereafter by continually hurling maledictions in my direction, consigning me to multifarious hells in a multiplicity of unpleasant ways.

"I have told you before not to worry in the least about Mamrabahen's curses. First of all, I am there to protect you. Second, everyone asks me about blessings and curses but no one bothers to ask me how long a blessing or a curse will last. Isn't it important to know? If you know that a certain curse will only be short-lived you need not go to much trouble to try to lift it. You need only keep quiet until the end of the time limit and then you are free. Likewise, if you know how long a blessing will last you will be able to know how long you have to make use of it to progress.

"To know how long a blessing or curse will last you must first know in which form of speech (*vani*) it was delivered: *Vaikhari* (oral), *Madhyama* (mental), *Pashyanti* (visual), or *Para* (telepathic) *Vani.* Oral curses and blessings are almost worthless because your tongue burns whatever it speaks. This is why speaking mantras aloud dissipates their shakti. Even speaking someone's name too much spoils its sweetness. Even saying 'I love you' aloud is far less meaningful or effective than saying it mentally, or looking at someone and letting the love flow through your eyes or, best of all, using telepathy. In the old days the real gurus would bless their 'children' with Para Vani. Those blessings would go directly to the target and hit the mark; their effects would last a lifetime and nothing else needed to be done. *That* is the power of Para Vani."

"When that man committed suicide because of Mount Everest's defeat, was his dying curse in some higher form of speech?"

"Very likely it was, even though he probably was not aware of it."

"But Mamrabahen cannot use higher speech herself?"

"How can she? She tries to do sadhana, but she has no *niyama* (internal discipline). As soon as she gets some shakti she gets angry with someone and shouts at them, which burns it away with her tongue. Or she goes with some man and screws it away with her lower mouth, or does something else that eliminates its effect. The time to get worried is when you are cursed by someone who does good sadhana, because she will put some of her shakti into that curse.

"This applies to blessings, too. Think of it this way: if you beg money from a beggar you will only get small change, because that is all he has to give you. This is like an oral blessing. If you go to a merchant and he is pleased with you he will give you a good amount, but he will still calculate how much he gives you according to how much he can afford to give. This is like a mental blessing. But if a king is pleased with you, well, the sky's the limit. Real kings know how to give. This is one reason why they call good sadhus *maharaj* (great king), because they know how to bless—and to curse. A saint or a sadhu can only really bless or curse you when they are overcome by love or by wrath. Then the force flows from them without their even being aware of it.

"You can know a lot about a saint from the results produced by his blessings. Think of Mukunda Babu, who in his earlier years was a schoolteacher. When Mukunda Babu was growing up his grandfather had gradually taught the boy the entire *Ram Charit Manas* (the version of the *Ramayana* composed by Tulsidas). After he got older Mukunda Babu used to recite this *Ramayana* here and there in his spare time, for which he earned a little money. Then a sadhu who worshipped Anjaneya blessed Mukunda Babu, and now the ex-schoolteacher lectures before huge audiences of people. People are ready to give him millions, but fortunately for him he accepts their money on only one day of the year. Tulsidas clearly did not write his book on Rama with the intention that other people would use it to make money. But by not demanding money for his programs Mukunda Babu limits his exposure to the negative karma of selling spiritual knowledge.

"Any blessing that you get has to filter through both your causal and astral bodies, causing certain of your karmas to project outwards for fulfillment. Because a good sadhu delivered the blessing Mukunda Babu's mind is kept firm so that he does not desire name, fame and so on. He is tempted, according to the Law of Karma, but he does not succumb to temptation like so many 'swamis' do. If he did succumb we would know that the sadhu who blessed him was a false sadhu."

"Do you know the sadhu that blessed him?"

"The sadhu was just an excuse, a medium through which the blessing was given. It was in fact Anjaneya Himself who blessed Mukunda Babu through the sadhu."

As if in thought Vimalananda paused, which permitted the flat to fill with street noise from two floors below. Then he continued: "Now I have given you a couple of good examples of saints' blessings. Here is an example of the power of a saint's curse: Kamran, king of Kandahar, was the brother of Humayun, Akbar's father. One day when Kamran was out hunting he shot a pregnant deer, who even though she was mortally wounded managed to struggle to the feet of Shri Chand Ji to die with her head on his foot.

"Now, Shri Chand Ji was no ordinary mortal. He was a great saint in his own right, and was also the son of Guru Nanak, who was a *Siddha* (perfected being). Shri Chand Ji was amazed that this doe had sought him out to die at his feet. He was so amazed, and so filled with love for her and for the Nature that had created her, that he blessed her from the depths of his heart. He was still in this mood of tremendous love when Kamran, who had been tracking the deer, arrived to claim his prize.

"Shri Chand Ji tried to reason with him, and explained that since the doe had come to him and taken refuge at his feet that he could not part even with her body. But Kamran was a cruel and unreasoning man, and he insisted. He was the king, after all, and was not used to people defying him.

"Then Shri Chand Ji was filled with such agony for the fate of the deer that it poured from him in the form of a terrible curse: "Your son will blind you, and make you beg in the streets before he murders you!" And it happened. In fact, Kamran was disemboweled."

"He shouldn't have insisted."

"No, and neither should you. If you are ever cursed by a real saint you have to expect the worst."

"And if a real saint blesses me should I expect the best?"

"You must. If an ordinary sadhu blesses you, expect an ordinary blessing that will last a short time. The effects of a great saint's blessing will last months, or years, or maybe your entire life. A Siddha's blessing gives you both worldly and spiritual benefits. At first you will prosper like anything. Then, after three or four years—seven years maximum—you will begin to feel, 'Why do I have all this? What is it for? Why should I not go out and live in the jungle?' And you will."

"And if a Rishi blesses you?"

"A Rishi's blessing lasts for lives and lives. Sometimes a Rishi, or some other *Mahapurusha* (immortal being), will give the blessing *Chirayur bhava!* ('Live indefinitely long!') If this meant that the person who was blessed should become a *Chiranjivi*, one who lives for millions of years at a time, then the whole world would be populated with ancient people by now. There would be no room for anyone new, which we can see is not the case. What this sort of blessing really means is that those who receive it will be reborn as humans every time they reincarnate. This gives them a chance to finish their jobs sooner, continuing their progression along the road to liberation through each succeeding birth without any further delays as animals or plants.

"A Rishi's curse is something unique because it always turns out to be a blessing in the end. It may plague you for many lives, but it will purify so many of your bad karmas that once you emerge from it you will become quite different. The curse makes all those bad karmas come out all at once.

"Will the curse on Mamrabahen cause all of her bad karmas to come out?"

"That is obviously happening already. But in order for such a curse to change you you have to admit your faults and stop performing evil karmas. Mamrabahen, on the contrary, is performing more and more evil karmas; she refuses to improve. I have been trying to improve her, but it is not working. You know, one of the greatest blessings you can obtain is to have someone near you who will always correct your mistakes for you."

"Is that why Birbal used to correct all of Akbar's mistakes, because he appreciated what Prithviraj had done for Chand Barot?" I asked, as the story of the great king and his loyal servant who had been reborn as the mighty Emperor Akbar and his closest confidant abruptly recalled itself to my mind.

"Perhaps."

"Surely Mamrabahen must be able to do something right."

"Oh, yes, she is quite clever. One thing she knows is pedigree; she can tell you the pedigree of almost every horse racing here in Western India. She also knows the sorts of influence that the various sires and dams have on their progeny."

"But the only good this has done her is to embroil her with jockeys."

"Yes, that long-ago curse has prevented her from ever being able to profit from her knowledge. It is so very difficult to escape from the effects of your karmas.

"This is a true story: There was a king who, having fathered no child during his first marriage, adopted a son. Sometime thereafter he married another wife who bore him a son. The second son's mother wanted her own son to suceed to the throne, and eventually, blood being thicker than water, she convinced the king to accede to her demand. But how to get rid of the adopted son?

"After some thinking the king decided to send the boy to his neighbor, a vassal king who did most of his dirty work for him, including murders. The boy carried a sealed letter from his adopted father to the vassal. The letter read: 'Give this boy *visha* (poison).'

"When the boy reached the river at the edge of the vassal king's city he lay down on the riverbank for a nap. The king's daughter happened to come down to the river, and when she saw the handsome boy on the bank she instantly fell in love with him. Seeing the letter he was carrying she opened it and read, 'Give this boy visha.'

"Looking at him with eyes of love she said to herself, 'What a fine young man! How could anyone, and his own father in particular, want to poison him? The king must have simply left out the letter 'ya.' He must have meant to write 'Vishaya'—and that is my name! So I am to be given to this prince in marriage! How wonderful! But I must correct this oversight.' She added 'ya' to the word 'visha,' replaced the letter, and awoke the boy.

"She then led him joyously to her father, who read the note and said, 'How fine! My daughter is to become a queen! They must be married immediately!' And so they were. The young couple was then sent back to the first king with many presents—jewels, elephants, and whatnot—and a note from the princess's father: 'King, you have done me great honor by marrying your son to my daughter and thus making a queen of her. Please accept these meager presents in gratitude!'

"When the boy's adopted father read the note he realized both that his plan had backfired, and that there was nothing he could do about it. If he were to make his natural son king after him the other king would be terribly insulted, and might disrupt the whole alliance system. So he had to keep his trap shut, and after he died his adopted son became king. And that was that."

"So everything is predestined?"

"By no means; there is such a thing as free will in the world. How much free will you have in any given situation, though, depends on how much you have used up in the past. Using your free will today creates karmas that become your fate tomorrow. Every time you use your free will to try to avoid your fate, to try to swim against Nature's current, you create new karmas whose effects will not always be obvious to you until much, much later."

"And presumably the more people you affect the bigger your karma, like the jockey who hooked Mount Everest. Which means that someone like Mao Tse-tung, what with the Cultural Revolution and everything else he has done to the people of China, is going to have an ocean of karmas to answer for."

"Without a shadow of a doubt. The more authority you have over people the more conscientiously you must exercise it."

"Lao Tse said, 'Ruling a great kingdom is like cooking small fish.'"

"And I agree with him. When you are a ruler you must be very cautious, for things that you might think of as minor can soon become major when you look at them from the perspective of the people you rule. If enough of them die cursing you with their last breath you'll be finished, done for, for ages. It is the rare person, like Akbar, who can endure the luxuries of princely life without being ensnared by them. But even he made some missteps—he was only human, after all, and no human is perfect. He may even be still be paying for some of these mistakes today.

"Tansen, Akbar's chief musician, was really Tansen Pandey. His father's name was Makaranda Pandey. 'Pandey' is derived from *panda* ('priest'), which means they were a Brahmana family. Makaranda Pandey was unsuccessful at siring a child until he started to perform devotional services for one *fakir* (Muslim religious mendicant) named Mohammed Gous who lived near him. After some time Gous became pleased with Makaranda. One day when he was in a peculiar mood he called the Brahmana over to him and spit in his palm, and then put the spit in a paan. He told Makaranda, 'Eat this and your work will be done.' He did, and it was; Tansen was the result.

"The other Brahmanas, bigoted as Brahmanas usually are, told Makaranda, 'You have swallowed the spittle of a Mohammedan, so now you have become a Mohammedan.' Makaranda replied, 'All right, then I am a Mohammedan.' And so Tansen was reared as a Muslim, even though he came from a Brahmana family. What do you have to say to that?"

"Nothing," I replied with bitter heat. "I have no more use for orthodox Brahmanas than I have for any other kind of Hindu fundamentalists. I have already had difficulties with Brahmanas who refuse me entry into certain temples, as well as Brahmanas who think that the secrets of Ayurveda should not be opened to me just because my skin is white. Whites may be racist, but there seems to be a vast amount of anti-white discrimination right here in India too."

"You are lucky that you have come here in the '70s," Vimalananda replied soothingly. "Twenty or thirty years ago it would have been nearly impossible for you to do what you are doing.

"After Tansen entered Akbar's service he was recognized almost immediately as one of the Nine Jewels of the court. He became famous throughout the kingdom, and Akbar was very pleased with him. Then one day when Akbar was feeling expansive he said to Tansen, 'Wah, wah, what a superb musician you are!' He was taken aback when Tansen replied humbly, 'Compared to my guruji I am nothing at all, O Refuge of the World. Yes, I am a good musician, but Haridas Swami, my teacher, is much greater than I. I sing for money and fame and to please you, but he sings only for God.'

"This piqued Akbar's curiosity. He loved excellence, so he told Tansen, 'You must request your guruji to come to my court so that I can hear him sing.' Tansen replied, 'He will never come here, Your Majesty. He cares nothing for the world's grandeur. But if you will come with me in disguise then perhaps we will be able to hear him sing.'

"Akbar went incognito as Tansen's guest to listen to Swami Haridas worship the Lord with song. Midway through the performance he was so overcome by Haridas's singing that he forgot himself and cried 'Subanullah!', which is a Muslim way of saying, 'Outstanding! A marvel of God!' Haridas then immediately knew that a Muslim was listening to his music, and asked Tansen who he was.

"Tansen said, 'This is the Emperor, and he is very pleased with your singing.'

"Haridas said, 'He may be the Emperor, but I do not sing for emperors.'

"Then, to show his humility, Akbar offered Haridas Swami a vial of priceless perfume from Persia. Haridas took it and poured it onto the ground in front of him.

"Akbar gasped, and forgot his humility. He said, 'If you were not going to use it you should have given it to Krishna.' Haridas said, 'Go and see.'

"When Akbar went to the Krishna temple nearby he found that the image was covered with the same essence which he had just poured out onto the ground. Then Akbar understood—a little—of what Haridas was. Akbar was fortunate in that he behaved as a servant toward God—and God was the only thing he ever respected in that way—and so he respected the servants of God. Here is another effect of having ample good karmas in your account. Good karmas give you the opportunity to be exposed to saints who will help you get your priorities straight by humbling you. This happened to Akbar more than once.

"Meanwhile, Tansen stayed on with Akbar. He was really a great musician, though he did have some major character flaws."

"Like what?"

"How about the vicious jealousy that led him to kill everyone, like Gopal Naik, who might remotely be construed to be a threat to him?"

I had no answer to that, so Vimalananda continued: "Tansen composed two *ragas* (modes of Indian music)—*Darbari Kannada* and *Miya ke Malhar*—especially for Akbar. If you play Darbari correctly you'll see an image of Akbar, sitting on his throne, raising a rose to his nostrils. Tansen was widely famous for his ability to sing the Raga *Deepaka* (the Kindling or Igniting

Mode). He had so thoroughly mastered Deepaka that when he sang it at dusk all the lamps in the palace would light themselves, automatically. When Haridas Swami left his body, certain courtiers challenged him to light the Swami's funeral pyre by singing Deepaka. Tansen's arrogance got the best of him, and he accepted the challenge. He was able to light the pyre, but it was too much of a strain on him. He immediately fell ill. He was engulfed in heat; he felt as if his entire organism was on fire."

"Do we think that maybe the evil karmas created by killing Gopal Naik and all those other musicians somehow influenced this malady?"

"It's very likely."

"I guess this served him right for being so egotistical."

"Yes; you might keep that in mind. None of the court physicians knew how to treat this sort of disease. For six months Tansen was in agony, roving aimless about the country, his very being aflame, looking for relief. As luck would have it—which means, as his karmas arranged it—he ultimately reached the small village of Vadnagar in Gujarat. As he dragged himself through its streets he heard beautiful music coming from one of the houses. He recognized the music as the Raga *Megha*, the Cloud Mode—and what better thing to put out a fire than rain! The singers were two sisters, Tana and Riri, and Tansen requested permission to meet them. When the villagers discovered that the great Tansen himself had arrived they advised the girls' father Kanchanrai to have nothing to do with this Muslim entertainer. They warned him that he and his entire family would become outcasts if they helped him in any way. In spite of these threats to his family Kanchanrai invited Tansen into his house. The girls sang Megha so well for him that he was cured. Tansen offered Kanchanrai immense rewards, but they were politely declined. For Kanchanrai and his family wanted nothing to do with the Mughal court. Tansen then returned to Akbar's court, where the Emperor was wonderstruck at his story.

"Then it became Kanchanrai's turn to experience the results of his karmas. The courtiers who had challenged Tansen to misuse Deepaka goaded Akbar to believe that it was Kanchanrai's disdain for the throne that had led him to refuse a reward. Now it became a matter of principle, and Akbar insisted on summoning the father and his daughters to the imperial court. When the villagers discovered this they told Kanchanrai, 'You see, we told you so. Now you too will become Muslims. Perhaps the Emperor will even take your girls into his harem.' In order to protect their honor, and that of their family and village, Tana and Riri snuck away from their home and commited suicide together. And we can be sure that they were not thinking pleasant thoughts about the Emperor as they died."

"Didn't Akbar regret what he had done?"

"Oh, he did, he did, much later; but what was the use of regret then? Two brilliant musicians, who like Tansen could control prana through song, were lost to the world. And why? Simply because Akbar insisted on having his way. Remember this, when you are tempted to insist on having things your way."

chapter four
TIMIR

IN EARLY 1978 I was introduced to Vimalananda's newest horse, a handsome compact colt named Timir, when I watched him win his first race. This occasion was also noteworthy for me—it was the first time I had been able to cheer home one of Vimalananda's horses—and I found winning to be as electrifying a feeling as he had promised it would be. For the first time I understood the seduction of that sensation, how for sporting types like Vimalananda each victory could be as thrilling as his first.

I got an even greater thrill a few weeks later on the day Timir gave jockey Hemant Pawar an armchair ride to the 1000th win of his career. As Timir catapulted past the finish line all the railbirds around us erupted into huzzahs for horse, owner and rider alike. Cama and young Godrej pumped Vimalananda's hand; Firoz clapped him hard on the back. I convoyed Timir's beaming proprietor down the steps toward the gate where his 'child' would soon appear. After all the losing mounts had returned dispirited Hemant brought Timir forward so that Vimalananda could grasp one side of his reins. Mr. Lafange, the trainer, then grabbed the other side, and the three humans gave the conquering horse his triumph by leading him ceremoniously back to the paddock.

Though I had previously spent time at the Bombay racing stables my visit there after that afternoon's last race was another first for me: the first day that I helped Vimalananda distribute tips to the grooms after a victory. The heroic Timir got his tip of carrots and alfalfa first, of course, for he was watching us as we arrived. Horses love to watch people, and their heads generally emerge from their stalls instinctively when visitors walk by. Timir was one of those horses who enjoy a telepathic ability to know in advance when a friend is headed for the stable; he always seemed to be expecting us whenever we showed up. After Timir and his handlers had been fed I lowered myself into a folding chair and took a good look at the community in which I would spend much of my next seven years. A groom served me tea. As I sipped it I thought, "I could easily get used to all this."

Though no other pleasure can really compare to afternoon tea in the Bombay racing stables I soon learned that, as in racing venues the world over, its veneer of gentility sits atop a compost heap of plots and paranoia, pride and jealousy, overconfidence and frustration and, above all, cash and the rumors of cash. Skillful players learn that "money makes the mare go," and that innuendo and deviousness can make the mare's owner gain a status in the racing fraternity that his mares may never gain on the track. Truth at the racecourse can be amusing and interesting, but the appearance of truth usually counts for far more than its reality. That afternoon in the stables, though, I was most struck by how far withdrawn we seemed there from the Bombay which surrounded us. It was as though the uniformed guards at the gates of that treed and flowered biosphere of repose brandished some sort of authority that prevented all encroachment from the never-sleeping metropolis beyond. Redolent of the good farm smells of feed and dung, the stables reverberated with the caws of the ever-watchful jungle crows, the gentle whinnies of the hungry horses, and the fraternal murmurs of their handlers. God must surely be here in this heaven: What could be wrong with this world?

A wave of Vimalananda's hand summoned me out of my reverie, and I lifted myself from my seat to be introduced to Dr. Kulkarni, the vet who looked after Mr. Lafange's horses. Laughing, Dr. Kulkarni said to Vimalananda, "Oh, so here's the American on your team. Now you'll be able to use American 'medicines' for your runners that the lab won't be able to detect."

"What a joker you are, Dr. Saheb," said Vimalananda with a smile. Everyone at the racecourse knew that Vimalananda dosed his horses with all manner of permissible Ayurvedic, homeopathic and patent medicines, and even some from the Arabic medical system known as Unani. Though he never told anyone but me and Roshni what he was giving, the results they produced were evident to all observers. Perhaps Dr. Kulkarni thought that in the elation of victory Vimalananda would let some secret or another slip, but he did not know as I did that Vimalananda never allowed himself to be carried away by any species of intoxication.

After some further racecourse small talk we drove back to our digs. It was a day or two later, as we were driving to the two-thousand-year-old rock-cut Mandapeshwar cave temples in North Bombay to perform some rituals, that an opportunity surfaced to ask Vimalananda the question that had been exercising my mind: "Did you know before you bought Timir that he had this sort of rnanubandhana with Hemant Pawar?"

"Knowing all rnanubandhanas with all beings is a hell of a job," he replied. "I *did* know, even before I purchased him at the 1977 Auction Sales, that Timir had the chance to shine out. His pedigree is solid, and he has brought good karmas with him to experience during this lifetime. I knew Timir would do well, based on his fitness, and knew how much Hemant wanted to win his thousandth race. I didn't ask Hemant to ride him, you know; Hemant came on his own to ask me. I've known Hemant since way back when he was an apprentice, years and years ago, and I know what a good eye he has. He would not ask for a mount unless he was confident that he could win on it. As soon as he asked me for the mount I agreed. It felt like the right thing to do, and it was."

"Due to the rnanubandhanas between you, him, and the horse?"

"What else could it be? There is nothing in the world but rnanubandhana. Rnanubandhana is created and destroyed according to the mandate of the Law of Karma. Please don't think that anyone can be exempted from the Law of Karma. There are exceptions to every other law but this one. When God Himself comes to Earth He becomes subject to the Law of Karma, so what about you and me? Even the Rishis have not been spared by the Law of Karma. The Rishi Durvasas, who was the son of the Rishi Atri and the extraordinary Anasuya, was always irate. He inherited this incredible irritability from the blessing of Shiva, who, when upset, is anger incarnate. It was Durvasas who cursed Shakuntala, the young girl who neglected to serve him when he came to beg from her. Shakuntala's only crime was that she was thinking so fondly of her husband that she could remember nothing else. Because of this curse the girl was separated from her husband for years. Eventually she realized that it was all for her benefit—but what a hard lesson it was!

"But Durvasas too met his karmic Waterloo. King Ambarisha and his wife loved Krishna immensely; every day Krishna Himself would come to eat the food they offered to their little idol of *Bala Gopala*, the Baby Krishna. One day Durvasas and thousands of his disciples came to Ambarisha's palace for dinner. Durvasas already had a bad reputation, and whenever he was in town everybody would quake and quiver.

"Ambarisha and his wife were busy feeding Krishna when Durvasas arrived on the scene. The queen politely told Durvasas, 'Maharaj, please wait until we put Gopala to bed, and then we will take proper care of you.' Durvasas, who had come to test Ambarisha, got wild. Ambarisha said, 'Maharaj, you have such a high respect for God that it really doesn't behoove you to lose your temper this way.' Durvasas snarled at him, and asked, 'Who is this God of yours?' He didn't know Ambarisha. How could he? He had come to Ambarisha full of the ego of his *bala* (might). Bala and *kala* (stratagem, finesse) rarely exist together in one person. Ambarisha could not compete with Durvasas's power, but he was full of finesse. As usual, finesse won."

"Out from the tiny idol of Krishna sprang Vishnu's divine weapon, the *Sudarshana Chakra*. It sped straight for Durvasas, who decided to run. The *Chakra* (discus) chased him over hill and over dale, through deserts and forests, through all the three worlds. When there was nowhere left to run to Durvasas hid himself in a lake. The Chakra hovered there above his head, whirring menacingly.

"Then Durvasas knew he was defeated. He said to Vishnu, 'I was wrong, O Lord. Please forgive me. What is my punishment?'

"Vishnu said, 'The fruit of ten thousand years of your penance is to be forfeited.' And so it was. Ten thousand years was not much to Durvasas, who had been doing penances for much longer. The worst thing for him was having to admit his fault.

"Durvasas had to pay dearly for insulting Ambarisha. But Durvasas is himself a great devotee of Krishna; how could he ever dream of insulting either Him or His other devotees? The answer is simple: It was the effect of Saturn. When Saturn's 'gaze' falls on someone it usually causes them hardships, often by making them do things they would never do under normal circumstances. The Rishi Vasistha lost all his sons because of Saturn. Due to Saturn the Rishi Vishvamitra twice lost the benefits of thousands of years of penance because of his dallying with Menaka. In fact, one result of Vishvamitra's dalliances was that very Shakuntala who Durvasas cursed with separation from her husband. The play of the Rishis is really unique."

"I thought you told me that if you can completely conquer 'what comes naturally' to you, then Saturn can have no effect on you, and that immortals like the Rishis have been able to truly conquer their own natures."

"True; but it is also true that even the most minimal attachment of your Kundalini Shakti to your body will interfere with your ability to control your own nature. So long as a Rishi remains embodied he must remain at least slightly attached to his body, and Saturn has to cast his glaze on every embodied being; there is no exception. Everyone in the universe has to falter sometimes. Even the Lords of the universe remain subject to the Law of Karma. Fate can affect any immortal being who becomes subject to the time, space and causation of our universe, no matter how tenuous or temporary that attachment might be.

"To know karma is to know fate; but fate is not such an easy thing to know," he repeated, as if to himself. "In fact, I doubt that anyone really knows fate fully. Even the gods are unable to fathom it. Do you know the story of Indra and his parrot?"

"No, I don't."

"Indra had a pet parrot. One day he got the thought, 'Someday my beautiful little parrot is going to die. But when will that day be?' This question started to prey on his mind so much that eventually Indra picked up his parrot and went to Brahma, the Creator. Indra asked Brahma, 'Great lord, when will my beloved parrot die?'

"Brahma replied, 'I am sorry, Indra, I am only the Creator. I don't know about things like death. But now I am myself curious, so let us go and ask this of Vishnu.'

"Indra, his parrot and Brahma went to Vishnu and asked the Preserver of the Cosmos the same question. But Vishnu responded, 'I am only the Preserver; I know nothing of destroying. For that we must go to Lord Shiva.'

"All four of them trundled off to put the question to Lord Shiva. But Shiva answered, 'Though it is true that I am the Destroyer I do nothing on my own initiative. I only act according to fate. When it is written in someone's destiny that his time has come then I am there to take him. If we want to know when the parrot is going to pass on we must ask Vidhata.'

"Indra, the parrot, Brahma, Vishnu and Shiva accordingly made their way to the residence of Vidhata—Fate personified. As soon as they entered his presence they asked their question, but Vidhata merely said to them, 'Look at the parrot.' When they did they saw it lying dead on its back, its little legs sticking forlornly upward. Shocked, the four gods asked for an explanation.

"Vidhata told them, 'It was written that the bird would die only when it, Indra, Brahma, Vishnu and Shiva all met with me at the same time. This was the only way in which the prerequisites for its death could be fulfilled. It was because the parrot's time had come that you, Indra, got the idea to come and inquire. Had you ignored that thought the parrot need never have died.'"

"And that was it? Indra and the Trinity learned a good lesson and had to go home parrotless?"

"That's right."

"Huh. . . . Is asking questions what comes naturally to Indra?"

"Of course. From the celestial point of view Indra may be the king of the devas, but in the context of the human body he represents *indriya*, which means sense organ. All that the sense organs do all day long is ask questions. They are always looking outside to hear, touch, see, taste and smell what is going on. If asking questions is not 'what comes naturally' to the sense organs I don't know what is. If Indra had been able to control his own nature he would have asked himself why he had asked himself that question. Then he might still have his parrot. Don't forget: your conquered senses are your friends, and your unconquered senses—the ones that you allow to do what comes naturally to them—are your enemies."

"All right, I can see that. Does this also mean that just as it was written that the parrot had to meet his quietus in the presence of the Big Bosses it was also written that Hemant should win his thousandth on Timir, and that I should be there to watch you lead him in?"

"It certainly seems that way, doesn't it? There is still a thing like free will in the world, but sometimes when the karmas have become very concentrated there is very little space for free will to operate. If this weren't the case how could astrologers ever predict the future accurately? We know that they can; you have experienced it yourself."

"True."

"When your karmas become very, very concentrated in a certain area no amount of effort can enable you to escape Saturn and cheat your fate." He laughed a quiet laugh. "R. D. Shah is a mathematical wizard and an amateur palmist who learned some of his palmistry from me. He is also something of the classic 'absent-minded professor.' If he is deeply engrossed in some problem he will go out into a rainstorm without any cover and will look up into the pouring rain without even being able to recognize what it is.

"One day he came to me so fired up that he could barely talk. I waited patiently for him to calm down, when finally he spit out: 'I've seen a palm which is so unusual that you must come look at it and tell me if I am interpreting it correctly.' He took me to the man whose palm he had read, and when he saw the palm again R. D. Shah suddenly told the man, 'You are going to murder someone within four days. Please come to my house so that I can make sure you don't.'

"None of the people there believed this prediction except me, for I did see murder written in his palm. The prospective murderer's best friend, who was sitting next to him, objected: 'I've known this man for years, and I can tell you that he would never murder anyone.'

"R. D. Shah asked for the friend's hand, looked at his palm for only a moment and gasped, 'You are going to be the victim! Oh, my—please get out of town immediately!' No one listened. They all probably thought he had gone crazy. But I didn't, because I had seen the victim's palm, too, and saw in it the same thing that R. D. Shah saw.

"R. D. Shah went to the prospective victim's wife, but she ignored him. Three days after the prediction was made the victim carried a large sum of money to the prospective killer, who promptly murdered the man for his trouble. When R. D. Shah heard of this he came to me and broke into tears. It was pitiful. He sobbed, 'I tried to prevent it but I couldn't do a thing.'

"On a whim R. D. Shah went down to the jail and looked at the man's palm again. He said, 'You will be convicted and sentenced to hang, but appeal the conviction! Your conviction will be overturned on appeal.' All of this took place exactly as predicted.

"When he was freed the murderer came to R. D. Shah for a third look at his hand. The verdict? 'You will become a *yati*, a Jain sadhu.' And it happened."

"And all this detail shows up in the palm?"

"No, the outlines are there, but the details have to come from elsewhere, from the palmist's intuition. Palmistry is after all a form of astrology, and in any form of astrology you can at best be right 85% of the time on calculation alone. For the other 15% you must use your intuition. R. D. Shah is a good palmist; he used his intuition, and it did not mislead him. In spite of all the warnings and implorings the murder happened just as predicted."

"Couldn't it have been forcibly averted?"

"Perhaps, if someone had used enough force. When you bless someone, you lighten their heavy load of bad karmas. Someone could have blessed the victim with long life. But we would have had to find someone who had enough shakti to give that sort of blessing and also had the desire to give it. And even if we had found someone like that what is the guarantee that the prospective victim would have been able to digest the blessing?"

"Digest the blessing?"

"Here is an example of what I mean. Sevadas Aghori was a very good sadhu, but he was so heavy that he could not even wash his backside after he defecated. He had a devotee named Chunilal who did this washing for him. When it came time for Sevadasji to die he called Chunilal to his side, gave him a stone, and told him, "Offer incense to this stone every day and you will always have just enough money to live on."

Chunilal told his guru, "No, Maharaj, I need more."

Sevadasji said, "It is not in your destiny to have more."

But Chunilal insisted, which caused Sevadasji to reflect over how Chunilal had done a very dirty job for him for so long. So Sevadasji used his power to create the sum of one hundred thousand rupees, which he gave to Chunilal. Chunilal took leave of Sevadasji, but he had not travelled even a couple of miles toward the city of Baroda when this money was robbed from him. Then he had to return to Sevadasji and accept the stone that had first been offered to him."

We had arrived at the caves, and were welcomed by a group of Vimalananda's spiritual "children" who were to worship with us.

"Do gurus give out knowledge the way Sevadasji gave out money?" I prompted as we walked toward the temple.

"There are only two ways in which you can get knowledge from a guru," responded Vimalananda emphatically so that his "children" could hear. "One way is via rnanubandhana. If the guru owes you some debt of knowledge from a previous birth, if you are his creditor, then he will have to pay you back. Where will he go? The other way is how Arjuna got the knowledge of the *Bhagavad Gita* from Krishna: *mat prasadat*, by God's grace. There is no third way.

"Look at how easily I step over this channel in the floor," he said as we entered the caves. "That is how easy it is when you have *kripa* (grace) from your guru: you step over the samsara from the physical to the spiritual without any difficulty. If there is no kripa you may slip and bang your foot, or trip and break your leg. When a guru gives kripa to a disciple it is spontaneous; the guru himself doesn't know how he does it. Krishna saw that Arjuna had pure love for him. When He also saw that Arjuna could not understand what He was trying to explain Krishna said, *Divyam dadami te chaksuh*: 'I give you a divine eye.' That was kripa, a spontaneous outpouring from the heart. The result of kripa is that the disciple's mind becomes utterly firm. Before kripa the mind will always be moving from object to object, but after kripa it becomes perfectly one-pointed. Kripa can be used only for spiritual purposes, and it cannot be spoken. Whoever says kripa can be spoken or willingly given is a fool.

"The same holds true for *kalyana*, which is mainly mundane and only slightly spiritual. Kalyana will improve your material life, but it will not make your mind very one-pointed. You cannot take from a guru anything more than what he owes you unless he gives you grace, either kripa or kalyana; and even if he gives you grace you may not be able to hold onto it, just as Chunilal could not hold onto the kalyana that Sevadasji offered him."

"This means," I offered, "that kalyana and kripa are varieties of blessings."

"Kalyana and kripa are," continued Vimalananda, "two of the many varieties of blessings. And kripa is really a wonderful thing; it is so wonderful to have a one-pointed mind! Does anyone really know the power of the mind? Listen to this story. Once in a certain kingdom the king had fallen ill. No one knew how to cure him; even his personal physician failed. The king became so wild that he called his prime minister to his presence and then told him, 'If you don't get me cured I'll have your head separated from your shoulders!' Kings can be unreasonable like that."

"So can yogis, fire and water."

"Right. The prime minister was no physician, and had no idea of what to do. He gadded about the city, trying to find a way to keep his head on his shoulders. As he wandered a madman stopped him and asked him what was wrong. When the prime minister explained, the madman asked, 'Are you prepared to spend a lot of money?'

"The prime minister replied, 'To save my head I'll do anything.' So the madman took him incognito to the biggest sandalwood merchant in the city. This fellow had completely cornered the market in sandalwood, but appeared to be in agony.

"The prime minister asked, 'What is wrong, my good man?'

"The merchant replied, 'My warehouses are so full of sandalwood that I will never be able to sell it all unless the king should die. If the king dies then everyone in the country will burn sandalwood in his memory. So I am praying twenty-four hours a day that that bugger of a king should die.'

"The prime minister immediately understood that this single-pointed concentration was the cause of the king's illness. He therefore immediately bought all the merchant's sandalwood. The merchant forgot about the king, and when the king became well he rewarded his prime minister handsomely."

"So in this case, at least, one man's forgetfulfulness became another man's salvation."

"It takes tremendous energy to remember things. This is why Kundalini never gets an opportunity to wake up in most people, much less rise. So long as your memory is strongly connected to your own karmas all of Kundalini's energy will be taken up just in the act of remembering who you are. And there are plenty of karmas for you to remember. Forget for a moment the karmas in your causal body; what about the ones in your greater causal body?"

"Huh?"

"Your greater causal body, or *mahakarana sharira*. Everything that has ever happened in the cosmos has left its mark there. Each action gets registered on each particle of Mind throughout creation and can be recalled to awareness. This is the Universal Memory. In order to make Kundalini wake completely you must forget to identify even with that; you require perfect forgetfulness."

"Perfect forgetfulness."

"Yes, because as She awakens you will gain access to the memories of all your past karmas. We call this *punassmriti* in Sanskrit. If you gain punassmriti before you are able to handle it—before you can digest what you will remember—then you might get trapped in those memories."

"So you don't think it is good to try to recapture the memories of your past lives, like some Westerners are now starting to try to do?"

"How will that help them? Fortunately most of these people will just hallucinate something and think it is real, and will build some complicated construction around it to entertain themselves. But a few will really tune into their rnanubandhanas, and those are the ones who will be in real danger. What do you think would happen if you were a mother who realized that your child had murdered you in a previous life? Would you be able to behave in a purely maternal way in this lifetime, and get beyond your desire for revenge? Or would you get stuck in that previous reality and keep the whole cycle of retribution moving along? I thank God for the magnanimity of Nature which causes us to forget almost everything of our past lives when we are born!

"But even perfect forgetfulness is a later stage. First you have to learn to remember. You haven't forgotten Jean Valjean, have you?"

"How could I?" Vimalananda could turn even *Les Miserables* to his purposes.

"After Jean Valjean was caught stealing the bishop's candlesticks the bishop protected him instead of accusing him. That one incident changed Jean Valjean for the rest of his life. That is why I remember, every morning of my life, that I am going to die. When you go to the smashan this is what you should tell yourself: 'As this corpse is, so will I be; forget not, forget not.'

"Now enough—it is time for us to do our work," he concluded, and we proceeded with our ritual. Though he sat after we completed our worship and joked with his other 'children' for a bit he showed no interested in resuming this conversation until we were on our way back to South Bombay. Then he began again: "You were talking of blessings earlier tonight, but do you have any idea of how many types of blessing there are? Each blessing is a karma, which means that each has its own consequences. Probably the simplest way for me to bless someone is to take away some of that individual's bad karmas—but if I do that then I will have to suffer those karmas myself. The Law of Karma is very strict: When there is an action, someone or some thing will have to experience the reaction. Taking on someone else's karmas is therefore a crude and unsatisfactory way of blessing. Not only will I make myself miserable, but I will use up all my shakti working off the bad karmas of only a few people. Then I will have nothing left for all the others who have rnanubandhanas with me.

"One way to bless someone which will cost me almost nothing is for me to rearrange that individual's karmas. If he or she is destined to suffer miseries to pay off some bad karmas I can arrange for some good karmas, ones which were supposed to ripen and emerge later, to emerge now. But once these good karmas are exhausted there will still be those bad karmas to pay off, and there will not be any good karmas left to cushion the blows. The last condition will then be worse than the first. This is obviously not much of a blessing, but some people I know who did not deserve wealth in this lifetime have demanded it from me and I have given it to them in this way. If they are sensible they will use this wealth to perform more good karmas, to rebuild their karmic credit balances."

"And if they don't they'll be finished?"

"Completely finished. Now, *Pitri Tarpana* can also be a blessing. Suppose you have an ancestor (*pitri*) who has been reborn as a horse who draws a carriage. Because you still possess some of his genes and chromosomes his consciousness in his new form is going to affect yours."

"How?"

"While he was living his ahamkara identified with his entire body. The only part of that body that remains after his death is that body's pattern of genes and chromosomes, a portion of which resides in you. Because everything that has ever happened in the cosmos has left its mark there, his 'mark' remains on those genes and chromosomes for as long as the pattern remains relatively intact. As long as his 'mark' is there his awareness will continue to resonate, to some extent, with those genes and chromosomes—which means that his awareness will be able to influence your awareness via the genetic material that he has bequeathed you."

"Oh my God! How long will that influence last?"

"Vedic tradition speaks of seven generations."

"Is this some sort of numerological number?"

"Not at all. Don't you remember how many times an ordinary horse must be crossed with a thoroughbred before its progeny can be registered in the thoroughbred stud book?"

"The eighth cross becomes a thoroughbred."

"Which means that the ordinary bloodline becomes effaced after—"

"Seven generations! Oh my God! So the people in the Bible were not just talking through their hats when they spoke of a sin being visited on their heads, and on their children's heads, 'up to the seventh generation.'"

"Not at all. Now, if your ancestor was some sort of a saint the influence of his awareness on you might be fairly positive. Otherwise it will probably not help you much, and might prove greatly detrimental. What *would* be helpful for you is to break your ties with him in such a way that you help him out as well. To do this you perform a *Tarpana* ritual, which forcibly draws that ancestor's spirit to you. Obviously it would be easier to do this if your ancestor were bodiless, but it can be done with him embodied all the same.

"When the spirit of your ancestor leaves the body of this carriage horse the body will drop down without warning onto the road. No one in the vicinity will understand what is going on. Someone may even accuse the horse owner of cruelty to dumb animals. During the ritual the horse will remain unconscious, and after it is finished the horse will jump up and start lurching about. Then at night, when no one is around, that spirit will leave the horse permanently to go to another womb, and the horse will die."

"And that breaks the tie?"

"Not at all; you still have his genes and chromosomes. But now he has moved up a little in the world of manifestation, so his influence on you will improve—a little.

"But this is only one of your many ancestors. My Senior Guru Maharaj used to say, 'When you know just by looking at a person all about his father, father's father, and so on, twenty-five generations back, and when you can tell what that person was in his last twenty-five births, and you can see into the future to what he will become in his next twenty-five births, then you may say that you have learned—a little bit. You have learned a fraction of what you can know.' What a mentor! Twenty-five generations is only the beginning; a real Rishi will know millions of generations, all at once.

"If I perform Pitri Tarpana for your forefathers and foremothers it will bless you by helping you to distance yourself from their negative influences. But an even subtler way to bless you would be to perform Tarpana for the Rishi who founded your *gotra* (clan). This will make the Rishi so happy that he will bless you from the overflowing of his love—and I will stay free of even the slightest stain of karma. Another way for me to bless you would be to worship your personal deity—your *ishta devata*—on your behalf. When your deity is happy you are bound to be blessed! You 'bless' yourself—you improve your own innate nature—every time you perform sincere worship of your ishta devata. You can also bless yourself when you personally worship the Rishi who originated your gotra, or personally perform Pitri Tarpana for your ancestors. In each case you change your consciousness by regulating the activity of certain of your genes.

"And what about curses?"

"There are many, many different ways to curse. Two of them are rituals which are common in South India called *Kegamati* and *Bhanamati*. They were so common when the British were ruling the country that a special police cell was created to deal with all the cases that occurred."

"You're kidding."

"Not at all. These rituals are usually performed only on individuals, but I have seen cases where an entire village was affected. In this village everyone worked hard and was as normal as could be during the day. After sunset, though, they would all take off their clothes and run caterwauling through the streets, stark raving mad. A daughter might show her vulva to her father, and her father might show his pecker to her. Everyone would be shouting and screaming bloody murder. Come daylight, they would all forget what they had done during the night, and start their normal lives again. These people's lives were thoroughly disrupted by the curse, but the only difference between their daytime and their nighttime lives was a shift in their awareness, a change in consciousness.

"No one can deny that human consciousness is dependent on chemicals. If it were not how would intoxicants and other psychoactive drugs affect us? Just a change of a few molecules and a whole new pattern is created. All you need is for a few cells to distend or a few tiny blood vessels to contract and the mind changes completely. You must have noticed how your attitude changes from moment to moment. At the office you may be tired, angry and upset, but most of the time you will forget all that as soon as you reach home, where you relax and enjoy yourself. There are many, many factors which affect your nature, your *svabhava*, but the whole thing boils down to control of the chemical patterns of the brain. How much or how little ahamkara self-identifies with your body, which determines how free Kundalini can be, is controlled by your chemistry. When Saturn wants to affect your consciousness all he has to do is make some minor alterations in your metabolism.

"This is why Aghoris are fond of intoxicants. As long as you remain in control of your intoxicant—as long as you are consuming the drug and it is not consuming you—you can direct it to alter your nature in any way you see fit. This is especially true of *bhang* (a preparation of marijuana leaves): whatever thought you hold in your mind stays there without effort. If you can concentrate on disengaging Kundalini from Her coverings you can make quick progress with the help of intoxicants—but they are useful if and only if you can control your mind. If your consciousness is inundated by intoxicants you are sunk, because then they will reinforce and intensify all the limitations of your nature.

"As long as your svabhava is not perfectly controlled you will be subject to Saturn's control, and believe you me, it is no joke to be able to control your nature. Even Shiva Himself was once affected by Saturn. When He and Parvati were married all the planets except Saturn came to bless the couple. Parvati took Saturn's absence as an insult and demanded that Saturn be instructed to appear. Shiva smiled gently and told Her, 'Goddess, why not leave well enough alone? It is better that he is not here. In fact, he has done us a special favor by not coming.'

"But Parvati was adamant—Shakti in Her awakened, uncontrollable form—and Saturn was obliged to come. He didn't stand in front of the couple; he just glanced at them from a distance. But as soon as Shiva saw Saturn He experienced his own true nature and went into samadhi. Saturn makes you experience yourself as you really are, down deep inside. Since Shiva's nature is pure consciousness, that is what He experienced. Shiva stayed in samadhi experiencing that consciousness for seven and a half divine years, and all during that time Parvati was livid. How could She enjoy holy nuptials with Her husband when He was deep in samadhi? When at the end of those years

He came back down to normal consciousness Shiva told Her, 'Now you see why Saturn was not invited to our wedding.'

"Then Parvati in a rage cursed astrology that it would never be 100% accurate without adding plenty of intuition to it. She also cursed those who make their livings by astrology that they would always be miserable beggars."

"Has that happened?"

"Many of the astrologers I know are in fact miserable, and some are literally beggars."

I also had seen some suggestive examples. "And this is due to Parvati's curse?"

"Yes, and also because they have forgotten much of the original knowledge of Jyotish. Parvati's curse is able to affect them strongly because of their weak intuition. Do you know the Sanskrit word for intuition? *Ishtabala*—literally, 'the strength of your *ishta devata*,' your personal deity. You won't be much of an astrologer unless you have a healthy relationship with a personal deity.

"In spite of Parvati's curse, Jyotish is still the best tool we have for predicting fate, because Saturn represents fate. It is good to be able to predict fate, which can overpower almost anyone."

"Shouldn't astrologers also worship the planets?"

"Why just astrologers? Worshipping the Nine Planets is a good way to control your nature. We in India worship the well-placed planets, to encourage them to assist us more vigorously, and try to placate the afflicted planets, to request them not to pervert our minds or lives. We respect the planets as Mahapurushas of the type known as *munis*. Like any other beings—Rishis, deities, your next-door neighbors—they respond positively to attempts to butter them up. A few of India's kings and yogis have even gained control, or at least influence, over eight of the nine planets by successfully completing *sadhanas* for them. But very few of these *sadhakas* (people who perform sadhanas) have ever been able to control the most powerful and difficult to placate of all the planets: Saturn.Only the very bold or the very rash attempt to control all Nine Planets, for when you fully control the Nine Planets you control the entire manifested universe."

"Not so easy."

"No, but it's been done. Ravana did it. Ravana was a Siddha; he had become immortal. His Kundalini was therefore completely under his control, which meant that Fate could no longer affect him. He had gained complete control of his *svabhava*, his innate nature. Control of his svabhava gave him the power to conquer the planets, including Saturn. After he conquered them he took them home with him and kept them face down on the steps leading up to his throne. He could have gone on for ages like this, since the planets could have no effect on him if they could not see him. But that would have obstructed the Rishis' play, so they sent *Narada*, the Celestial Troublemaker, to solve the problem.

"Narada went to Saturn and said, 'You are the most powerful of all the planets, but here you are lying face down in front of Ravana's throne unable to do anything about your condition.'

"Saturn replied, 'Because I am face down my gaze cannot fall on Ravana, so I cannot affect him. Advise him to turn me over and I will do the rest.'

"Narada understood, and went to search out Ravana. After praising him to the skies Narada suggested to Ravana that he might like to turn the planets over, so that he could enjoy their misfortune more fully. Ravana liked this suggestion, and as soon as he turned the planets over onto their backs Saturn's gaze fell on him, and his mind became perverted.

"Now, Ravana knew the effects of Saturn as well as anyone else did; something came over him to make him agree with Narada's suggestion. *What* came over him is another question. Part of it was his own svabhava, his innate nature. He was a *rakshasa*, and *rakshasas* always love to humiliate their enemies. But when he was in complete control of his svabhava how could he lose this control in an instant for no apparent reason? Perhaps it was the words of Saturn, spoken to him through Narada. What is clear is that as soon as Ravana turned the planets over Saturn's gaze fell upon him, and from that moment on his intellect began to be distorted.

"The first effect of Saturn's gaze on Ravana came via his wife. One day she enquired of her husband, 'You are now immortal, which is fine, but when will you ever be free from having to exist?' Ravana said to himself, 'Oh my God, I've forgotten about that!' He realized that his wife was right. So long as he was immortal he could never hope to improve further. You must die if you don't want to stagnate. Ravana was trying to change his innate nature to become one of the gods, but Nature would not permit him to do that, because it would disturb Her balance. So Ravana's intellect *had* to be altered. There was nothing wrong with Ravana's desire to die, of course, but it would never have occurred to him had not his intellect been impaired.

"It was his previous penance of Lord Shiva that had made Ravana immortal in the first place, so Ravana went back to do more penance of Shiva. After long, hard penance Ravana again gained a vision of Lord Shiva. Shiva asked him, 'What do you desire?'

"Ravana told Him, 'Lord, please give me some way to die.'

"Lord Shiva looked at him askance and said, 'I'm very sorry, but you should have thought of this earlier. I have already blessed you with eternal life, and you know that whatever I say must come true. How can I go back on my words now?'

"But Ravana insisted, and Shiva eventually gave in. He said, 'All right. I can't revoke my boon, but I will amend it: *Parastri haranam, Ravana maranam*.' (Ravana will die when he steals another man's wife.)

"Ravana was shocked. He said, 'Lord, I am King of Lanka, and I must set an example for my people. If I take someone else's wife my subjects will follow suit, which will make me the cause of much misery and immorality. I could never stoop so low as to do that.'

"Shiva replied, 'Rama, the incarnation of Vishnu, is going to be born on Earth. You will take His wife, and He will be forced to kill you. Then, dying at the hands of God Himself, you will go to the heaven meant for warriors who die on the field of battle, and your merit will be great. Moreover, your death will act as a warning to anyone who would be tempted to steal another man's wife.'

"And so it happened. It was only because Ravana was such a great devotee of Lord Shiva that he got the opportunity of enjoying such an auspicious death. If Shiva, the god of death, cannot make His devotee die well then what is the use of Shiva? Because no one knows this everyone thinks Ravana stole Sita out of lust. If that were the case would he have kept her a prisoner so long in the grove, unharmed? No, he would have had his way with her long before."

"Orthodox Hindus think of Ravana as a total blighter."

"Don't mention those idiots to me; what do they know about the *Ramayana*? They only know how to parrot what someone else has told them."

"So was it Ravana's fate to become immortal and then to die?"

"It would seem so. He had performed tremendous penances in order to achieve immortality, and he never would have been able to complete them unless he had been fated to do so."

"So his death was fated too."

"It was, and there is a good reason for it too. He and his brother Kumbhakarna were originally *Jaya* and *Vijaya*, Vishnu's two doorkeepers. Once they foolishly insulted the four Rishis known as the Sanatkumaras, who cursed the pair to fall to Earth as demons. Vishnu then promised that He too would be born on Earth to redeem them. First they were born as Hiranyaksha and Hiranyakashipu, and Vishnu killed them in the Boar and Man-Lion Avataras respectively. Then they became Ravana and Kumbhakarna, who were killed by Vishnu in his Rama incarnation. Then they incarnated again, and Krishna killed them. Curses and blessings, for seven births at a time.

"It was a curse that caused Rama to lose Sita in the first place. When Parashurama met Ramachandra they fought, and Parashurama cursed Rama."

"Parashurama was the sixth Avatara of Vishnu, and Ramachandra was Vishnu's seventh Avatara. It doesn't seem very spiritual for Vishnu to fight Vishnu."

"*Parashurama* ("Rama-with-the-Axe"), who is immortal, is a Brahmana, and Ramachandra was a Kshatriya, a warrior. Because Parashurama's father had been killed by a Kshatriya Parashurama vowed to use his battle axe to rid the earth of warriors. He did it, too; he did it several times. As soon as he heard of Ramachandra, the powerful young Kshatriya, a clash between them became inevitable.

"Ramachandra defeated Parashurama handily, though, and took Parashurama's power away for Himself. Then Parashurama, irate at being defeated by a upstart youth, looked at Ramachandra and said, smiling ironically, 'All right, my child, you have taken my Shakti. It doesn't matter. But you will be thrown out of your kingdom. You will lose your own Shakti,'—meaning Sita—'and you will have great difficulty in retrieving her.' And so it happened. Without that curse there would have been no *Ramayana.*"

This was not the version of the *Parashurama-Rama* story that appeared in either the Sanskrit *Valmiki Ramayana* or Tulsidas's *Ram Charit Manas*. In both of those texts Parashurama came to Rama upset that Rama had broken Lord Shiva's bow. Although Parashurama wanted to fight Rama, Rama refused to fight and thus pacified Parashurama gifted his shakti to Rama.

Since it did not seem apropos to object to his choice of story at that moment I asked instead, "If Rama took away all of Parashurama's shakti how did the old man have any left to curse Rama?"

But he was ready for me: "If Rama had taken *all* Parashurama's shakti Parashurama would have fallen dead right there. But Parashurama is immortal, so obviously some of his shakti remained."

"Some sort of core, personal shakti remained, and Rama merely took away his 'discretionary' shakti, you mean?"

"Something like that. Parashurama's words had the effect of a curse. He was so upset that his emotions took control of him and he spoke from his heart. He may not have even meant to do it; it may just have been something that was pressing on him so strongly that it had to come out. But when it came out it had enough force behind it to come true.

"Besides, Nature wanted Parashurama to lose his shakti somehow or other. Both he and Rama were avataras of Vishnu, but Parashurama had already finished the work that he had been sent to Earth to do. Rama was *adhikara* (fit, apropriate) to take on the older avatara's sakti, and he needed that extra shakti to be better be able to do his own work, which was just beginning. It was only a matter of Nature's finding a way to transfer that shakti from the one to the other. In this case a curse did the job; in some other situation it might be a blessing."

All I could say in response to this was, "This business of blessings and curses is really complicated."

"I'll say! Here's an illustration from my own life. A poor musician named Damle once came to me for help. He was paralyzed from the waist down, and maintained himself by tutoring pupils for a few rupees a month. When I saw him something came over me and I kicked him. I don't know what happened, but after that kick he could walk again. Then I told him, 'A young woman has just started studying music with you. Please ask her to marry you. You and she can then teach classes together, and she will be very lucky for you. You will have plenty of money.' He listened to my words and married her, and they were happy.

"All this happened years ago. Then one day a few weeks back I suddenly got the thought, 'I wonder how Damle is? Why don't I go see him and check him out?' I had helped him out, but I was wondering if the blessing had been sufficient. How strong a blessing is, is determined by how many of those bad karmas disappear or are reshuffled for later experience. Changing someone's destiny is not a joke. If there is a tremendous load of bad karmas, even a strong blessing may only make a dent in them. This is why they say *garib ki naseeb garib hai*: a poor person's destiny is to be poor.

"When I arrived at his house Damle greeted me with every mark of respect. Eventually the conversation came around to him, and he told me, 'All is fine with me and my family that way, except that some one or another of us is always sick. My wife and I make plenty of money, but it all seems to go to the doctors.'

"I had been afraid of this. Too many bad karmas. I told him, 'I really love your music. Please play Kedara Raga for me, and let us see what happens.' I knew that if he could play Kedara well that something would come over me again, and he would be benefitted. But his destiny was such that he never got around to playing it for me. So I had to leave him to his destiny. Beware of fiddling about too much with other people's destinies, my boy, or you might end up like Sheikh Salim Chishti!"

"At least you didn't follow his example, and bless Damle and his wife to have a child."

"Thank God! But that probably wouldn't have been necessary anyway. Poor people, even in rich countries like America, always have many children. It is easy to be born into a poor family because there are many spirits who have such a heavy load of evil karmas that they are destined to be afflicted on Earth. To be born poor into a large family in a cruel, dangerous environment will make any soul miserable. It takes plenty of luck—good karmas, blessings—to be born into a rich family; look at how long it took John F. Kennedy to get a son. All across America people who can't have children are literally purchasing them from other countries, including India. Think what sort of karmas those children must have: born in poverty as an orphan, then whisked away to opulence. If you are meant to enjoy wealth, if Nature desires it, then you will have it whether you want it or not, and no one can stop you from getting it.

"When India was rich it was the same way, which is why Akbar could have a son only after Sheikh Salim Chishti blessed him. After all, how many people can accumulate enough good karmas to be born Emperor of the World? Very few. The being who became Akbar's son Salim had many good karmas, but not quite enough to be born as Akbar's son. In order to be born he needed that extra push in the form of the saint's blessing. But what about all the bad karmas? They still had to come out, and when they did they corrupted his mind. He became an opium-eating drunkard who was not at all worthy of his father.

"Akbar himself was born as the result of a blessing, but the circumstances were different. After his father Humayun had been driven from his throne and was roving about in Sindh he met a good fakir, who understood something of what was going on. When the fakir, who knew Prithviraj Chauhan's capabilities, perceived that Prithviraj needed a womb in which to be born, he decided to endow his daughter with a matchless son. He gave her away in marriage to Humayun, and then blessed the couple by saying that their son would rule as Emperor of India.

"To be born as the child of a deposed ruler is not so difficult. To be born into power and luxury is much harder and a much harder situation to 'digest.' In fact Akbar's chief disappointment in life was his son Salim, the very person he had gone to so much trouble to bring into his life! He always called Salim 'Sheikhu Baba' in honor of the fakir whose blessing had caused the boy to be born. By the time Salim was in his mid-thirties he had despaired of ever succeeding to the throne, because his father's health seemed indestructible. He took to heavy drinking and, his mind was addled by intoxicants, his ears were swayed by evil counsel. He rebelled against his father, and set himself up as King of Allahabad. Eventually he marched on his father's capital city, and soon two armies, one his and one his father's, were arrayed facing one another, ready to fight.

"This time Akbar, who had indulged his son in everything throughout his life, had had enough. His wife sensed this. Before every battle Salim's mother would worship Akbar's favorite sword and then present it to him. This time as she handed the sword to her husband she said, 'My only request is that you spare my son's life.'

"He told her, 'You have forgotten that a wife should think of her husband first. You are more attached to your son. All right, for your sake alone will I spare his life.'

"Out on the field of battle the two antagonists met. Akbar told his son, 'Sheikhu, why do you want all these men and their families to suffer? The quarrel is between you and me. Why don't we fight it out together? I am an old man, and you are young and strong. Whoever wins can take the kingdom.'

"In his drunken foolhardiness Salim agreed, and the two men fought as both armies looked on. Within a few minutes Akbar, who was an old wrestling crony, had pinned Salim, who was no fighter, to the ground. There is nothing worse than to be humiliated in front of those you command, and Akbar knew it. He told his son, 'Now, shall I kill you? No, I won't. I have promised your mother.' He had Salim thrown into the dungeon and took his wine and opium away from him for four days.

"Then he sent for his son, who was thoroughly chastened, and made him Crown Prince. But Akbar's enthusiasm for life had been snuffed out, and within a year and a half he died, having realized the futility of pomp and worldly glory."

"That must have been when he came under the influence of Saturn."

"Yes, that was when his fate caught up with him."

"I have tried to explain your theory of karma to various of my friends," I said, resigned to being dim, "and many of them ask me, 'If this business of action and reaction is true, and if you kill me today it is because I killed you sometime in the past, how did this all begin? What was that first karmic debt?'"

Vimalananda smilingly answered, "That first debt is the first step in the creation of the universe: the projection of the *Adya Shakti*, the original Shakti, Nature, the foundation of everything. Because she projected from the Absolute, She owes the Absolute everything, beginning with Her very existence. Debts multiply from there as She tries to reunite with Her source, the Supreme Shiva. Because She feels incomplete on Her own She craves reunion. When this transcendent, cosmic Shakti merges again with Her Lord Shiva there is nothing left to support creation, and the universe dissolves. This is called *pralaya*. When your Kundalini Shakti—your own ahamkara, the thing which self-identifies—merges with her personal Lord Shiva then you cease to exist as an individual. This is *laya*, dissolution of your false identity in the ocean of the Absolute Reality. Laya, which is *pralaya* on the microcosmic scale, involves withdrawal of all your projections back into their source. After laya occurs there is no karma, because no individual remains to self-identify.

"Every action including passivity contains karmic activity. Passivity is active in the sense that it is a conditioned state, which makes it part of Shakti. The cosmos exists so long as Shakti exists; without Shakti there is nothing, not even Shiva. Without Shakti *shiva* (auspiciousness) becomes *shava* (corpse). You keep asking me about the Kaulas; now listen carefully: Only after you have realized Shava in your life will you be fit enough to understand Kaula.

"Everyone is lecturing on the *Bhagavad Gita*, which Krishna recited to Arjuna, but does anyone really understand it? Take the first two words only: *Dharmakshetre kurukshetre*. How can a *kurukshetra*—a place where actions, or karmas, are performed—be a *dharmakshetra*—a place of *dharma*, of righteousness and holiness? It seems to be a contradiction until you think it through clearly. First, what is a 'kurukshetra'? Your heart, which is continually beating—'kuru, kuru, kuru.' Your heart can become a place of dharma, a '*dharmakshetra*,' in only one way, and that is by taking Lord Krishna's advice: 'Go ahead and perform karmas, because you were born to do them, but leave the results to me.' What he means is, you can write as many checks as you like on the Bank of Karma—but don't sign any of them! You don't have enough credit in your account to pay for all the karmas that you perform, but Krishna does. Let Him sign the check instead. Then you will be free—free not from action but from your self-identification with your action. This is the essence of the Gita. Turn the word *gita* (song) around and you get *tyagi* (renunciate). What you have to renounce is your ignorant self-identification with your actions. Right now you are a *kshetra* (a field of activity), and what you must become is a *kshetrajna* (a knower of the field). Only through *jnana* (wisdom) can dharma arise.

"But just telling yourself that you are not going to self-identify with your actions will not work. Your ahamkara must self-identify with your body, even to a small extent, for as long as your body exists. Otherwise none of your essential bodily processes would be able to continue to work, which would spell the end of your physical being. But this self-identification, which creates more karma, is often karmically fatal. Ahamkara is free to identify with anything She likes; there is no guarantee at all that she will only self-identify with beneficial things. Even identification with mental images can be dangerous, because any image with which your mind self-identifies gains the power to affect you. Sadhana is essential because sadhana gives you a beneficial image for ahamkara to identify with, an image which once empowered can help you tremendously.

"When you worship a deity and completely self-identify with Him or Her your ahamkara will no longer find it easy to self-identify with the actions of your body. If you can completely identify yourself with your deity He or She will then do all your work, and karma will not be able to touch you. When an

Aghori eats meat and drinks wine, for example, he doesn't bother about it. He thinks to himself, 'Because of rnanubandhana the body must do these things. I offer it all to You.' But if when you eat meat you think, 'Oh, how delicious! I like it,' then you are lost. Finished! Karma will cling to you like mud. It is better to be like the lotus, which rises out of the mud but is not defiled by it. Mud cannot stain or soil a lotus. As long as you fail to self-identify you can remain a witness to everything you do while your body continues to fulfill its rnanubandhanas for as long as it continues to live. But is it so easy to act without self-identification? Try to enjoy sex without self-identification and you will see how hard it is."

"Is it better then to enjoy vicariously?"

"Not much better; that can become a karma too. Have you ever heard that saying in Marathi which refers to a certain well-known Maharaja of yesteryear: *Malle chode, mallerao raje?*"

"I haven't heard it."

"It is really untranslatable, but it roughly translates, 'The wrestler does the pumping and the king gets the pleasure.' As he got older this king could no longer sustain an erection. He still liked sex, though, so to get some vicarious enjoyment he would order one of his wrestlers to screw a woman in his presence. The sort of gratification that the Maharaja got from this kind of sex did in fact create less karma than if he had gone out and had sex himself—had he been able to do so. But he still collected some karma from having ordered the couple to copulate. And what if he decided to go around and secretly spy on couples who were engaged in sexual embraces? That invasion of privacy without being asked would also be a karma. Only if the event happened in front of him without any request on his part could he be completely free of all karmic attachment to that sexual act—provided that he didn't mentally self-identify himself with the wrestler."

"And if he did?"

"Then he would be participating in the karma. Karma is a matter of self-identification."

"So better to avoid sex altogether."

"Maybe—but that can also lead you into trouble. We say in Hindi: *Tapeshwari se rajeshwari, aur rajeshwari se narakeshwari* (penance to riches, and riches to ruination). The first part of this saying means that the Law of Action and Reaction causes a yogi who does severe penances in this life to be reborn as a prince, or as the scion of a very rich family. If you have done a really good job of penance you may get a chance to be reborn into a family of yogis, where you will be able to continue right from where you left off. However, as Lord Krishna says in the Bhagavad Gita, this is rare. Usually it is *shuchinam shrimatam gehe*—rebirth in splendor—in which case you will be able to discover your dharma, your proper job in life, only through your guru's grace.

"But what happened to *ante matih sa gatih*? If you die planning to continue your penance won't you do so, since the thought you have when you die determines where you will end up?"

"But who says that the very last thought you have before you die will be for more penance? If you have spent your entire life restricting yourself you'll probably be thinking of those restrictions when you die. But thinking of a restriction is really a thought of the thing you are restricting—which is where you will proceed."

"So doing *sadhana* (spiritual practices) in this life is no guarantee that you'll be doing it in your next life?" An alarming prospect.

"No, there is no guarantee at all, because of the Law of Action and Reaction. When a sadhu stringently restricts his food during one lifetime Nature will say to him in his next life, 'Since you denied yourself so much last time around you will now have the most delicious foods.' If he lived naked or in skins or rags he will wear silks and gold brocades encrusted with jewels in his next birth. If he lived in a cave or out under the sky Nature will give him a palace to play in. And if he tied up a loincloth and never went with a woman in this birth then in his next birth he will be chased by women even during his childhood, and will be introduced to sex very early. All of this holds true for women too.

"The result? Well, unless the child is very special he will be unable to remember anything of his previous life. Instead he will become enthralled by all the beautiful sense objects that Nature will give him. Ma is so magnanimous; She never frees anyone from the world so long as they continue to desire it. Becoming enmeshed in Maya the child will remember nothing of his past penances; he will not realize that he is now a ruler or a rich man because of his past austerities. During his life of luxury he will enjoy his karmic pension until all his good karmas are finished. After he dies all the evil karmas that he performed during his riotous life of indulgence will catch up with him, and he will fall into hell. And hell is not out in space or under the ground somewhere; hell is right here. Hells are types of wombs, some of which can be really terrible. Only after most of these evil karmas have been burned away will he then be qualified take birth in the world again, though not necessarily as a human. So watch out! You may get yourself into trouble if you try to go against Nature, even if you only mean to speed up your own progress, unless you have a good guide who will keep his eye on you."

I had by then developed confidence in Vimalananda's competence in matters arcane. He impressed me at our first-ever meeting when he answered all the questions on my ethnographic questionnaire (which was the tool I was using to fulfill the conditions of a project funded by NEH to investigate Ayurveda in Poona) before I could even ask them. Months later, after I had tied my loincloth too tight, he showed me how to tie a tobacco leaf to my swollen testicle to relieve the swelling (and grinned an I-told-you-so at my nausea when I left the leaf on too long). He taught me to follow instructions by creating a persistent and vexatiously itchy skin rash after I had a glass of milk at Shernaz's house on a day when he had specifically told me only to drink water there until further notice.

Once he saw that he had my obedient attention he included me in some of his experiments, like the one with the packet of ash from a Tantric homa in Kashmir. He had me mix a pinch of the ash into hot milk every night for a week, and when I did a pack of howling dogs showed up outside my dormitory room punctually at 1 A.M. on each of those seven nights to serenade me. Greatly though my sleep-deprived fellow students groused, they never discovered the source of these visitations. Nor did I, for though Vimalananda was pleased with the results of his experiment he said no more, when I enquired as to its significance, than, "My idea was to introduce to you a certain ethereal 'presence,' and that has been done. Your concern should be with getting your work done. If you need to know more than that this 'presence' will tell you itself, in due time."

It was because I wanted my work to be done expeditiously that I turned to Vimalananda when a spirit who had harassed me during my first year at the college returned after a sabbatical. Long afterward I learned that the college hostel had been built on land that had previously served as a Christian cemetery, but when I was first assaulted a few months after my arrival there my assailant's provenance was a complete mystery. During an attack, which would come when I entered that no-man's-land between wakefulness and sleep which is called in Sanskrit *tandra*, the entity would jump without warning onto my chest and squeeze the breath out of my lungs. Though enfeebled with fear during the initial encounter I somehow realized that my only avenue of rescue was to awaken, and somehow I did that when next it beset me. Fear quickly became animosity; soon I was driving the thing away by angrily repeating in that twilight state a mantra taught to me by a yogi. After some months the shade went on furlough. When it resumed its predation I complained to Vimalananda, who merely said, "It won't be back." And it hasn't, since.

I had had a generalized faith in Vimalananda from the moment I met him, but the seemingly unrelated permanent departure of the weird spirit and the unforeseen arrival of the barking dogs convinced me that his knowledge of the ethereal world was unparalleled. He quickly became the helmsman of my voyage through Indian society as well when he saved me from official censure after my Sanskrit professor had finagled me into making unnecessarily disparaging remarks about the near-moribund state of Ayurvedic teaching and practice at the time. When to his demonstrated expertise in both the physical and non-physical realms I added the marvelous erudition he used to expand my perceptual skyline in every subject I raised with him, I became persuaded beyond any reasonable doubt that I had found in Vimalananda an exemplary friend, philosopher and guide.

chapter five
SCARLET RUBY

STONEY FAILED TO GET into foal at Vitu Karve's stud farm even in early 1978, due at least in part to Vitu's unwillingness to spend much money on her feed. Vimalananda soon decided to send her elsewhere, but where? All the other stud farms insisted on seeing the color of his coin. When things seemed bleakest Nature stepped in, as She usually did for Vimalananda in a pinch. This time She arrived in the form of Mr. Gokuldas Madhavdas, a friendly industrialist and race horse owner growling his way through life. Gokuldas, who to my eye most resembled a mature and knowledgeable frog, was introduced to Vimalananda by Gokuldas's shy niece Prabha, who brought her angelic voice to Vimalananda for training on a regular basis. On hearing of Stoney's dilemma Gokuldas insisted on attempting to prevail on Erach Ghasvala, a dapper Parsi who owned a stud in the South, to accept Stoney into his farm on favorable terms. This was a boon in itself, but the icing on the cake—in Hindi we say "the fragrance on the gold"—was that Scarlet Ruby stood in Erach's yard.

Vimalananda had once owned an unofficial share in Scarlet Ruby. Though he was but a part-owner, he had involved himself in all facets of the horse's training throughout his racing career. Scarlet Ruby's record speaks to the value of Vimalananda's participation: win after effortless win, including some of the Classic races. Once he retired to stud Scarlet Ruby made a name for himself as the first stallion foaled in India to sire a significant crop of winners. Though now long in the tooth he continued to sire successful foals, and Vimalananda, thinking perhaps of how fine it would be to see the offspring of a tryst between two of his most beloved equine friends, decided without hesitation to try to engineer their union.

This necessitated negotiations with Ghasvala who, like us, had a decided fondness for Black Dog, a blend of premium Scotch which is sold only in the

Indian subcontinent. During a meeting over Black Dog in Bombay, Vima-lananda proposed to Erach that he accept Stoney on a contingency basis. After her first live foal, who would go to Vimalananda, she and all her future progeny would become Ghasvala's property. Ghasvala countered by suggesting that if he decided to accept Stoney he would give Vimalananda half of the first live foal. Vimalananda understood him to promise a half-share in the second as well. Ghasvala then hied himself back to Bangalore, promising a swift decision.

I didn't attend that meeting and wasn't much engaged in these delibera-tions. When I next arrived in Bombay the matter had come down to the wire, for Vitu was insisting that we decide immediately whether or not Stoney would be staying with him for the rest of the year. In fact, if Ghasvala did not accept her as a brood mare that very night there would be no choice but to leave her in Vitu's hands for another potentially fruitless year. While Roshni and I sat near the phone anxiously awaiting Ghasvala's call Vimalananda nonchalantly launched into a numinous discourse for that night's avid listen-ers, a cohort from the group of a dozen or so "spiritual children" who regu-larly came weekday evenings to listen to Vimalananda deliver his "talks."

I was becoming antsy, and said, "Ghasvala hasn't called yet."

Vimalananda replied, "Pipe down, will you? The night is not yet over."

"But what are you going to do if he doesn't call?"

"I'm not going to worry about it at all. I am relying on Nature to arrange something for Stoney, and I am confident that Nature will not let me down."

"You may not be worried, but I am about to start biting my nails."

"Calm down, my boy, it's all a matter of fate. Stoney will end up wherever she is destined to be. I am confident for many reasons that she has a good destiny, and that wherever she goes she will be happy."

Vimalananda then began to sing a *bhajan* (devotional song), and ten or fif-teen minutes later came Ghasvala's call accepting Stoney. After Vimalananda laid the telephone receiver in its cradle he looked at me with an imperious grin and said, "Nature didn't let me down after all, did She?"

The assembled spiritual "children" then all smiled at me condescendingly, as if to cluck, "You doubted because you lacked faith." Their smiles chafed me, for though Vimalananda sometimes praised these "children" for their spiritual fervor, both to their faces and to his other acquaintances, he was in private quite aware of their limitations. "Bashermal," he would say to me in a reflective moment, "is the foundation of this group. He has learned well, and now spends all his free time traipsing around the countryside performing *homa*. There is nothing wrong with this; it is a good thing. But he could learn even more if he spent more time with me. After all, I was the one who taught him to do homa in the first place. His little bit of knowledge has gone to his head.

"It is the same with Kalubhai, who keeps trying to impress me with his astrology. He has developed what he believes to be a foolproof system to make money at the racecourse and has become a regular racegoer, even though I have told him more than once that in all my decades of gambling that I have never seen a foolproof system. He thinks he knows quite a bit, and sometimes I have had to be harsh with him, because I don't want him to ruin himself. This has hurt him, I know, but I simply can't be a sugar-coated quinine tablet. Better he should be hurt a little bit now and learn his lesson than to have someone else burst his bloated balloon later, which might hurt more. Doshi comes to me mainly to try to impress me with his supposed spiritual achievements and experiences, and Harshbhai and some of the others come mainly to get favors—marriage of their sons and daughters, improvements in their finances, expansion of their factories.

"I advised Natvarlal not to get married because it is not in his destiny to be happily married. Then his relatives started to pressure him, and reminded him how dreary life can be when lived alone. In the end he gave in, and came eagerly to me to get my blessing. What could I tell him? I told him, 'Go ahead!' Now he comes to me complaining about his household problems, and about his health. His eyes were always weak, and now that he is losing semen regularly his sight is getting even weaker. But what can I do? I gave him my advice and he didn't take it. Marriage is like a wooden *laddu* (ball-shaped sweet): if you bite into it you get splinters in your mouth, but if you don't bite into it you spend the rest of your life wondering how it must have tasted.

"Then there is Bhogilal, who really does very nice sadhana, and doesn't have enough money to get married even if he wanted to. He is friendly with a good sadhu, who keeps telling him to come live in the ashram and forget his foolish little job, which barely pays him enough to live on. In the ashram he would be fed, clothed and sheltered, and could do sadhana all day long. What could be better for him? Here is God telling him, 'Come, my boy, I want you to do sadhana, I have made all the arrangements,' but does he move to the ashram? No! He is afraid to leave the safety of his circle of relatives and friends. Also, somewhere deep in his heart he still thinks he might be able to get married one of these days. So he stays on where he is and does his sadhana. But half of his mind is on the pinups he has on his walls, and that half induces him to masturbate. How will he ever be able to build up enough shakti to make spiritual progress if he won't stop having orgasms for at least a few months? It's a waste, I tell you, a real waste of good potential."

It was the same story with the other "children," like Dr. Martanda, who would come to Vimalananda with the intention of showing off his Ayurvedic knowledge. Usually, though, the doctor found himself being taught something new, as he did on the day he flourished under Vimalananda's nose a small plastic envelope containing a small brown object labelled "camel nose insect."

"Doctor Saheb, have you just been in Rajasthan?" asked the galvanized Vimalananda, without even breaking conversational stride. "Look, Robby, camel nose insect! Anyone who has ever spent much time around camels knows that a male camel becomes uncontrollable when he goes into rut. When he becomes really excited he will evert his soft palate—bring it all the way out of his mouth—and then trumpet his virility so that the entire neighborhood can hear. Doctor Saheb, would you please imitate that noise for my Robby?" Dr. Martanda hereupon begrudgingly produced a truly remarkable noise by grunting loudly while vigorously shaking his head from side to side. I saw Vimalananda stifling a smile.

"At this point," Vimalananda continued, "you must beat the camel severely about the head and neck until he calms down. Otherwise he will break his chain and run amok, trampling people and other animals. Once he calms down he will begin to sneeze, and out from his nose will come lots of white worms. Only the virile camels have these worms, and the most virile produce the most worms. The worms die immediately, and dry into the state that you see this one in. We use these in Ayurveda to treat respiratory ailments and menstrual maladies. Am I right, Doctor Saheb?" Dr. Martanda could only shake his head "yes," in amazed silence. At first I had some doubts about the veracity of this rather too far-fetched story, but when years later on a camel safari in the Rajasthan desert I made enquiries I found that all its details checked out.

Vimalananda tried periodically to make his "children" understand the error of their ways, but they mostly preferred to continue in the way they were going while he mostly preferred not to interfere. "Give them enough rope and they will hang themselves," he would say. "Because Nature loves me She loves my 'children' too, and does much of their work for them. But many of them have come to expect me to force Nature to solve all their problems. Why should I? I did my sadhanas for my own benefit, and for the benefit of those who love me for myself. This is why I am mainly interested in paying off my existing rnanubandhanas with these so-called devotees. They believe they are doing something great if they bring me sweets and flowers now and again. They think that I should recognize the 'depth' of their devotion and be prepared to do whatever they ask of me. Do they think I am going to become their slave? Ha! If they are sensible they will take advantage of what I have to offer; if not, well, once the debt is paid I'll go my own way and they can go theirs."

Parekh, who owned a transport company, was one of the few lower-maintenance devotees. He neither claimed to be something he was not nor pretended to be smarter than he was. Whenever Parekh would send us lunch unannounced we would know that he had a problem—one of his trucks had gone missing, perhaps, or maybe he wanted to convey a grossly overweight payload. He would inevitably arrive a few hours after his food did, and would begin to massage Vimalananda's legs while he explained his trouble. Vimalananda would then speed off in his astral body to ameliorate the problem while the massage was going on, and Parekh would sail home afterwards confident that his most recent difficulty would soon be a thing of the past.

As Vimalananda and I sat playing chess a few days after one such transaction he told me, "Parekh is one of the few sensible people who come to extract work from me. He never tries to show off. He knows he is coming to beg and he comes humbly, which I appreciate. Next, he doesn't disturb me while I am doing the work; on the contrary, he helps me out by his massage." He paused to checkmate me charmingly as I helplessly marvelled yet again over his prowess at the game. Or rather his prowess at arranging prowess for himself. Though he had been chess champion of his college Vimalananda could still be beaten by another well-trained player when he was playing on his own. But when he called a disembodied grandmaster into his body while he went elsewhere on an astral errand he was quite unbeatable. His favorite 'substitute' player was Paul Morphy, whom he claimed had reincarnated as Bobby Fischer. Both men specialized in "the play of the knights," the skillful use of those pieces to interdict the opponent's movements. I never grew tired of watching Vimalananda's seemingly disorganized chessmen suddenly sweep invincibly around the board like an armored whirlwind. Occasionally when he was thoroughly preoccupied elsewhere I could wear down his concentration sufficiently, by using the Indian strategy of never moving a piece to any square where it has no support, to win a game off him. But those occasions were rare.

"You know, Robby," he continued as I reset the board for the next game, "all these swamis talk about samadhi as the highest goal, but I think they are fools. What is the use of these spurting samadhis, anyway? Fine, you go off into a trance, but when you drop back down to earth you are just as you were before. That sort of samadhi state stays separate from the normal waking 'you.' I think it is much better to retain consciousness on this plane even while you shift your main focus to other realities. Here I am playing chess with you, but as I play I can go to America to check on how your parents are doing, or I can visit *Patala* (the underworld), or the planet Venus, or my Guru Maharaj, or wherever I please, and still sit here acting as if I know nothing. To be truly aware you have to know what is happening far away today, what has happened here long ago, and what is going to happen anywhere in the cosmos during the coming decades. But all the while you continue to function effectively in this time, space and causality. Awareness on all levels at all times—that sort of enlightenment has some use."

This sort of awareness was particularly useful to those students like me who approached Vimalananda for help during their exams, for every student who did so inevitably scored well. It was best to advise him in advance, but even when informed after the fact he seemed able to influence results. Shernaz's daughter Arzoo, whom I was tutoring at his behest, made it a post-test ritual to stand before him with a hang-dog look, telling him timidly that because of some stupid errors she would not do well in a certain subject. After chiding her a little for her carelessness Vimalananda would tell her, "Don't worry about it; wait and see the result." After she received that assurance Arzoo would without fail score best in that subject in which she had done the worst.

Though he never explained to me how he manipulated examinations Vimalananda was forthright about the means he used to help one of his friends with her piano recitals: "She likes to give performances, but they make her so nervous that she slips up in her playing. I want to help her out, because she is my 'child.' Every mother wants her child to shine out. The *Chaya Purusha Siddhi* is very useful for this sort of thing. *Chaya* means 'shadow.' You achieve the Chaya Purusha Siddhi when you can bring your own shadow to life and gain control over it. This is not a very difficult siddhi to attain, really; the main restriction is that you have to repeat the mantra at a certain time of day while you sit on a riverbank. Once you have achieved this siddhi you can send your shadow wherever you please and it will do your work for you. When performance time for my friend comes around, for instance, I simply send my shadow to the concert hall to stand behind her, and transfer some of my confidence to her. Then she plays confidently, and her show is a success."

The University of Poona's Ayurvedic examinations, which spanned a three-week period every year and a half, consisted of a dozen or more three-hour periods of writing long-hand answers to essay questions, followed by half a dozen practicals. These became real torture sessions in the 107°F heat of April 1978. On their completion I made tracks for Bombay, ready for what I felt was a well-earned vacation. There I found Vimalananda in an excellent mood, for Stoney was finally in foal. Shortly thereafter Arzoo made her first trip to Bombay, and Vimalananda decided that we should all have an outing to Tirthakshetra, our favorite hot springs. Arzoo stayed at Harshbhai's house, where she was stung by a wasp on the inside of her thigh on Sunday, the day after her arrival. Too embarrassed to tell anyone she suffered silently until she reached Vimalananda's flat on Monday, when Vimalananda noticed the pain on her face and forced her to disclose her misery to him. "Let's solve this problem right now," he said. "Robby, go get me the broom!" Was he going to sweep the pain away, I wondered? Yes he was—he had Arzoo spread her legs modestly, and then stroked the swollen area with the delicate tips of the grasses that compose this sort of broom. Arzoo and I were both amazed, for *voila!* the pain disappeared instantly, and the swelling began to subside.

But there was no time for awe; we had to be off on our excursion. The most famous of the several hot springs near Bombay are at Vajreshwari, near Ganeshpuri. At that time Tirthakshetra was little known and rarely frequented. The first two of its four pools are too hot for anything except cooking, so as soon as we arrived we would put our rice and dal into a small cloth bag and leave it to parboil in pool no. 1 while we coddled ourselves in pool no. 3. On this occasion we enjoyed both a good soak and a pleasant lunch, and were reluctantly wending our way back toward the city, jugs filled with mineral water, when our automobile conked out. Though Vimalananda tried over and over to start it the battery continued to die, and soon was dead. There we were in the middle of an unfamiliar jungle, miles from the nearest town. Night was falling. For ten minutes we tried to start the car by pushing it, to no avail.

Vimalananda then opened the car's hood and stared concentratedly at the engine. After he closed the hood he paused for a few minutes, and when he again sat behind the wheel and turned the ignition key the engine started instantly, as if nothing was wrong. We drove uneventfully back to Bombay, saved yet again by "Nature." As soon as we reached home the car quit and would not start for anything. We discovered the next day that the starter solenoid was burnt out. Vimalananda sent me down to make an offering to Anjaneya, saying, "You should be thankful to Anjaneya that you are here in Bombay now. If not for him we might still be out by the side of that road." I accordingly made a beeline for the Anjaneya temple near the fire station, to praise Him for saving us the previous evening. While there I also sent up an orison of thanks to Nature for sending me such an intercessor as Vimalananda, and a plea to keep him interceding for me indefinitely.

June 1978 found the winds of change, spawned perchance by the impending monsoon, sweeping across our string of horses. When he took up racing again after a hiatus of more than two decades Vimalananda's first trainer had been the genial, foul-mouthed, owl-faced Maneckjee, and his first horse the grey Zomaral, which he owned half and half with his trainer. Shortly thereafter Stone Ice arrived, and after old Maneckjee's death both horses went along with Scarlet Ruby to Maneckjee's son Zubin to train. They remained there until the day when Scarlet Ruby was sent to stud and Zubin neglected to obtain for Vimalananda his portion of the money due him for his "unofficial" part share in the horse. Vimalananda, who was quick to react to unfairness, lost his temper and predicted that Zubin's charges would do poorly during the upcoming Hyderabad season.

When Vimalananda would occasionally prognosticate for trainers or owners who did not know him well they would often think him drunk or insane even when those predictions later came true. But Zubin, who had planned multiple winners in Hyderabad, knew enough of Vimalananda's influence with Nature to realize what sort of predicament he was in when these winners failed to materialize. A few months after this prediction of drought Vimalananda met Zubin at a party in Hyderabad and greeted him with, "So, my boy, how goes your season?"

"What season?" asked Zubin, jauntily. "I am here on a holiday!" Then Zubin meekly buttered up his owner over the evening until Vimalananda magnanimously proclaimed, "I will permit you to win one race, on the last day." Zubin did in fact win one race in Hyderabad that year, on the last day of the season. He then quit training altogether.

Vimalananda's horses were thereupon transferred to one Appagaru. When a year later Appagaru went off to train in Bangalore, the horses went to Mr. M. Lafange, where they sat when I arrived on the scene. Lafange was not a bad man, but he was cheap. From the beginning he tried to save money by scrimping on his horses' rations and on the straw they used for their bedding. I never much liked him, but so long as he catered to Vimalananda's whims I at least endured him. In 1978, though, two new owners entered his stable and Lafange got too big for his britches. Plans were therefore afoot, initiated by the ever-scheming Dr. Kulkarni, to transfer Vimalananda's horses to the care of Mr. Tehmul Antia, a handsome scapegrace whose charming wife Dinaz did everything she could to make us feel that we would be welcome in her husband's stable. Tehmul could only get a trainer's license if he could show to the Club that he had a minimum of six horses under his care, and Vimalananda's string of six—Zomaral, Elan, Repay, Kamaal, Timir and Bajarangi—would enable him to comfortably satisfy that requirement.

I completely lost my sympathy for the Lafanges on the morning I went to request Mr. Lafange to appear before Vimalananda in his hotel room, that by his contrition he might avoid the loss of Vimalananda's horses. When I reached Lafange's home I found no one there but his wife, who replied to my query with some asperity: "Mr. Lafange cannot come to Mr. Vimalananda whenever he is summoned! He is busy with his other owners."

"Fine," I said, and left in a huff, thinking, "He'll soon have plenty of free time for those other owners." I arrived at the hotel ready to present my case in detail, only to find that Vimalananda had already made his mind up to shift from the world of Lafange's rnanubandhanas to Tehmul's karmic milieu. Mrs. Lafange's fresh insult provided us a convenient excuse for moving on, and we prepared a story of innocent lack of recourse: "We wanted you to come to settle things, Mr. Lafange, but you were busy with your other owners."

In the end it was Lafange himself who did the deed, when a day or two later Roshni called him from Bombay and he told her that everything was just fine with the horses in Poona. Thoroughbred horses are a finicky lot, each with its own idiosyncrasies; Elan, for example, would only take her carrots grated. The trainer was expected to take care of these individual requirements, and was paid for doing so. Shortly after Roshni called Vimalananda to report that all was well Arzoo, who acted as our spy at the Poona stables, called to report that all was in fact not well. Arzoo notified Vimalananda that the horses were getting no carrots or other treats and that there was a shortage of bedding straw. Vimalananda promptly called Roshni back and accused her of shielding Lafange. Roshni promptly "got wild" and called Mr. Lafange, but got through only to Mrs. Lafange, who told her that all was well. Roshni then called both husband and wife liars, told Mrs. Lafange that Mr. Lafange was "dead" to her, and hung up.

To tell an Indian woman even in jest that her husband is dead to you is a dreadful insult, for it acts as a sort of request to Nature to bring that death about. Being an Indian woman Roshni knew very well that Mrs. Lafange would be sure to retaliate. Indeed, when Vimalananda called Lafange in the evening to patch things up Lafange told him, "Take your horses out of my yard!" Lafange expected that Vimalananda would then beg forgiveness for that slight, which would allow Lafange some moments of self-righteous satisfaction before he would grudgingly permit the penitent to scrabble back to his fold. Little did he know that Tehmul was waiting to step into his place, that to Tehmul those horses swiftly went. Then, after it had become too late for any entreaties, the Lafanges realized that they had lost their fount of golden eggs. Had Roshni not lost her temper the horses might still be with Lafange, for Vimalananda usually harkened to supplication as readily as did Prithviraj Chauhan. Lafange was predictably livid when he discovered the defection and refused to speak to Dr. Kulkarni ("that traitor!") for weeks thereafter.

"At least," said Vimalananda on his arrival in Poona at the end of the drama, puffing contentedly on a cigarette, "Lafange now has some other owners. I've been wanting a new trainer for some time, and one of my reasons for waiting so long to leave has been Lafange's lack of horses. Every time

I hinted that I might shift Lafange or his wife would come to me whining about how poor they are and how they would be ruined without my string. I don't hate the man, so I didn't want to destroy him. But I am really glad to be free of him and his mokul."

I had dropped in on the Lafanges only once before, in the company of Vimalananda during the 1977 Poona season. On that occasion he had drawn my attention to a large rock that sat completely covered with the red powder called *sindura* smack dab in the middle of the parlor of the small flat the Lafanges called home. "Yes?" I asked him with my eyebrows. "Mokul," he whispered. After we left he explained to me that a *mokul*, which is a sort of Muslim angel, had taken up residence in that rock, and that while the Lafanges were aware of the good he could do them they couldn't seem to comprehend the ill he could cause if he weren't pleased.

"I am glad to be free," Vimalananda continued, "because the Lafanges are always asking the mokul to do things for them and keep trying to bribe him by offering him this and that. But because the mokul doesn't appreciate their greedy attitude he is never in a very good mood, and so their prosperity is never very good."

"Aren't they asking for trouble by fiddling about like this with an ethereal being?"

"And how! They're in way over their heads. They don't comprehend anything of how the mokul thinks, and I am very much afraid they will just continue creating trouble for themselves until they are destroyed. I tried to explain to them how to take care of the thing, but they wouldn't, or couldn't, listen. Then I told them that I'd get rid of him for them. But they think he is going to be their ticket to the big time, so they refused that too. It's so ironic; they don't know what to do with him but they insist on holding onto him."

"Like a baby pulling a dog's tail."

"That's right. Even if he is a good dog he will probably bite you if you annoy him long enough. Then why should you cry about it when he does?"

"This is all the Law of Karma at work again, I suppose?"

"What is there in life but the Law of Karma? My concern was not to be dragged down with them, and now that Nature has given me a way to exit gracefully I have taken it gladly. I know that Tehmul is no saint either—have you looked closely at his physiognomy?—but he owes me something, since I have helped him get his license. Also, he is inexperienced, which means that he won't interfere too much with me—at least for a while. Hey, Arzoo!"

Arzoo had, after putting some rice for our lunch in the pressure cooker, come to the front room to listen to the latest in the Lafange saga.

"Why is it that after an hour of cooking we have not heard any whistle from the pressure cooker's safety valve? Shouldn't the cooker's pressure have built up by now?" Arzoo agreed that it should have, and we all filed into the kitchen to probe the mystery. There was the cooker, cooking merrily, but not a sign of any pressure.

Arzoo then clumsily blurted out a confession: "Now I remember! I put water in the vessel with the rice but I forgot to add water into the bottom of the cooker. Now it's too late; the rice must be burned." She began to hyperventilate and wail: "What if the cooker is damaged? If it is damaged my mother will kill me!"

"Oh, pipe down," said Vimalananda genially as he took charge of the pot, and when he opened its lid there sat perfect rice steaming fragrantly within! "Your mind was on my talks instead of on your cooking, but because Nature loves me She loves my 'children' too, so long as they don't get too big for their breeches. But don't try this stunt when I'm not around or you'll be saving up to buy a new pressure cooker! It's time you learned to concentrate on your work."

I knew that admonition was meant for me as well, for I had just been officially made Vimalananda's racing agent and was now expected to handle much of his business both at the stables and in the offices of the R.W.I.T.C. As it was my responsibility to ensure that there was enough money in each horse's account to cover that month's B.T.F. (Basic Training Fees) and race entrance fees I quickly made friends with most of the office staff and, since I also handled the matter of the vet bill, Dr. Kulkarni quickly became my friend. Many of the other trainers also began to acknowledge my presence, having concluded early on that I would only work so hard for Vimalananda's benefit if I were his (probably wealthy) silent partner. I did what I could to foster this useful misapprehension, which helped to open the doors of the racing fraternity to me.

And what an unusual world that fraternity was! There were the "big" trainers, like Ardeshir Rustomjee, who kept in their own stables the Club limit of 60 horses but controlled more via their villeins. After thoroughly drilling these bright and seemingly pliant assistants in their training methods the big trainers would "lend" them enough horses to be individually licensed. The owners who trafficked with these assistants would then be confident that even though their horses were not officially saddled in the master's stables the master's eye was on them nonetheless.

Next came the mid-size and small trainers, some quite talented, who had never accumulated quite enough good press or good fortune to join the ranks of the big boys. A few of these were private trainers, who trained horses for a single owner. Some trainers were ex-jockeys whose knowledge of how both to boot home and to hook horses made them really expert players of the game. Param Singh, who began mid-sized but soon graduated to bigness, was one of my favorites in this genre. Both he and his able assistant Nusrat Hassan, who afterwards also became a major trainer, had great respect for Vimalananda and always made it a point to chat with me as well.

Near the bottom of the heap of trainers sit the *masalawalas*, who are satisfied only when they can make their charges win at long odds. A *masala* is any mixture of spices that is used to flavor food. Each Indian recipe has its own masala, without which the dish falls flat. Similarly, each horse or mare requires its own pattern of "spicing" in the form of track work, veterinary treatment, handicap and the like for her to create a tasty bet for her owner and trainer. A racecourse masalawala, who specializes in "cooking" horses that no one else would "eat," works overtime disseminating disinformation to ensure a glorious repast for himself and his friends.

Masalawalas will do anything to get their horses fit enough for a good gamble. Sometimes masalawalas take healthy horses and sedulously hook them for months together until they drop so far out of the public eye that no one will take a flutter on them even when they look fit enough to run a good race. Sometimes they take broken-down plug horses and patiently return them to racing fitness, and sometimes they experiment on defective, neurotic or uncontrollable horses with unorthodox training methods. Whatever his preferred methods you know a trainer is a real masalawala when you can never tell that his horses are on the job. Foremost among the masalawalas during my time was Mohammed Mustapha, who was ably assisted by his son Mashallah, 'Mashie' for short. They invariably greeted me as I walked by, and invariably never gave me the slightest idea of what they were up to.

Owners also come in large, medium, and small sizes, the smallest of them owning only a part of a single horse. It is widely rumored that some big owners enter the racing business for the express purpose of gaining tax relief by losing money, for horse racing is reckoned in India to be an "agricultural undertaking" which attracts favorable tax rates. It is said to be an open secret that many owners launder their "black" (illegal) money by betting heavily, for once the government tax is paid on a bet any winnings therefrom become "white" (legal) money. Regular bettors in those days abated their tax burdens by opening special accounts with bookies . When a "1 + 4" owner told his bookie that he wished to bet Rs. 100 the bookie would write "Rs. 100" in his book and would charge tax on that amount, but would calculate the owner's bet as Rs. 100 + 400 = 500 and would pay off on that amount. For a "1 + 9" owner the tax was paid on Rs. 100 and the wager became Rs. 100 + 900 = 1000. "Mad" bettors who wagered hundreds of thousands of rupees on a race placed those sums with private, often illegal, bookies, and any winnings from those bets remained wholly unlaundered.

Horses belong to one of five handicap classes in Western India. Two-year olds enter the system in Class V-A and are promoted or demoted as they win or lose. Those who live up to their potential rise to the ranks of the crème de la crème who occupy the top handicaps of Class I, and those who are but nags tumble down to Class V-B, where they become masala fodder. Our Timir, for instance, was a reliable Class III horse who after flirting briefly with Class II remained in and continued to win races in Class III throughout his career. The biggest tests of talent in Western India are the Classic races, which are terms races that are at least theoretically open to horses of any class. At that time the Classics included the Indian versions of the 1000 Guineas, the 2000 Guineas, the Oaks, the Derby and the St. Leger, and the R.W.I.T.C. Ltd. Invitational Cup. The big trainers handle most of the Classic winners and Class I horses, leaving only the dregs of the upper classes to the mid-size brigade. The masalawala eternally plays his horses between classes V-B and V-A, with the occasional foray into class IV.

Tehmul's yard, which sheltered horses from all the classes, soon became my own classroom. There I watched horses schooling and lounging, spurting and galloping, loosely rolling and gently trotting. I discovered that work in the sand is good for horses with dinky joints, and swimming benefits those whose bodies are stiff. I learned how horses are fed and groomed and their stables cleaned, and was introduced to bog spavins and bone spavins and shin splints, and how to treat them (one of the best ways to treat shin splints being to wash the area repeatedly in the horse's own urine). I saw how swollen joints were chemically blistered to reduce them and how tendons that had bowed out were "pin-fired" to create thick bands of scar tissue to hold them in place. I learned to extract useful rumors from the current of vulgarisms and ribaldries that circulates like irrigation water from yard to yard, and to note without overt comment the many inequities and grievances as they accumulated. I studied jockeys for falsehoods and inconsistencies as they dissected a defeat with the owner and trainer, aware that they were already thinking of their next rides as they described their last ones. In between I rewarded myself for all this work by sitting in awe of Nature's plan, as I watched the late afternoon sun shine on necks and flanks and hindquarters that rippled with quivering well-tuned muscles as the horses gambolled and tit-tupped through their evening walks.

Tehmul notched his maiden success as a trainer on August 15, 1978, India's 31st Indepedence Day. His first winning mount was our milestone-maker Timir, who won in a spectacular dead heat. As he passed the winning post an infuriated Vimalananda snapped, "Had Shernaz not disturbed me last night Timir would have walked this race!" Shernaz had disturbed him to tell him of

Arzoo's high fever; he resented the distraction not because he did not care for Arzoo but because Shernaz by this time in her life should have known how to deal with a fever. Arzoo's fever, which turned out to be typhoid, went on for weeks—as Vimalananda had predicted some weeks earlier in the wake of an amazing event.

One ominous afternoon a monkey climbed in through the front window of Shernaz's house and advanced to the middle room where Arzoo lay sleeping on her bed. Next to the bed stood a full-length mirror, and when the monkey saw himself therein he saw a rival. He probably threatened that opponent a few times before he lost his temper and threw an uppercut at him, a punch which broke the mirror and lacerted his hand. His screams of panic and fury awoke Arzoo from a deep sleep into the terror of finding herself lying alone, flecked with mirror shards, covered with the blood of a monkey who raged just a foot or two from her bed. When Vimalananda was told of this he said solemnly, "This bodes very ill for Arzoo's health. I will try to avert it, but I think she is about to fall seriously ill," and so she did. She also recovered completely, thanks to Vimalananda's nursing.

Timir continued to create landmarks in the lives of his affiliated humans when the young, talented, personable Homi Mehta became a full-fledged jockey by winning his 40th race on his back. Everyone loved Timir. Though he tended to be somewhat testy his behavior was generally genteel. Most male horses who are not expected to win Classic races are gelded early on to keep them tractable, but Timir had escaped the castration knife because he was a "double rig": neither of his testicles had ever descended into his scrotum. Another reason male horses are caponized is to keep them from wasting their energy in masturbation, which becomes quite the fixation with some of them, as it did with Repay, the horse who had begun the 1978-79 season as Vimalananda's great hope. Repay was unusual in two ways: while most horses sleep standing up he would instead make up a nice bed in the straw for himself each night, and lay down to sleep; and he had a striking predisposition for self-fellatio.

Many of Vimalananda's horses showed some sort of sexual peccadillo. Elan, for instance, who had returned to racing from stud, would regularly become so aroused by any well-hung stallions nearby that she would begin to swish her tail and gush fluid from her vagina, which did away with any interest she had in her work. But Repay's was a rare and strange case, for every other horse (in India at least) masturbates by rubbing against a handy surface like the door of his stall. Even Dr. Kulkarni, who had seen most every equine aberration, was perplexed: "It's astounding," he informed Vimalananda. "At first I could not believe it when the groom told me that he was sucking himself off, but it is true. We have tried to stop him with a ring, but he refuses to quit until he has an orgasm. In fact, it has now become a daily habit. I know you don't like to cut your horses, but I don't think you have a choice in this case." Unwilling to give up just yet Vimalananda instructed the groom to continue trying to interrupt Repay's persistent sperm-swilling, first with the ring, which was positioned on the end of his penis to hinder erection, and then by applying bitter herbs to his organ to discourage him from taking it into his mouth. Neither of these expedients worked, though, and eventually a reluctant Vimalananda had to agree with Dr. Kulkarni's assessment. Repay was emasculated in the spring of 1979.

During this period of our protracted focus on semen Vimalananda found one day the occasion to enlarge on its nature and importance, and on the implications of its wastage. "You must know," he began one evening after an afternoon of viewing the recalcitrant Repay at the stables, "that the word *shukra* means semen in Sanskrit."

"I do," I replied.

"And you know that *Shukra* is also a name for the planet Venus?"

"Yes. The texts also state that the planet Venus, is the guru of the *asuras*. In that context they call him *Shukracharya* (*Shukra* + *Acharya* [teacher] = 'Venus the Guru'). When the texts say 'asura,' do they mean the asuras who are the enemies of the devas? The asuras that some people call 'demons'?"

"Yes, those asuras."

"Who are supposed to live under the earth, in Patala?"

"Well, not exactly. Patala is on a different plane of existence from our Earth, an astral plane. The asuras are a sort of degenerate race of astral beings. The devas, who are also astral beings, are willing to help us humans if we know how to properly propitiate them. The asuras are much more selfish, and use their power to delude other beings into believing what the asuras want them to believe. A lot of this 'flying saucer' business has to do with the asuras. They like to play around with humans, pretending to be divine while they experiment on us. Some deluded people even worship the asuras—but they usually regret it in the end.

"Asuras are very fond of indulging themselves with meat, alcohol, and sex. I like to call asuras *shukra-charya*, 'those whose behavior is motivated by semen,' because they believe in using sex freely for enjoyment, and don't mind wasting semen. That is why asuras worship the god Brahma, the creator. The planet Venus is called 'Shukra' in Sanskrit because Venus is in charge of sexuality. 'Shukracharya' can thus also mean 'Semen-Teacher,' which is quite an apt way of translating Venus's name."

"Why?"

"Because Shukracharya possesses the *Sanjivini Vidya*, the knowledge (*vidya*) of return to life (*sanjivini*). That is, he can bring the dead back to life, which he does with the help of semen. Sanjivini Vidya is so great that you can take a corpse, bury it, and make a contract with Mother Earth to keep it inviolate for up to six months. Then you can still bring it back to life after that six months, with the same soul, same personality, and same karmas, good for another hundred years."

"Isn't this what some sadhus do?"

"When an Aghori is about to die he will find someone else who is on the threshold of death and will then enter that body. This is called *para-kaya-pravesha*. Through it you can live on and on and on. But it is different from *Sanjivini Vidya*."

"I keep hearing stories about the Sanjivini Vidya. What exactly is it?"

"Good question. If you want to know about Sanjivini Vidya you should ask Shukracharya directly. All I will tell you about it right now is that is has something to do with semen. You've heard of cloning, haven't you? Sanjivini Vidya is a sort of super-cloning, in which thousands or millions of beings can be produced from a single spermatozoon. But it is not that simple to perform.

"Sanjivini Vidya mainly utilizes the subtle form of semen—the ojas—instead of the physical sperm. The asuras are very practical, and they are very interested in physical semen, so they follow Shukracharya. And he in turn tries to get them to go beyond the physical semen to the ethereal ojas, from the mundane into the more subtle regions of being. It is one facet of the eternal play of guru and disciple.

"Sanjivini Vidya interests me because of the role it played in an incident which happened long, long ago. Its repercussions are being felt even today, so listen carefully! The asuras are so jealous of the fact that the devas are allowed to run the cosmos that they do nothing but plot wars against the devas to challenge them for dominion of the universe. All the wars have the same result: the devas are defeated until they seek help from some superior being, like Shiva or Vishnu, Who helps them regain heaven."

"Why should the devas always lose first? Aren't they the good guys?"

"They are good, but they are also complacent. They are easily satisfied with their achievements and have no interest in progressing further. This makes them vulnerable to the asuras, who are always hungry for more, always willing to try something new.

"Why not just have a universe without asuras, since they're so much trouble?"

"Because you can't have devas without asuras. The devas balance the asuras and vice versa, which is natural. Without asuras the devas would let the universe stagnate. Nothing would ever change, because the devas believe in the status quo. Asuras believe in change, and in fact the devas change only when the asuras force them to change. But the asuras are so selfish that if they were allowed to rule the universe they would quickly demolish it. You cannot trust asuras with authority because even though they can achieve great things they also create great chaos. Like children they can be both very kind and very cruel. They can perform terrific austerities, penances which the devas could never dream of doing, but when their austerities produce shakti they always misuse it. Fortunately for us not all asuras are experts at sadhana. Most asuras are very foolish, in fact. They can follow the rules and restrictions of sadhana nicely for a while. But then, because they have no inherent sense of purity, they dissipate the shakti they are building up by breaking their own rules. Thank God that they do, for otherwise they would still be running the universe, and it would be in a terrible mess!

"During these wars with the devas the asuras had a distinct advantage in that any of their number who were killed in battle could be brought back to life again. The devas lacked this advantage because their guru Brihaspati, the planet Jupiter, lacked knowledge of the Sanjivini Vidya, which was Shukracharya's exclusive preserve. The devas knew that they would always be in danger of being conquered by the asuras as long as Shukracharya alone had this power, so they decided to employ subterfuge. They sent Kacha, Brihaspati's son, to Shukracharya to learn the Sanjivini Vidya by trickery.

"When Kacha reached the city of the asuras and informed Shukracharya of his intention to learn Sanjivini, all the asuras warned Shukracharya against it. They knew that if Kacha learned that vidya the devas would be able to use it against the asuras in battle.

"But Shukracharya told them, 'I will never turn away anyone who comes to me for knowledge. The devas have humbled themselves sufficiently to send the son of their preceptor to me, and he will study.' The asuras had to keep quiet in front of their guru, whom they relied on to provide them with the energy to enjoy the things they valued most in life: good food, good wine, and plenty of combat and sex. They kept quiet to his face, but behind Shukracharya's back they grumbled.

"Kacha was such a brilliant pupil that he attracted the attention of Devayani, Shukracharya's daughter, who promptly fell in love with him. Shukracharya encouraged his daughter's suit because he knew that she loved Kacha purely. The word kacha means the loincloth a boy wears during his period of study while he is celibate. So when I tell you that soon Kacha and Devayani were 'married by the ceremony used in heaven' I mean that Devayani divested Kacha of his loincloth—and with it his sexual continence.

"This development alarmed the asuras even more, for now their enemy was wooing their preceptor's daughter. Thinking it best to get Kacha out of the way once and for all they waylaid him one evening in a lonely place, killed him, and left his body for the wolves. When Kacha didn't come home at night Devayani was very upset. Even Shukracharya was concerned, and by using his yogic powers he was able to discover that Kacha had been murdered. With the help of Sanjivini Vidya he brought Kacha back to life.

"But asuras do not give up so easily. They waited for another opportunity and before long took Kacha unawares again and killed him again. This time they pounded his body into a paste and mixed it into sea water. Again, however, Shukracharya revived him, because of Devayani's tears.

"The third time the asuras decided to make sure. They killed Kacha, burned his body, and dissolved his ashes in a bowl of wine. Then they offered the wine to Shukracharya to drink. Shukracharya drank it, exclaiming as he did, 'Victory to the asuras!'

"Again Devayani cried and cried when Kacha did not come back to her. This time Shukracharya tried to reason with her: 'Daughter, the asuras will never permit Kacha to remain alive, and I cannot continue to revive him. It is better that he stay dead.' But she was adamant; she told her father bluntly, 'I cannot live without Kacha.'

"As he prepared to employ the Sanjivini Vidya yet again Shukracharya got the shock of his lifetime when with his yogic hearing he heard Kacha tell him, 'Wait, I'm inside you!' With his yogic vision he discovered Kacha to be inside his own belly. Now he was really in a fix. If he brought Kacha back to life he himself would be torn to bits as Kacha emerged from his abdomen, and Devayani would lose her father. If he did not raise Kacha from the dead Devayani would lose her lover. What to do?

"Shukracharya decided that he had no choice but to teach the Sanjivini Vidya to Devayani. As he taught it to her Kacha, listening from inside his belly, learned it too. When Devayani pronounced it to resurrect Kacha Shukracharya's belly burst open and he dropped to the ground dead. Then she pronounced it again and revived her father.

"Shukracharya looked at them both solemnly and said, 'Well, I never wanted things to work out this way. Had the asuras not been so stupid this never would have happened. I curse them for their stupidity!

"'I am also to blame for falling prey to the desire to drink wine. This desire clouded my perception, else I would have been able to see Kacha in the cup before I drank it. I curse wine-drinking, because it causes one to give out secrets which should never be given out!

"'Kacha, now you are as good as my son, because you have been reborn from my belly. You and Devayani are my own. I want the two of you to get married.'

"Kacha said to him, 'Gurudev, I cannot. You yourself have said that I am now like your son, because I have been born from your belly. If I marry Devayani now it will be like the marriage of a brother and sister. Moreover, I now have what I was sent here by the devas to obtain. I must therefore now go back to my real home.'

"Devayani said to him, 'So you loved me only for that purpose. You deceived me. Go then! But I curse you that your knowledge will never be of any use to you!'

"Kacha replied, 'Even if I am unable to use my knowledge I can teach it to others, and they can use it. But I curse you in turn that you will never find a man of transcendent wisdom to marry; you shall have to marry a king or a prince.'

"And that is what happened, to each of them. When like Kacha and Devayani you are full of shakti because of having done lots of austerities any curse or blessing that you pronounce must take effect. However, the force of these curses drained all the shakti from Kacha and Devayani so that neither could make use of the Sanjivini Vidya even if they wanted to. Shukracharya's knowledge was thus saved.

"Whose fault was this debacle? Mainly Kacha's. He came to Shukracharya as a stooge of the devas to steal knowledge, which is forbidden. Also, he used Devayani. He led her along when he was interested only in the knowledge and not in her. And when he knew he was in the wrong why should he have cursed her? He should have kept his mouth shut, and accepted the results of his actions. But his wounded ego made him lash back at her, which compounded his guilt.

"Now, a subtle mind will ask, 'Why did it happen that both Kacha and Devayani were overcome with the desire to curse, which made them both forget the Sanjivini Vidya?'"

"Yes, why did that happen?"

"It is simple: Shukracharya perverted both their minds with the help of a certain *siddhi*; he *forced* them to curse one another. He did this not because he was being selfish with his knowledge; in fact he had planned all along to teach it to Devayani since he really did love Kacha as a son. But both still had imperfections—Kacha's deviousness and Devayani's sensuality—which convinced Shukracharya that he had to prevent them from obtaining the knowledge until they were fit to use it properly. Knowledge placed into the wrong hands always causes problems. So Shukracharya made the best of a bad situation by ensuring that both of them would be born on Earth, which is what happens to those from the heavenly spheres who lose their shakti. They will have to remain on Earth until their imperfections disappear; then they will both remember Sanjivini."

"That could take a while."

"Is Shukracharya in any hurry? He believes in doing a thorough job since there is no question of the limitation of time. But then he is no ordinary being; he is a Muni, a Mahapurusha. In fact he is a one-eyed Muni. He lost his other eye because of *Vamana*, Vishnu's avatara in the form of a dwarf Brahmana."

"And how might that have happened?" I greatly wished to know how his version of Vamana's story differed from the textual ones.

"You know that the devas and the asuras once churned the Ocean of Milk to obtain *Amrita*, the nectar of immortality. At that time Vishnu helped the devas, led by Brihaspati, to defeat the asuras, kill their king Bali, and steal all the Amrita. This was a karma for which the devas later had to pay. As guru of the asuras Shukracharya was also the guru of their king. After he used Sanjivini to bring Bali back to life he worked to enable Bali to conquer the devas in turn. Eventually Bali triumphed, and Vishnu, the Preserver of the cosmos, could do nothing to protect the devas. How could He? He had broken his promise, given at the time of the Churning, to provide the asuras with some of the Amrita they had worked so hard to obtain. This caused Him to forfeit His right to help the devas on this occasion. Karma is karma, after all; it shows no favoritism, not even to the gods themselves.

"But in order to protect dharma Vishnu had to somehow return control of the cosmos to the devas, so He devised a ruse. He arranged to be born as the Vamana Avatara. Immediately after His birth He approached Bali at Bharuch (the ancient Bhrigukaccha), on the north bank of the holy Narmada River.

"Just then Shukracharya was causing Bali to complete a great sacrifice that would reinforce his position as ruler of the cosmos. At the end of every sacrifice offerings are made to Brahmanas, and Vamana was filled with such profound spiritual radiance that Bali decided to make his offerings to this tiny ascetic. When Shukracharya perceived that Vamana was in fact Vishnu and had come to take the kingdom away from Bali, he warned his disciple not to give anything to the dwarf. But Bali was determined, and said to his guru, 'When the Lord Himself comes to me as a beggar and requests something of me won't it increase my glory to give it to him? Whatever the outcome I will get to see Him in His true form, and I will get His blessings.'

"When he saw that his disciple was prepared to rebel against his order Shukracharya cursed Bali to fall into Patala, deprived of all his wealth and glory. Bali willingly accepted his mentor's curse, and when he told Vamana to ask for whatever He wanted Vamana replied, 'All I want from you, O king, is as much land as I can cover in three steps.'

"Bali said, 'That will be a truly paltry gift. Ask for more!' But Vamana insisted, so Bali resolved to give three steps worth of land to Vamana. To seal his promise he prepared to offer a *dana vrata*, an oath of donation. The central act of this sort of vow involves pouring water onto the ground. This makes the Earth and Water Elements witnesses to the pledge. It is very dangerous to make such an oath, because if you break it Earth and Water will turn against you. Then any body of water you come across may try to drown you, and the earth may literally slip out from under your feet."

"As in an earthquake?"

"Yes. It is better never to make any vows, because they can land you in very hot water. It is much wiser just to play it safe by doing your best without promising never to fail. It is very difficult never to make any mistakes. In fact, every human makes mistakes, which is why I tell people never to worry about their mistakes. Worry is not useful. What *is* useful is to make different mistakes, to learn from your mistakes so that you don't keep making the same ones over and over again."

"Was Bali wrong to go against his guru's order?"

"Shukracharya thought that he was. But Bali was determined to give Vamana what he had requested, and was ready to swear to that effect. From his side Shukracharya was equally determined to ensure that his disciple did not lose his kingdom. As the moment for the oath approached Shukracharya shrank himself to miniscule size and entered the spout of the water pot. When Bali tried to pour the water out onto the ground, therefore, nothing came out.

"Vamana knew what was going on; how could He not know? He took a blade of *darbha* grass, which is so sharp that it can cut your finger, and stuck it into the spout. The blade of darbha poked out Shukracharya's eye and his own blood spilled out onto the ground to seal the oath. After the oath was taken Vamana expanded from His dwarf body into a being of enormous size. With His first step He covered the entire Earth, and with His second step He covered the rest of the universe. Then He looked down at Bali and said, 'Now, where shall I put my third step? There is no place left to put it. You have broken your promise.'

"But Bali said, 'No, Lord, I am still here. When you put your foot on my head you will have encompassed everything.' Vishnu smiled at Bali's cleverness, and did so. In this way Bali got the great blessing of having Vishnu's foot placed on his head. Vishnu awarded Bali immortal life in exchange for his gift of the cosmos. Bali still rules his subjects down below the surface of the earth. No one realizes it, but an offering to the Earth is really an offering to Bali."

When you have propitiated King Bali you have accomplished more than half your task. Sacrifice is called *bali dana* in Sanskrit because you are in fact making an offering (*dana* = gift) to Bali. It is his job to be propitiated in this way, and to reciprocate by assisting you in what you want done.

"Isn't it wonderful? Vishnu came to Earth as *Varaha*, the Sacrificial Boar, to save the Earth from the asura Hiranyaksha. Then He returned as *Narasimha*, the Man-Lion, to save Prahlada from his father Hiranyakashipu, Hiranyaksha's brother. Next He came in the form of the diminutive Vamana to beg the three worlds from Prahlada's grandson Bali." "What a rnanubandhana He had with that family! And what an outstanding pedigree, that produced so many Grand Champions."

"Yes, they were all unique. Bali was smarter even than his guru Shukracharya when it came to donating heaven and earth. After all, how often does the Lord Himself come to beg? Only once so far in the history of the cosmos. It was an opportunity not to be missed, and because he took advantage of it Bali became immortal."

The doorbell drew me briefly to the door, after which Vimalananda resumed his exegesis: "Look at how difficult it is to know what is a curse and what is a blessing! When Bali disobeyed his guru Shukracharya realized that his disciple's term as ruler of the universe was over. Shukracharya's curse that sent Bali to Patala was therefore a blessing in disguise, because Patala is Bali's natural homeland."

"You mean that by his curse Shukracharya ensured that Bali would make it home again, no matter what happened with Vamana."

"That's right. And what of Shukracharya himself? What does it mean that his eye was poked out? With two eyes we see duality. By putting out one of them, in the esoteric sense, Vishnu gave Shukracharya a vision of undivided Reality. This was Vishnu's blessing to Shukracharya, not his curse. See how the devas love to play about!

"The play of the devas is part and parcel of the play of the Rishis. Shukracharya, who was the son of the Rishi Bhrigu, made the asuras so powerful that only Vamana, who was the creation of Angiras Rishi, could save the devas. Angiras Rishi also happened to be the father of Brihaspati, the guru of the devas, who was also the great rival of Shukracharya. So in reality all of this was the play of Bhrigu and Angiras."

Vimalananda stopped long enough for a thorough stare in my direction. Then he continued, "A good guru will always try to do the right thing for his disciple, as Shukracharya tried to do for Bali. But what if the disciple refuses to cooperate, or is so addicted to intoxication that he commits *guru droha* (offense or treachery against the guru)?"

He stopped for me to answer, so I said, "I guess the guru will have to curse the disciple, like Shukracharya cursed Bali."

"Actually your guru will not even have to bother cursing you if you perform guru droha, because that very action will act as your curse. In Bali's case the curse turned out to be a blessing simply because he had Shukracharya for a guru, and because he disobeyed his guru specifically for the purpose of satifying the Lord. Most disciples who perform guru droha, however, do so out of ego, and because they self-identify with their action it truly has the force of a curse.

"Guru droha is really a terrible thing. Blindness from birth is one of the effects of guru droha in a previous incarnation; so is depigmented skin. Albinos and people who have leucoderma (vitiligo), which we call *shwitra* ('white leprosy') in Sanskrit, are obviously depigmented. But even those people whose skin is simply very pale—a condition which is often associated with affliction of the Sun in the horoscope—have also been cursed in the past by their gurus. Many, many Westerners have white skins, don't they? The white race—the 'palefaces'—have lorded it over the dark races for almost five centuries now. They have tried to brainwash us that we are inferior because our skins are darker than theirs. But I think they are inferior, because they can't take the sun, neither literally nor figuratively. Why figuratively? Because in Jyotish the Sun stands for the Soul, and who is the guru if not the embodiment, for the disciple, of the Supreme Soul, the Eternal Absolute? Guru droha is so terrible because it is a rebellion against the authority of Reality. Many of our 'modern' Indian boys and girls think it would be fantastic to marry a white girl or boy—but I think they are crazy."

I glanced reflexively at my own pale skin.

"It is no surprise that Westerners mainly find false gurus. When you have cheated your own guru in the past why should you not be cheated in now? You get what you pay for; that is the Law of Karma."

"So why is this? Why do most of the people in the West want knowledge from the wrong motive, and get only cheats as gurus?"

"Why? Because most Westerners are asuras at heart. All the celestials, including the asuras, have to go somewhere when they fall down to earth. Many of the asuras—who are very fond of indulging themselves with meat, alcohol, and sex, remember—have been born in the West, where they continue to indulge themselves. Occasionally one of them wakes up, a little; but because asuras are egotistical they conclude, as soon as they learn a little, that they know everything. Almost as soon as they learn how to meditate they start calling themselves gurus. But what do they really know of Indian wisdom? Nothing! They are still just probing our spirituality now. They will be learning spiritual things from us for the next 500 years. Even the dog of one of our

Rishis could teach them for one hundred years and still have more to teach. Westerners are so far behind us in spirituality that to shine out among them is nothing. It is child's play for our so-called swamis to go abroad and try to impress all the monkeys over there with their so-called knowledge. I can tell you one thing: A real guru will come to the Westerners only when they decide that they are ready for real knowledge, and they invite Shukracharya."

"And just where will they go to search for Shukracharya?"

"They won't need to search for him; when they are sincerely ready he will appear. They are his disciples, he is responsible for them. It is a great blessing to be guru or king to a bunch of asuras, because you are in a position to improve them. Unfortunately they tend to fall back into their old habits very easily, since their innate natures cannot change. Even Shukracharya tires of them now and again. I call people asuras when even though they have the desire for sadhana they cannot seem to follow the basic rules of discipline. I am willing to try to help such people out, but most of them are by no means ready for spirituality yet and I grow tired of them too."

I thought of one of Vimalananda's well-loved spiritual "children" from the West who while reading the *Upavana Vinoda*, a text on the Ayurveda of plants, remarked a little too flippantly how its pages prescribed that certain weird things be planted under trees to make their fruits or flowers grow to the size of an elephant's trunk. Though this sort of conjecture seemed harmless enough for me it occasioned a violent cloudburst from Vimalananda, who insisted that I write this errant fellow and advise him to try these substances on himself, that he might develop an elephant-trunk-sized penis. Chastened and distressed by his faux pas the 'child' wrote back to discover how to again enter Vimalananda's good graces only to find that he was already there, for Vimalananda was always enthusiastic to forgive.

But do not forget, for the *Upavana Vinoda* contretemps provided him yet further fuel for occasional anti-Western commentary: "Part of the problem lies in the way Western culture has developed. The West is so utterly contrary to the East in so many ways that it is no wonder that people from the two areas cannot understand one another. For example, Indian dance focuses more on facial expressions than does ballet. In fact, the best Indian dancers can display all the possible emotions with their faces alone. Or consider *haute couture*. Until recently in India a man's honor rested on his turban and his mustache. If you were to shave off a Rajput's mustache or take his turban from him he would never be able to bear the shame; he would commit suicide. But today we have adopted the Western trait of judging everyone by their footwear. Nowadays the first thing anyone does is to look down to see what sort of shoes you are wearing, and whether they are properly shined.

"And what of sex? We in India, or at least a few of us, still know how to enjoy sex. And I don't mean just the Tantrics, whose sexual practices are as far ahead of the foolish things that your American 'experts in tantric sexuality' write about as the sky is distant from the earth. Even our rulers understood sexual refinement. Take the Emperor Akbar: not only was he noble, he was versatile to boot. He invented *biryani*, the famous dish of meat and rice, and *jelabi*, the well-known sweet. He even developed his own variety of mango as well. You can still find Aam-e-Akbari and Aam Jehangiri, the varieties of mango that he and his son developed, in a few parts of North India. Back in Akbar's day the imperial gardeners would feed these trees blood, saffron, marijuana, musk and various other substances while they were growing. These things would gradually percolate into the tree's fruit, and turn its flesh a beautiful saffron color."

"Blood?"

"Yes, the best fertilizer for mangoes is blood; that's where much of the blood from the slaughterhouse in Deonar ends up." Deonar is the Bombay suburb which hosts Asia's largest slaughterhouse.

"So when I eat a mango I may in effect be drinking blood?!"

"Yes, and when you eat a banana you may be eating a rat, because the best fertilizer for banana trees is dead rats!"

"Eeuuw!"

"The Law of Karma, my dear boy, the Law of Karma. Anyway, one mango from one of Akbar's trees could give you a beautiful intoxication that would last for an entire day. Now, Akbar's enjoyments were as refined as his fruit. When he was interested in loveplay he would take half of one of those intoxicating mangoes for himself, and would send the other half to his favorite wife. She would know from this that the emperor would be calling on her that evening and would prepare herself accordingly. In the evening both would eat their slice of mango, and by the time they met they would both be nicely excited. Then they would have a beautiful loveplay.

"That was the sort of refined sex that Akbar enjoyed. Do we find such sexual refinement anywhere in the West? No, and it is because sex has become so free and so common over there. You see a girl, you like her, you go up to her and say, 'Hey, how about a nice screw?' No preliminaries, no romance. Sex in the West is now seen as nothing more than a bodily function which you should relieve whenever you feel the need to do so. No wonder perversions are so rampant in the West. Once you have stripped all the mystery and the emotional excitement from sex what is left but the technique?"

"You're not trying to tell me that we will find sexual refinement anywhere in India, are you?"

"Oh, no; forget it! At least Westerners are not so inhibited as today's Indians are. Today's Indians are hopeless when it comes to sex."

"Haven't you always said that there are a few Westerners who could learn how to perform Tantric sexual sadhanas properly?"

"Yes, I have; but the question is, will they be able to do without sex long enough to gain control over it? They live their lives so fast that they think everything can be done instantly; they have no patience. Most Westerners today believe that all their desires, and their sexual desires in particular, should be gratified immediately. But there is nothing speedy about refinement; it takes time and restraint. Refinement occurs automatically in all aspects of life, and especially in sex and in spirituality, if you just slow down. Westerners think the spiritual urge can be gratified in the same way that they gratify their sex urges. No wonder that most of them end up with fake gurus."

"Do you have a theory as to why these differences between East and West?" I knew he must.

"The reason for all these cultural differences is the great difference in the svabhava, the inherent nature, of Westerners and Easterners. There are three main traits inborn into a Westerner. First, he wants to make money and become a millionaire; his god is money, no doubt about it. Second, he wants to enjoy what he earns; he sees no reason to save it. Third, he calculates: first phase, second phase, third phase. These three traits explain why so many Westerners try to mix commerce and spirituality.

"Once a sadhu was invited to the USA. The American who was seated next to him in the plane became curious—a shaven-headed fellow in saffron robes sitting in the next seat—and asked, 'Excuse me, sir, who are you?'

"The sadhu answered, 'That is just what I am trying to find out: who am I?'

"The American then realized that he had come across an intelligent fellow, and asked, 'How are you searching?'

"The sadhu replied, 'By means of "*Om.*"'

"The American realized that there was some potential there; like most Americans, he was a good businessman. When the plane stopped in London he phoned ahead to his people in New York and told them to meet the plane at the airport.

"After the plane took off again the American said to the sadhu, 'Please put your hand on my head.' When the sadhu did so the American intoned, 'Om, Om, Om. I am now your disciple. You must instruct me.' The sadhu didn't know exactly what to think.

"There was a crowd of people to meet the sadhu and his new disciple once the plane landed in New York. The poor sadhu didn't know that it had all been arranged beforehand; he thought it was spontaneous, so he went along with it. Pretty soon he was lecturing one day, holding a meditation camp the next, and so on. 'Om' pillowcases came onto the market, along with 'Om' books and so many other 'Om' products.

"After doing this for some little while the sadhu said to his American promoter, the man he had met on the plane, 'What have you done to me? When I'm not talking I'm meeting people individually, and we are always flying off to some city or other. I have lost all my peace of mind. I want to go back to India.'

"The 'disciple' said, 'But Swamiji, why go back now? You have $2 million in the bank.'

"Swamiji said, 'What is the use of $2 million when I have no peace? You be my chief disciple, take all my money, and run everything. I am going back to India to get my peace back.' And that is what happened. He got his peace back and the American took over the business, made a lot of money, and enjoyed his life."

"Which means he was cashing in his good karmas."

"That's right. America is perfect place for withdrawal of good karmas because it is the place where this effect of commercialization is most pronounced. Why? All because of the gravitation in that part of the world."

"Gravitation?"

"Yes, the quality of the gravity there. For that matter it's all due to our gravity, and to something in our water, that India has always been a special place, that everyone here different. India can never go completely communist because our people are stoic. Because they believe in the life beyond they try not to create problems for themselves in this life if they can help it. If belief in the after-life had not been there we would have gone communist long ago. During the 1942 Bengal famine, which even Western historians agree was a man-made famine created to fill the pockets of certain businessmen, people would sit starving outside fancy hotels in Calcutta and beg food from those emerging after ten-course meals. It never occurred to those starving people to get together and storm the hotel and steal the food. Even though they died like flies they never tried to grab for themselves. Why? They remembered the Law of Karma. These people had every right to steal and eat but they didn't. That is India."

"So is everyone in India a saint, even the beggars?"

"Far from it! Some of the greatest evil in the world has been perpetrated here, like that engineered famine, and the Visha Kanyas. What I am getting at is that most people in India even when they are miserable still know that they are suffering from the effects of previous bad karmas. This makes them think twice and three times before reacting to their misery. India is a deposit counter for good karmas, at least for most of our people. We believe in the life hereafter and work towards it. Now we too are suffering from the effects of the American disease, but originally we in India believed in stock-piling our good karmas and using them only when there is real need. We had the same philosophy about money too. Even now most Indians prefer to save rather than to spend. Did you know that an English scholar has estimated that one-third of the world's total wealth is buried under the desert in Rajasthan? From what I have seen there I think he may be underestimating the amount. It may be more, but it is certainly not less.

"The Western countries, and America in particular, are withdrawal counters for good karmas. You might say that most of the people there are enjoying their karmic pensions. They have suffered and toiled over many lives and now they are getting the result—and wasting it away. Some are doing some sadhana, I grant you, but only a few are doing penance compared to the number who are frittering away their penances.

"Think of the word *saha*, which means to endure, to go patiently through hardships without rebelling. When you invert saha you get *hasa*, which means to laugh. If you endure all your evil karmas at the beginning of your life then you can achieve your goal and live comfortably at the end of your life. Then you will have nothing left to do but laugh like a madman because of the overwhelming joy of it all. But if you enjoy yourself at the beginning of your life and waste all your good karmas you will find that your end is lamentable. And since what you are thinking about when you die determines your next rebirth—*ante matih sa gatih*—your future birth is likely to be lamentable too. It is always better to endure whatever fate throws your way. You will definitely receive your reward—eventually. But if you try to laugh now you are heading for sorrow in the end. Don't forget the old saying: 'He who laughs last laughs best.'

"When all of America's good karmas have been used up then only their bad karmas will remain, and you don't know what will happen. Westerners don't know what they are heading for. Because they are rich they can purchase more luxuries and kill more animals than poor countries like ours. But when the time comes for them to pay it all back they'll be ruined, I tell you, ruined. We are seeing the decay already. Look at television. It is a extraordinary thing which has become an emotional addiction for millions of people. So many people, with Westerners leading the pack, get all their emotional stimulation from TV. This is frightening, because many Westerners now live machine-like lives; even their love is machine love. Westerners have become so dependent on their gizmos that they can't live without them, just as we cannot live without our servants. They have become slaves to their machines.

"When you have a servant you must always be sure that the servant knows who is boss; otherwise the servant will take over. Here in India we are slaves to our servants. They can tyrannize us and we humor them because we need them to get our work done. Westerners think they have solved this problem by building machines. It is true that machines can't go on strike, don't take tea breaks and have no emotional problems to interfere with their productivity. But machines are also living beings, in a sense. The machine says, 'So, you've created me to be your slave? All right, now I'll control you.' And that is just what happens. It is the Law of Karma.

"Westerners have created a modern machine-filled world for themselves, which is fine. But in the process they have lost much of their humanity, which is a much more terrible thing than losing your life. So I thank God that India is still a poor backward nation for the most part. We still possess part of our humanity. We still have our traditions to fall back on, and our peculiar approach to life. I think India is a fine country to live in, because we have everything, good and bad, over here, and you are not protected from anything. You have no choice but to learn to deal with everything, sometimes in the most disgusting circumstances."

"Perhaps Saturn, who is the power behind those of your experiences that you never wanted to experience, has some sort of special relationship with India?"

"Of course he does, and why not? At least over here we worship him as a God. The few Westerners who even think about Saturn call him a devil! If you were he where would you like to be?

"Westerners have spent decades trying to protect themselves from unpleasantness, but they, like us, will eventually have to learn to deal with reality. Saturn will force them to do so. Now they are intoxicated with their machines and addicted to their pleasures, but like all other intoxications these will not last. An Aghori may take intoxicants and indulge in sex, but such activities always remain under his control; no good Aghori ever lets any intoxication control his mind. Addiction to anything but God is a sure path to misery; addiction to God is the only path to happiness."

THE CITY of DELUSION
chapter six

AS BOMBAY'S IMPORTANCE in my life accelerated I increasingly understood why Vimalananda had had to leave his life of many years as a itinerant sadhu and resettle in his hometown. Bombay was so crowded for him with tangled heaps of rnanubandhanas that nothing less than physical residence there would suffice for their unravelling. People daily arrived at his doorstep to confront him with shopping lists of cravings to be satisfied, but few of these solicitants showed any concern for him or his condition. Most were little more than embodied karmic debts who were striving to entrap him, and few of this group appreciated interference from his own Jaya and Vijaya (Roshni and me). Fortunately none of them possessed the power of the Sanatkumaras, or their curses would have kept Vimalananda busy preventing his doorkeepers from falling deep into Patala. Roshni's strategies and protocols may have differed from mine but our ends were the same: to preserve as much as possible of Vimalananda's energy from being suckled from him by these smarmy vampires and to keep conditions in the flat from going completely cattywampus.

Vimalananda's spiritual "children," except for Parekh, usually came to glean wisdom from him by night. The day's callers were of a more mundane genre: a continuous and occasionally entertaining parade of musicians, astrologers, doctors, lawyers, businessmen, politicians, impostors, vagabonds, wastrels and cranks, all seeking some species of profit. Many of them were experts in their fields, like Sayed Sahib, an Arab who occasionally introduced Vimalananda to oil sheiks. When I first met Sayed Saheb two enormous glass jars had just been delivered to Vimalananda's residence. Sayed Saheb spent most of his hour there eyeing the jars as if trying to figure out how much he could make by selling them. When he finally left I asked Vimalananda who he was.

"Sayed Saheb? Oh my, as a con man he's tops! You've heard of people in California and Florida back in the '30s selling people a tract of scrub forest and calling it an orange grove? People talk about such things, but Sayed Saheb has actually done it, right here in India. He actually painted lemons on the trees in order to do it!

"His most successful swindle was the way he separated the Saudis from their jewelry. Some members of the Saudi royal family wanted to quietly dispose of some family treasure; Sayed Saheb assured them that he easily could handle the transaction in Bombay, no questions asked.

"The Saudis flew into India in their private plane and landed at a small airstrip south of Bombay. Sayed Saheb had arranged everything; all they had to do was hand over the gems and take the cash and off they would fly again. Now here they were on the runway, the Saudis with their jewel cases and Sayed Saheb with a suitcase full of money, which he opened to show them that there was no hanky-panky going on.

"All at once there was a clamor of sirens. 'It's the police!' shouted Sayed Sahib as two jeeps filled with his accomplices brandishing guns sped toward the plane. As Sayed Sahib grabbed the baubles he thrust his suitcase into the hands of the startled Arabs and told them, 'Quick, take the money and fly!' Which is what they did, and once they were in the air and headed back to safety what did they find when they opened that case? Newspaper! Bundles and bundles of newspaper cut to the appropriate size, with a 100-rupee note on top and on bottom to make the bundles look legitimate."

"They must have been pretty irate."

"Irate! If they had ever been able to locate Sayed Sahib they would have dismembered him, after first flaying him alive. But he was lucky, and he escaped that time too."

"So his good karmas haven't completely run out yet."

"Not yet." And probably they would not, so long as he kept Vimalananda happy. Sayed Saheb also pursued legitimate businesses. He always insisted on giving Vimalananda a cut of the money that he made from a sheik who had been impressed with Vimalananda's talents. A pattern developed: Sayed Saheb would offer, and Vimalananda would demur. Then Sayed Saheb would tarry until Vimalananda left the room for some reason and would then hide a bundle of bank notes for us to find later, Easter-egg-like.

Another of Vimalananda's associates, Sidi Saheb, used his restaurant as a cover for his various less-than-legal activities. I appreciated Sidi Saheb for teaching me the approved Bombay way of politely handing a cigarette or *chillum* to another smoker by using three fingers. Vimalananda did not appreciate it when from time to time Sidi Saheb would try to test him by bringing him some marijuana or hashish laced with arsenic, aconite or some other poisonous intensifier. Vimalananda would smoke it and be troubled by the mixture for a while, but he would send most of the noxious effect to Sidi Saheb, who would land in the hospital for a few days as a result. This would temporarily calm him down.

Sidi Saheb, who was a great worshipper of Shiva, built next to his restaurant a Shiva temple with a full-time priest to perform worship there. When the priest was discovered in flagrante delicto with a woman inside the temple there was a hue and cry whose volume increased the next morning when the priest's dismembered body was found inside the shrine. "Lord Shiva became angry at his fornication and punished him," was the explanation. It was rumored that when Sidi Saheb would put out a contract on a rival he would arrange to have the victim's corpse cooked into a curry which he would then feed, with due philanthropic fanfare, to the widows and orphans of the community. The poor loved Sidi Saheb, the police hated him, and his rivals feared him. To Roshni and me he was just one more act in the ongoing Vimalananda Circus.

One performer in that extravaganza whom I found personally distasteful was Shantilal the musician. Though he was a talented singer his speaking voice was almost as obnoxious as his personality, which grated through a paan-stained face that looked like nothing so much as a deteriorating jack-o'-lantern. I was easily peeved by the arrogance in his voice when he talked to me. It did nothing for my mood that every time he arrived I was forced to go downstairs and fetch him a cup of specially-prepared cardamom tea. I came to resent this service. When the ringmaster noticed my attitude he quickly set me straight.

"What are you so upset about?" Vimalananda asked with some vexation. "Your rnanubandhana with Shantilal requires you to minister to him. You are merely paying him back. Is that such a big deal? Pay him back now and get it over with if you don't want to have to come back and take care of it later. Besides, he is an interesting case study. Think about him for a moment. He is a walking hospital. Right now his main problem is arthritic knees. Modern medicine can give him relief in a few days, but within a couple of weeks he will relapse. Ayurveda would cure his problem permanently, but it would take at least six months—and he wants quick results.

"Now, I am interested in helping Shantilal because I too have a rnanubandhana with him. Forget past lifetimes; I owe him from when he helped me out at a very critical period in this lifetime. When my son Ranu died I had no money to cremate him. Shantilal had just been paid for some singing he had done and when he saw how miserable I was he gave me his whole paycheck. Only then I could burn my son. I paid Shantilal back afterwards, of course, but how can I forget that at a critical period in my life he was there to help me out? Other people might forget, but I cannot. I cannot adequately pay him back with money when his gift to me was more than mere money. Even Ranu, wherever he may be, still owes Shantilal a little something for arranging to dispose of his old body.

"I must pay Shantilal back for the sincere, compassionate love he showed in helping me out in time of need, but I don't want to take his karmas on myself. The main cause of his arthritis is a whore he has been visiting. He spends his money on that whore instead of on his family. Because of too frequent sex his ojas is very low and his joints have become weak. Too much sex usually hits you first in the knees.

"I have tried to persuade Shantilal to give this woman up. Even Nature has tried: Once when they were in bed together they were both burned, as if by a cigarette, in their private parts. But nothing has worked. Meanwhile, I have to think of the Law of Karma. Even though I don't approve of his activities I still owe him this rna. Healing him helps me pay off the rna, and I am interested in dying with a clean balance sheet.

"I think that the best way to handle this situation is to locate a spirit who has some rnanubandhana with Shantilal. The spirit of Shantilal's father, who was very unhappy because he could not see his son before he died, will do nicely. Now that he has become a spirit, he is ethereal and can enter Shantilal's body without Shantilal's knowledge. When? Near dawn, when Shantilal will be in a deep, deep sleep. Then, because the old man is in an ethereal form he can literally 'blow' the impurities out of the body, from the knee joints to begin with. Gradually, Shantilal's entire body can be cured.

"Now, Shantilal is still wasting his energy with that prostitute, so he may recreate his arthritis again—which will be his problem. Meanwhile he gets what he wants, which is relief. His father gets what he wants, which is to be with his son again. And I am also happy, because my rnanubandhana with Shantilal is settled without any overt action on my part."

Vimalananda shook his head. "Unfortunately Shantilal has never been able to prosper by knowing me. Last year I finally forced him to sing Kedara Raga for me, and now he has for some unknown reason started going on pilgrimages to all the holy places, which he has never done before. In fact, he has become so 'holy' that when I told him I was thinking of going to visit the States again he told me, 'Why do you want to go to that land of sex and meat-eaters? What is wrong with our own country?' He forgets that I have seen much of our own country while he was busy all during his life enjoying illicit sex.

"He doesn't ask himself why he has suddenly started going on pilgrimages, because he is too egotistical to do so. But he should think about it. He doesn't have sense enough to think of such a thing himself, preoccupied as he has been with women and what is underneath their saris. His mind is being forcibly turned towards God, so that at least when he dies he may remember God. That will give him at least a chance for a good rebirth—*ante matih sa gatih*—no matter what sort of evil karmas he may have done in this life."

"Pilgrimages are good then?"

"Very good."

"Is this why saints go on pilgrimages?"

"No, a good saint's mind is already turned in God's direction. Saints go on pilgraimge mainly to enjoy the presence of their beloved deities, and to purify the pilgrimage places where their Beloveds live."

"Which need to be purified after people like Shantilal visit them."

"Unfortunately, yes. Hence the theft of King Krishnadevaraya's emeralds from that temple in the South."

If I rarely welcomed Shantilal's advent I was inevitably delighted when Chotu, one of Vimalananda's oldest friends, would present himself at the door. Once arrived Chotu would roost with us for the day, ruminating over old times in Vimalananda's dairy and at his rock quarry. Like the day when Vimalananda nearly killed himself in a runaway truck; or the time when he was experimenting with explosives and accidentally sent a multi-ton rock scudding through the air like a cannonball all the way to the next island.

Roshni and Chotu used to be bridge partners when they played against Vimalananda and Mamrabahen. One day the two of them connived to stack the deck in such a way that they bid and made a little slam. Vimalananda, at first skeptical, became furious when they divulged their secret. Then he shuffled the cards himself, and thumped them down on the table. He had Chotu cut the deck and Roshni deal, and as soon as he picked up his hand he laid down a grand slam. Then he asked them how they liked it.

Chotu would always demand to be fed when he came, and Vimalananda would always oblige with his usual brilliant cookery. Vimalananda loved to cook, and fed his Beloved through the mouths of whatever people, animals, or plants might be handy. One memorable Vimalananda monologue began on such a day, when lunch preparations had just begun. Vimalananda was just saying, "There is no escaping the Law of Karma. Your karmas may provide Dr. Shantilal Mehta, India's premier surgeon, to care for you, or they may give you Dr. Gomes," when Chotu began to cackle.

"Dr. Gomes?" I enquired

"Dr. Gomes," explained Chotu, "was the manager of the rock quarry. He really handled the labor very well, but he was almost always drunk. Most of the time when the boss here would send me out to look for Gomes I would find him lying senseless in the gutter. Having him as a manager was convenient because he would treat the workers for free. Every injection he would give them would develop into an injection abscess, so when we would see laborers walking around rubbing their arms we would know that Gomes had been up to his tricks again."

At this point the doorbell rang and in flounced Miss Motibahen Bambhani, toting as usual her multiple containers of home-cooked lunch. None of us cared for Motibahen, not even Vimalananda, but giving proper respect to the food also implied giving respect to the cook, and we were at least polite to her until she left. Then Vimalananda said, as he stared at her vegetables, "Who does she think she is trying to fool? She makes a big show of her devotional service, but we all know what is on her mind. She pretends that she is chaste, but you can see from her face that she is enjoying regular sex, probably with her 'friend' Mr. Ginwalla."

"With him?" I asked unbelieving. "She must be fifteen or twenty years younger than that old Parsi."

"That is precisely my point. Do you think they are having an affair because she loves him truly? Forget it! She stays with him because he is so useful to her. She must have seduced him, probably after first feeding him to the gills, and now she has him dangling from her pubic hair. She thinks she can similarly entice me into bed with her and then tow me around by my cock. She doesn't know that I have escaped from much worse traps than hers."

He sighed. "I don't like to toot my own horn, but very few people with real spiritual credentials have ever been able to stay in Bombay for very long without being ruined. Even the best of sadhus have been affected, if only in a small way. And sadhus who have not perfected themselves are lost once they come here, completely lost. This is why I call Bombay *Mohamayi Nagari*, 'The City of Delusion.' Did you know that the very ground on which Bombay is built is cursed?"

"You mean that blessings and curses can affect land and water too??"

"Yes, they can. In fact, tradition states that the entire Konkan, the whole southwest coastal strip of India, is cursed. Whole districts of Eastern India are cursed. The Tapti River, which flows through Surat in Gujarat, is cursed.

"Specific villages are also sometimes hexed. Once I took some of my friends to such a village. During the day it was deserted, and seemed harmless enough. As night fell I drew a circle with a mantra around our group and warned them that I would not be responsible for what would happen to any one of them who dared to step out of the circle before daylight. That night the spirits of the people who had lived there when the village was cursed came to harass us. They harassed us all night long, shouting, 'Come one step outside and we will make you just like we are!' By morning my friends were thoroughly shaken, let me tell you. They forgot ever again to ask about the nature of spirits.

"In Bombay's case the curse affects the minds of everyone who lives here. Part of the effect comes via Bombay's gravity, part from our drinking water, but quite a lot of it comes from our food. All the food that is grown and cooked in this area is affected by the curse. When people eat this food they partake of the effects of the curse and fall prey to delusion."

"And this curse is separate from the faults of food that are due to the avarice of the farmer, the middleman, or the merchant, the unthinking hurry of the cook, and the forgetfulness of the eater."

"Yes, and those faults just reinforce the curse."

"This curse presumably makes people like Miss Bhambani and Mamrabahen worse than they normally would be."

"Naturally."

"It must disturb even the great Chotu," I said impishly, and Chotu bellowed in mock offense.

"Yes, even Chotu."

"Haven't you and your family also been affected by this curse?"

"For fifteen generations we escaped it and thrived in Bombay, thanks to the blessing that was given to our ancestor Seth Sagal Shah, and the protection that our own personal deities provided us. Our family traded with China and dealt in silk and silver. We made money fairly by adding a fixed 10% of cost to the price of our goods as our profit. We were pretty well shielded from misery until my father's brother's mind was degraded by greed and our fortune disappeared."

"How did that happen?"

"Well, as the eldest of three brothers my father was the head of their joint family. All went well until he inherited a great deal of tainted money from his father's brother, who had earned it through his legal practice. Shortly thereafter one of my father's two brothers demanded the division of the loot. The case went all the way to the High Court, where millions of rupees were wasted in legal fees."

"Amazing! The money that came in from legal fees contaminated even the good money you were making from your business. Is this a matter of the 'one bad apple can spoil a whole bushel' rule?"

"That's right. Bad money can easily contaminate good money."

"But still, if your family was protected how could your uncle's mind have become subverted?"

"He fell under the influence of his wife Putlibai, who was the daughter of a bookkeeper, an accountant—and what will an accountant think of other than accounts? She pestered him to get a full accounting of his share for so long that he was eventually led astray, and estranged himself from his brothers. She was doing this mainly for herself, of course, not for him. She had not grown up with money and had no idea of how to live with it. Why, when the car came for her on her wedding day to take her to the wedding she sat on its running board instead of inside it—she had never been in a car before! And what did she get for all her pains? She became notorious for being the destruction of the family fortune. How can I say notorious? Well, the High Court case was named after her and even now everyone who studies the law of joint families studies that case, the Putlibai case."

"I still don't quite understand how your grandfather's mind became so disturbed that he permitted the wedding to occur."

"Nothing is permanent, not even a saint's blessings. Obviously our period as a prosperous family had ended, and we had to disappear from the scene. Nature needed a pretext to terminate our prosperity using Putlibai as Her instrument.

"That does not amaze me. What does amaze me is that we could carry on in Bombay for as long as we did, for fifteen generations. Partly it was because we were householders. It is easier to try to neutralize this kind of curse when you are a householder. But when you are a sadhu the effects of such delusion are truly profound. If it is hard for you and me to avoid the negative influences of Bombay you can imagine how hard it must be for someone who has renounced the world in the pursuit of God.

"I personally know the truth of this story: There was a good sadhu at Mount Abu who once cured a Marwari lady of tuberculosis by using nothing but ash from his fire. After a year of, 'Please, Maharaj, just this once,' he finally agreed to come to Bombay for a brief stay with the lady's family. A good sadhu knows that he has to pay back his hospitality, in part to try to negate the effects of the food he eats. So this fellow told the lady's husband, a wealthy cotton merchant, to lock him in the toilet for twenty days. When he came out he told the merchant to buy all the cotton he could find in the market, and to sell it only when the sadhu directed him to do so.

"Before long the merchant had cornered the market. The sadhu had himself locked in the toilet again, this time for a month—no food, no water, nothing. When he came out he told the merchant, 'Sell!' He sold, and made one hundred million rupees. Do you know how much money that is? This was almost fifty years ago, so it would be equivalent to more than a billion rupees today (tens of millions of dollars).

"When a Marwari makes money he becomes deliriously happy, and this merchant was no different. He started to feed the sadhu with rich food cooked in *ghee* (clarified butter), and all the finest sweets. Before long all this heavy food had an aphrodisiac effect on the poor sadhu. All alone for years in the jungle, eating nothing but roots and fruits, drinking only water, and never toying with any woman. The result? He got entangled in an affair with the merchant's wife.

"When the merchant found out about the affair he was in a quandry. He couldn't insult the sadhu who had given him all that money, but he didn't want to go on being cuckolded either. He decided to be generous. So he hired a goldsmith's daughter and gave her to the sadhu to enjoy. Soon the sadhu was enjoying both her and the wife. He had been in the forest a long time, so he had plenty of appetite for sex.

"This went on for so long that the merchant finally became exasperated. One day he told the sadhu, 'You stop this nonsense now or I will call the police!'

"The sadhu lost his temper and said to him, 'Fool! Have you forgotten that I made you? My penance is finished now, true, but I have enough left for one last curse: Become a beggar!' Overnight the merchant became a beggar. Before long he died, still a beggar. The sadhu took the two ladies with him and supported himself and them for several years by making Ayurvedic medicines. But he was completely ruined as a sadhu, all because he came to Bombay in Kali Yuga.

"So many sadhus have been ruined that way here in Bombay. Sadhus are easily fooled by devious people. This is partly due to action and reaction—a sadhu is trying to reach the heights, so there is always a tendency to plummet—but it is mainly because he has become unsophisticated. He has begun to act like a child, or a dunce, or a demon, and like an animal he can be easily ensnared by those who are still sophisticated, particularly when they start to feed him.

"If you think about these things long enough you will eventually begin to wonder about eating."

"Wonder what?"

"Wonder, 'Why should humans and animals have to eat at all, if eating is such a dangerous business? Why shouldn't they live like plants and get all their nutrition from the sun?'"

"Well," I offered, "other than the obvious scientific reason, which is that you cannot get enough energy from the sun fast enough to move around as much as animals move around, I don't know."

"If we did not eat what would we do with the Law of Karma? Without karma and rnanubandhana how would the play go on? They are essential parts of the world. Do you have any idea of how thoroughly rnanubandhana permeates our lives? Look at this paint on the wall. Even it has a rnanubandhana with me. When that rnanubandhana is finished it will flake off, or I will get the idea to repaint it. Even the stones that make up the floor have a connection. How can you explain it except via the Law of Karma? Or think of a fly who is born and then dies within a few seconds. What sort of karma did it do to force it to take birth for such a short period, or even to take birth at all? It is all perfect when you consider rnanubandhana.

"And don't delude yourself to think that plants do not perform karmas. What do you think their roots are doing? While absorbing water they may be annihilating so many millions of bacteria. Every living being is subject to the Law of Karma, except the man who has learned to do without food altogether, either from the upper mouth or from the lower mouth, the genitals. Such a being is a *Vayu Ahari*; he lives on air alone, and gets his prana directly from the atmosphere and the sun. Until then, though, you have to eat, and eating is as much a karma as is collecting food to eat."

"So what is the answer?" A certain sense of resigned despair at the puissance of the Law of Karma flitted through my mind.

"To begin with, always try to eat with people who owe you food, karmically. To pay back a debt of money is very easy; such a rna is quickly dispensed with. But how can you ever pay back a debt of food? Once that food had entered your circulation and been converted into the very tissues of your body how can you ever requite it? Repaying such a debt could bankrupt you."

"Bankrupt your shakti, you mean."

"Yes. This is one of the reasons that a good sadhu will never take food from anyone on a regular basis if he can avoid it. This is also the reason I try to avoid eating other people's food."

"Except Motibahen's."

"This is my point. If I have a rnanubandhana with her that will best be fulfilled by eating her food then that's what I need to do. A sensible person who cannot avoid eating will take food only from those who have appropriate rnanubandhanas with him. That way he will not create new rnanubandhanas with people who might project their own delusions onto him. At least this way you can get used to one set of delusions and become immune to them. And besides, do I encourage Motibahen to bring her food over here?"

"No."

"Correct. I prefer to eat my own food, which I cook whenever I am in the mood to do so. Home-cooked food is always better for anyone, which is why Bombay has the dhabawalas." The *dhabawalas* are men who bring hot home-cooked lunches to hundreds of thousands of workers in Bombay every day. "You can look at the dhabawalas if you want proof that it is not impossible to live in Bombay without scuttling yourself. It just requires some effort, and the dhabawalas are willing to make the effort. They have never gone on strike and have never been known to molest any of the ladies whom they collect lunches from. And why not? Because they are devotees of Vitthala; they spend all their spare time worshipping Him. When their minds are full of Vittala how can any base thought disturb them?

"One reason I like to stay with Roshni is because I like to eat Roshni's food when I am not in the mood to cook. Roshni's food is tasty and does not disturb my mind. Why? Because she is serious about her sadhana. She repeats her mantra while she cooks, which gives the food a beautiful spiritual vibration. Also, she feeds me out of love and not because she wants to extract something from me, as most people do. There have been so many like Miss Bambhani who have tried to ruin me over the years, but I have not yet scuttled myself. I was born in Bombay; I know the ropes."

"But why then," I interrupted, "do you continue to live in Bombay, when staying here means you have to cope with this curse and all these other problems?"

"Ah, my boy, that is the Law of Karma," Vimalananda replied sadly, his gaze drifting momentarily off into the distance. "I have my karmic debts to pay off. There are so many types of rna: debts to your parents, to your teachers, to the knowledge itself. One type of debt is to the place you were born in. Once I've paid off all these debts, goodbye! But until then I have to remain. When your foot is trapped underneath a stone you don't pull it out abruptly, if you want to preserve your skin. You lift the stone carefully, little by little, and little by little you remove your foot, ever so slowly until it is freed."

"What about the people who come along and try to step on the stone while you are trying to remove your foot?"

"Well, you have to be prepared for them. Years ago my Junior Guru Maharaj came to me and said, 'You had better watch out, babuji—he always called me 'babuji'—someone is trying to use black magic to kill you.' I had not expected this. I knew I was in danger. In those days one of my aunts was trying to do away with me for my inheritance. She had tried to have me killed before, more than once, by various methods. But by using black magic she was upping the ante.

"I told him, 'Pah, Maharaj, don't worry about it even for a moment.' He loves me so much that he was very concerned for my welfare. But he knows I can take care of myself when it comes to black magic.

"I made some inquiries from an ethereal friend and found out that my aunt had hired Balam Bhat to do the work. I have always been blunt and outspoken, so I went myself to Balam Bhat and came to the point: 'Balam Bhat, you have been our family priest for decades. You presided over my naming ceremony, the first cutting of my hair, my first meal of cooked food. How could you ever dream of lifting your hand against me, when you have looked upon me as your own son?'

"At first he denied it, but when I persisted he flew into a rage and said things like, 'Who do you think you are? I will finish you off!'

"Then I said, 'All right, go ahead and try,' and went to the smashan. I told my friend, 'You were right, it is Balam Bhat who is trying to do me in. What shall I do?'

"My friend told me, 'Don't worry about a thing; let me handle it.'

"And how he handled it! Next morning there were twenty-three corpses to be disposed of: Balam Bhat and twenty-two of his relatives."

"My goodness!"

"Yes, it is unfortunate that it had to end that way, but Balam Bhat had asked for it. Besides, his death prevented him from incurring the karma of killing me."

"Didn't you have a mountain of karmas to deal with, though, from initiating the whole process?"

"Naturally. Even though I never explicitly told my ethereal friend to do in Balam Bhat and his whole family I did authorize him to handle the job, which makes me responsible for what happened. But I escaped from those karmas too. In fact, I offered all the victims as Nara Balis! Thank God for my mentors; they taught me how to deal with such things."

"So you were saved again, as usual."

"Why not? If you take life here as a challenge you'll decide to succeed at it or die trying. Why be frightened? But since Bombay is such a dangerous place, in so many ways, you have to be sure to always use stratagem (*kala*) instead of force (*bala*) to pay off your rnas, if you don't want to be sunk."

"This is why you are fond of Birbal."

"Yes, that is why. He was a master of stratagem." Out came a sudden chuckle that started a story: "You know, many of Akbar's courtiers hated Birbal passionately because he was so close to the emperor. They schemed day and night over ways to do away with him. No matter how hard they tried to catch him off guard he would almost always outsmart them. For example, when one of them told Akbar that Birbal claimed to be able to read minds Akbar asked Birbal to demonstrate this power. Birbal replied, 'Your Majesty's mind is much too subtle for someone like me to read. But I do know what everyone else is thinking. They are thinking, "May God bless our Emperor to rule over us in power and prosperity for many years, and may his fame spread far and wide." Isn't that so, O members of the court?"'

"I suppose all the courtiers then had to agree that Birbal could read minds."

"Could they do anything but agree?"

Three laughs merged above the remains of our food. We moved into the sitting room, and as he sipped his tea Vimalananda continued: "Another time they thought they had a foolproof plan. It required an accomplice, so they recruited the royal barber with the help of a huge sum of money. A few days later while he was shaving the sovereign the barber slyly said, 'You are enjoying yourself in such luxury here, my liege. Don't you ever wonder how your father must be passing his days in heaven?'

" 'What a fool you are!' said the emperor. 'How do you think I would be able to enquire about my father's status in heaven?'

" 'I know a magician, Great One, who can send anyone to heaven while still alive to check up on our dead ancestors.'

"Akbar stroked his mustache thoughtfully, then said to the barber, 'Make the necessary arrangements, and send someone immediately to bring news of my father.'

" 'I will do so immediately, master,' said the barber. 'But we must send an important and experienced person on this errand, someone who will know just how to act in heaven, and how to find your father.'

" 'Hmm,' said Akbar. 'Who do you have in mind?'

" 'Why, Prince Birbal, O Refuge of the World,' replied the wily barber.

" 'Birbal!' boomed the king. "Why Birbal?'

" 'No one in the world is as clever or wise as is Birbal, Your Majesty,' offered the barber obsequiously." Who else will be a fit ambassador from your court to the court of heaven?'

" 'Hmm,' said Akbar. 'All right, we will send Birbal. But just exactly how do you plan to do this?'"

" 'What we will do, your worship,' said the barber hastily, sensing success, 'is to put Birbal into a special house built in the smashan. Then we will set the house on fire. Because of the powerful mantras this great sage will recite, the fire will not kill Birbal. Instead, it will take him straight to heaven, alive and unhurt. I have been there myself on a visit, more than once.'"

"It sounds like the barber was embellishing the script."

"He was probably salivating over the bonus he had been promised if this scheme actually worked."

"Did Akbar believe any of this?"

"No, he knew what sort of man his barber was."

"Wasn't he concerned, though, that Birbal might not be able to escape and would be burned alive?"

"He probably was concerned, but he also knew that Birbal could take care of himself. Besides, he wanted to teach all his jealous ministers a good lesson, and he enjoyed keeping Birbal on his toes.

"Birbal arrived at court the next day to find a rude surprise awaiting him, for Akbar ordered him to get ready to go to heaven straightaway. When he heard the details of his mission, Birbal immediately recognized the nature of the trap and knew who had set it. He thought for a moment and then said, 'Your majesty, when I am ready to go to hell for you going to heaven will be a pleasure. But if I am to go I will need quite a lot of money to make my preparations.'

" 'You may have as much money as you need,' the Emperor assured him.

" 'Also, I will need time to make arrangements with my family before my departure,' said Birbal.

" 'How long will you need?' asked Akbar.

" 'Three months,' replied Birbal, and this period was granted to him.

"Now Birbal had some breathing time. He gave the money to his wife as insurance, just in case he should fail to escape. Then he set out to save himself. He began by planning out a tunnel from his house to the smashan. All night long he would dig to extend the tunnel, and each day he would work in the smashan preparing the hut he would need for his voyage.

"Birbal finished the hut and the tunnel just a few days before the end of his three-month grace period, and on the appointed day he called on the emperor and declared that he was ready to go. He was then taken in a gala procession to the site and entered the hut, which was just atop the tunnel. The pyre was then lit, and the fake saint began to chant ostentatiously. Birbal had cleverly selected the greenest wood that he could find, so it did not take long for a mammoth cloud of smoke to accumulate. Under the cover of this smoke he crept off through the tunnel to his own house, taking care to fill in the mouth of the tunnel as he went. He waited there silently in hiding for three months, without cutting his hair or beard. In fact, he was gone so long that Akbar was worried that he actually was gone for good."

"Well, Akbar had put him in mortal danger, so it served him right, didn't it?"

"Yes, I'm sure Birbal deliberately prolonged his stay in hiding, just to rub some salt in the wound. When Birbal did return to the court after those three months he made a sudden, dramatic appearance there. Akbar embraced him in ecstasies and said, 'How are you, my dear friend? How was your trip, and how is heaven?'

" 'It was a long, dangerous trip, your majesty, but somehow I managed it and made it back here to give you a report.'

"'Don't keep me in suspense, Birbal, tell me how my saintly father is doing!' said Akbar loudly, playing to the gallery.

"Oh, he is very well, my lord. All is fine in heaven.' And Birbal went on and on, describing the glories of the angels and the luxuries of the blessed. Then he concluded with, 'But there is one thing...'

" 'What is it?' said the emperor anxiously, while all the courtiers showed their great concern.

" 'Well,' said Birbal, 'Your father gets everything he wants—good food, elegant clothes, beautiful women, all the comforts. He is sad only about one little thing.'

" 'What is it?' asked Akbar impatiently.

" 'He told me not to bother anyone about it,' said Birbal, stretching out the suspense.

" 'But now that we have found a way to reach heaven,' said the Emperor, 'we can send anything to him from here,' and all the courtiers nodded in agreement.

" 'Welllllll,' said Birbal, 'your papa said that he gets everything he asks for in paradise—except for a good shave.'

" 'What,' asked Akbar amazedly, 'has no dead barber yet reached heaven?'

" 'No, sire,' said Birbal, 'none so far.'"

I had to interrupt: "What an insult to barbers!"

"Well, Birbal really wanted to make the barber twist in the wind. He said, 'Look at my appearance, lord. Wouldn't I have shown myself to you clean-shaven if I could have located a barber? I even had trouble recognizing your father, his hair and beard were so long. He sends you his blessings, and he did request you—if it was no trouble . . .'

" 'What request? Tell me immediately!' Akbar thundered.

" 'Your father asked you to send him a good barber, if you can spare one.'

" 'But of course,' said the emperor grandly. "In fact, let us send this noble barber of ours! It is he who showed us how to reach heaven, where he has visited more than once, and he deserves to return there now.' And that was the end of the barber."

"Did Akbar really have him burnt alive?"

"It's hard to say. Some versions of this story say that the barber was burned. Others say that he avoided becoming a nice roast by confessing everything, that he then spent most of the rest of his life in the dungeon for attempting to murder Birbal. Whichever was his fate it served him right, which proves my point. If Birbal had tried to use force to save himself his enemies might have been able to gang up on him and kill him. He used deception instead and was saved. I myself use deception freely so that, God willing, those whom I love and who love me will continue to be saved."

"Even the ones who fight with you?" I tossed in provocatively.

"Yes, even people like Roshni and her family."

Roshni, who had meanwhile arrived home from work and was knitting peacefully in her chair, glowered at him lovingly over the tops of her glasses.

"Doesn't deception imply karma?"

"Karma is everywhere. But if you deceive people without literally lying to them, like Yuddhisthira did—*naro va kunjaro va*—then the karma is much reduced."

Asvatthama, the son of Guru Dronacharya, shared his name with an elephant. When during the great war that the *Mahabharata* chronicles it looked as if Dronacharya had become unconquerable Krishna directed that the elephant Asvatthama be killed and that a rumor be spread that it was Asvatthama the man who had died. After hearing this rumor a worried Dronacharya came to Yuddhisthira, whose name was a byword for truthfulness, to ask if his son were dead. Though the two of them were fighting on opposing sides Dronacharya, who was Yuddhisthira's weapons guru, knew that Yuddhisthira would not lie to him. Indeed, Yuddhisthira loudly replied to Dronacharya, "Asvatthama is dead!" Then, following Krishna's instructions, he added in a whisper, "*Naro va kunjaro va* ("either the man or the elephant"). Dronacharya, who could hear only the first phrase, wrongly concluded that his son was dead. This knocked all the fight out of him and he was himself killed shortly thereafter, which benefitted the cause of Krishna and Yuddhisthira. But even though they represented the letter of the truth Yuddhisthira's words had the impact of a lie. Due to that deception Yuddhisthira had to start walking on the ground again, instead of walking a foot above it as his unwavering adherence to truth had previously permitted him to do. If that was the effect of "much reduced" karma I hated to think what might have happened to Yuddhisthira had he performed overt *guru droha* by openly lying to his guru.

"What I really don't understand about this story," I said to Vimalananda, "is why the karma for lying didn't cling to Krishna instead of to Yuddhisthira when it was Krishna Who forced Yuddhisthira to violate his personal dharma by speaking what amounted to a lie."

"It is very simple," replied Vimalananda. "Krishna didn't identify with His advice to Yuddhisthira and Yuddhisthira self-identified with his deception to his guru. Krishna was *Yogeshvara*, the Lord of Yoga. Karma rolled off Him just like water rolls off a duck's back. He would create a situation, watch it being played out, and still remain a karmically-aloof observer. Wah, Krishna, wah! No one can know every aspect of Your play!"

Vimalananda glanced momentarily at Roshni and Chotu before continuing: "Anytime you act with self-identification, my boy, a karma is created no matter how noble your motives. And rnanubandhanas can multiply rapidly when your karma involves putting your neck out to try to save someone. This is something I know only too well. My dear old friend Faram, Roshni's late father, really loved me and used to look after me; I in turn had looked after him. I even postponed his death more than once. You can ask Chotu about it if you like." Chotu nodded gravely.

"Unfortunately, towards the end of Faram's life something happened to his mind—it was Mahakala, Death Personified, inciting him—which made him become very argumentative with me. Not only that, but he cheated me more than once. I warned him several times that he was playing with a live wire, but he persisted. He had always been obstinate.

"After a lot of this there came a time when I had to go to Delhi. I warned him not to eat fish, beef, or pork while I was out of Bombay. You see, he was a Parsi, and they eat everything. I also exhorted him not to curse me in any way, because I knew this would be the excuse Mahakala would use to take him away. And I told him, 'I know you're not going to listen to me, and that you are going to eat meat and abuse me. Don't worry, though; even after you die I'll look after your children.' I promised his wife and children that as soon as he died I would come immediately no matter where I was, and I made them promise not to remove the body until I got back. Then I left.

"After finishing my work in Delhi I went down to a certain sacred mountain in South India. No females are permitted there, and no men dare ascend it except on one day during the year—Maha Shivaratri. On that day they go up the mountain early in the morning, worship at the Shiva temple, and come right back down. It is not a mountain for the curious or the insincere."

When I first visited this mountain, a month after Vimalananda's demise, I discovered that on one Maha Shivaratri not too long before two hundred men had lost their way in the fog and died of exposure. It was apparently a hell of a job to get all the corpses down off the hill.

"There are dense elephant jungles on this mountain, filled with plenty of dangerous wild animals. There is also a huge bull elephant; he and I are the best of friends. Whenever I would go there he would sit near my fire and play with my hair using his trunk. He is not really an elephant, of course; he is something else entirely.

"There I was on the mountain sitting at my fire, keeping track of all my loved ones 'long distance' with its help, when suddenly I saw the dead body of my friend Faram. Then I saw that he had eaten fish and had called me all the foul names in the book ending with, 'I never want to see his blessed face again.' As soon as he spoke those words he keeled over and died. When I saw that I knew he was dead."

"You didn't wonder if the vision was true?"

"The fire never lies. Ethereal beings may stretch the truth on occasion, but the fire will never be false to you. I was sure he was dead and was plunged into despair. How would I ever get back to Bombay in time for the funeral and fulfill my promise to his children? The promise was the action. Now I was experiencing the reaction. I have always believed that promises are meant to be kept, but here I was on a mountaintop far from civilization. I would have to hike down to the road, catch a bus to the nearest town, and then find a train or plane. All that would take at least a couple of days. I had to be in Bombay in a matter of minutes. It looked impossible.

"While I was worrying over this my elephant came up to me, nuzzled me with his trunk, and asked, 'What's wrong?' I explained everything, and he told me, 'I'll see that you get back to Bombay immediately. But first you must promise me that you won't bring this fellow back to life.' He knew my habits. There was no other way, so I promised him. Another promise, another karma.

'Close your eyes,' he told me. When I opened them I was on the landing in front of my friend's flat in Bombay. The door was open.

"I was a little shaken to think that I was back in Bombay, but there was no time to lose. I rushed into the flat. Roshni met me and with tears in her eyes told me that her father's body had just been taken away just minutes before. I rushed to the Tower of Silence in pouring rain. Ask Roshni; she'll tell you." Roshni nodded her assent.

"The Parsis believe that the fire is polluted if it touches a corpse. They neither bury nor burn their dead. Instead they expose them in a place called the Tower of Silence for the vultures, crows, rats and other scavangers to polish off. They perform plenty of rituals before the body is taken into the tower— otherwise how could the priests make a living?—but once the bodies are laid out on the marble slab inside they get eaten all the same.

"According to their traditions no non-Parsi is supposed to even look at the body of a dead Parsi after it has been washed. I have never cared for such bigoted traditions, so I went in straight away. I think I am still the only non-Parsi ever to enter a Tower of Silence. All the mourners were shocked, but no one could prevent me. I went up to my friend, kissed him, and said, 'Well, old boy, I couldn't save you this time. But don't worry, I'll look after your kids.' The priests sat there aghast, but all they could do was to cough suggestively while they fanned themselves, as if their fire was troubling them greatly. I ignored them; how can you take a priest seriously if he is afraid of his own god?"

Roshni, Vimalananda and I would drive past the Tower of Silence from time to time, mainly on those occasions when we went to eat at Tehmul's residence up on the top of Malabar Hill. The building in which Tehmul stayed used to be part of the garden of the bungalow in which Vimalananda was raised. Half-a-dozen high-rises have since sprouted in place of the bungalow, and the hyper-rich now pay $10,000 a month or more per flat for the privilege of calling Malabar Hill home.

"Was it your promise to Faram that has made you a part of Roshni's karmic family?" I queried, glancing over to see if this would get a rise out of Roshni.

"No," Vimalananda scowled with a grin, "I already had a complicated rnanubandhana with Faram which brought me into contact with Roshni and her other family members long back. But this promise did cause me to have to begin to stay with this family in order to save it. And that has led me into a whole new series of rnanubandhanas, with Parsis in particular.

"The original home of the Parsis was ancient Persia, which some of us call *Vasistha Bhumi* ('the land of the Rishi Vasistha'). Ages back Vasistha Rishi went there and taught the Persians how to worship the fire. For centuries they practiced their religion sincerely. Then almost 1400 years ago Caliph Omar led the Muslim invasion of Persia, and who abetted his conquest? The Zoroastrian priests! They betrayed the secrets of the country's defence to him. The Zoroastrian religion has some good techniques for obtaining siddhis, and had these priests could have supported their own king by using their occult powers. If they had Omar might never have been able to conquer their country. But the priests were tempted by money, and invited Omar in. And what was the first thing he did after conquering Persia? He executed all the Zoroastrian priests that he could catch! He was an orthodox Muslim, and like many orthodox Muslims he sincerely believed that all other religions are false and should be eliminated. The few Parsi priests who survived fled to a ship and sailed here to India. What other country would take them? Our doors are open for everyone: the Parsis, the Jews, everyone. India is a big garbage dump for all the religions that have no place left to go."

"So the Parsis landed here and started to thrive again."

"When they reached India they landed at Sanjan in Gujarat. On hearing of their arrival Jadavji Rana, the king of that region, sent them a bowl filled to the brim with milk. That was his message to them. The message read: 'My kingdom is already full of people, and there is no space for any more.'"

"Now what to do? Fortunately one of the Parsis, Dastur Meherjee Rana, had a brilliant idea. He took some powdered sugar and added it very carefully to the milk, so that no drops spilled out. Then he gingerly laid some rose petals onto its surface. This was his reply to the king: 'Your majesty, we are so few that we will blend in among your people as easily and invisibly as this sugar dissolves in this milk, and like the sugar our presence will "sweeten" your domain. Like the rose petals we will provide you beauty and fragrance without being any burden.' When Jadavji Rana 'read' this message he said to his advisors, 'This is a man of subtle intelligence! This is the kind of man that we need in our kingdom. Let them remain!' And ever since then the Parsis have done well for themselves here in India, because of stratagem, not strength."

"You seem to really like the Parsis in spite of all your ranting about them and their priests."

"Does he have any choice?" an aroused Roshni asked sharply. "He is part of our family now, he has become one of us!"

"Quiet, you!" growled Vimalananda affectionately. "I may be one of you, but I will never become a Parsi, even if I could. And I can't, thank God, for even though the Parsis are a miniscule minority they still refuse to permit conversions. At least they have not abandoned their fire worship. But very few of today's Zoroastrians have any real affection for their god the fire. Most of their priests have forgotten the true meaning of their religion, and all they have left are empty rituals. But they do know how to extract money from the people. Suppose some part of your body is removed in an operation. Whether it is a wart, a finger, or your penis, an orthodox Parsi must spend thousands of rupees for special ceremonies for it. And what is the holiest substance to Parsis? Bull's urine, processed in a certain way, which is also fabulously expensive. Was any of this Zoroaster's idea? No, it was all an invention of the priests. The priestly classes in every religion are always scoundrels."

"If Zarathustra's religon has been despoiled by its priests hasn't Hinduism also been distorted by some of its priests?"

"Our Vedic religion has been absolutely *ruined* by its priests, the Brahmanas. Could the Muslims have ever sacked Somnath (a famous Shiva temple in the Western Indian state of Gujarat) if the priests there had not been corrupt? No. Even now most priests do all sorts of rituals without having any idea of what it is they are doing or why they are doing it. But they still collect hefty fees for what they do, just because they are Brahmanas. It was the lawgiver Manu, who came along much later than the Vedas, who invented all this business of Brahmana supremacy. You don't find it in the original Vedic tradition. Back in Vedic times the Rishi Vishvamitra even decided that there was no need for any restrictions about the intermarriage of castes after he married a *dasyu* (a member of an outcaste group). Vasistha Rishi opposed him in the beginning but eventually had to go along."

"Why?"

"Vishvamitra was born a Kshatriya, and had been a king before he became a Rishi. His motto was, 'Succeed, or die trying!' Vasistha was a Brahmana, and Brahmanas always believe in going with the times, because they are beggars. If they don't give allegiance to the king how will they be fed? It was the same principle that led the Zoroastrian priests to try to strike terms with

Omar. Even now the Parsis will support whoever is in power—first Jadavji Rana, then the British, and now the Indian government. They are opportunists, just like our Brahmanas. Vasistha, who was a Rishi, cared nothing for money, fame, or any other such worldly prize; but he did understand that discretion is the better part of valor. He followed Vishvamitra's lead and eventually he even became the guru of a group of dasyus: the Zoroastrians!"

"You don't have much value for Brahmanas, do you? Haven't they done any good at all?"

"I draw a distinction between the real Brahmana and the Brahmana by birth. Listen to this Sanskrit *shloka* (verse): 'By birth everyone is a *shudra* ("one who performs laborious work"), by samskaras you become a *dvija* (a "twice-born"), by learning you become a *vipra* ("one who shakes with ecstasy"), and by knowing the Absolute Reality of the Brahman you become a *brahmana*. I bow down again and again to those true Brahmanas, the knowers of the Absolute. It is they who have made India a spiritual powerhouse."

"But you don't seem to care much for *Adi* (the original) Shankaracharya."

"Although the original Shankaracharya was a famous philosopher and evangelist of Vedanta, he was still only a *jnani* (a knower of Reality). He was not a *vijnani*, a Siddha. Although he was a great man he did commit some blunders."

"Everyone makes mistakes."

"Yes, but everyone does not set out to change the world. At first Shankaracharya was afraid of Ma. He preached that Shakti was to be rejected and only *Shaktiman*, the Controller of Shakti, the Ultimate Absolute, was to be worshipped. He somehow forgot that it is utterly impossible for Shaktiman to exist without Shakti. Ma had to teach him some hard lessons, in Kashmir and Mithila—remember the Mandan Mishra episode?—before he could realize this."

"What happened in Kashmir?" When Shankaracharya went to Mithila to challenge the knowledgeable Mandan Mishra to a debate he was on the point of winning when Mandan Mishra's wife insisted that Shankaracharya debate her as well. She began to speak on sex, a subject about which the celibate-since-birth Shankaracharya knew nothing; he had to plead for a recess to learn about it. Leaving his physical body in a cave he used his astral body to reanimate the physical body of a recently deceased king. He then used that body to learn all about sex with the willing help of the women in that king's harem, who thought their liege had risen from the dead. After he had collected enough knowledge Shankaracharya departed the old king's body, reinhabited his own, and returned to Mithila to complete Mandan Mishra's defeat. But Mandan Mishra's wife got the last laugh when she reminded Shankaracharya that he had taken a vow of celibacy. Becaue he taught that only consciousness is real it was his consciousness that had taken that vow.

But in order to win the debate he had enjoyed sex with his consciousness, albeit in another body. Thus he had broken his vow.

"Well, Shankaracharya was touring around in Kashmir, preaching his doctrine of non-duality and saying all sorts of wrong things about shakti. Now, Kashmir is a stronghold of Tantra, one of Ma's chief haunts. The very word *Kashmir* is a corruption of the Sanskrit *Kshira Bhavani* ('Ma's Milk'), which is the snow that falls there. Shankaracharya was playing with fire when he went there to insult Ma.

"One morning as he was about to begin his talks an old woman came up to him and said, "My son, quit this slander of Shakti; were you not born from a woman?" When he started to preach to her she disappeared.

"At noon the same thing happened, but with a middle-aged woman; he ignored her too. In the evening, a young girl came to him—notice how She has been getting younger with each appearance—and told him, 'Great Sage, if you don't stop defaming Shakti you are headed for big trouble.' Still he ignored her—until he developed a sudden, intense case of diarrhea which lasted until he woke up out of his stupor. What was Ma to do? She had tried to persuade him to change, but when he refused she realized that he was set in his ways and that only a good karmic purge would do. After taking all this strong medicine that Ma had to dish out to him Shankaracharya finally learned his lesson. Now the Shri Chakra, the greatest *yantra* of Shakti, is worshipped in all his monasteries.

"But God wasn't finished with Shankaracharya yet! Next Lord Shiva took His turn with him. Shankaracharya was bathing one day in the city of Banaras, which is Shiva's home, when Shiva took the form of a *chandala* ('dog eater'; the lowest of the low) and splashed some water on Shankaracharya. No Brahmana likes to be touched by an outcaste or by anything that has touched an outcaste, and Shankaracharya said testily, 'Oh chandala! Take care of where you splash!'

"The chandala said, 'Maharaj, of what should I take care? You teach that the world and everything in it, including our physical bodies, are unreal. The touch of that water on your flesh must therefore be equally unreal.'

"Shankaracharya was momentarily taken aback by this answer, but then he recovered and said, 'I was speaking not of your body but of your samskaras.'

"To this the chandala replied, 'If my samskaras reside in my body how can they be any more real than it is? And besides, are we not bathing in the *Ganga* (the River Ganges), whose waters remove all sin? If this is true its waters must negate my evil samskaras as soon as they touch me.'

"All of a sudden Shankaracharya realized with Whom he was talking, and fell at the chandala's feet. Shiva had taught him yet another good lesson.

Shankaracharya was still discriminating on the basis of purity and impurity, and Lord Shiva showed him that the real purity is internal."

"Which I suppose is one reason why Lord Shiva drinks poison."

"Yes. Lord Shiva drinks poison, but never lets it fall lower than his throat. That way He is always in perfect control of the poison's effects. Lord Shiva is called *Nilakantha* ('Blue-Throat') because all the poison He has consumed has turned His throat blue. Do you know the name of the poison He drank on the occasion of the churning of the Ocean of Milk?"

"*Halahala.*"

"Which is a word composed of two other words: *hala* and *ahala.*"

"Which basically mean 'shaking' and 'nonshaking.'"

"Right. Mahakala kills you by shaking you—shaking your Kundalini's self-identification with your body and mind. If you could remain unshaken under all circumstances you would never need to die. Aghoris take intoxicants to teach themselves how to remain unshaken. If you hallucinate or lose control in any other way when you take an intoxicant know that the intoxicant has 'shaken' you. *Halna nahi* ('never get shook') should become your mantra.

"The best way to to avoid being 'shook' is to follow the path of bhakti. Shankaracharya was a jnani. He knew how to do a few things, which is nice, but he forgot that God knows how to do all things. Isn't it better to surrender to God and let God take care of everything? When Mirabai was given poison by her husband she first offered it to her beloved Krishna, Who transmuted that poison into nectar. *That* is the way to live your life, the way that Baba Chandal Das lived his."

"Baba Chandal Das?! The 'Servant of the Dog-Eater' Baba?"

"Yes, Baba Chandal Das was the great devotee of Lord Shiva in His *chandala* form. Can anything be low to a dog-eater? When this saint would arrive somewhere he would shout to the Lord, 'Baba Chandal Das! My bhakti, Your shakti—Your inspiration, my words—that's how my work gets done! Baba Chandal Das!'

"Baba Chandal Das was the real thing. But Shankaracharya was not Baba Chandal Das and only learned a little from what Lord Shiva as *chandala* could have taught him. Shankaracharya's fundamental error was to spend his life moving about in India defeating people in debate."

"How so?"

"He taught *Brahmam sat, jagan mithya*—the Absolute is true, the Relative is false. But if the Relative is false and you are debating in the Relative you are just raising falsehoods to defeat falsehoods. What is the use in that? Moreover, if as he taught there is only one Reality of which everyone is a part then who is debating whom? Can the One debate with the One?"

205

"Uh, well, no. But at least Shankaracharya wrote a number of beautiful hymns, like the *Saundarya Lahari* and the *Bhaja Govindam.*"

"Yes, he wrote beautifully, and I appreciate his work. But was he fully aware of the implications of what he wrote? Take just one example: he wrote, 'Bad sons are sometimes born, but there is no such thing as a bad mother.' Esoterically, this is quite true. Reverse *atma* (soul) and you get *mata* (mother). The Atma or Soul never leaves the body as long as it is alive; in fact, the body only lives because the Atma is within. This makes the Atma a good mother. Her son is the body, which is always a bad son because it is always getting embroiled in the *samsara*. But no matter what evil thing the body does its mother the Soul never forsakes Her child. Only a physical mother can be a bad mother. A woman who has not realized the Ma within her is a bad mother. So in the mundane sense Shankaracharya was wrong in saying there is no such thing as a bad mother. In Kali Yuga there are bad mothers everywhere, though bad sons are still more common than bad mothers."

"I'm not sure that I see your point here."

"My point is this: The writer of that verse was himself a terrible son. Shankaracharya was still a young boy when he wanted to run away from home and take the vows of *sannyasa*, renunciation of the world. His mother naturally refused him permission to go out and ramble about the world. Any real mother will feel protective of her child, and Shankaracharya's mother was a good mother.

"But Shankaracharya was determined to leave, and decided on a different course of action. He had been sent into the world for the specific purpose of establishing the orders of sannyasa, and he had been born with certain siddhis to assist him in this work. One day when he and his mother were down on the banks of the river he used his siddhis to trick her. He created an illusory crocodile which gripped his leg firmly and began to drag him into the river. You know the ferocity of crocodiles.

"Shankaracharya called out to his mother in mock fright as the fake croc tugged him down, 'Ma! Ma! Save me! Give me permission to take sannyasa and then I can be freed! Otherwise I am doomed!' Can you imagine the intensity of the terror that attacked his mother in that moment? It was like a knife being pushed into her chest and slowly rotated in her heart. She had no choice; she gave him permission, and off he went."

"So he deluded her, which sounds a lot like what Yuddhisthira did to his guru. But what was Shankaracharya supposed to do? He had to go and fulfill his mission, didn't he?"

"But did he need to to cheat his own mother in order to achieve his purpose?" There were other ways in which he could have made her agree. It was he who decided to force the issue, to have things his way; that made this act his personal karma. And look what has happened because of this evil karma! His followers have imitated his example, and from Shankaracharya's time onwards most of these followers have been bad sons, and cowards. Because they are afraid to meet the world on its own terms they hide from it behind their saffron robes. What was the use of Shankaracharya's siddhis? They got him what he wanted in the short run but tarnished the results of his life's work in the long run. This is the difference between a jnani and a vijnani. Let this be a lesson to you: Unless you are very, very cautious the use of siddhis may have consequences that can persist for centuries or even millennia."

Dusk was falling as Harshbhai appeared at the door to end our afternoon of private audience. As I listened to this "spiritual child" describe to Vimalananda his marriage plans for his daughters I reflected on the siddhi warning. Here was Vimalananda, judiciously employing his many siddhis to keep slowly, slowly disentangling himself from his rnanubandhanas with people like Harshbhai. Trying simultaneously to keep from losing his skin and to avoid generating any new karmas as he dispensed with his expiring ones, Vimalananda lived with an elan and a *joie de vivre* that could only arise from his moment-by-moment recollection of the imminence of death. Love of the Deathless was the root from which blossomed his love of we who are doomed to die, and I found that the deeper I probed his love the less of a bottom I could find to it.

chapter seven
REPAY

OUR GREATEST TINGLE during the Spring 1979 Bombay Race Meeting was the announcement of a blessed event: the debut in our world of Stoney's first foal, a colt whom Vimalananda promptly named Redstone. The spring's most unusual incident, however, occurred midseason when Vimalananda felt obliged to exercise yet another of his siddhis to deal with Behram, the husband of Shernaz and father of Arzoo. He had unexpectedly and inopportunely arrived in Poona from Iran just in time for Navroz, the ancient Persian New Year's Day which many Indian Zoroastrians still celebrate.

Vimalananda hurried to Poona a few days after Behram's arrival and summoned me to Shernaz's place. I arrived there to find him sitting in Shernaz's front room, smoking and remonstrating with her. Seeing me he smiled with some cynicism and said, "What a life I lead! Is it my job to take responsibility for everybody's evil karmas? If you knew this family's whole history you will know what I am up against. Here is Behram, a boozer and womanizer, who used to spend all his money on himself and beat his wife if she asked for any. When it came to the stage that he had decided to desert Shernaz and the children I lost my temper. I came here when he was out and told Shernaz to give me two matchsticks, which I tied together with the help of a mantra. Then I told her, 'Take these. If Berham can ever leave you as long as you have these I will cut my own throat.' That was more than twenty years ago and they are still together—and so are the matchsticks." Shernaz proudly showed them to me.

"Times were tough then, so I told Shernaz, 'Every day when you go to the little corner where you pray you will find ten rupees. That money is meant for food for you and your children. As long as you don't misuse it you will continue to receive it, every day of your life. The day you start to act funny that will be it.'

"For years ten rupees appeared daily. She used that money to help keep the wolf away from her door. Sad to say, though—and I'm saying it in front of her—her intellect eventually became perverted . . . "

"No, it wasn't that way at all, I . . . "

"Yes, perverted," he insisted as Shernaz strove to defend herself, "I know what I am saying; don't try to deny it. Did you or did you not start to waste that money on liquor, meat, cinemas, and other such trifles?"

"But that was all for the children . . . "

He cut her short: "But you were told it was for food, weren't you?" But she continued to try to justify her actions, and Vimalananda, seeing her uncontrite, overrode her and continued: "One day there was no money there. She came to me to complain but I told her: 'I warned you. If you have bungled I can't help it. Now you please do without.'

"And what about your *maasi* (maternal aunt)," he said to Shernaz, annoyed, "what about that dog that I gave her? When she and her husband," he said to me, resuming his narrative tone, "were passing through a difficult period I gave them a small dog. So long as the dog remained in their house their fortunes skyrocketed." Back to Shernaz: "And what about the day your maasi cut her wrists? It was only because the dog set up a howl that people were drawn there and saved her."

Back to me: "Unfortunately she or her husband made a mistake one day, and the dog disappeared. It ran away and was never seen again. Then she came to me for another dog. But I told her, 'You don't get *halvah* (an Indian sweet) whenever you please. You had your chance, but you were not meant for it. Now forget it. Anyway, your work was done; you got your prosperity. Now hold onto it.'

"After I joined the matchsticks together for Shernaz, Behram got a steady though low-paying job and started sending money to his family. Eventually he went to the Middle East, where he started to earn lots of money. Now he has just landed here and has announced that he will never go back to work. He feels it is time for him to relax and live off his children's earnings.

"But the rest of the family doesn't agree with him! Ask Shernaz, Arzoo and Sohrab and they will all say, 'Send him back!' So now what should I do? If I don't interfere he will become comfortable here and their lives will become hell—and I hate to see that happen to any of my 'children.' And if I do interfere, well, there'll be some karma involved. We'll see what happens."

Our talk then turned to horses and courses until Behram made his appearance. That night we drank Behram's Scotch. The next night Vimalananda, who had carried a bottle of Scotch with him from Bombay, brought his bottle over to Behram's house to offer him drinks in celebration of his return to India. After a couple of drinks Behram's tongue began to wag freely as he explained all about his plans for his retired life. He was in the midst of describing his plans for his new life in India: "Sohrab has a job, Arzoo will be out of school and then can get one, and we should be able to live comfortably on what they earn . . . " when all at once Anjaneya entered Vimalananda's body and gave that poor wretch a withering glance. Behram stopped short in mid-sentence, looking dazed and confused. After a few moments he pulled himself together and said, "No, no, my children should continue as they have been. I will go back and see that they enjoy life at my expense. I am proud to be able to take care of them."

All of us spectators were simultaneously stunned and pleased, but we took great care to show no emotion whatsoever lest Behram change his mind yet again. Vimalananda left for Bombay the next day, and it was only a couple of weeks later, after Behram had departed for the Middle East and Vimalananda had again appeared in Poona, that anyone even dared to mention the events of that evening.

Vimalananda was bemused by the whole episode: "What an unexpected turn of mind, to have him change his tune in mid-sentence, eh? Isn't it amazing what Anjaneya can do?"

"Are you sure you didn't put something in his drink?" I asked suspiciously. "It was so sudden, such an abrupt reversal of plan."

"Are you talking out of your wits, Robby? You were drinking from the self-same bottle; you tell me. Was there something in the Scotch?"

"You know very well what I mean."

"Well, nothing physical was added to the Scotch; what was added came from elsewhere. The nice thing is that Behram thinks he changed his mind on his own. That pampers his ego and makes it less likely that he will change his mind again any time soon. He's the kind of guy that likes to make a decision and stick with it, even if it is the wrong decision. Tamasic people are like that."

Shernaz then began to thank Vimalananda profusely, but before she could pick up steam he derailed her: "Anjaneya did the job, didn't he? You'd better thank him instead of me. But now that your work has been done it's time to have some fun. Let's celebrate! If you had gone to some sadhu or fakir to do your work he would have taken your money and had you bow down to him and told you to leave. But I am not a sadhu or fakir. I don't think you'll ever run into any sadhu or fakir who is such a toy to be played with."

"So is that what you are," I asked, pleased, "a toy?"

"For those who love me I am. Everyone in the world is miserable, all due to the effects of their karmas. Why not try to lighten things up?" At Vimalananda's instance we then enjoyed some drinks, helped him cook a delicious dinner, and ate together in the midst of what he called a "laughing spree."

Poona allowed Vimalananda time for repose and enjoyment, for fewer people came to disturb him there than when he held court in Bombay. He thus had more occasion to "lighten things up" in the lives of his local loved ones. He delivered his tales with impeccable timing, and his jokes were always in good taste even when they were vulgar. Many of them came from the classics: "Sanskrit is a *samskaric bhasha* ('well-bred language')," he would say. "Even its dirty jokes are refined. Here is one: Once a young man wanted to make a living in the king's court as a poet. No one values poets nowadays, but back then kings made careers in poetry possible. When he arrived at the gate that led into the king's palace, however, the young man found that he never could seem to catch the king's attention. The monarch was always surrounded by big important pundits who did not like any competition and so kept the king perpetually entertained.

"After a few days of this disappointment the young man became frustrated, and wrote on the wall at the king's doorway a bit of Sanskrit verse. I'll translate it for you: 'The king's door is like a vulva, and the pundits are like a penis. They enter and exit over and over again, enjoying great bliss, whereas I, like the testicles, must remain outside, eternally squeezed between the two.' Note the hidden meanings as well. By comparing the king's entranceway to a vagina he also meant that the king was being 'screwed' by the ambitious pundits. By comparing the pundits to a penis he was suggesting that they had all the intelligence of a pizzle; and so on.

"When the king emerged from his palace the next day and saw this bit of doggerel he was struck by its sophistication, and asked who had written it. When the young man was produced in front of him he congratulated him on his sagacity, and welcomed him into his court as a full-fledged poet."

Another favorite 'anecdote' of Vimalananda's, which is even today current in Banaras, addresses the important question of, "How can we know that the famous poet Kalidasa was the he-man of his time?" The answer: Kalidasa was one day wandering partly clothed along the banks of the Kshipra River when he came across a bathing beauty. Embarrassed, the girl quickly covered her breasts with one arm and her pubic region with her other hand. Simultaneously overcome with both passion and inspiration, Kalidasa composed a poem in a flash: "O fortunate young woman, who can cover with but a hand her nakedness. O unfortunate Kalidasa, who even after grasping himself with both fists finds that two fingersworth yet remain to be concealed." Wide-eyed at her vision of his manhood the girl cried, "O my yes!" We thus have her testimony that he was the he-man of his time.

Vimalananda's teasing was also refined, particularly when he turned his truly unrivaled linguistic abilities to its service: "Once I lived in a place where my neighbor woman, whose name was Dhani, used to do nothing but gossip all day long. I used to call her 'Mrs. Wagging Tongue.' At first I ignored her, but finally I got so fed up with her that I decided to teach her a lesson. You know how much I like to sing. Well, on that day I composed a new song: *Dhani gappa mare, sa ni gappa mare?* ('Dhani is gossiping, why is she gossiping?'). And I began to sing it loudly.

"When Dhani heard it she confronted me. She asked me what I thought I was doing. I told her innocently, 'All I am doing are my vocal exercises. You know how to sing an Indian scale, don't you? The scale goes *sa re ga ma pa dhi ni sa.* I am singing nothing beyond those syllables.' And then I began to sing even louder and more ardently, *Dha ni ga pa ma re, sa ni ga pa ma re? Dha ni ga pa ma re*, and so on, until it was obviously that she understood me. I had no trouble with her gossiping thereafter."

Vimalananda also liked to demonstrate that ordinary speech can also work wonders when delivered judiciously: "On one occasion, as Dr. Martand and Arzoo and I were driving outside Poona, we saw so many grapes growing alongside the road that we became hungry for some. We stopped where we saw a heavy-set man working in his vineyard, and Dr. Martand insisted on approaching him for us. But when he tried to show off his knowledge by telling the man how unhealthy he looked the fellow told him, 'Get out of here! I won't sell you anything!'

"Then I told Arzoo to go address the farmer as *pahalwan* ('wrestler'), and to speak to him sweetly. When she did he told her, 'Not only can you have some grapes, my girl, you can have them for free. But don't give any to him,' he said, pointing at Dr. Martand, 'he can't have any at all!'"

Vimalananda obligingly placed his talents for communication at my service when during June and July of 1979 I busied myself with my mother, who had come all the way to India to see for herself my condition and to scrutinize the crowd I had fallen in with. Vimalananda, who regularly reminded me of my rnanubandhana with my parents and the need to fulfill it gracefully, acted the part of host to perfection. Training all his powers of persuasion on her to convince her of the worth of my studies, he first saw to it that her Bombay tour was a red-letter one, and then set us up with his friends and associates in other parts of India. She and I travelled together pleasingly for five weeks, capping our circuit with a last visit with Vimalananda. She departed confident that I was indeed in good hands, and I could then reoccupy myself with racing.

There was no laughter in Repay's life that summer, for he had lost his gonads and was now expected to start earning his corn bill. He had dropped down into Class V-B during the period when he was quaffing semen, but now that he was not preoccupied with his penis his interest in racing improved dramatically. By August 1979 he had become fit enough for a hard gallop, which Vimalananda and I drove down to Poona to watch. We had Tehmul schedule it before dawn, that we might watch Repay work without betraying his fine fettle to any tipsters or gamblers. We followed the same procedure at every morning gallop: a swing by the stables to inform Tehmul of our arrival and to make a quick check of the horse before he set hoof to track, a sprint to the stands to take split timings for each furlong (200 meters) of the run on our stopwatches, and a sprint back to the stables to check the horse's wind and legs as he highstepped his way back in. When the grandstands at a racecourse are empty and a single horse flies down the track bunching and releasing his muscles in the exhilaration of the sprint, you can hear otherwise inaudible sounds that can be remarkably diagnostic: the whoosh of the galloper's body, the thud of his hooves, even sometimes the grunt of his breathing. On this occasion we both heard and saw Repay do an outstanding job, and no one but us seemed to notice him. The chances for a quick coup seemed to multiply before our eyes.

Too enthused over our prospects to immure ourselves immediately in the hotel, we breakfasted idly at the Club, and then reported again to the stables. It was a beautiful forenoon at the Poona racecourse, a day to laze now that the early work was done, and Dr. Lobo, a friendly chap who was one of the official Turf Club veterinarians, was sitting in Tehmul's yard. As we chatted Dr. Lobo, who knew a little of Vimalananda's reputation, delivered up a challenge by saying that he doubted that all the stories that people told about yoga could be true. Vimalananda glanced at me and I shrugged my eyebrows. Then Vimalananda asked Dr. Lobo to participate in an experiment. He asked the vet to feel his pulse, and while the man was holding his arm Vimalananda went on and on about 'the many unusual things that happen here in India.' The vet was a man with a dark complexion. When I saw his face become rapidly pallid I knew Vimalananda must have stopped his heart. This being a tremendous strain on his body I waited only a few seconds before wigwagging to him to quit. He took pity on me and complied, and as he continued to chatter away cheerily his pulse normalized and the color drained back into Dr. Lobo's face.

In short order the vet found some excuse to depart, and after he left Vimalananda laughed in triumph. I objected, perfunctorily: "Was the showing off really worth the exertion?" He dismissed me with, "His reaction was priceless! It was worth it just to see how funky he became. Now he will not prattle on about what yogis can or cannot do!"

Racing in Poona was much more relaxed than racing in Bombay. For one thing, the track is not an island of green in a sea of skyscrapers. In Poona broad tree-lined streets cluster about the racecourse and in the east the Empress Gardens offers a thickly arboreal vista. For another, Vimalananda being an outsider in Poona had only a few chums to chat with among the local racegoers. One of the more notable was Poona's premier Chinese dentist, Dr. Wang, who came like clockwork every week with his wife. We appreciated his occasional work on our teeth and would always smilingly offer whatever information we had when he would smilingly ask which horse we favored.

But the Wangs did not sit with us, for in Poona there are but two enclosures: the Members-cum-First and the Second. When Mr. Lafange had been our trainer we sat just above the Members' boxes, on benches which though outfitted with green cushions were benches nonetheless. With our switch to Tehmul our status improved, for he had a friend whose box was almost never used. We now arrived on the Poona racing scene like royalty circulating among commoners and seated ourselves among the hoity-toity rather than with the hoi polloi. To the right and below our box was the Indian gentleman who had married his European nurse; a bit further down sat the Maharaja of Gwalior. Far in front perched the wanton Bapsi, who cuckolded her seemingly-impotent husband Porus with whomever she could. The box to our immediate left was usually occupied by the face and the cigar of the delightful Maharaja of Mudhol, our favorite among the racing gentry, with whom we spent many a pleasant evening over drinks and dinner after a rousing afternoon at the track.

Perhaps the least aesthetic of all our new neighbors were the obese Mr. and Mrs. Kumar and their obese daughter. They wanted nothing to do with us po' folk, which made me qualmless about dubbing them "The Three Pigs." Mr. Kumar's had a way of perpetually rejamming a gigantic cigar into his mouth which wonderfully reinforced, like the apple wedged into the maw of a suckling pig destined for the oven, his own porcineness. Even Vimalananda had to agree that they were three of the most hog-faced humans that he had ever seen. Rumor had it that they made most of their money in "leather currency," which is a euphemism for the flesh trade. It was easy to believe this to be true of the cruel-mouthed Mrs. Kumar, a sow who looked hungry enough to cannibalize the runts from her litters.

We enjoyed many a joke at the expense of the Three Pigs, but there is justice in the world, alas, and soon it became evident that Mr. Pig's beady little eyes had homed in on Repay. Kumar was no fool, and he could see that Tehmul and Vimalananda were cooking up a masala for the first win of Repay's career. Kumar had access to vast sums of money, with which he could drive Repay's odds down with or without us; this made it a case of "do we want the porker inside the tent pissing out or outside the tent pissing in?" Tehmul brokered an agreement and Kumar did all the betting. When Repay scooted comfortably home in September as a 7-to-1 outsider I sat silently watching when Kumar arrived at the stables after the race, plunked down our share of the winnings (about $10,000), and left to tend to his other "investments"—or perhaps to dip his snout down into his dinner trough. His profit would have been at least ten times as much.

I opened my jaws after Kumar had departed: "Repay did a pretty good job of 'repaying,' didn't he?"

"Why do you think I agreed to name him 'Repay'?" replied my contented mentor. "I knew that he had that sort of rnanubandhana with me, that he would be able to amply requite his debt, to redeem his pledge. I had no fear of that; I was only uncertain of when it would happen."

"And you're not sorry Kumar got in on the deal?"

"Not at all. Remember, always distribute your karmas! Sharing your good fortune creates 'partners in karma.' It spreads the karmas around, which reduces your own burden significantly. It is better to share your profits with good people, but if you can't have good people then use whoever God sends you—within reason."

Back at the hotel redemption continued to occupy his mind: "We have been talking casually about 'repaying' and 'redemption,' but do you know what a serious matter it is to redeem? Probably the best blessing, the best gift of all, is the gift of fearlessness. When you give fearlessness you tell that person, 'Look, you must endure your karmas yourself, but I can give you the courage to endure them.' In fact, there used to be a sadhu in Girnar named *Abhayananda* ('Bliss of Fearlessness') who was ready to give fearlessness to anyone. He didn't last long, though; how could he? Such behavior interferes with the Divine Plan.

"Fearlessness is a great gift, but it is not redemption. To redeem is to say, 'I will bear your karmas for you'—that is the highest. Very few can do this, or even want to do it. Ramakrishna Paramahamsa, who was a truly great saint, only took someone else's karmas onto himself in three cases; only three and no more. No, in all history there has only been one Redeemer: my Jesus. And He had to pay very dearly for taking all those karmas; He had to be crucified.

"A few years ago the Pope came to Bombay. Imagine that! I went with Roshni's mother to see what would happen. There was a mammoth crowd. The Pope drove up in a Mercedes, got out, raised his arms and said: 'Repeat after me: That which should have been done by me has not been done by me; that which should not have been done by me has been done by me.' We all repeated it. Then he said, 'By the power of the Holy See I absolve you of all your sins.' Roshni's mother was very impressed by this drama. But does the Pope really think that it is so easy to absolve everyone's bad karmas? When Jesus tried to do the same thing for the Jews He died a most terrible death. This sort of painless absolution of sins is all a delusion, as of course is the infallibility of the Pope. Were the Popes who ordered the Crusades or the Inquisiton infallible? Or the ones who ordered young boys to be castrated just because the church wanted some sopranos? Was any of this Jesus's idea? I think not!"

"Jesus was the One Who could say, 'Come unto me.' He was the only One Who ever could say, 'Come, I will suffer for your sins. Forget them, and live a new life.' One look from those eyes of His and you melt completely; all Rajasic and Tamasic qualities gone! These Christians harp on sin, sin, sin, and by teaching sin they perpetuate it. They have forgotten the teachings of Jesus. Jesus said, 'Forget your sins! Give them to Me, and I will wipe the slate clean. You start over, and never return to them.' And what agonies He had to endure for taking so many karmas over onto himself; my God! But He endured them willingly. Not even Krishna did what Jesus did, and that is why I will ever love Jesus. He was the real thing."

Rajas and Tamas represent respectively an overwillingness to act and an underwillingness to act. Should both these tendencies disappear from the mind nothing would remain but that state of quiescent clarity known as Sattva. I too love Jesus dearly, and my own emotions rose to my eyes as I watched the image of His smiling face coalesce in my mind. How deep was His clarity, to sustain Him throughout His ordeal! I asked, "Didn't Jesus also die on the cross to teach us to bear each other's karmas in the same way that He bore ours, even to a reduced degree? After all, if you love your neighbor as you love yourself, and if everyone is really an emanation of God, then you are ultimately me, and when I take on your karmas I am effectively saving myself."

"That is precisely what so many great Christian saints have done. They have worshipped Jesus by giving back to Him the gift that He gave to us: the gift of compassion. It's so wonderful!

"Jesus could create such a marvelous play, such an unprecedented lila, because He was the emanation of a certain Rishi. All the avataras of Vishnu, like Rama and Krishna, emanated from Rishis; in fact, Jesus and Krishna emanated from the same Rishi. But look at the difference in their play! Krishna was *Gopala*, the 'Protector of the Cows.' 'Gopala' also means 'He Who Restrains His Senses,' and this is what Krishna taught to His devotees. Jesus, on the other hand, was the Good Shepherd."

"Does this mean that if Krishna was the Gopala Jesus was the *Meshapala*, the 'Protector of the Sheep'?"

"Yes, I suppose so." He laughed, momentarily nonplused. A rare pleasure! My *bon mot* had struck home. Then he shot back, "But why Shepherd? Because of the sheep mentality of most people. Like sheep people easily become lost in the wilderness of the world; that's why they need protection. Jesus is prepared to go out into the wilderness to save those sheep, to search for them until He finds them and carries them home with Him. This is why there is no need for intelligence in Jesus's religion, which is one of pure love. In fact, you can hamper your progress in your sadhana of Jesus if you use your intelligence. You simply have to be ready to follow wherever Jesus leads you, in perfect faith that as long as you follow Him you can never go astray.

"The main difficulty with everyone is that they have no faith. Jesus used to complain about this all the time. One way in which animals are better than humans is that they have no conscious self-interest; they do not anguish all the time about what happened in the past and what is yet to come. Humans forget that God is doing everything for us already so there is no need to prepare anything. It is only because of our ill fate that any of us worry. If we didn't worry we would be perennially happy, for we would accept whatever God chose to offer us according to our karmas. But the weight of our karmas interferes with our happiness. It causes us to plan and anticipate, and to experience anxiety and worry. Look at how we planned Repay's run and worried over its outcome, when we could have just relaxed and let God do His work. This is why a saint is the only truly happy person. A real saint has gone beyond worry.

"Here is a question for you: Millions of people bathe in the external River Ganga every day. All the authorities—the saints, the holy books—say that bathing in the Ganga washes away all evil karmas. If this is true, why hasn't everyone who bathes in the Ganga become enlightened by now, since you become 'enlightened' when your karmic burden is lightened?"

"Good question. I don't think I know why."

"Well, let's assume that you bathe in the Ganga and come out perfectly clean of karma. But as soon as you step out onto the riverbank you start to perform new karmas again. *Voila!* There you are, right back in the soup. Which is why there is no escape from the Law of Karma until you change your consciousness. Though we humans imagine that we are in charge of our destinies, fate is far more complicated than you can even imagine."

He settled back with his Scotch while *ghazals* emanated from a well-worn recording of the famous vocalist Begum Akhtar, and began again: "Even Rishis can be bewildered by Fate. Consider the case of Parashara Rishi, who was an authority on Jyotish, a subject which is nothing more nor less than the knowledge of the play of the Nine Planets. One day as Parashara walked through a fishing village on the River Yamuna a realization struck him like a flash of lightning. He saw that a child conceived at a precise instant on that day would become one of the greatest of sages, and a redactor of the Vedas. A

Rishi can give birth to thousands of beings simply by wiping the sweat off his forehead, but Fate perverted Parashara's mind. He decided instead that he should enjoy sex with a girl himself and father a child through copulation. That this would cause him to lose the fruits of centuries of his penance did not occur to him at the time.

"As Fate would have it a beautiful young fishergirl named *Matsyagandha* ('Fishy Odor') was standing nearby. She was not an ordinary girl; her father was a king and her mother was a celestial damsel who had taken the form of a fish as the result of a curse. She was called Matsyagandha because her body smelled fishy."

"Only to be expected if your mother was a fish. But I read that her real name was Satyavati."

"Maybe so, but I call her Matsyagandha. Parashara hailed her and explained his plan without any hesitation. Back then people were not as embarrassed about such things as they are today. The girl readily agreed to his proposal, thinking, 'To become the mother of a Rishi's child is a rare blessing!' But she told him, 'It would not be good to enjoy sex right here in the village. Let us go out onto the water.' So they got into a boat and went out into the middle of the water, where Parashara created an island for their lovemaking. Then when Parashara approached her she said, 'The sun is witnessing our play. Please request him to turn away.' So darkness fell at the precise moment when the child had to be conceived.

"After their loveplay was over Parashara was pleased, and granted Matsyagandha the boon of permanent body fragrance. Thereafter she was called Yojanagandha ('She Whose Fragrance Can Be Smelled at a Distance of Eight Miles'). The child, who was born the same day that he was conceived, was Krishna ('Dark-Complexioned,' due to the darkness at his conception) Dvaipayana ('Born on an Island') Vyasa ('The Complier'), who is commonly known as Veda Vyasa ('Veda-Arranger'). Besides reworking the Vedas Vyasa composed a number of literary masterpieces, including the great epic of more than 100,000 verses known as the *Mahabharata*, and the sublime story of Lord Krishna that is the *Shrimad Bhagavata*. If Vyasa had never been born, none of these stories would ever have appeared in our world. But isn't there something strange about all this?"

I drew a blank.

"Why did he ever get the idea to write these stories down? Does a Rishi have any use for the written word? None whatsoever; he always prefers to use Para Vani—telepathic speech. But Vyasa was the son of a Shudra girl; Shudras are mired in the awareness of the physical. It's natural; they have to toil hard to earn a living, and their minds focus on their toil. The only reason that the thought of a physical representation of his knowledge even entered Vyasa's mind was this mundane influence on his intellect. Vyasa was born as he was because Nature wanted that all this should be written down for the benefit of those of us who live in Kali Yuga. Parashara's intellect was perverted precisely because Nature needed the offspring of a Brahmana and a Shudra to redact the Vedas and create the *Mahabharata* and the *Shrimad Bhagavata*. Isn't Nature wonderful?

"This is another reason why the caste system is no longer applicable in its original form. Even today no orthodox Brahmana will accept into his family any son of a Brahmana father and a Shudra mother—but that was Vyasa's parentage. And what he accomplished no other Brahmana could accomplish. Does this make him better or worse than an orthodox Brahmana? Neither; he is what he is, a distinguished immortal.

"Vyasa was once asked to father children on two princesses. He agreed, and like his father before him decided to use sexual intercourse instead of some other method to fulfill his commitment. Why did he prefer physical sex? Because his consciousness was affected, even if minimally, by the fact that he had been born as the result of a sexual act. Look at how deep and long-lasting the effects of sexual karma can be! Unfortunately, Vyasa's preference for sex created some unintentional karmas of its own. The first princess was so terrified by Vyasa's imposing demeanor that she paled when he embraced her. This caused Pandu, her son, to be born pale. The second couldn't endure Vyasa's intense aura and closed her eyes, which caused her son Dhritarashtra to be born blind."

"Was it that simple?"

"It is that simple when you're dealing with a Rishi. A woman takes a man's shakti when he ejaculates into her, and nourishes that shakti with her own shakti to create a child. When the woman and the man have more or less equal shaktis, as they usually do when they are both humans, their shaktis will have a more or less equal influence on the child that results. But a Rishi is not a human. A Rishi is a super duper who has super shakti, and only a similarly super woman will be able to unite with him as an equal. Any human woman who tries to unite with him will function mainly as the mold into which he pours his shakti. If the woman doesn't open herself to him completely the Rishi's shakti will not penetrate her evenly. The 'mold' will thus not be completely filled, and wherever the shakti doesn't reach there will be a deficiency in the child."

"O.K."

"The first princess was then requested to return to the Rishi for another try at producing a healthy crown prince. But she wanted no more of that, so she secretly sent her servant girl instead. That girl had no inhibitions, and was so pleased that she was going to enjoy sex with a Rishi that she surrendered herself completely to him. Through her surrender some fragment of Vyasa's super-qualities were transmitted through her into the fetus, who became her son Vidura. These qualities made Vidura clairvoyant from birth."

"Let me get something straight," I interrupted. "The *Mahabharata* war was fought between the five sons of Pandu and the one hundred sons of Dhritarashtra, which means that it was actually fought between two sets of grandsons of Vyasa."

"Precisely."

"My my, a civil war that was really all in the family. No wonder Vyasa had to write the *Mahabharata*; it was a family history."

"Yes, but there's more. One of Pandu's five sons was Yuddhisthira. Another was Arjuna, the great warrior who was Lord Krishna's great friend. Arjuna sired Abhimanyu out of Subhadra, Krishna's sister, and Abhimanyu died in the war because Arjuna had stolen Subhadra. But before his death Abhimanyu had impregnated his wife Uttara with Parikshit, and it is thanks to King Parikshit that we have the *Shrimad Bhagavata*. The *Shrimad Bhagavata* was transmitted to Parikshit by the Suta, who heard it from the great Rishi Shukadeva, who heard it from his father Vyasa."

"Shukadeva being yet another of Vyasa's children."

"He was the most amazing of Vyasa's children, for he was not born from a womb. He escaped the taint of copulation by springing instead from the rubbing of the *arani*, the sticks used to create fire for Vedic sacrifices. This is why he is called *Araniputra* ('Son of the Arani'). Because Shukadeva was not born as the result of sex he did not discriminate according to gender. Celestial damsels would throng to him as he roamed naked in the jungle. They would feel completely relaxed with him because he never showed the slightest trace of awareness of their sexual identity. But if Vyasa approached the women would quickly hide, for they could feel that he saw them in a different way."

"Even though he was also pure-minded."

"Yes, even though he never lusted after them, Vyasa's awareness was ever so slightly sexual, because of his birth. That was enough to make a difference.

"Vyasa created the *Shrimad Bhagavat* for his own pleasure, and for the pleasure of his son Shukadeva. He might never have released it to the world had he not wanted King Parikshit to obtain *moksha* (liberation) by hearing it. Parikshit had been cursed by a Rishi to die by being bitten by a snake. As the king listened to the Suta recite the *Shrimad Bhagavata* for seven days Parikshit released his attachments to the world, and welcomed death when it arrived."

"Why would Vyasa want Parikshit to obtain moksha?"

"Why wouldn't he? He wanted to wind up the karmas of that branch of his family, and what better way to do it than arrange for his great-great-grandson's liberation?"

"How would that help the family?"

"Haven't you been paying attention? If you can help yourself out by doing Pitri Tarpana for your ancestors, you can help your ancestors out even more by becoming liberated. It's the same sort of thing."

"Are you saying that Vyasa released the *Shrimad Bhagavata* into the world just to save his great-great-grandson and to improve his family's karmic pedigree?"

"That was his immediate purpose, but by doing so he also ensured that it would be handed down to posterity."

"How did that happen?"

"The Suta, who was present when Shukadeva recited it to Parikshit, later retold the *Shrimad Bhagavata* to a group of sages who had assembled in the Naimisharanya. These sages and their disciples were responsible for introducing the *Shrimad Bhagavata* to the rest of the world. You should only read or listen to the *Shrimad Bhagavata* when you are ready to abandon, temporarily or permanently, the mundane outside world, as those sages who had withdrawn from the world into the Naimisharanya did."

Though the *Naimisharanya* is a forest in North India, some writers have proposed that the word also be read as the 'forest' (*aranya*) of 'blinking' (*naimisha*), which would refer to the inside of the human body. A sojourn in the Naimisharanya would then imply a turning inward of the normally outward-pointed senses, to heighten awareness of the inner cosmos.

"And like Parikshit," Vimalananda continued, "you must cultivate your interiority if you hope to enter into the inner, astral world of the *Shrimad Bhagavata*. What does *Parikshit* mean?"

" 'Tested.' " Technically speaking, *parikshit* means "surrounding, extending," as heaven and earth extend out to surround us, but I knew that Vimalananda was thinking of the word *parikshita*, which means "tested."

"Exactly. Only when a disciple is completely tested is he eligible to be taught. You should understand from his name that King Parikshit had gone through the grind. He had become thoroughly prepared for the knowledge that was given to him. Anyone who wants to get the real juice out of the *Shrimad Bhagavata* needs to be prepared to self-identify with King Parikshit when they listen to it. When you hear it you need to be able to temporarily 'become' Parikshit, which you will only be able to do if you have been painstakingly 'tested.' "

"So King Parikshit was delivered this wisdom via the Suta. I thought *suta* was just a word that means 'son.'"

"Suta does mean son, but it also means the metal mercury, a woman after delivery, a charioteer—it has so many meanings. Because it is a Sanskrit word all these meanings must be related. You are a student of Sanskrit; you tell me what these things have in common."

"Well . . ." I was stuck.

"They are all carriers. They transport essence around in the world until it reaches the point where it can manifest. Think it over."

"They deliver things? They represent the cosmic courier service?"

"Yes, they deliver. The Suta's father was the charioteer Romaharshana, who was personally killed by Lord Krishna, seemingly by mistake but in fact as a blessing."

"How was that?"

"Have you ever heard that 'the father lives on through the son'?"

"Yes."

"A child transports the essence of its parents—their genes and chromosomes. Romaharshana was not pure enough to act as a fit vehicle for the *Shrimad Bhagavata*, but when Krishna killed him He purified him. This made Romaharshana's son pure enough to deliver the *Shrimad Bhagavata* to the world. Romaharshana must have already been quite an advanced soul, otherwise he would not have even been fit to be killed and purified by Krishna Himself. But he was not quite pure enough. What does *romaharshana* mean in Sanskrit?"

"Horripilation; goose flesh; the body hairs stand on end."

"Which is caused by cold, fear or some other strong stimulation, including spiritual experiences. Romaharshana was highly evolved, but not quite evolved enough to transport this particular shakti."

"Did Lord Krishna's act of killing Romaharshana serve as a sort of Pitri Tarpana for the Romaharshana family?"

"Yes, if you want to look at it that way."

"Well, Romaharshana's death paved the way for the transmission of the *Shrimad Bhagavata*, which has benefitted millions of people. Some of those benefitted are bound to bless it and its writers, and some percentage of those blessings are bound to flow to those who arranged to 'transport' it to us, no? Sort of an ongoing astral royalty payment?"

"I think we can be confident that the *Shrimad Bhagavata* has enormously benefitted everyone who was involved in bringing it to light in our world, and all their ancestors too. It particularly benefitted Parashara, who by siring Vyasa made it all possible. And Parashara certainly needed some benefit, to help counteract the karma that he incurred by inseminating Matsyagandha. While it was very good for the world that Vyasa was born, it did not do Parashara much good to have enjoyed sex with a Shudra. That act entangled him in the play of her karmas, which were of a pattern quite different from his. These karmas forced Parashara to take birth again to experience the repercussions of his act. Every taint, and especially that of copulation, must be erased."

"Is copulation such a big taint, then?"

"Do you remember that you once asked me about a certain Vedic sacrifice in which beer is brewed?"

Months had passed but he had not forgotten. "Yes, the Sautramani sacrifice. I had asked you why the ritual text specifies that the barley from which the beer will be brewed must be taken from a eunuch."

"Here is your answer: The Rishis who created this sacrifice intended the barley to be collected from someone who is a born eunuch, not from a eunuch who has been cut. A natural eunuch has not even been exposed to the energy of sex, much less the experience of copulation. Such a person has the potential to be the living embodiment of the *nirakara tattva* ('The Principle of Formlessness'), because what is sex about if not the creation of new forms?"

"But even a natural eunuch only has the 'potential' to embody formlessness. Didn't the Rishis expect the sacrificer to locate someone who had realized this formless potential, and not just find any old barley-donating natural eunuch?"

"Exactly! Our Rishis were not fools. What possible use would an ordinary eunuch have been to them? The essence is what counts, not the outer garb."

"Is this the sort of thing that Jesus was talking about when he talked about someone who makes himself a eunuch for the kingdom of heaven's sake?" I was thinking of Matthew 19:12.

"Yes, the same sort of thing. And remember that in this context Jesus says that this is not for everyone, but only for those who properly understand it."

"Maybe for those 'who have the ears to hear'?"

"And the eyes to see."

"Oh. . . So—the copulation taint was strong enough to force Parashara to take birth yet again."

"It was. Unfortunately, Parashara's personality in his new body was rather dull. His father tried to teach him many things, but he failed. Exasperated, he asked his son, 'Why can't you learn anything I try to teach you?'

"The boy answered, 'I do not know, father. I suppose it must be due to my past karmas.'

"The father got wild on hearing this from his dull-witted son and told him, 'You had better get out of here and go do Gayatri!' So the boy went out into the forest.

"Here the father's intellect had become perverted. How could the boy help it if his past karmas were bad; and what father would begrudge his own son his past faults? Parents are there to forgive, not to curse. But without this order from his father the boy would not have succeeded so quickly. His father probably did not know it, but it was important for Parashara to do sadhana of the sun. Why? Because Parashara had deliberately sent the sun away on that fateful day when he had impregnated Matsyagandha."

"So even that was a karma?"

"A big karma; you have to be very careful when you play about with the Nine Planets. The boy found himself a good spot and made a hammock of twelve stout ropes made of creepers, braced with three cross ropes. He strung his hammock between two trees and sat on it, with a fire beneath him, repeating the Gayatri Mantra. Every year he cut one of the ropes, so that after eleven years he was balancing on a single strand.

"When the twelve years were almost up he said to himself, 'If I don't succeed at perfecting this mantra and obtaining a vision of the sun god at the end of these twelve years there will be nothing to do but put an end to myself.'

"But deities are not cruel; they are really very kind. On the last day of his penance he saw a sadhu approaching him. The sadhu had an unworldly, effulgent glow about him, and the boy realized that the sun himself—*Surya Narayana*—had come to him in human form. He bowed to the sadhu, and Lord Surya said to him, 'So, my boy, what do you want?' The boy asked for proficiency in astrology. Why would he ask for this? Both because of his previous expertise in astrology as Parashara—that influence was beginning to re-exert itself—and because who better than the sun to teach astrology?

"Lord Surya then blessed him, saying, 'Your name will last as long as the sun and moon exist as the greatest-ever expert in astrology.' Then he disppeared, and the boy left his place of penance. When he reached his home his remorse-filled father recognized him, and tearfully said, 'I don't care if you are a dud or not, please come and embrace me.' When the boy responded with a beautiful Sanskrit verse his father realized that, yes, he had indeed been doing Gayatri all this time, for Gayatri is the mother of Sanskrit. Over the course of time this boy, now called *Mihiracharya* in honor of his penance (Mihira is one of the names of the sun), became a gem at the king's court.

"When the king's son was born the court astrologers were directed to predict his fate. All except Mihira said that he would live long, rule wisely and enjoy his glory. Mihira alone said, 'The boy will die at age three, on such-and-such a day, at this exact moment, gored to death by a *varaha* (wild boar).'

"The king said, 'Please, Mihira, everyone else has said something good. Kindly change your prediction.' Mihira replied, 'I am sorry, O king, but it will happen as I have said; that is his fate.'

"The king built a seven-story building and put his son on the top floor surrounded by a strong guard so that no boar could get to him. When the appointed day arrived the king and all the jealous courtiers were waiting to see Mihira proved wrong and then punished.

"Exactly at the given moment the flagstaff on the seventh story of the building broke and fell on top of the little boy who happened to be playing below it. Atop the flagpole sat the king's symbol, which was a boar's head made of solid gold and weighing more than eighty pounds. When this image landed on the child one of its golden tusks pierced his chest, and he died instantly.

"Mihira said to the shocked king, 'O king! The boar has killed the boy, as I predicted.'

"The grieving king replied, 'You are the wisest of my astrologers. In honor of this brilliant prediction I now name you *Varaha* (boar) *Mihira*.' Varaha Mihira went on to write many well-known treatises on astrology. His system follows Parashara's system, though, with only a few principles changed here and there."

"As it should; after all, he had only recently been Parashara."

"But even Varaha Mihira did not realize the significance of his words when he spoke of Fate. Fate is so powerful that even things which seem impossible become possible if they are meant to be. And even stronger than Fate is God. As they say in Hindi, *khuda meherban to gadda bhi pahalwan*: 'If God is gracious even a donkey can become a wrestler.'"

"Even Jhendu Kumar?"

"Quit baiting me! Yes, even Jhendu Kumar, but if and only if God went along with his schemes. But God is not going to do that, so you can forget about it. And so can he!"

"At least God was kind enough to let Repay finally repay you."

"Nature is very kind to me, Robby; that's all I can tell you, that Nature is very kind to me. There is absolutely nothing that God cannot do; I have seen it over and over again in my life. This is why I pray day and night for more bhakti, because I know that if my devotion is truly sincere God will provide me with whatever it is that I need.'"

After my final grueling round of university exams in the fall of 1979 I proceeded to Bombay and watched Repay continue to win there during the early months of 1980. Around this time Vimalananda bought Onslaught, a reliable Class I horse, from Boman Hansotia. Though Onslaught had never won for

Boman he did for Vimalananda, and it began to seem that all our horses were doing well—even Bajarangi, the last horse Vimalananda had purchased when he kept his string with Lafange. In one of his more egregious transgressions, Lafange had insisted that Vimalananda purchase this horse, and Vimalananda had regretted his acquisition ever since. "For one thing," he would say, "his color is liver chestnut, and everyone knows that liver chestnuts rarely keep good health." In Bajarangi's case, at least, this was true. Jockeys would complain that when they sat on him he would try to move his back out from under them, as if they were causing him pain. No one could discover any obvious pathology or do him any good, not even Dr. Singh, the eccentric vet who sought to prove his expertise at equine massage by flaunting at us his copy of the *Turaga Samhita*, a Sanskrit treatise on horses.

I had meanwhile been studying Ayurvedic herbology at the college, and I came one morning to Vimalananda with a proposal that we try on Bajarangi a local preparation of *bhallataka* (*Semecarpus anacardium*), an extremely poisonous fruit which when appropriately manufactured often shows good results in such varied afflictions as goiter, paralysis, and infertility. At his wit's end over Bajarangi Vimalananda agreed, and being dutiful experimenters he and I decided to try some of this restorative as well, just to see what it would do. The horse got two tablespoons, and Vimalananda and I took a half-teaspoon each.

The medication, which had in fact not been properly prepared, gave the horse extreme colic and us two humans extreme skin rashes. At least Tehmul could report that Bajarangi, who luckily survived, became significantly more spirited afterwards than he had been before the medicine, though he was still uneasy when mounted. Vimalananda and I also noticed vastly improved zest and energy.

Vimalananda's skin being darker than mine, his rash disappeared a mere two or three days after he began to ingest the antidote. A bhallataka reaction is always more severe in a white-skinned individual, though, and even with the antidote it took a full two weeks for my skin color to fade from bright pink back to normal. Everyone at the college thought I had been fiercely sunburned, but it was just the effects of urushiol, the poison in bhallataka which is also the poison in poison ivy, poison oak, poison sumac, cashew shells, mango skins, and Chinese lacquer. It was a poison ivy rash but from the inside out, which meant that I felt the intense itching about an inch below the surface of my skin. It like the pinkness gradually faded with the antidote, but it cost me a couple of sleepless nights of vain attempts to scratch it. "Thank God we knew what was the main ingredient in this concoction," said Vimalananda to me, once it became clear that my reaction would indeed disappear. "I once treated a woman who had been secretly given bhallataka. No ordinary remedy could give her any relief because no one had suspected the truth. She suffered for two full years from its poison before she came to me and got the specific antidote."

Bajarangi was a real preoccupation during much of 1979, and by the spring of 1980 we were ready to throw in the towel on him when the enterprising Dr. Martanda happened to drive us to the stables one afternoon. We escorted the doctor from stall to stall introducing him to Vimalananda's "four-legged children" until we reached Bajarangi, where we recounted our woes in full. "What?" said the doctor. "Such a minor thing, and no one has been able to deal with it? It is obvious that he lacks marrow in the bones of his back. Since the Marrow Tissue is the foundation of Shukra he must have a deficiency of sperms, which has kept his vitality low." Great, I thought. Repay couldn't get enough of his own sperm, and Bajarangi doesn't have enough to go around. "I can cure him," said Dr. Martanda, "with just two doses of medicine. All you have to do after I dose him is to feed him the soup made from one dozen goat thigh bones, and I can guarantee you a cure."

"Dr. Saheb," said Vimalananda smoothly, "horses have no gall bladders, and feeding him something as fatty as marrow soup will give him colic that will kill him."

"Don't worry yourself in the least," replied the ever theatrical Dr. Martand. "I guarantee that no harm will come to him."

Vimalananda and I looked at one another until at last he said to me, "What do we have to lose?" Though Tehmul was not pleased with this proposal at all he agreed to permit the doctor try his potion, for he realized that if anything untoward did happen we would at least be able to collect on Bajarangi's insurance money. The groom was therefore ordered to proceed to the market and buy the appropriate bones. The next morning Dr. Martanda arrived at the stables promptly after the morning work to administer the first dose, Tehmul standing by expecting calamity at any minute. But Bajarangi showed complications neither that day nor the next, and the next jockey to mount him testified that the horse was no longer doing his previous "dance." The goat marrow had presumably filled his bones, for his track work improved weekly. The day that he actually ran a race was one of the highlights of our season. Vimalananda laid no wager on this horse who had let us down so often in the past, but we were just happy to see him out competing with his fellows on the grass.

After running once or twice more Bajarangi still showed no signs of wanting to win, so we disposed of him. After the fact Vimalananda questioned the wisdom of his decision to name our "sperm-deficient" horse *Bajarangi*, which is the Hindi version of one of the Sanskrit names of Anjaneya. He had hoped in vain that carrying such a name would make him want to live up to the standards of his namesake and run well. Now Vimalananda speculated that the opposite might have been the case:

"It is always good to name your child after God; that's how Ajamila was saved. Do you recall? When death came for him he called for his son Narayana, but got through to Lord Vishnu, Narayana Himself. I had no intention of commercializing Anjaneya's name when I named my horse Bajarangi, but it is possible that it might have seemed that way to the Law of Karma, since he was racing for money. This might in fact have been one of the factors that prevented his progress. It is so difficult to know the Law of Karma in detail!"

"And impossible to know in its entirety."

"Completely impossible, even for the Rishis. It didn't seem like a bad idea to me at the time because Anjaneya has helped me advance my career in the past. During my salad days as a pro wrestler it was the power of Anjaneya that sustained me. Could I have ever done it on my own? Ha!" Anjaneya, who has from His birth been the patron deity of wrestlers, continued to sustain Vimalananda even in my era when he would challenge to arm wrestling the young Maharashtrian wrestlers who used to come to him to get his blessing for an upcoming bout. Invariably the heart patient in his mid-sixties would easily defeat the youthful musclemen, and when they would shamefacedly admit defeat he would tell them, "Don't worry, my boy; which human can withstand the power of Anjaneya? Remember this, and when you return to your village don't forget to pay your regards to the temple of Anjaneya there," a temple whose new image had been purchased by that very Dr. Martanda who had treated Anjaneya's equine namesake.

The Ayurvedic internship program at the Tarachand Ramnath Charitable Ayurvedic Hospital depleted my 1980 spring and summer. Aside from the odd weekend in Bombay I could meet Vimalananda only when he came to Poona to pay a visit to his "four-legged friends." A few of my instructors made regular pilgrimages to his hotel during his stays, hoping to mop up for their own practices the odd treatment tip that Vimalananda would occasionally spill. They were intrigued with his knowledge of herbs and minerals and with his ability to diagnose people by taking his own pulse; he was intrigued with the possibility that he might somehow get some of them to think originally for a change. Aside from Dr. Vasant Lad, though, few of these physicians impressed him.

Vimalananda, who appreciated Dr. Lad's devotion to his guru Hambir Baba and his personal deity *Ganesha* (the elephant-headed remover of obstacles), assisted him and his family in various ways. This favoritism made some of the other faculty members, who regarded Dr. Lad's station in life as being beneath theirs, determine to take from Vimalananda the assistance that they felt they deserved. As these men had no deep interest in Ayurveda, Jyotish, Tantra, or any other form of classical Indian wisdom, Vimalananda protected himself creatively from them. For example, after Dr. Potdukhe brought his father to Vimalananda one day to ask his help in reversing a chronic intestinal infirmity, Vimalananda said, "Oh, it can be fixed all right—I can guarantee it—but if it is he will lose all his money. Which will it be: health without wealth or wealth without health?" After they left Vimalananda confidently predicted that he would never see them again, and he never did.

The crassness of the bulk of these doctors disappointed Vimalananda acutely. He expected that anyone who had been blessed with the opportunity to imbibe Sanskritic learning ought to evince the same broadness of mind, quickness of wit, and keenness of awareness that seemed to come effortlessly to him. A lack of "art, grace and culture" in otherwise knowledgeable men and women always seemed to disgruntle him. In 1980 he responded to the only invitation he ever received from my college with an address to its staff that went something like this:

> It is no surprise that no one wants to learn Ayurveda nowadays since no one is teaching the real meat of Ayurveda. If you really want your students to understand Ayurveda you must teach them that there are only four things in medicine: *duhkha, duhkha ka karana, karana ka upaya, aur upaya ka anta* ('misery, the cause of misery, the remedy for the cause, and the end of the remedy'). As Ayurvedic physicians we want to liberate our patients mostly from physical sorrow. This means that we must be fully conversant with the structures in which diseases develop: the *dhatus* (tissues) and *malas* (wastes). Teach your students why diagnosis of disease is usually by mala. The wastes are produced during the metabolic processes which produce the tissues, which means that if you know the malas you will know the dhatus.
>
> Unfortunately you people overlook many of the malas, like dandruff. Even examination of dandruff can yield significant information, in particular about the bones, given that head hair is an *upadhatu* (secondary tissue) of bone. In a way the bones are a bridge between the astral body, which is the mind, and the physical body. Bone is governed by *Vayu* (the Air Element), which also appears in the body as prana; what controls prana controls the mind, and vice versa. Also, as a tissue, Bone is the foundation of Marrow, which is the foundation of Shukra, which is the foundation of ojas,

which is the foundation of health. Know dandruff in detail and you can know the patient's health.

If you want good health you must nourish your tissues well, which means you must nourish the tastes in your body. When you lack tastes your metabolism is affected. Even if you lay a big meal before a sick man he will not be interested; his taste is not there. Lack of taste within the body causes a patient of jaundice to lack appetite. Disturbance of the inner taste process causes the appetite to be lost in fever. Ayurveda is the only medical system which describes medicines for supplying to the body the tastes which it lacks; teach your students that!

Actually all the tastes are inside, but we look for them outside, in our food. Our job as physicians is to create the proper taste within a sick person so that proper tissue nourishment will resume and natural immunity in the form of ojas will increase. This is why we use medicines; not just to suppress disease, like the allopaths do, but to return the patient's balance to normal. Your great Ayurvedic author Charaka learned about medicinal herbs by watching what animals ate when they were sick. Students should learn in the same way. You should teach them how to make the plant talk to you, how to make it tell you, "These are my qualities, my tastes, and my useful parts, and I am useful in this disease." Those who really know Ayurveda know that every plant has a thousand uses.

Teach your students why we like to use plants for our medicines. Plants and animals complement one another nicely. Plants breathe in carbon dioxide and breathe out oxygen, while animals exhale carbon dioxide and inhale oxygen. Teach them all the details of how to collect medicinal plants. When you inform them that plants should never be collected at night, tell them the reason why. Plants breathe at night, and if you collect them then it is like strangling them. If you strangle the plant, do you think it will be interested in trying to help you help your patient? Teach your pupils how one plant antidotes another. Teach them the secret uses of apamarga (*Achyranthes aspera*), tulsi (*Ocimum sanctum*), and bilva (*Aegle marmelos*), plants which can make you clairaudient and clairvoyant. Teach them the limitations of herbs, and why we also use medicines made from minerals. Above all, teach them the real meaning of *Rasayana* (rejuvenation; literally, "the Path of Rasa"), because it is only through *rasa* (taste, juice, emotion) that rejuvenation can occur.

All the assembled physicians nodded sagaciously and thanked him for his comments, but when we were alone again Vimalananda shook his head with resignation and said, "Is it any wonder that Ayurveda is in such a desperate state today? Your professors seem to be good people, by and large, but most of them simply do not know Ayurveda—so how do they think they are going to teach it? They don't even know the simplest things about Ayurveda, such as how to develop your body. What is the use in knowing about Ayurveda if you can't even develop your body?"

A wrestler was talking. I asked, "What method do you like best for body development?"

He replied, "It depends on the individual. *Bhang* works well for many people. Wrestlers who live in Banaras have made a science of how to use bhang as part of their training regimen. After their morning workout they will bathe in the Ganga, get a two-hour massage, bathe again, eat well, and take a nap. On arising they will defecate, to lighten their bodies and minds, then bathe again, then get yet another massage, then take bhang. They eat when the intoxication of the bhang is at its height. Try it; your body will develop amazingly."

"We do not expect, though, that using bhang like this is going to help them free Kundalini from its constraints."

"How could it? In fact, it will make ahamkara identify even more firmly with the body. But you have to decide what you want to do with your life; only then can Ayurveda help you. If you want to go the way of awakening Kundalini using bhang then you have to use it in another way, which I am sure that your professors are also unaware of. Do they have any idea of the real way to perform rejuvenation? Do they know that while herbs can make you live 400-500 years you can go on almost indefinitely if you know how to use mercury? Do they know that you can extract copper from peacock feathers, and mercury from bilva leaves? Or that alchemical gold shows different results from mined gold when seen in the mass spectrometer? They teach chemistry at your college, but do they know anything at all of the real *Rasa Shastra* (alchemy)? Have they ever heard of, much less seen, the many ways to solidify mercury? Or the few ways in which you can make mercury *agnisthayi* ('fire-fast') so that it will not melt when placed into a fire? The true alchemy, my boy, is not even easy to understand, much less do. I wonder how many of your instructors are even interested in understanding it.

"One way in which I am different from most doctors is that most doctors—not all, but most—see sick people as money-making projects. I look at them with Smashan Tara's eyes instead, and see them as my own children. When I can help someone escape from a disease I feel as if I've helped cure my own son or daughter. I love to do that, but I don't want anyone to know how I'm doing it. Why should they know? If they're sick they should be interested in the result, not in the process. And if they're doctors I don't *want* them to know how I do things. If they learn they will just go out and commercialize my knowledge; they will use it to earn money from sick people. Besides, can they ever know how many days and weeks of hard work it took me to learn what I know? This is why I always like to try out new methods of treatment, so that no one will be able to pinpoint exactly what I am doing.

"During one period of my life I used to give an ounce of castor oil to every sick person who came my way. No one had any reaction or got diarrhea from it. On the contrary, everyone got some relief from the ailment they had brought to me. One lady who watched me do this to various people decided to be smart. She tried to do the same thing herself, but none of her patients ever responded. In fact, they invariably got worse. Then she came to me and demanded to know why this was happening.

"I asked her in response, 'Who told you to do this?'"

"Then what did she say?"

"Nothing; what is she going to say?"

"Obviously," I said, "something other than the castor oil was doing the trick."

"Obviously," he echoed. "In fact it was something ethereal, something that used the castor oil as a medium through which to exert its effect. Castor oil is itself a wonderful medicine, but this ethereal thing could have used any medium. One day my friend Faram was suffering from intestinal colic. To help him out I picked up the first bottle I could reach on the shelf and gave him two pills from it. The pain disappeared. When I was out of Bombay a few weeks later the pain recurred, and Faram looked for the bottle to dose himself again. This time he looked at the label and discovered that it was a hormonal preparation meant for regulating his wife's menses. He flew into such a rage that he threw the bottle out of the window!"

"He must have had some choice words for you when you got back."

"He always had choice words for me—but then I always fired him too. That's the way our friendship was." To be "fired" in Indian English is to be chewed out, dressed down, or similarly raked over the coals.

"You know, Faram's wife suffered for years with excessive menstrual bleeding. She would bleed for twenty days out of the month. She tried everything, but got no relief. Finally she came to me one day and said, 'Look, I've had enough. I just can't stand it anymore. I am going to go and get a hysterectomy.'

"I told her, 'All you want to do is stop the flow, isn't it? Then why do you worry? Drink this water,' and I handed her a full glass. She drank it, and her menses stopped from that day onwards.

"Whenever I look at a woman I see Ma, and I can't bear to see Ma in pain. One day when I was at a friend's house I heard moaning from the next room. I asked him what the problem was, and he said, 'Oh, it's my sister. She's been in labor for the whole day, and there has been no progress so far. I'm not sure whether we'll need to do a Caesarian or what.'

"I told him, 'Give me a shiny metal tray, one of those German silver ones you are so fond of.' I traced a *yantra* on it with my finger. He asked me what I thought I was doing, because he couldn't see anything on the tray. I ignored him and went into the room where the girl was lying on the bed. I showed her the tray. She couldn't see the yantra either, but within a matter of minutes the child was born. *That* is the power of yantras."

"Now I understand why all these old friends of yours keep pestering you to heal them or their family members. It's because they know your capabilities."

"Having learned a few of my capabilities they are trying to capitalize on them, for their own benefit. Some of them have even told me that I should start healing the sick en masse. But besides the fact that the fame from such programs would ruin my life, what about the rnanubandhana? I have to have an appropriate rnanubandhana with someone in order to heal them."

"Is that true of any doctor?"

"Yes, and of any astrologer, or any other professional who wants to do help someone out. But there are so many people with whom I have rnanu-bandhanas that if I tried to heal all of them at once I would run out of shakti before very long. I'm not Jesus, and I have never claimed to be a '*bhagavan*.'

"Sometimes even my own karmas become too much to bear, and I've even had to use some funny business to cure *myself*. I don't like to do it, because I believe that it is better to suffer now and be free of the burden of your karmas rather than to hide from them. After all, they are sure to catch up with you anyway, eventually. But in a crisis you do whatever is necessary.

"Some years ago a Dr. Durandar lived in Bombay. Somehow or other he had lost his son and nearly went mad as a result. Afterwards he began to treat me like I was his son. He was always coming around to see how I was, and to check on my health. He would give me medicine whenever I needed it—and sometimes even when I didn't. When I needed antibiotics he would usually give me an injection of penicillin, but one day when he was out of penicillin he gave me streptomycin instead. I had never taken streptomycin before and once had a severe reaction to it: high fever, rigors, the works. I thought I was done for. I called some of my friends who all sat around me crying, thinking I was going to die. So did I. Faram was abusing me, as was his wont. The days he didn't abuse me I would ask him, 'What, my child, I have heard none of your beautiful language today; are you ill?' That would start him off again, insulting my family members with the foulest of words. I enjoyed it; it was his peculiar way of expressing his love for me.

"Just as Faram was abusing Dr. Durandar left and right for giving me the injection Dr. Durandar unexpectedly arrived to check on his patient. I couldn't let him see me in this condition—when he looked at me he saw his son, and if he saw me near death now it would be a second big shock for him that might prove fatal. So somehow the fever disappeared and I became perfectly normal again. I complimented him on his treatment, made him happy, and showed him the door. As soon as he left the fever returned, and Faram started to abuse me again!

"Then I lost my temper. I told Roshni to bring me her quilt. It was a beautiful brown satin quilt which her father had brought to her from Burma, and she never lent it to anyone else. It was so precious to her that she slept with it each and every night, but as soon as she heard that I wanted it she handed it over to me. I told her to cover me with it, and after about five minutes I threw the quilt on the floor. I was perfectly all right—but the quilt was hot; all the fever had gone into it. There it lay, literally shivering by itself on the ground. I told Faram, 'Be careful now: whoever uses this quilt next will get the fever.'

"Then Faram abused everyone loudly and, shouting out the Parsi equivalent of 'Not in my house!' had Roshni throw it out the window."

"And that was it?"

"That was all; I was cured. Don't ask me how."

"But if somehow you transfered your fever to the quilt, where did your karmas go? They must have somehow gone into the quilt too."

"Something like that."

I cringed slightly, thinking of whoever must have picked it up, and then said to him, "So the moral to the story is never pick up anything from the street!"

"Especially not in India!" he laughed.

chapter eight
REDSTONE

VIMALANANDA'S INTEREST IN his spiritual 'children' had been corroding for some time, for they were proving to be no more dedicated than Shankaracharya's 'sons.' It waned yet further on the morning that he had a visitation from Doshi's wife. She and Doshi had come to Poona that weekend to accompany us for some homa nearby, and were staying in the hotel room that was next door to Vimalananda's. Apparently these two, conniving perhaps with some of the other 'children,' had decided that it was time for Vimalananda to part with some of his Tantric sexual knowledge. Mrs. Doshi had therefore knocked at Vimalananda's door braless, her sari barely covering her sagging middle-aged bosoms, to beseech this expert for a Vajroli practicum, or at the very least a how-to course in Lata Mudra. It was very difficult for me to see how the evidently dissolute Mrs. Doshi could have any chance to succeed at Lata Mudra, a practice in which two sexual partners invoke Lord Shiva and his Grand Consort Parvati into their bodies before they dally together. How then could she even dream of Vajroli, in which you use your genitals to suck up your partner's secretions during intercourse?

As I remembered Vimalananda's often-repeated advice—"Just slow down and refinement occurs automatically, especially in sex"—it became obvious that the contrapositive must be equally true: "Just speed up and coarseness will overtake you, especially in sex." I was racking my brain for some worthy comment to offer my offended mentor when Vimalananda spat out, "Who does she think she is? Does she think I'll see her naked boobs and lose control? I've seen much better than hers, and I'm still in control!"

Calming him down with sweet words being now quite out of the question I decied to try discharge the rest of his repugnance at her wasteful haste by first intensifying it: "Maybe," I said, "she thinks she's become some great Bhairavi," a Bhairavi being the female in a Lata Mudra partnership, to which he replied, "Bhairavi, my foot! Can you be a Bhairavi if you are completely lacking in *niyama*? To succeed at any sort of sadhana you first have to learn to say NO to the things that are preventing you from making progress. Roshni has been able to make some progress in her sadhana because she's learned the three stages of 'no.'"

"The three stages of 'no'?"

"Yes. The first stage is n-o—no. No! If that doesn't work, move up to g-o—go. Go! Get lost! That will usually work, but if it doesn't, then you have to get tough, and you say F.O.! F.O. is bound to do the trick."

The Doshi incident multiplied Vimalananda's ire with my recently inaugurated semi-romantic liaison with one of my fellow Ayurvedic students. He was unhappy that I spent time with this girl that I could have spent meditating or studying instead; he was concerned that some indiscretion of ours might be seized upon by my enemies at the college and used to attack me; he was wary of having the girl's reputation ruined, particularly if we became physically intimate (which she and I both realized would be highly unwise); he did not care much for the girl herself.

It was in this rather vitiated climate that, not long after the Balam Bhat-Faram-Shankaracharya discourse, he sat me down and said to me, "Your *Sade Sati* is about to begin."

His tone of voice alarmed me, though the words themselves were not overly sinister; *sade sati* means 'seven and a half' in Hindi. I tried to sound plucky: "The 'seven-and-a-half'?"

"Yes. The Sade Sati is the seven-and-a-half year period during which Saturn will afflict the Moon in your horoscope." This was sounding less and less pleasant. "In Jyotish we respect the Sun as the planet of light, but we regard its effects as harsh; its light 'burns' you. The Moon's light, however, cools and nourishes you, which makes the Moon the most important planet in Jyotish—after Saturn. When Saturn, the planet of dryness, constriction and disappointment, transits the Moon it pinches off the flow of life's juice and promotes desolation."

Not a very attractive prospect. I tried to keep my gorge from rising.

"How is Saturn," I asked slowly, to throttle down my racing mind, "going to affect me?"

"It will affect you in the same way that all the other planets affect you: by its subtle gravity. The planets you see in the sky are gross, physical structures that have a minor effect on us. But each of these gross planets is the physical reflection of a subtle planet whose gravity affects us strongly. Saturn's subtle gravity spares no one: not his fellow planets, not his fellow devas, not even his father the Sun. Even the Rishis are affected. By nourishing the Sun the Rishis are able to direct the influence of the Sun on themselves and on the world in general. One of the many benefits they gain thereby is some control over Saturn. But only some, for even they sometimes fall under Saturn's shadow. As long as they exist on the earth even the Rishis have to be concerned about Saturn. Think of Parashara; even he did not escape, in spite of being an expert in astrology."

"Great! So now I'm finished. What is going to happen to me? Should I make out my will?"

"No, but I may need to. One of the main effects of the Sade Sati is *Chatra Bhanga*."

" 'The Breaking of the Umbrella'?"

"Exactly. An umbrella is a very useful thing, right? It keeps the sun and rain off your head; it protects you from the elements, from the outside world. The parents and grandparents of a small child form its umbrella. Sade Sati tends to cause those relatives to be 'broken'—to disappear from the scene somehow."

"By dying, for example?"

"Yes, or going to jail, being kidnaped, or simply running away. Roshni's Sade Sati begins when yours does, because her Moon occupies the same constellation that yours does. You and Roshni both treat me as a father, which makes me doubt that the effect on me is going to be very good. Your parents and Roshni's mother will probably also be affected." Prescient words these: Vimalananda died midway through this Sade Sati, my mother came very close to death a few months thereafter, and a few months after that Roshni's mother died, well before the period ended for the two of us.

"Is there anything at all good about the Sade Sati?"

"Well, the best time for you to perform any sadhana is when Saturn turns his 'gaze' on you, when the influence of Saturn predominates in your horoscope. If you cooperate Saturn can make you experience great spiritual heights. You should always respect Saturn, but never be afraid of him. Orthodox people are afraid of Saturn; they treat him like the Devil incarnate. But if they really are so pure why should they be worried about Saturn?"

"What should I do?"

"One approach to problem planets is to wear gems and perform rituals to placate them. Another approach is to have full faith in your deity and request Him or Her to take care of everything. I prefer the latter approach, except that when it comes to Saturn you really have to have absolute faith in your personal deity if you want to be protected. If your faith is not total Saturn will still be able to affect you. You may therefore want to diminish Saturn's effects—not eliminate them, which is not possible, but at least reduce them. To do this you can either worship Saturn, or you can worship Shiva, especially in his incarnation as Anjaneya.

"Look at that photo of Anjaneya there on the wall. Do you see the mace he holds on his shoulder?"

"Yes," I replied with unnecessary peevishness.

"I have told you before that Anjaneya's mace controls all the planets except Saturn, who is controlled by His tail. But what does that mean? 'Hanuman's mace' is the name of a *mudra*, a hand gesture, which is nothing but a part of *nyasa*. Nyasa is a way to place the deity you are worshipping into your subtle body so that your deity can pervade your being. A sadhaka makes his internal temple sacred by means of nyasa so that his beloved deity will find it inviting to enter him. When you can properly perform 'Hanuman's mace' and you use it with the appropriate mantra Anjaneya can enter you. Then He can do the work of controlling the planets instead of you. Until you have realized Hanuman in yourself this mudra will give only minor results. Once Anjaneya performs that mudra through you, though, the control will be perfect."

"I have not yet realized Anjaneya in myself," I said with real contrition. "I will continue to worship Anjaneya, but the results I will obtain are bound to continue to be limited. Is there anything I can do in addition?"

"Yes, there is. You should read the *Shani Mahatmya* ('The Greatness of Saturn'[2]); that will help you too."

Impressed by Vimalananda's seriousness I went out straightway to get myself a copy of *The Greatness of Saturn* and began to read it. As if by way of reinforcement—Nature confirming the rightness of this act—Saturn popped up for me on my very next trip to the race track.

"You see that old fellow over there in the Maharashtrian dhoti, vest and hat?" said Vimalananda, pointing downwards between races. "That is Deshpande, from Poona. One year he bought a foal that had something wrong with its palate. Whenever it tried to eat it would regurgitate some of its food. Every vet who inspected it said it was incurable without a complicated operation. All of us, including me, thought Deshpande was a fool for wasting his money on it. But he knows some Ayurveda and worked wonders on that horse, I tell you, wonders. He named it Akhlakh, and it won races for him."

"Akhlakh!" I said loudly. "That's the name of the horse from *The Greatness of Saturn*, the one that carried King Vikramaditya away into the sky when he sat down on its back!"

2. *The Greatness of Saturn*, English translation of the *Shani Mahatmya*, published 1997 by Sadhana Publications.

"Very good! Now why Deshpande would name his horse Akhlakh is completely beyond me, unless he thought that somehow that name was going to make it fly down the track."

"Maybe he thought it would make Saturn happy."

"Maybe. If only it were so easy to satisfy Saturn."

Saturn was still much on my mind as I prepared at Vimalananda's behest to leave for the United States and begin to lecture on Ayurveda. He had already forced me to write one little book which Dr. Martanda had volunteered to publish. He had also arranged for a dinner meeting in Poona to introduce me to various newspaper reporters who reciprocated for the good food and copious drink they were served by dutifully writing glowing accounts of my genius. I had no desire to leave Vimalananda to go to work in the West, but he kept reminding me of the rnas to my parents and my homeland which remained outstanding, rnas which I would do better to pay off now rather than later. "And besides," he would say, "think how happy it will make your parents feel for you to make a success of yourself! Don't you think they must be worried about whether or not you'll be properly set up in life before they die? Don't you want to take that load of their minds?"

One day when he was going on in this vein I interrupted him with, "But I'm going to a country filled with asuras, where the food will be totally impregnated with commercial gravity. I'm no saint; how am I ever going to save myself from being ruined?"

"Don't worry, my boy," he said compassionately, "I will always be there with you. Whenever you are troubled remember Anjaneya. With Anjaneya's help you will never get bogged down in the quicksand." Then he added, as if in afterthought, "If only all those monkeys over in America would worship Anjaneya they might save themselves from being stuck also."

He had compared Westerners to monkeys before, but I took this reference to heart, and testily asked him, "Aren't people in India monkeys too?"

"I know what I am saying," he replied serenely. "Listen now to why I say it. Though Ramachandra, the seventh of Vishnu's Avataras, has long since left Earth His dedicated devotee, the immortal Anjaneya, remains. So do the blessings that Lord Rama gave while He walked on Earth, blessings whose effects can be felt even today. I take my mind back to the Dvapara Yuga, perhaps a million years ago, when Rama made three promises. The first was to Jatayu, the eagle who tried to rescue Sita from Ravana without even knowing who She was. Rama promised Jatayu that in Kali Yuga he would be worshipped and adored as perfectly humane, even though a bird. By temperament eagles are killers, but Lord Rama gave Jatayu the powers of sympathy and compassion, to shelter all under his wings. Rama even took Jatayu's head in His lap when the old bird died, which is something He did not even do for His own father Dasharatha.

"Whose symbol is the eagle? America's. America is the first country to help anywhere in the world in time of famine, flood or other disaster. Americans are generous by nature and love to give to others who don't have enough. And they do it just for the sake of doing it. Not for gain, but because it is to be done, just as Jatayu did for Sita. Some say that in Kali Yuga the giving of gifts is the highest form of religious merit. As Americans have given a great deal they have collected considerable spiritual benefit. Yes, they have also made mistakes, like Vietnam, but they have still done more good than anyone else has. So, America is Lord Rama's blessing to this Earth through the eagle Jatayu.

"Rama's second promise was to the monkeys who built the bridge to Lanka. They were blessed that in Kali Yuga they would become great inventors and innovators and would rule the world. This also refers to America. The Americans are ruling the world and are responsible for most of the great inventions that have so radically changed the world. I call your fellow countrymen monkeys because they are descended from monkeys. Even they believe that they are descended from monkeys! But now they have forgotten their ancestry and are experimenting on monkeys. The curses they are receiving from their monkey brethren are rapidly eroding this blessing that Lord Rama gave them.

"The third promise was to Sita, that women will come forward in Kali Yuga. And America is the leader in making women the absolute equals of men. This is why I say that America has been triply blessed. I am so fond of America because of these blessings, not because of its riches or power, neither of which will last forever. They may not last very much longer, in fact, because America is wasting both its riches and its power at a very high rate of speed. Still, the Americans have Rama's three blessings, and also blessings from Ramakrishna Paramahamsa and Swami Vivekananda. So they will continue to thrive—for a while.

"Now, was no one else blessed by Lord Rama? Well, Russia was; otherwise how could it have ever become a superpower? Russia's symbol is the bear. The bear Jambavant did help Lord Rama in His quest for Sita, but not as much as the monkeys did. This means that Russia will never have ascendancy over America. Thank God for that; I hate communism!

"Another reason that America is strong can be discovered in numerology. How many states does America have? Fifty: $5 + 0 = 5$. Mark my words, if the United States ever adds another state they will be asking for trouble. They use five-pointed stars on their flags, military vehicles, etc. Five is the number of *Guru*, or Brihaspati—the planet Jupiter—who is the world's protector. And five is also the number of magic and mystery. The Greeks used to go into battle with their word for five painted on their shields. Also, the American flag has thirteen stripes: $1 + 3 = 4$. Four is the number for foundation, so their foundation is firm. As I always say, if the foundation is strong the building will last; if not it will surely fall."

"Surely you prefer the six-pointed star to the five-pointed star?" Vimalananda used the six-pointed star as the yantra in the bottom of his firepit when he performed homa.

"They are different, but they are both good. The Jews call the six-pointed star the Star of David, and David was no fool to use this star. It is one of the reasons that the Israeli army always wins. You may not have noticed, but a six-pointed star also appears in the Great Seal of the United States, made out of thirteen individual stars."

"So America's foundation is good."

"*Most* of it is good. But they have performed some terrible karmas also. Don't forget that the Americans came into possession of America by theft. Armed robbery, in fact; they used firearms. Shouldn't armed robbery be a prominent part of their lives today? And since they stole the country by using the Fire Element, shouldn't they be made to suffer by the Fire Element? We see it already: the whole world is warming up, there are forest fires and droughts everywhere; and if there is ever a nuclear war much of the world will be incinerated.

"And what about drilling oil wells and sucking oil out of the earth? The Americans have taught the world how best to prospect for oil and how pump it from the ground efficiently. Oil is the earth's blood, so shouldn't they have their blood sucked in return? They must, and look what their medical science is doing to them: it is sucking their blood. Every time one of them goes to a doctor he gets at least one blood test. One thing is for sure: when all these karmas catch up with them they will truly be ruined. The question is, when will these karmas catch up with them? So long as the Americans can just remain true to their heritage and remember to be generous they will continue to prosper. Whether or not they are able to do so will depend on how well they can improve their own innate natures, their collective *svabhava*. It will also depend on how well their good qualities can continue to function in the face of the powerful distortion that the weight of all their evil karmas is creating. Thanks to Lord Rama's blessings there is still some hope for them."

Silence descended for a few moments before he continued.

"I tell you, Robby, there is very little to karma besides blessings and curses. Read the *Ramayana* and the *Mahabharata* and you will find blessings and curses on nearly every page, just as you find in your Bible too. I have already shown you how blessings and curses worked in the case of Prithviraj and Akbar. Now listen to how a blessing influenced a famous Western ruler.

"Long ago there lived a Rishi who was a *Kurma Guru*. From the outside he would sit silently like a tortoise (*kurma*), seemingly inactive. But on the inside he would secretly watch what his disciples were doing and would help and nourish them from a distance. In that ashram lived Shabari, an old Shudra lady who used to sweep and scrub to keep the place clean. One day the Rishi's pet disciple came by and felt compassion for her. He asked her, 'Ma, do you do any kind of sadhana?'

"She replied, 'My son, I am just a poor illiterate woman; I know nothing of Sanskrit.'

"The boy told her, 'Ma, even if you can't recite the Veda you can still call on God. You just repeat, "Master, when will you come? Master, when will you come? I am making everything clean for You." Repeat this all the time, when you are doing your work and when you are at home, and you will see the result.' He gave her this phrase as a mantra in her mother tongue so she would be able to pronounce it. Whatever a Rishi gives you to recite is a mantra, no matter what language it is in or whether it is grammatically correct or not. *That* is the power of a Rishi.

"Every day, all day long, Shabari repeated her mantra. She did it so long and so well that when Lord Rama, who was God incarnate on earth at that time, came that way He stopped to meet her. He even had to accept her gift of jujube fruits to Him. You see, in a Rishi's ashram all work according to their capabilities and all get results. Isn't that the way it should be? The Rishis never refused anyone if they were sincere.

"Shabari was so thrilled that Rama had come to her that she wanted everything to be perfect for Him. In order to make sure that Rama would enjoy each fruit she wanted to test them to make sure that they were sweet. So she bit into each *jujube* and tasted it first before giving it to Him. Now, as you well know people in India never offer any food to anyone else that they have already tasted. You would never offer such food to a guest, and most especially not to your Lord and King; that would be one of the gravest of insults."

"And Shabari didn't know this?!"

"How could she not have known it? The upper caste people around her would have reminded her of it regularly. But her joy at seeing the Lord Himself was so immense that she forgot everything except wanting to do her utmost to please Him. When Rama looked inside Shabari and saw the depth of her devotion and sincerity, He ate those berries joyfully.

"Rama then blessed Shabari that she would rule as a queen in her next birth. This is the Law of Karma again: first the austerities, then the rewards. She had to wait many centuries until a good opportunity presented itself, but eventually Shabari became a queen. In fact, she became Queen Victoria, the Empress of all India. Even though her penance was not of a quality that would have enabled her to become an Indian ruler, she did have the qualifications to become queen of a nation of asuras. The real reason that England, which is a nation of Shudras and *Mlecchas* (barbarians) as far as we are concerned, was allowed to rule over us was so that Shabari could rule India by ruling England. Because Shabari in her incarnation as Victoria had a vague remembrance of her previous life some of her previous qualities shone through. This explains why she always believed in religious toleration. She was a well-loved queen, and people still remember her here favorably. Why, there's even a Victoria Memorial in Calcutta."

"And Victoria Terminus on the Central Railway right here in Bombay!"

"Precisely. Now, after she died Queen Victoria must have descended into some lower womb. This became inevitable because she did not persist with the austerities which had brought her to that position. Wasn't Queen Victoria distressed in her last days? Here again is the Law of Karma: you do austerities which result in great enjoyments, but then the enjoyments make you forget to continue you austerities and down you go. *Tapeshwari se rajeshwari, aur rajeshwari se narakeshwari:* penance to riches, and riches to ruination."

"She needed someone to guide her; where was her guru, the Rishi's disciple?"

"Well, he had no desire to be born in the West, so she had to go there on her own. But he must still be around somewhere, looking after her from afar like a good Kurma Guru should. The Rishis never forsake their 'children,' even after both they and their 'children' have left their bodies. There is no limitation of time, space or causation when it comes to love. If Queen Victoria had really been lucky she would have had the kind of positive influences around her that Akbar had around him when he became Emperor. Despite his blood-stained heritage he had so many saints blessing him, and had such good samskaras from his past birth as Prithviraj, that he was able to overcome his inborn svabhava. Akbar was truly lucky in that like Birbal almost all of the people around him were unique, and amazing."

"Except his children."

"No, not at all," retorted Vimalananda, annoyed. "If his son Salim was his greatest disappointment one of his greatest satisfactions was his daughter Taj. His pet name for her was Dilaram. She was a very simple girl on the outside, but very deep within. Once Akbar asked her, 'Why don't you ever dress up well to impress the members of my court?'

"She replied, 'But I am wearing twenty costumes,' and to prove it she took all of them off one by one. When the last was removed she stood there with her hands covering her breasts, not her genitalia.

"Akbar accosted her furiously: 'Shameless girl! What do you mean by standing like this before me? Where is your modesty?'

"She replied, 'But father, you have seen me without clothes many times when I was young. Since then these have grown,' she said as she indicated her breasts, 'and this,' she said, indicating her vulva 'has not. So I must cover these.'

"What could Akbar say then? She was right. Another time she helped him win a crucial game of chess. You know, Akbar was an expert chess player, what is called a *shatarangi*—he could think one hundred moves ahead. For enjoyment he would use courtiers as chesspieces on the big chessboard of in-laid stone that he ordered laid out in his courtyard. You can still see it at Fatehpur Sikri.

"On this occasion he had rather gone overboard. He was playing with one of his viceroys, and was so confident of his superior skills he had bet the viceroy his kingdom, with the added bonus of Dilaram for a wife. Unfortunately Akbar was having an off game, and at one point he had to stop and think hard. He realized that unless he thought of something sensational that he would be finished—checkmated—after his next move.

"Then Dilaram came to him and showed him how to win the game. She spoke in a couplet: 'Move your rook like this, and he will have to move like this; he has no choice. Then move your pawn forward two squares and he will be checkmated, and you will not lose your Dilaram.'

"Akbar did as she advised, and won. He tried to make her accept so many things as a reward, but she refused everything. She never married, and when Akbar died she left everything and went to Gokul, where Krishna lived as a child. She was a great devotee of Krishna. When she got to Gokul she said, 'Here, Krishna, I have come to you.' And she merged."

"A Muslim devotee of Krishna?"

"Is that so hard to believe? Rasa Khan, the author of some of the greatest devotional songs of Krishna ever written, was also a Muslim. So was Khan-i-Khanan Rahim, the son of Akbar's boyhood adviser Bairam Khan. Rahim was something else entirely. When he was governor of the province of Avadh he used to bestow gifts with his hand uplifted and his eyes downcast, to show that God was the real giver, not he."

Rahim's wife, Aram Banu Begum, was Akbar's daughter.

"It was well known in court that though a Muslim Rahim had become a devotee of Krishna. Some of the more bigoted Muslim courtiers were therefore always scheming against him, hoping to trip him up in some way so that he would be humiliated. After a number of abortive schemes they came up with a metrical plot and proclaimed a poetry completion contest. In this sort of competition the first line of a couplet is given to which a second line must be appended. The prize goes to whoever creates the best second line, the line which best fits with the first. This sort of challenge, which has been used in India since ancient days, was also used to identify someone who had long been missing, or in hiding. In such cases the line that would be publicized would be the first line of a couplet known only to the seeker and the person sought.

"The first line that was concocted for this competition was *kaffir he wo jo khyal nahi islam ka*, which translates something like this: 'Whoever does not believe in Islam is an infidel.' The bigots were sure that they had Rahim now. If in his second line he spoke favorably of Krishna it would be a direct insult to Islam, and he could then be accused of blasphemy. If on the other hand he spoke favorably of Islam everyone would know how weak his devotion for Krishna was, and how willing he was to compromise his principles. His opportunism and his fear of loss of position and freedom would thus disgrace him. Rahim frankly did not like the idea of such a trial by verse. But for some reason Akbar insisted, giving Rahim no choice but to accede to his sovereign's wishes.

"The fanatics could hardly wait for the month to pass until the day of Rahim's dishonor, but soon enough that day arrived. All the poets who assembled before the Emperor spoke glowingly of the greatness of Islam and the perfidies of the unbelievers. All, that is, except Rahim, who was kept for last, that the suspense might magnify the expected stigma. But when it became Rahim's turn everyone was dumbfounded when he took the given line as the second line of his couplet, not the first. His couplet became:

Khyal he wo lam, gesu mere pyare ghanashyam ka.
Kaffir he wo jo khyal nahi islam ka.

Belief there is in that '*lam*' that is formed by the locks of my beloved Ghanshyam.
A heretic is anyone who does not believe in this 'lam.'

"Rahim had created a verse which actually praised *Ghanshyam* (Krishna) by making a brilliant play on the Arabic word *Islam*, which can mean in Hindi 'this lam' (*is lam*). The Arabic character for the sound 'lam' is a stroke that looks something like the silhouette of someone's hair. Rahim could thus legitimately take the word *islam* to mean 'these locks of hair,' and could then say that the only true infidel is whoever fails to have faith in Krishna's hair, that is, in Krishna Himself.

"All the zealots were of course quite discomfited by this sudden turn of events, but what could they do? He had beaten them fair and square. The Emperor was overjoyed that Rahim had acquitted himself so brilliantly. But when he summoned Rahim for congratulation Rahim told him, 'Your Majesty, you became Emperor thanks to my father, and it is partly thanks to my worship of Krishna that your rule has been maintained. To my knowledge I have never given you any cause for censure, and yet to test me you sanctioned this competition. Now I have lost interest in your court, and I am leaving your service.' Despite Akbar's pleas he left, and then Akbar's real problems began."

"This was not exactly a curse?"

"No, Rahim was too noble a man to curse anyone, certainly not the man whose salt he had eaten for so long. No, he simply withdrew the prayers for protection which he had been regularly offering up all during the time that he had been in Akbar's service. Without those prayers Akbar began to experience the effects of his own karmas more strongly. Akbar still survived for a while longer, for he was lucky enough to have been blessed by a number of saints. The Mughals as a dynasty had even been blessed by one of the Sikh gurus. But when some of the later Mughals tortured the later Sikh gurus the Mughals lost that blessing. This led them to eventually lose India to the British.

"And how do you think the British lost India? They might still be ruling here now were it not for three curses, delivered to them by three kings that they had treacherously overthrown and sent into exile. One was King Thibaw of Burma, who was such a good sadhaka that he could even perform a little Vajroli. Another was Wajid Ali Shah, the ruler of Avadh, who had so perfected his sadhana that Krishna Himself would come and dance before him. And the third was the last of the Mughals, Bahadur Shah Zafar, who was a true poet. His last poem was a heartbroken lament for his fate: 'How ill-starred you are, Zafar, that for your burial you could not even obtain two yards of earth in the bylane of your beloved,' namely India. At one time he had 'owned' all of India; now he retained not even six feet worth of his cherished country in which to be buried. And it was all because of the Britishers. Can you imagine the anguish that he and the other two rulers must have felt as they died? Anguish that was strong enough to bring down the British Empire? *That* is the power of a real curse. So long as Victoria ruled the Rishi's blessing protected her in her position as Mistress of India. As soon as she died these curses were free to exert their effects since none of her successors had the kind of blessing that she had had. Curses and blessings: the Law of Karma. Remember that, my boy, when you are over there in your country."

∾

My departure for the United States at the end of August 1980 coincided almost to the day with the start of my Sade Sati. During my absence from the scene Vimalananda continued to procure horseflesh, beginning with Redstone, whose other half he purchased from Erach Ghasvala. He also obtained in partnership with Tehmul a very likely-looking filly that he named Meherunnissa in honor of the Emperor Akbar's daughter-in-law.

Kamaal slipped out of Vimalananda's hands in early 1981. After cooling his hooves in first Lafange's stables and then Tehmul's yard without ever notching a win, we had sent him to be trained by Lalloo Dalal. Lalloo, who was a friend of Tehmul's, had approached Vimalananda with a promise to make Kamaal win, and there seemed no reason not to let him try. Lalloo trained mainly for Nawab Saheb, a refined member of the minor Muslim nobility who sold jewels to pay for the corn bills of his horses that ran in colors resembling some peer's livery. One of Nawab Saheb's daughters became very friendly with Lalloo; they were seen everywhere together. It was rumored they were having an affair. Wags commented that such an affair was a sensible use of her time, for it gave her a crow's nest view of Lalloo's plans for Nawab Saheb's horses.

Despite Dalal's promise Kamaal seemed to owe nothing to Vimalananda, for he continued to lose even there. But when Vimalananda requested Lalloo to send Kamaal back to Tehmul's yard Lalloo refused to do so until all his arrears had been cleared, and he counterattacked by demanding immediate settlement of his unpaid bills for extras. Vimalananda being just then exceeedingly low on cash he had little alternative but to transfer Kamaal to Lalloo in payment of those 'arrears,' which seemed suspiciously high. Immediately after the transfer Lalloo shifted his horses east for the Hyderabad season, where Kamaal won without further ado. That sudden win created great suspicion in all our minds. Lalloo's explanation was a model of innocence: "For some reason the horse decided to take the bit at last. All my hard work on him finally paid off; I only wish it had done so while you still owned him." Though we might doubt him we had no way to challenge his version of the story, for horses are not machines.

Just before I arrived India again in October 1981, Vimalananda lost his beloved dog Lizoo, who had simply grown too old to continue to live. Vimalananda, who valued love above all else, was hit hard by the loss of this being who loved him purely and unconditionally. I tried to soften the shock of this blow by taking him on a round-the-world tour in December 1981 and January 1982. A sparkling win by his new filly Meherunnissa on December 26 while he and I were at my parents' home in New Mexico raised his spirits sufficiently to spur some of his old enthusiasm. He became so merry, in fact, that he was able to convince my teetotaller parents to sip a little champagne in Meherunnissa's honor.

Back in India in January 1982 Vimalananda went to Bangalore to settle with Ghasvala for the other half of Stoney's second foal. He was accompanied by the scheming Miss Bambhani, who was making noises about entering the racing business herself. But once in Bangalore, Vimalananda discovered that Ghasvala had understood their agreement to be for a half-interest in the first foal only, not the second. Ghasvala, moreover, wanted considerably more for that second foal than Vimalananda was willing or able to pay. As a sop Ghasvala offered him a good deal on another filly, which Vimalananda accepted reluctantly. His heart was set on Stoney's new foal, and he also questioned whether this other filly's action (foot-joint configuration) was a little too upright to be healthy. Ghasvala assured him that this would be no problem. Vimalananda named her Ramakda ("Toy"). Though she did endear herself to us with her 'toy-like' ways her upright action did in fact interfere with her running, which did nothing to endear Ghasvala to any of us.

In February 1982 Vimalananda took me to meet his Junior Guru Maharaj for the first time. He had not dared introduce me before, for he knew what Guru Maharaj could do to me if he lost his temper. In fact, Vimalananda had sent me off to the United States suddenly in May 1977, ostensibly to reconnect with my family, just days before Guru Maharaj arrived unannounced in Bombay for his first visit there since 1959. Even then Vimalananda refused to let Guru Maharaj in the door until Guru Maharaj promised that nothing would happen to Lizoo so long as he remained there. Lizoo had become a dog due to Guru Maharaj's curse, after all, and Guru Maharaj wanted to close out his karmic account with her to free himself of that rnanubandhana. On his part Vimalananda wanted both to retain the love of his doggie as long as he could, and to continually remind Guru Maharaj of the repercussions of this curse.

Guru Maharaj had migrated back to his place of residence before I made it back from the United States that year. After completing such a journey he would not venture off his hill again for at least twelve years. If I was to meet him I thus had no choice but to proceed to his mountain. Vimalananda accompanied me to protect me, as he had previously protected Lizoo, and to get Guru Maharaj to agree to give Redstone the same kind of riderly treatment that he had given Stone Ice a decade before. Vimalananda wanted this in trade for doing some unspecified but essential work that Guru Maharaj wanted done. But Guru Maharaj was not ready to deal, and we had to leave empty-handed.

At the door Vimalananda said to Guru Maharaj, "At least do something for my boy here; do some *Rakta Shuddhi* (purification of the blood) for him!" At this Guru Maharaj, whose love was truly unparalleled, stared at me with studied bluster, pulled hard on my hair, and started to sting me with slaps about the body. "So, you want Rakta Shuddhi, do you?" he shouted, and after he had finished his work he said, "OK, that's Rakta Shuddhi!"

A beaming Vimalananda hugged me as we walked toward the car.

"What was all that about?" I wondered aloud.

"Rakta Shuddhi—great! He's removed a number of your karmas that have been perverting your mind. You'll be much improved now, whether you like it or not."

I began to think that Vimalananda had partially turned me over to Guru Maharaj, as if saying, "I don't know what to do with this one, Maharaj; you handle him." As time went by I discovered the truth of this surmise; Guru Maharaj later told me that he had had to promise Vimalananda that he would not kill me while he was improving me. However, in the coming years Guru Maharaj took pains to harass me over such things as my then girlfriend and my diet, and came near to causing me serious grief in the imbroglio over Aghori Baba's stick—which is another story.

As Vimalananda and I drove away from Guru Maharaj on the day of that last meeting they were to have in the flesh we saw two pigs coupling—a sight which sent Vimalananda into a rapture of joy: "Guru Maharaj has not deserted me yet! Redstone will win very soon!" And so he did.

Shortly after Redstone's first win I was sitting with Vimalananda in Bombay when Erach Ghasvala called with the sad news of sudden deaths of both Stoney and her new foal. I feared Vimalananda would become distraught, but he was actually happy: "She is free now," he said, "to take a better rebirth, to continue her development. Shouldn't I be overjoyed about that, if I truly love her? Moreover, I now have her son Redstone with me, so the karmic link continues.

"And besides, Erach didn't deserve to have her. He agreed to take her not out of love for her but because he thought he'd be able to make lots of money off her children. Breeding animals for sale is a big karma, even if you are not raising them for slaughter. This is why I never bred my Lizoo. I had no place to keep all her puppies myself, and if I had given them away I would not have been able to keep track of what was happening to them. If one had gone to a family that tortured it I would have had to bear most of the blame, first because I had arranged for it to be brought into the world and then because I placed it with that family. Animals are as big a responsibility as people. Or maybe bigger, in that they can't speak up for themselves." Though I knew that Vimalananda had had some hand in the unexpected demise of mare and foal—I had seen him at work too often to think otherwise—he never admitted any complicity.

Now that Redstone was the only son Stone Ice would ever foal Vimalananda paid even more attention to him, and while we continued to pamper all the horses by bringing them carrots, apples and other treats Redstone received extra-special pampering. One reason that Vimalananda liked Redstone was a certain whorl of hair located in an auspicious spot on his body. He was also overjoyed that Redstone was not an *asrudar*, a 'horse who will make you cry.' In such animals the whorl on their foreheads is so low that they can see it. An asrudar makes you weep by mangling your prosperity; either it will personally bankrupt you by losing when you have bet on it heavily, or it will make money for you even while it is causing your business to fail. Stone Ice's perfect star on her forehead, well above the line of her eyes, was one of the things which made her lucky. Vimalananda, who had learned what he knew of horse markings from a Maharashtrian nobleman, the Chief of Jat, would point out such signs to me when he saw them. One strongly propitious combination is the *panchakalyana* ("five auspicious markings"), which is defined as a horse who sports four white socks and a white forehead blaze.

The American Stud Book, a copy of which I had brought Vimalananda from the United States, spurred his interest in Redstone's possibilities yet further. He would spend hours pouring over the permutations and combinations created by such noble progenitors as Potooooooooo (Pot8os, or Potatoes) and Waxy, or studying the ramifications of the fact that about 90% of all thoroughbreds are descended from a single stallion named Eclipse who was foaled during an eclipse and never lost a race. We pondered such questions as coat color inheritance—chestnut, bay, brown, black, grey, red roan and blue roan—and why most of the issue in the line of a horse named Geranium had light-colored eyes. Equine, human and divine lineages became a favored topic of our conversation as he enhanced my knowledge both of horseflesh and of the genealogical complexities of Indian myth.

Ancestry even crept into seemingly unrelated subjects, as it did on the evening of a day during which we had discussed with a vet effective treatments for the 'sand cracks' that afflict the hooves of certain horses. Vimalananda began that evening by musing on the nature of the Three Gunas: *Sattva* (equilibrium), *Rajas* (activity), and *Tamas* (inertia). Devas basically have Sattvic intellect, asuras Tamasic intellect, and humans Rajasic intellect. To advance spiritually you first replace Rajas and Tamas with Sattva in your consciousness, and then use Sattva to conquer Sattva itself, that you may go beyond the Gunas. Good karma is basically something that helps free you from your rnanubandhanas and the bondage of Rajas and Tamas; bad karmas have the opposite effect. Enlightenment lies beyond the influence of all of these gunas.

As he was meandering along in this vein inspiration suddenly hit him, and he slipped into story mode:

"It happened once during the reign of Caliph Haroun el-Rashid that three marijuana-smokers who were sitting in the main bazaar of the city of Baghdad started to have a loud argument about which of them was greatest. They made such a noise that they were called in before the caliph, who asked them who they were."

"Who were they actually?"

"They were actually Sattva, Rajas and Tamas. Now please listen. The first said, 'I am an expert on horses' pedigrees.' The second said, 'I can tell everything about a man from his face.' When the caliph turned to the third that man said, 'I think it will be better if I don't tell your majesty who I am, because if I do you will have my throat cut.'

"This man's cheek immediately enraged the king, who ordered all three to be confined until he had some opportunity to test their abilities. The first two were housed together and received a regular ration from the palace kitchen, while the third, still smiling, was kept alone and got nothing to eat.

"One day, when the caliph was in a peculiar frame of mind, he sent for the three and told them he was ready to take up the matter of their examinations. He brought out a horse and asked the first man if it was purebred.

"After looking it over the man told the king, 'Definitely not!'

"The king became wild and said, 'How can this horse, which is a present from the Shah of Iran, not be purebred? Tell me how you know or you will die for it!'

"The first man answered, 'I merely looked at the crack in his hoof. All forest animals have cracked hooves. This horse must have also come from the forest, where the rough ground has caused this crack.'

"The king was so shocked that he could say nothing further. He then turned to the second man and said, 'Now, am I of royal lineage or not? Tell me my true lineage!' He was thinking that he would hear that he was of the family of the daughter of Hazrat Imam Hussein. Imagine his reaction when the second man prefaced his remarks with, 'First promise me that you will not punish me for my bluntness,' and said upon receiving that promise, 'You are the son of a cook.'

"The king drew his sword, just as he had after the reply of the first, and said, 'If you cannot prove that impossible statement you will surely die.'

"The man responded calmly, 'Please ask your mother.'

"The caliph rushed to the harem, found his mother, and with drawn sword and eyes reddened with anger demanded, 'Who was my father? The late king, or a cook?'

"His mother looked at him compassionately and said, 'My son, your father was very old when we married. He could never produce children, and it greatly worried me that there was no heir to the throne. While I was wondering what to do I noticed a young cook in the kitchen, strong and handsome to look at. You were conceived after we slept together.'

"The sobered caliph returned to his court and said to the second man, 'You were absolutely right, but how did you know?'

"The man answered, 'It was very easy, your majesty. You sent us rations of food while we were being kept in your palace. No real king would keep an account of how much food his guests were eating; only a cook would.'

"Now the speechless king had nothing left to ask the third man—who was really Sattva—so he was given leave to go with the other two, without ever disclosing his own special capacity. After all, a spiritual man should never disclose his capacities to anyone. And the caliph learned the lesson of his lifetime."

The lineage question took a turn for the somber when in spring 1982 the war for the Falkland Islands began. This conflict, coupled with the ingratitude of certain Americans of his acquaintance, caused the lovely positivity that Vimalananda felt towards Westerners—which had swelled during his recent world tour—to evaporate with the sizzle of water on a hot griddle. While in the army he had commanded Gurkhas, and was proud of the way they acquitted themselves during this invasion. But he was contemptuous of the operation as a whole: "The Brits have been very lucky in this war," he observed sourly, "to have America helping them. Otherwise their entire invasion fleet would have been sunk by now by the Argentine Air Force. The Americans were very clever: they sold the right bombs to the Argentines, but gave them the wrong fuses. Without the right fuses how would they explode? Would the Americans have dared to do this to anyone else? No, Thatcher was very clever. She played on Reagan's prejudices by subtly suggesting to him that the Anglo-Saxon countries should stick together, and Reagan fell for her bait hook, line and sinker.

"But Thatcher is no Victoria, and if she thinks that war can salvage for Britain what is left of its empire she had best think again. The Law of Karma is no respecter of persons, places or things. Britain would have been wiser to recognize that its day in the sun is past, and to gracefully yield her position of pre-eminence. Had the United Kingdom settled with the Argentine government its grateful populace would have showered the Brits with blessings, which they urgently require. Instead, Thatcher has opened herself and her country to the effects of still more curses, which will enlarge their burdens of karmic debt. This war is going to cost both of them dearly, karmically as well as monetarily."

"But what about the karma of the Argentines? They must have done something to deserve this?"

"They must have; that is the Law of Karma. Their soldiers killed in the field were destined to die at the hands of those Brits and Gurkhas who invaded; that is fairly straightforward. As for the Argentine generals, well, think of the mountain of evil karmas they had created for themselves by causing so many innocent people to 'disappear.' Those karmas had to catch up with them some day."

"But this defeat is just the beginning for the generals, isn't it?"

"Oh yes; they have plenty of blood on their hands. They have a lot to suffer yet; the Law of Karma will take good care of them, just like it took care of the Shah of Iran."

"You are speaking now of the most recent Shah of Iran? The man who is said to have installed a solid gold toilet on his personal jet?"

"Yes, that Shah. Do you remember that he staged his coronation at the ancient Persian capital of Persepolis?"

"I do."

"Persepolis had been a deserted ruin for hundreds of years until the Shah got it into his mind to be crowned there. He wanted to show everyone that he was the legitimate successor to the great Persian emperors of yore, like Cyrus, Darius, and Xerxes. But he forgot to ask himself whether those great rulers would enjoy having their ancient citadel invaded by some inconsequential nincompoop. When the Shah's antics aroused the spirits of those monarchs from their sleep of death they asked themselves, 'Who is this pip-squeak who dares to strut about comparing himself to us?' When they looked down on him they saw not a king but the insignificant son of an insignificant cavalry officer who had made himself Shah after a palace coup. All they could hear when this Shah spoke was the barking of an insolent pup. The impudence of this 'Shah' who lacked everything that is *shahi* (regal, majestic) so infuriated the dead emperors that they cursed him. Those were the curses that ended the Shah's reign, just as surely as the curses of King Thibaw, Wajid Ali Shah, and Bahadur Shah Zafar destroyed the British Empire. If the Shah had remembered who he was, and not tried to pretend to be something that he was not, he might be ruling Iran today."

"Would it have made a difference if the Shah had actually had some pedigree, if he had actually been descended from conquerors?"

"It might have; at the very least, it would have made him understand the gravity of the situation into which he was thrusting himself."

"Do we think it was Saturn who put this coronation idea into the Shah's mind?"

"Who else could do it? The Shah's good karmas had obviously run out, and it had become time for him to experience the results of his myriad evil karmas. *Vinasha kale viparita buddhi*—'when the time for your destruction arrives your mind becomes perverted.'"

"And Saturn is just the being to pervert it for you."

"That is his job."

"He certainly does it well."

"Remember that whenever you remember him."

After Redstone's next convincing win, in the late spring of 1982, Vimalananda began to suspect that he had a horse who could "go a long way off," i.e. who could win one of India's Classic races. The horses entrained for Poona shortly after, and on our way to inspect them there he shared his feelings with me: "You know, Robby, I thought I had lost my will to live—but I haven't; not yet! There's life in the old boy still! And for this I have to thank Mamrabahen. I never wanted to get back into racing, but she forced me to return. She did it for her own purposes, no doubt, but just as I blame her for some of my problems I have to thank her for some of my enjoyments, which are due at least in part to her insistence."

He paused as if in thought, then began again abruptly: "Some years back a certain sadhu lived in Girnar with a few disciples. One day he decided to go off a little way into the jungle and sit in meditation. He was really a good sadhu, and after a short while he was doing so well that Indra became frightened and decided to send an apsaras down to disturb him."

In the mythology of the Puranas Indra is always sending some *apsaras* or another down to disturb some sadhu or other, for a hard-working sadhu who performs enough penance may be elevated by the powers-that-be to the Indra-state, and every Indra will try to protect his own position.

"The apsaras appeared in front of him to tantalize him, but he was so deep in meditation that he didn't know what was going on around him. Then she used a siddhi to become tiny, and started to dance on him. Still no effect. First she danced on his body, then on his face, and then she jumped onto his matted locks. At last the sadhu felt a disturbance, perceived what was going on, and lost his temper. He said to her, 'Become a female monkey!' Immediately she became a female monkey.

"When she realized what had happened she began to cry, but he told her to keep quiet and not to worry. He took her back to his ashram and ordered his disciples to feed her sweets and good food whenever she was hungry. Not long after that the sadhu left his body, and the monkey lived on in the ashram. When the monkey died she was cremated, and her memorial was placed next to that of the sadhu.

"Look what happened here: Even though the sadhu escaped falling prey to the blandishments of the apsaras he still created some karma for himself, but lost some of his shakti by losing his temper. Similarly, a whole train of karmas has been initiated because of Mamrabahen, but now at least with Redstone there is a chance that we will see some good results of all our work. Nature is so kind!"

He fell silent as we entered the *ghats* (hills), where all his concentration would be needed, and had me toss a coin, as all drivers did, to the little shrine at the foot of the chief hill. The Konkan coastal strip that contains Bombay is connected with the Deccan Plateau where sits Poona by a road which climbs two thousand feet in the space of a couple of miles. At the time that Vimalananda and I drove it together it was a two-lane highway crowded with the usual Indian transport panoply of trucks, buses, cars, motorcycles, bullock carts and the occasional stray bicyclist, pedestrian and animal. Climbing the ghats was exceptionally stressful because of the need to maintain forward momentum without collision and without overheating the engine. My sensory awareness became effortlessly heightened when riding with Vimalananda on the ghat section of the Bombay-Poona road as he meticulously preserved gaps between our vehicle and those on the opposite side of the road. I often watched him merrily miss oncoming conveyances by literally no more than an inch or two. "Gauging," he would say, "it's all a matter of gauging. When your gauging is good you can drive confidently," whether it be on the road or through life. I had no anxiety as he gauged his way through the ghats since I knew well how well he could control his car; but when we reached that last inch the self-preservation instinct would still send a surge of adrenaline through me anyway, to remind me of my mortality.

One day as we were driving back into Bombay from Poona Vimalananda was so busy chatting with our guest, a horse owner named Willie D'Souza, that he failed to notice that the traffic light in front of us had turned red. In some amazement Willie and I watched Vimalananda forget to stop, but we were less astonished than was the man who had begun to cross the street at about the same time that we barreled into the intersection. Resentment, incredulity, and inspired aggravation flitted in succession across his face as he hurdled out of our way. I was not concerned for his life (Bombay pedestrians are fleet of foot) but I was somewhat troubled that Vimalananda was not too troubled. Seeing this, and eyeing the startled D'Souza, he commented as he drove on, "You should know by now, Robby, that someone is there to prevent me from getting into serious trouble even when I goof. And the fellow was not even in serious danger; he had plenty of time to escape. But the look on his face, that was priceless!

"I had a much worse problem the day I was driving down the road, right here in Bombay, when all of a sudden without any warning whatsoever both front wheels fell off! I was shocked, I tell you, shocked! There I sat in the middle of the road, holding my useless steering wheel, as I watched my wheels speed away from me. One ended up safely by the side of the road, but the other one rolled all the way across the street and bowled over a bystander. He had to be rushed to hospital, but fortunately was not too seriously injured." D'Souza and I were now impolitely laughing at the vision of two wayward wheels fleeing the stunned Vimalananda. "There is no security in life, I tell you," he went on. "One minute you are standing there calmly, minding your own business, and the next you are lying in the street, flattened by a runaway tire!"

The next day as I helped Vimalananda cook lunch I was again reminded of his command over gauging. After we put the food on the fire and went to sit in the other room Vimalananda said, "There is really no end to what you can learn. You know how much I love to cook; and many people have enjoyed my food. I think you will agree with me on that."

"I have always enjoyed your food."

"And you know that I have an advantage no Western chef has, thanks to the blessings of Annapurna, the goddess of food. Did I ever tell you what happened when Faram's wife burned the meat?"

"No, I don't think you have."

"Well, she burned it absolutely black. She charred it. Faram, as usual, lost his temper and started to shout at her. In the interest of family harmony I told him to shut up, and told her, 'Ma, please wash all the pieces of meat with soap and water.' She couldn't help laughing, and said, 'Do you know what that will do to it?' I said, 'It's spoiled anyway, isn't it? So just wash it and don't argue with me please.' She washed it, I cooked it, and it came out perfect, without even a hint of burned flavor."

I had seen his wizardry in the kitchen first-hand, close up, so I believed this story instantly.

"Oh, and by the way, Robby, the food is cooking a little too fast; turn the fire down just slightly."

Whenever I put a pot on the fire in a kitchen run by Vimalananda I knew that I could safely leave it to cook on its own, in the absolute certainty that the moment anything went wrong with it he would tell me. This was the power of his gauging.

I adjusted the fire, then thanked him for his care. He took a histrionic whiff of air, said, "Yes, it is. Sometimes when other people are cooking," he chuckled, "they try to show off how expert they are. I don't like show-offs, so I can't help but have a little fun. When they turn away from the food for a moment I will shout, 'Quick, turn off the fire, the food is burning!' and before anyone will be able to get there the food will be burnt!"

I laughed too, and was about to tell him what a show-off he was when he retorted: "Well, if they have the ability they can show it off too; who will stop them? What I object to is fakery, pretending to be something you are not. If they were so smart they should be able to turn down the fire from where they are sitting just as easily as I can turn it up."

Vimalananda's intolerance for pretenders had more than once before inspired him to show me just how little the run-of-the-mill 'swami' in India really walked his talk. "Such people show a trick or two and mislead the public into thinking they are some sort of super-dupers," he would say, before cutting another godman down to size. "I know one who claims to talk to Parashurama face-to-face. Now, Parashurama is a real Bhagavan, God incarnate, one of the Ten Avataras. Anyone who sees Parashurama loses all interest in worldly things and spends all his time alone. His only answer to people's questions will be, 'Leave me alone!' Why? Because that is Parashurama's nature. Parashurama, who is also known as Bhargava, loves to be alone. He lives almost exclusively on the astral planes and above. Bhargava is also continuously moving, which means that his devotee would also go on the move. If he doesn't, and if he says he wants money and an ashram and all sorts of other things, is it logically possible to conclude that he talks to Parashurama face to face? You tell me."

"Haven't you ever pretended to be something you're not?" I asked in mild pique one day after such a diatribe.

"Of course I have," he said, with a laugh at himself as a memory reared up within him. "Once I was staying with a friend at a Dak Bungalow," which is a sort of rest house for visiting dignitaries that the government maintains in small towns that lack hotels. "A barber had come to shave me, and when he had me lathered up he said, 'You know, sir, you look just like Chandramohan,' who was a famous movie star of that time. He was a good actor; if you ever get a chance, Robby, go see the movie *Pukar*. Chandramohan does a beautiful job of playing the Emperor Jehangir in that film.

"I don't know what came over me, but when the barber said this I smiled and nodded and pointed to myself as if to say, 'Yes, I am Chandramohan.' I never actually said in so many words that I was—that would have been too deceptive—but I didn't correct his misimpression either. The thought that he was shaving the great Chandramohan fired up the barber, so he did an excellent job on my beard. After he left I thought the charade was at an end and I lay down to take a nap.

"I had forgotten, though, that I was in a small town. In Indian villages and towns the barbers act as the news networks. When my companion woke me in alarm from my nap I looked out the window to find the entire Dak Bungalow surrounded by anxious fans, all hoping to see or touch or be touched by the great Chandramohan. It was a hell of a job to extract ourselves from that situation, let me tell you! Ever since then I have thought many times before trying to pretend that I am something I am not. But even in the Chandramohan case I only imitated an actor, not a saint. To imitate a saint is to ask for *real* trouble. Don't forget the sadhus in Girnar!"

"What happened to them?"

"Some years back one of the Nawabs of Junagadh (the principality at the base of Mount Girnar) got so fed up with all the fake sadhus and fakirs who were crowding Girnar that he had his men round them all up. Then he addressed them: 'You shameless idlers! How dare you lie around all day pretending to mediate! I know that most of you are criminals and good-for-nothings. If you are real sadhus, prove it to me! Show me a miracle! If you can't show me a miracle you are going to have to start working for your food!' None of the men was a real saint, so none of them could perform a miracle. The Nawab accordingly had his soldiers put each of them in front of a *chakki*, a grinding stone, which they had to turn by hand all day long, grinding grain into flour.

"All these phoney holymen bellyached like crazy as they worked, but now it was too late for them to get by just by pretending to be pious. Finally one really good sadhu who had escaped the Nawab's dragnet came to hear of their humilation and came down the mountain to confront the Nawab."

"Who was he?"

"I don't know." I could see that he did.

"This sadhu told the prince, 'Even if these fellows are crooks you were wrong to lock them up.'

"The Nawab, who had no intention of letting some sadhu presume to tell him what to do, replied, 'Since you have such a soft spot for these slackers why don't you go join them in the hoosegow!' The sadhu shrugged his shoulders, and accompanied by a police escort went to the prison, where he addressed the inmates: 'When I look at you I am ashamed to be wearing my *girwa* (ochre-colored renunciate's clothing); you have stained it so with your hypocrisy! What kind of sadhus and fakirs are you? When the Nawab asked for a miracle could none of you oblige? Stand back!'

"Then that sadhu shouted, '*Chakki chalo! Dhana piso!* (Turn, grindstones! Grind the grain!).' At that, all the stones began to turn on their own. Amazed, the jailers ran to summon the Nawab, who was appropriately impressed by this demonstration. He told that sadhu, 'Yes, you are the real thing; you can go.'

"The sadhu replied, 'No, Nawab Saheb, I can't go alone; everyone must come with me.' Though the Nawab was reluctant to let the frauds go he could not deny the sadhu, and had to set all the sadhus and fakirs free. As they left the jail the good sadhu told them, 'See that you perform your penance properly from now on. If you fail again, you will be expelled from Girnar!'"

"Did that lesson reform all those lazybones?"

"Yes, for a while."

"Until their natural svabhavas reasserted themselves?"

"Well, it is very difficult to conquer your nature, even after you have devoted your life to your sadhana. Fortunately someone is always there to test anyone who claims to have his nature under control."

Vimalananda's love of staging practical examinations of putative saints led him one day to take me with him to pay a call on a *baba* ("saintly person"). Our visit was a stopover during a test-drive of a used car that Vimalananda was thinking of purchasing, and the hour we spent cooling our heels before we could see the great man did nothing to improve Vimalananda's temper. Still, as soon as we were ushered into the august presence Vimalananda bowed to him, very low, to show humility. This pleased the baba a great deal. Then he asked Vimalananda what sort of business he was in, and Vimalananda replied, "The machinery business."

"Oh," replied the baba, "machinery business *very* good business." Then he opened his hand, and some ash poured out onto our expectant palms, for he was one of those people who make things like ash appear from thin air. I collected both heaps of ash in small pieces of paper and folded them into little bundles, which I put into the car's glove compartment after we had said our goodbyes. I accidentally left them there when we returned the car, and within the week that car got smashed both from the front and from the rear. Shortly thereafter the baba had a heart attack and later came down with other diseases. Vimalananda claimed not to know how any of this happened, calling it a coincidence. If so it was a truly conspicuous coincidence; I was mightily impressed.

"I began by touching his feet," replied Vimalananda when I brought up the subject, "because in India when you meet a saint you always touch his feet. Touching shows humility, but more importantly it allows you to steal some of the saint's energy. Generally energy enters the body through the head and exits through the feet. A true saint is the embodiment of his deity and the energy emanating from him is the energy of that deity. By touching a saint's feet you collect a little of that energy, which purifies your own consciousness and makes it more subtle. The saint loses some of his own peace of mind by this, which is unfortunate for the saint; this is how many saints go bad. First they achieve a good state, maybe by doing hard penances in strict seclusion. Then when they come back into the world they start absorbing the confusion and attachment of their devotees, and they too become worldly. A sensible saint will never let anyone touch his feet except on special occasions, like Guru Purnima.

"Anyone with subtle intelligence who touches a saint's feet will be able to learn a great deal about that saint's innate qualities. Touching this fellow's feet was my first test; I wanted to see how sensible he was and how much energy he had. He unfortunately scored zero on both counts. Next came the question of my 'business.' If he had any kind of real power at all he should have been able to know that I was in the race horse business and not the machinery business. But he had nothing except ash, which did not impress me. There are so many ways in which to produce ash and trinkets from what seems to be nowhere. It's too bad that the old man is unwell, but he should have known better than to try to show off. I am just sorry for the poor car; that ash was the cause of its ruination. Now you see how sticky karma can be!"

"Don't you think you were a little hard on him?"

"Hard?! I was hard on Taat Maharaj. *Taat* means 'gunny-sack,' which is what this fellow wore. One of my friends brought me to Taat Maharaj by telling me he could sit in samadhi for hours at a time while his followers sang and chanted. I didn't believe it, so I went to have his *darshana* (the viewing of a saint or deity). Sure enough, I could see that he was merely closing his eyes and fooling everyone. On top of that I was supposed to bow down to him! While I waited there I examined the room carefully and came up with a plan. Back at home I sharpened the point of a long iron nail until it was razor sharp. A few days later I returned to Taat Maharaj and got into the line to touch his lotus feet. When I got to the head of the line I bent down, raised the nail high above my head, and jabbed it into his foot. My God! What a howl came from that charlatan! His bellowings even drowned out the warbles of his singers."

"Wouldn't most people have responded to a nail in the foot even if they were in samadhi?"

"No, not if the samadhi is genuine. A person who is in samadhi has no knowledge whatsoever of the outside world so long as he remains in samadhi. If Taat Maharaj had actually been in samadhi he would have felt nothing from that nail, not even a pinprick. But he was just pretending, so he felt it all. Everyone was so stunned that I had time to rush out the door to where an accomplice was waiting in the getaway car, and off we sped. I don't like to think about what might have happened to me had I been caught!"

"Was there no karma involved in that little escapade?"

"There is karma involved in every activity, but this karma was worth it to me to see that imposter unmasked. I do have certain advantages in this department—the advantages of knowing my own karmas and rnanubandhanas—and I can assure you that he deserved what he got from me. Unless you know your rnanubandhanas, though, and know how to negate your karmas, never try any stunts like this!"

Knowledge of his rnanubandhanas and how to negate them seemed to spur Vimalananda into action when one of the doctors at my college sang the praises of one Dada Maharaj, who was reputed by some in Poona to be a great saint. "We must go have his darshana," said Vimalananda enthusiastically when he heard this news.

"Hah, so now this fellow's time is up," I replied with some sarcasm.

"Robby," said Vimalananda, feigning hurt, "am I that bad? Just because you have seen a few coincidences should you always make fun of me when I go to meet some 'saint'? What about Madhavbaba?"

Vimalananda's appreciation for the genuine article caused us always to visit Madhavbaba Patil whenever he came to Poona. Madhavbaba, who lived some two hours or more south of Poona in Narsobawadi, had been so thorough in his sadhanas that now he spent all of his time in some world other than ours, lost in contemplation of his Beloved. Vimalananda, who had known Madhavbaba for many years, respected him as a good sadhaka, and for his part Madhavbaba, who never appeared to recognize most people but blessed all indiscriminately, always recognized and remembered Vimalananda.

But I knew Madhavbaba was different, and indeed, my prediction regarding this Dada Maharaj proved to be true. When first we went to Dada Maharaj he met us perfunctorily and informed us that he had no time for us. Perhaps we didn't seem sufficiently important to him. The very next day, however, he called us back, and personally welcomed us when we came, explaining that he had been soundly remonstrated for his gaffe in a dream the night before and wanted to make amends for his negligence. He verbally pictured for us his spiritual adventures in Rishikesh, when he had seen angels ascending and descending divine staircases, and then described such other visions as seemed to impress his raptly-listening retainers. But as we sat listening politely I could see from the set of Vimalananda's eyes that he felt his work there to be completed. His interest in Dada Maharaj evaporated as promptly as it had developed, and the old man did in fact die just a few months later.

During the 1982 monsoon Vimalananda spent even more time than usual in Poona, focusing most of his energies on Redstone's progress. During the monsoon it is easier to focus on almost anything in Poona rather than in Bombay, when the rain falls like Thor's hammer onto the backs of anyone unwise enough to get caught out in a downpour. Once or twice each year it rains 18 inches or more in a single day. Then the overworked storm sewers, which can ordinarily handle up to a foot of rain daily, overflow to send nine months worth of accumulated muck into the laps of the luckless commuters scurring back to homes glazed with mold and mildew. The Poona monsoon, by contrast, is better behaved: it rarely rains more than a drizzle during the day, reserving most of its deluges for the evenings and nights. The rare heavy rain there is at most 7 or 8 inches. Poona during the monsoon is like an English city during a warm spell: temperate, green and inviting. It is at its pleasantest then, and the racing is cool and elegant.

When Redstone won yet another race, this time on the Poona course's verdant turf, Vimalananda determined to try him in the premier "run-up" race for the Classics: The Colonel Pratap Singh of Jodhpur Cup. Part of Vimalananda's fondness for the race derived from its namesake, Colonel Pratap Singh, sometimes known as "the Bayard of India," who was one of Queen Victoria's aides-de-camp and who helped lead the Indian Army in France during the First World War. The only problem, he told me, was that it was supposed to be a "hoodoo" race; no horse who won it ever seemed to win any of the Classics.

"A 'hoodoo' race?" I asked. "You mean races can be cursed too?"

"Anything can be cursed," he replied. "Houses, cars, clothes. What about the Hope Diamond? I wouldn't have it even if it was given to me. First of all it was pried loose from a stone image in a South Indian temple, which was hardly likely to put the deity from whom it was stolen into a good mood. And look at its history! Calamity has followed everyone who has ever possessed it. That in itself should be indication enough that it is cursed. So why not races?"

"Do *you* think the Colonel Pratap Singh Cup is a hoodoo race?"

"Whether or not it is I have decided to run Redstone in it. If he can't win it it will just prove that he's not Classic material anyway. Why live in fear? Better to go for broke!"

And so we did. As the countdown for the Big Race ticked by we exhaustively evaluated Redstone's trackwork, fitness, appetite and general mood, and kept our fingers thoroughly crossed. In our spare time we made excursions to those local beings, human and ethereal, with whom we had beneficial rnanubandhanas. One evening we drove to the Sindhi colony in Aundh, near Poona, to meet a family related to one of Vimalananda's 'children.' These people were bickering among themselves continually, and suffering from one disease after another. When Vimalananda visited them he immediately detected the problem: a large banyan tree nearby. No one dared to sleep under the tree at night, for it had a 'reputation.' Vimalananda changed all that, as he has done with the many other trees around India which have become his friends, and asked the head of the household to offer incense to the tree each week.

The man, who must have thought he was very clever, offered incense daily instead until the spirit in the tree came and stood in front of him and asked him what his intentions were. This terrified him enough to remember Vimalananda's words, and to revert to a weekly offering. "Now everyone in the house is well," Vimalananda commented, "all the family members cooperate with each other, and the warehouse of the family business is never empty. No matter how much is removed from the warehouse something always remains there. Many other people have seen this tree, offered it incense, and obtained results. Now the family is happy with me, and the tree is also happy with me—and their combined blessings add all the more to my karmic account balance as we prepare for Redstone's test."

The greatest time-squandering of the entire process centered around Das Bapa, a Tantric from Gujarat who claimed to be able to ensure Redstone's success. Vimalananda was always on the lookout for someone who could give him the reliable race results needed to make money at the track so that he could evade the karma of divining the results himself. He followed the path laid out in a Marathi saying: *pavnyacha sota ne vichu maar*: "Kill the scorpion with the guest's staff." Why soil your own walking stick with the scorpion venom of karma if you can soil someone else's? (Substitute "penis" for "staff" if you prefer the ribald interpretation of the word *sota.*) He had interviewed quite a number of candidates: astrologers, mediums, and one fellow who brought with him a little boy and a dark scrying glass for the boy to gaze into. All these previous contestants had flopped abjectly, however; no matter how expert they might be for other people in other places they always failed with Vimalananda. Perhaps it was coincidence, or perhaps it was not Vimalananda's destiny to win that way. More likely it was Vimalananda, teaching them valuable lessons.

Das Bapa had been brought to us by Mr. Bundaldas, a semi-nobleman with delusions of efficacy. The Bapa made tall claims of having magically fixed bullock races and stuffed ballot boxes by ethereal means. After Vimalananda saw some of his capabilities at first hand he lost some of his preliminary doubts about the man's potential. But he was under no illusion as to the source of Das Bapa's powers: "I do not doubt that he has done good avishkaras before," said Vimalananda. "He has been possessed by the likes of Mahakali and of Anjaneya. But you haven't forgotten what happened at the caves, have you? He claimed he was going to do an avishkara of the spirit of the great Guru Gorakh Nath. But Gorakh Nath was there just part of the time; the rest of the time it was just some ordinary little spirit playing about.

"But of course how could we have expected more? Should we imagine that Gorakh Nath, who is immortal, has nothing better to do than to commune with such a mediocre mortal as Das Bapa? And that too, someone with so much karma on his hands? To do much of their work Das Bapa and his own guru have tortured many many *dakinis* (the spirits of women who died in pregnancy or childbirth), and have not even spared the spirits of tiny babies. You just have no idea of how horrible is the price you have to pay if you fool about with these rituals."

"How about the karmic implications for us if he does some work for us?"

"First, he has offered to do this work of his own accord. He is thinking of some way to eventually profit from us, of course; he is not trying to help us because he loves us. But that's not the point. The point is that I didn't ask him to the work, which makes an immense karmic difference. And besides, we first need to see whether or not Nature will permit him to do anything for us before we worry about how to apportion karmic blame or praise. Right now Das Bapa is dancing on the strength of that spirit named Bhima Bapa that he keeps with him. Well, we can stop that, and then we'll see how much water he's swimming in."

"Is digging up dead babies and pregnant women some sort of very primitive Nara Bali?"

"It could be, but it is not in the way that Das Bapa does it, because he is not offering those spirits to Ma. He is enslaving them for his own use. It is true that from one point of view everything is sacrifice, including devotion, yoga, and even magic. But Das Bapa's kind of sacrifice is very selfish, and the karma for it will stick to him like glue. This is why the best sacrifice, the best Nara Bali of all, is the sacrifice of your own self. Offer yourself and all you possess, including your most precious possession—your life—to Ma, and She will save you. But she is not going to save Das Bapa. Just wait until these spirits get their revenge, and then you will see how far away from Nara Bali Das Bapa is."

Das Bapa was far away from us in Poona during the next ten days, three-quarters of an hour away in fact, holed up in the quiet of the Fruitwala Dharamsala in Alandi testing out his predictive methods. Each day Vima-

lananda sent me grumbling to Alandi astride Arzoo's motor scooter to enquire after Das Bapa's health, ask about any necessities to be brought to him
or his assistant from Poona, and remind him by my presence that we were expecting results. To me it was a complete waste of two hours each day, as I was
becoming surer and surer that Vimalananda was planning to have Das Bapa's
head on a platter.

Das Bapa and his man Friday resurfaced in Poona just in time for his first
quiz, which took place on the race day that fell on the Sunday before the Big
Race. We had expected a straightforward list of winners, and what we got was
Das Bapa insisting on accompanying us to the track so that he could "exam-
ine" the runners. It was embarrassing to be seen with him, and galling to have
to listen to his "advice." Though he did predict one winner, or maybe it was
two, neither was unexpected based on nothing more magical than fitness and
form. While he and his cheering section of one crowed over this glorious success it became clear to the rest of us that all that was left to do with him was to
boot him out of our lives as graciously as possible. This task was now more
difficult as he had begun to protest confidently that after seeing the track he
now had the necessary "range" to do a good job of predicting the results of
the next week's races. We packed him off to Alandi again without delay, to
"refine" his technique.

During this week Vimalananda thankfully did not force me to make fruitless runs to Alandi. Instead he sent me to plumb Redstone's prospects at the
Bhuleshwar Shiva temple. Vimalananda's first journey to Bhuleshwar had
been with Dr. Lad; they had set out in search of a different temple, but took
the wrong road and discovered Bhuleshwar. When I accompanied Vimalananda on his second Bhuleshwar trek we took a different wrong road, up
the wrong hillside, following the pavement even after it turned to dirt and
then became a track. When we pressed ahead we found ourselves alone and
roadless on the hillside squarely amidst a flock of goats. A sweetly-smiling
young goatherd then fortuitously appeared to navigate for Vimalananda as
he backed up the hill and down to the paved road, whence we drove off to
find the right road, and the shrine.

On our third expedition we reached the right hill, but in the deepening
twilight took the wrong fork of the road at its base. We then found ourselves
ascending by the old road, which had been condemned. It was much too late
to turn back when our thoroughfare suddenly deteriorated into a steeply-
climbing uneven field of fist-sized rocks without any semblance of a guard-
rail. Only the sum of our collective good karmas, the weight of our tank-like
Austin Cambridge station wagon, and Vimalananda's determination, pluck,
and driving skill got us up that hill—but clatter up it we did, and enjoyed our

darshana. Thereafter, having learned from our experiences and having passed these tests that Shiva (or whoever) had set for us, we made regular, safe outings to the sanctuary.

Bhuleshwar's architecture, which is unique in that region of Western India, suggests that it was built as a fortified Tantric monastery, though no one knows who the Tantrics were or how long they remained in residence there. Whoever it was that held the fort in the latter part of the 18th century appears to have run afoul of India's then paramount power in the person of the Mughal Emperor Aurangzeb, who dispatched his relative Shaistha Khan to crush their resistance. Shaistha Khan presumably invested the base of the hill and laid siege to the monastery, which cannot have held out for very long since its sole source of water is a small cistern within a bat-infested cave. On some fateful day the remaining residents must have sallied out to be slaughtered; the astral scent of violent death is thickly palpable in the vicinity. Enough local people have seen enough spirits of the unquiet dead there that none of them stays overnight at Bhuleshwar if they can avoid it. When I once spent ten days there meditating in the old guardhouse I could at night clearly hear faint sounds of battle wafting up to me from below and felt acutely the nearby presence of ethereal warriors. On one memorable evening a ghost outfitted in battle armor went so far as to career through my room. He paid no attention to me and sped on without stopping, engrossed as he was in his ancient, unseen tussle, submerged in his memories of killing and being killed.

Devout visitors to Bhuleshwar walk first down to the cistern to wash their feet and hands, taking care not to drink its water before filtering it through a cloth to remove any lurking Guinea worm larvae. Then they follow from the cistern to the temple a path that is lined with stone heads and torsos that Shaistha Khan's men hacked from the monastery's walls. Only vestiges survive of the erotica that once adorned the temple's exterior. Much exquisite sculpture still remains within, including scenes from the *Ramayana* and *Mahabharata*, a giant bull, and a female Ganesha, but here also the raiders savaged the figures, and most of them are missing limbs.

Inside the sanctum sits a stone *Shiva linga* (phallic symbol of Shiva) which is unusual not for its shape or size but because it can be lifted from its base. Such lingas are ordinarily regarded as worthless, but at Bhuleshwar water perpetually seeps from some unplumbed shaft into the small cavity which the linga covers. The *pujari* (ritual priest), after removing a little of this water for the worshippers to sip as Shiva's blessings, places into the cavity a small metal dish filled with some pieces of the bananas and milk-sweets that have been presented for offering, and closes the cavity with the linga. Then everyone sits patiently, sometimes for several minutes, for a peculiar scratching sound. Once the sound both comes and dies away, the linga is again removed, and *voila!* some of the offerings have disappeared.

Our first thought was that some sort of rodent must be entering the cavity to eat the food, but on close inspection we discovered that none of the holes within the cavity are large enough to admit any but the smallest of mice. Moreover, we on occasion offered the sacred-to-Shiva *bilva* leaves, which were also "consumed" by this mysterious beast—and what self-respecting small animal would choose bitter leaves over sweet treats? It was a mystery over which we expended much conversation.

We lost interest in what was taking the food on the day we realized that the quantity taken could provide answers to questions. When everything was taken the answer was an unqualified 'yes'; when one or two pieces remained the answer was 'yes, with limitations'; and if only one or two pieces were taken the answer was 'limited success.' No pieces taken? An unqualified 'no.' This mode of divination could be used for lost objects, employment opportunities and most any other enquiry provided that everyone there focused on a single query. Once Vimalananda determined to use Bhuleshwar as an oracle for his runners I was making regular, fatiguing pilgrimages to the spot. Never over the many months that I consulted it for this purpose were its predictions wrong: everything taken meant 'a winner'; a few pieces remaining indicated that the horse would win some stakes money, by placing second, third or fourth; and only one or two pieces taken, or none at all, meant 'the horse finishes well back in the pack.'

On this occasion everything went smoothly: my bus was on time, clouds shaded me from the sun during both my walk up and my walk down, the marvelous tree behind the temple sported a excellent complexion, and each and every piece of my offering was lifted. I consequently went into an excellent humor, as did Vimalananda when he heard these details. Our frame of mind remained thus until the following afternoon when we happened to run into one of the Stipendiary Stewards as we were leaving the stables. This conspicuous gentleman peered over his nose at us in a way that he presumed to be dignified, smiled disdainfully, and observed to Vimalananda that he was very courageous to enter his "nice little horse" in such a "big race." I saw fury infuse Vimalananda's face as he controlled himself and said something neutral like, "He will acquit himself well, God willing."

Back in the hotel he said to me coldly, "When this is all over I'm going to have a good laugh at the expense of everyone who thought I was a fool to enter my 'nice little horse' in such a 'big race.' I'll enjoy it as much as Birbal enjoyed humiliating Mullah Do Pyaza."

"What?"

"Haven't I told you that story before? Mullah Do Pyaza was one of the *hakims* (Unani physicians) in Akbar's court."

"*Do pyaza* means 'two onions.' What were his two onions: his testicles?"

"Probably. Like most of his fellow courtiers Mullah Do Pyaza hated Birbal with a passion, and was always looking for ways to show him up. One day he had a brain wave. He enlisted one of Akbar's concubines, promising her that the Emperor would start to pay her more attention if she would cooperate.

"An agonized screech rent the air on the appointed morning as Akbar conducted business in his court. There was a thoroughgoing commotion as two servants carried in the concubine, who had 'swooned.' 'She's been bitten by a snake, Your Majesty!' they shouted. 'She's dying! What can we do?'

"Sure enough, there on her arm were two puncture wounds which looked suspiciously like those made by a snake. The Emperor's heart was overcome with compassion. He cried out, 'Can no one save her?'

"Up sprang Mullah Do Pyaza, who yelped, 'Fear not, Your Majesty, I am here!' Then he grabbed the concubine's arm and began to suck the 'poison' out of the 'bite,' making a melodramatic pause now and again for effect. When he was finished he told Akbar, 'I think she is out of danger now, my liege.'

" 'Thank you, oh thank you, Mullah Saheb,' exclaimed the relieved emperor. 'You will be richly rewarded for your gallant services.' Then he turned to Birbal and said, 'Thank goodness Mullah Saheb was here; you were of no help at all.'

"Birbal was nobody's fool. He had already figured out what was going on. That taunt hardened his heart against the Mullah. He pondered his revenge carefully, and patiently awaited a fit moment to carry it out.

"That moment came on the Emperor's next hunting expedition. After a hot afternoon of riding down game Birbal signalled to Akbar that he needed to empty his bladder. After dismounting and assuming the stance he promptly began to shout, 'Oh, I'm dead, I'm a dead man now!'

"Akbar shouted back, 'What's the matter!'

"In obvious pain Birbal whimpered, 'Your majesty, while I was making water a snake bit me on my member. Now I'm done for!'

"Akbar looked around him, spied the Mullah, and said, 'Mullah Do Pyaza, you saved the life of my concubine by sucking the poison out of her arm. You must do the same for Birbal. He is my most trusted companion; I can't do without him!'

"The Mullah tried to make some lame excuse, but the Emperor would have none of it. Seeing that there was no alternative, and knowing that Birbal had got the best of him, Mullah Do Pyaza got down off his horse. He walked over to Birbal, bent down in front of him, and went to work. As the Mullah kissed Birbal's penis in submission Birbal whispered to him, 'So, my child, are you enjoying this little drama now as much as you enjoyed the act you arranged in the palace?"

All in the room enjoyed a good horselaugh over that one, and after I had calmed down I asked, "Are you so sure of your four-legged 'child' that you are now ready to predict success?"

"Almost, but not quite. Let us see after his spurt tomorrow."

The spurt, which was the sort of little half- to three-quarters-pace gallop over three furlongs that gets administered as a "lung-opener" to a racer three days before his race, went off well, for Redstone was as fit as a well-strung fiddle. Though Vimalananda still refused to speak definitively he did begin to relax, as if the race was already over and his "boy" had done the job.

It being a terms race there was no handicap to anguish over, and on the eve of the race there was little left to do at the stables except to sit watching Nakhodaji, the ever-smiling Rajasthani farrier, shoeing the next day's runners as the other horses walked their perpetual circles around the stable buildings. A few horses need to wear steel horseshoes on an outing, but most horses get shod just before a race in aluminum racing plates that are much lighter and thinner than the steel shoes they require for daily wear and work. After the race the farrier routinely changes the aluminum shoes back to steel.

Nakhodaji's intermittent hammering puncutated the persiflage that Tehmul and Dr. Kulkarni were exchanging over tea as they studiously attempted to avoid extra speculation over the outcome of The Race. Only three other runners were left in it—"Everyone else is afraid of the jinx," claimed the loquacious Dr. Kulkarni—and everyone wondered whether the meager field would hamper or enhance our boy's chances. When Redstone's jockey Chirag arrived to formally discuss strategy he was admonished to run a conservative race by keeping Redstone second behind the horse setting the pace. If the pace was too slow for Redstone Chirag should take him to the front, but only far enough to have a clear passage at the bend. Chirag nodded his agreement, and left to meet the trainers of his other mounts. We departed only when no one remained to talk with. Back at home we spent the rest of the evening in a last perusal of the records of the four runners, trying to determine which would best be able to carry the 57 kilos over the 9 furlongs (1800 meters) of the Colonel Pratap Singh Cup. We went to bed early, and after a good sleep, a good breakfast and a light lunch we proceeded with due temerity toward the racecourse, eyes open to omens.

My first meeting with Vimalananda had taken place on the day that his mare Elan won her first race for him. Vimalananda had gone on to become the most important influence in my life. I regarded that initial win as a particularly good portent for me. The interest in omens that had been awakened in me by the crash of the monkey's fist into Arzoo's mirror intensified unexpectedly one afternoon during 1979 or 1980 on the eve of a race in which Vimalananda had a runner. Vimalananda and I were sitting peaceably in Tehmul's yard at the Bombay racing stables mulling over the morrow when our gaze turned to a gang of crows who traced a sinister circle around something on the ground about fifteen or twenty meters away. Suddenly Vimalananda jumped up and yelled, "Quick, Robby, go scare off those crows!"

Vimalananda believed emphatically in feeding crows, and daily left food for them outside his Bombay kitchen window. One peculiarly hook-nosed crow became friendly and confident enough to eat from the palms of our hands, and feeding him became one of my Bombay joyances. For Vimalananda to request me to disturb crows was thus uncharacteristic enough to snap me to attention. When I rushed over to shoo the birds away I found that they had been harassing a dying lizard. Vimalananda moseyed up behind and stared at the lizard for a compassionate moment before he turned to me to say gloomily, "Well, my boy, our mare will finish in the money tomorrow, but now I don't believe that the old girl can win. If only we'd noticed this sooner and actually saved the lizard we'd have been guaranteed of victory!" As he predicted our mare did indeed place the next afternoon.

The sight of such a sign before Redstone's Big Race would have winched us up into a heaven of confidence, but we saw nothing out of the ordinary that day, neither on our way to the track nor as we walked to the stands. The first few races went by uneventfully. Though Das Bapa had come near to groveling for another chance to appear there in person neither of us had wanted to have to deal with him, so he had had to send his list of choices of uncertain value. I was not surprised that none of his picks before the Big Race came true. While I noted that he had selected Redstone as the winner of the that race he must have known that it would have been suicidal for him to do otherwise.

Now Vimalananda rose and repaired for the Paddock. I stood at the Paddock's edge, eyeing the four horses as they filed in. Before security had become so tight I would sometimes flash my badge and go backstage to watch the trainer and grooms perform the saddling ritual and administer final touches, like the tweaking of a forelock to make it lie straight. I saw that scene now in my mind's eye as the four runners, two with braided manes, began to parade around their owners and trainers who stood in their business suits tense with expectancy giving last-minute cautions to the jockeys in their silks and white breeches. Vimalananda had taught me how to tell something of a horse's fitness by the sight of his muscles, and it was clear to me that by that criterion ours was the fittest in this field. Everything went smoothly as the horses came into the Paddock's center to be mounted by their riders and then filed out to head for the track. Diverse criteria for success flitted through my mind as I tried to evaluate our prospects. One indicator of failure, which I had found to be reliable in seven or eight cases out of ten, was to see a horse drop dung while parading in the paddock or walking to the starting gate. That Redstone's bowels did not move in either locale removed one worry from my list.

As the horses wended their way to the gate I pondered the other things that might go wrong. Sometimes a horse who dumped his rider and got loose on his way to the post would gallop away half his energy before he could be caught and remounted. Sometimes one fractious horse would kick another as they were being loaded into the starting gates; sometimes one horse would take so long to be loaded that the others who were already in the starting gates would become fractious themselves. Sometimes a horse would bolt early from the gates again and again, producing a string of false starts that could dishearten other horses and distract their riders. Horses sometimes got left at the start, and some horses just unaccountably got spooked or went sour or hunkered down in obstinacy and refused at the last minute to race.

After what seemed manifold eternities all the horses were loaded. I at least had to concentrate on slowing my breath as my excitement tightened its squeeze on me. Just then, at what was the very last of moments, as the starter lifted his flag and Vimalananda and I prepared to stand to watch the gates open, up popped the ferret-faced waiter whose palm was always open for a tip, bringing us two cups of steaming tea. My heart teetered on the brink for a moment, and then sank down into my dress shoes: tea with milk! Milk, the harbinger no augur wishes to see! Was this last-minute omen going to negate all my work at Bhuleshwar? As I bent down to whisper to Vimalananda, "Does tea signify what milk does?" the flag dropped without warning, and the race began! I shoved my forebodings to the rear of my mind as I whipped up my binoculars and watched Redstone get a good jump out of the gate. It was Saturday, September 18, 1982.

All horse owners are captivated as a race kicks off by a seductive moment or two in which they begin to taste the attainment of their long-cultivated expectancies. Disappointments, recriminations, and prolonged autopsies of what actually happened and what might have been await all but one of them at the finish line, but at that moment of the start the owner's heart and horse leap together. Though I was but a lowly racing agent, that alluring feeling and I were familiars, and I think both I and my owner held our breaths for the first few furlongs of the Big Race and relaxed into respiration only when we saw that all was going well. The track had some give in it after a recent watering; some observers later commented that it might have been a bit overwatered, and that there should have been false rails. Redstone was second coming out of the gate, and stayed there as the field passed the first few distance poles. Two furlongs, four, then six; we could see that Redstone was handy, and that his competition was still more or less even with him.

Everything was happening according to plan, but I continued to think contingencies. What if the jockey fell off? Race jockeys ride above their saddles, enhancing their speed by leaning forward with their weight above their mounts' shoulders even though this pose increases the likelihood of a fall. But no fall occurred. As the sound of the thunder of horses's hooves began to catch up with the vision of their movement we saw them approaching the bend, and began to urge jockey and horse on with our screams.

The straight is very short in Poona, and when we saw Chirag take a good turn and then start to quicken his mount it suddenly became clear to both of us that he was going to win! Now a bellow mounted from the racing public to mingle with ours as Redstone flashed passed us to cross the winning post a length and a half clear of his nearest rival. The third horse was two lengths further away, and the best pedigreed horse of the day a bad fourth. As Chirag sat back in his saddle and began to slow his mount we stopped shouting long enough to think the same thought: Redstone, our "nice little horse," had done it! I momentarily took back all the nasty things I had thought about Kumar when he leaned over to congratulate us. Mudhol Maharaj was beside himself with fervid glee. Our nearest neighbors wished us well, but most of the other racing patricians glared at us sourly from their boxes, sure that we plebians had no business winning major races.

We ignored these costive disapprovers as we strode down the steep steps to where the beaming Tehmul stood. Some owners become temporarily mute or manic when their horses win, but Vimalananda was a model of evenness and self-possession as he responded to the acclaim of his friends and well-wishers until Redstone arrived. When the whole group started back to the Paddock my shrieks of praise fused with those of the partisan crowd to roll billow-like above all heads—and then it was over. Then all the trainers and owners and bettors and bookies who had had something riding on this race that they had lost let their shoulders sag definitively as they sighed over their fates and began to concoct the excuses that would soon be demanded of them.

I strode back to the Paddock rail, where I saw Tehmul's ferment express itself in his post-race duties: the supervision of the undoing of the saddle's girth buckles, the inspection of the legs, the fond pat on the nose. Though this might have been merely a Classic tuneup race Tehmul had not yet won any Classics, which made this win a good omen for him as well. After the white ball was raised to signify that no objections had been made the results were confirmed and the photos were snapped as the Stewards presented the Cup. We then remounted grandstands that for the rest of that day's races—only one of which Das Bapa's choice won—remained atwitter at Redstone's celebrity.

After the last race and the obligatory stop at the stables to distribute tips and feed treats to our hero of the day we retired to the hotel for congratulatory Scotch—an assiduously preserved bottle of Black Dog—and for the first of many retellings of the story of Redstone's Brilliant Run. A few days later the race video arrived, and over the next week we must have relived the race visually at least a dozen times, watching Redstone's action, noting Chirag's technique, trying to divine how our "nice little horse" might fare against stiffer competition. The pundits were sure it was a fluke; one turf weekly dubbed Redstone the best horse of the day but sniffed, "he is certainly not of the super class," and lamented that for the second year in a row the Colonel Pratap Singh Cup had been lifted by an outsider.

Super class or not our horse had won, a fact which now lured me into what became a maelstrom of omenological fantasies. Though the events that led up to the Big Race had been filled with all sorts of contradictory presentiments which seemed almost to nullify one another, the revelation that hot tea presaged an entirely different outcome from milk began to exercise my mind. Vimalananda, like Carlos Castaneda's Don Juan, looked to omens as "agreement from the world," clues of Nature's approval or disapproval of proposed human action, and he shared his knowledge of these generously. Useful tokens are often simple: to see milk being brought toward you is usually inauspicious, while water or yogurt brought toward you is normally auspicious. To see a sadhu walking toward you suggests a reduction in prosperity, with a shaved-head Jain sadhu or a Jain nun being a strong sign of likely loss, while seeing meat, fish or a corpse being carried toward you is a strong sign of impending gain. Most any event can presage something or other, but as I was soon to discover one event becomes a herald for the future only when your attention has consolidated around a specific question that requires resolution from Nature.

Omenology bounded squarely to the fore of my consciousness during the very next week as Vimalananda and I were travelling together by shared taxi from Poona to Bombay. When Vimalananda declined to drive to Poona we would usually travel by taxi. Though the taxis normally carry four passengers he and I would often pay for all four seats that we might enjoy privacy during the three-and-a-half- to four-hour ride. When we reached the taxi stand that evening and there were no other potential passengers we sat in the taxi at the head of the queue and prepared to depart. Just then a harried-looking man clutching a briefcase rushed up and begged permission to take the front seat. We had no objection, and since it would save us a little money we invited him in.

As we drove away the taxi driver announced self-importantly, "We will stop for fifteen minutes each in Lonavala and in Khopoli."

"You are only supposed to stop in one or the other place, and for half an hour," remonstrated the man in the front seat with a nervous promptness.

"I know the rules," responded the taxi driver severely, "The rules say stops may be had in both places, and that is how it will be. If you don't like it please take the next cab."

This shut the man up so abruptly that we were drawn to observe him. He was a singularly unimpressive specimen of humanity, and the peculiar combination of anxiety, preoccupation, distrust and cupidity which oozed from every pore of his blowsy visage had transformed his natural lack of comeliness into a positively ill-favored mien. Suspicion arose in two minds as one as we in the back seat began to question his identity, and his reasons for clasping his attaché case to his bosom as if his whole future were contained therein.

When we stopped as the driver had promised at Lonavala the front-seat man hopped out and promptly disappeared, to reappear only after half an hour. The rest of us were annoyed but said nothing. At Khopoli, after the driver ostentatiously anounced, "Fifteen minutes," the front-seat man disappeared yet again, and when twenty-five minutes had gone by without a sign from him the driver came to the table at which Vimalananda and I sat post-snack. He said, "I can't continue to wait around for this fellow. I'll give him five more minutes. If he doesn't show his face by then I am going to go on to Bombay, and he can come by the next cab. If we leave now will you bear witness of his shenanigans for me at the taxi stand so that I don't get into any trouble?"

As neither Vimalananda nor I were averse to giving this oaf a jolt we readily agreed to this plan. After requesting the people at the restaurant to inform the man that we had left we sped off, the man's briefcase lying untouched on the front seat. "I knew there would be trouble with this man as soon as I saw him," said the driver in the beautiful Urdu of the refined North Indian city of Lucknow, "which is why I didn't want to take him with us. When his face did not please me how was he able even to sit in my cab?" Aha! I thought. As a student of physiognomy I knew exactly what he meant. Something was obviously improper about the man, something that violated the canons of auspiciousness, an unsuitable something that should have alerted us to the likelihood of trouble with him. Nature had somehow limned this inappropriateness onto his face, and had we heeded the message of his facial language we could have spared ourselves his company.

Had we done that, though, we would have missed sampling the feast of our taxi driver in full extemporaneous flight. By turns self-congratulatory, fearful, indignant and overconfident, his monologue entertained us all the way to the Bombay taxi stand, where he was so pleased with our witness for him that he insisted on buying us paan and cigarettes as treats. We learned then that when the front-seat man had discovered that we had departed with his briefcase he had first clawed at his heart as if it might stop beating. Then, after regaining his composure, he had phoned Bombay in a frenzy to tell the taxi dispatcher to hold his briefcase as soon as it arrived. We three agreed that something illegal must be involved, which made it even less comprehensible why he would leave his briefcase unattended in the taxi while he galavanted about.

Struck by the momentous nature of this affair I was soon seeing so many omens that were so thoroughly empty of significance that Vimalananda felt obliged to warn me not to get so worked up over divination by auspices. His warning came in the form of a story:

"One day, when Akbar woke early, the first person he saw was a one-eyed *dhobi* (washerman) scrubbing clothes in the Yamuna. While he was wondering what kind of omen this was the washerman happened to look up, and bowed when he saw the emperor. Later in the day Akbar tripped on the steps of his palace and bumped his shin; a bee stung him in the garden; the empress was taken ill; and there was a fire in the kitchen which delayed his lunch. 'An ill-omened day,' bawled his yes-men. 'Who did you see first thing this morning, Your Majesty?'

" 'I saw the one-eyed washerman.'

" 'His face is inauspicious; put him to death!' they squealed. Out went a posse of soldiers to arrest the hapless washerman.

"Birbal, who had heard the entire exchange, took the man aside to give him a piece of advice as he stood trembling in the court waiting for the emperor to appear and pass sentence. After Akbar arrived and told the washerman how unlucky his face was the man replied humbly, 'Begging your pardon, Lord, but I must ask you whose face is really more unlucky: mine or yours?'

"All the courtiers were aghast at the man's impertinence, but Akbar gestured them into silence. He said, 'What precisely do you mean by that?'

" 'Well, my liege, yours was the first face I saw this morning, and now I'm about to lose my head.' Akbar laughed in spite of his attempt to remain solemn, and asked the man, 'Who put these words into your mouth?'

" 'Why, Birbal did, my lord.'

" 'Well, my good man, Birbal has saved you,' said the emperor as he ordered that the washerman be rewarded for his trouble."

"Was Akbar really about to have the man executed for being unlucky?"

"Probably not—but you can never tell with kings, yogis, fire, and water."

Having gleaned from this that being mesmerized by signs and portents can easily deteriorate into karma-creating superstition I again turned my spare neurons to racing, which had by now shifted back to Bombay. Our reappearance at the Mahalakshmi Racecourse in the fall of 1982 was a festive occasion. Led by Cama and the Godrejs the residents of our home bench greeted Vimalananda heartily and demanded a stride by stride account of the famous victory. Kalubhai also showed up to offer his felicitations. He continued to come listen to Vimalananda's "talks" in the evenings, but though we also ran into him now and again at the track he and his numerological charts sat elsewhere. It might have been shame over his refusal to take Vimalananda's advice, or maybe he was simply determined to prove Vimalananda wrong.

Vimalananda's new-found enthusiasm for life got an extra shot in the arm when the erstwhile Maharaja of an erstwhile state on the Kathiawar Peninsula of Gujarat flew us out to one of his palaces to discuss the making of a film there. We and the film's provisional producer were treated to a concert by the Maharaja's court musicians, a poetry reading by his court poet, and gourmet food cooked by his two Paris-trained chefs, served at the Maharaja's usual dinner time of 2 A.M. During this junket I got the opportunity to boat over to the small island on which Vimalananda's ancestor Sagal Shah had lived fifteen generations earlier. There I saw the very mortar and pestle in which Sagal Shah's wife had mashed the brains of their son Chellaya during the famous incident when Lord Shiva came to the couple in the form of a cannabalistic Aghori to test their devotion. Back in Bombay Vimalananda began to contemplate some of his old projects that he was now ebullient enough to think of reviving. His most important project, however, continued to misfire, for after his strenuous race Redstone seemed to be talking longer than normal to recapture his peak of fitness.

An exhausting race can take everything out of a horse; we didn't want to wreck Redstone by racing before he had recuperated fully. Even worse would have been to have him break down during a race and have to be put down then and there; it happened from time to time. I still vividly remember the day that a horse dislocated his fetlock right in front of me as I stood at the rail watching his race. I was paralyzed with horror as his entire hoof and the joint above it came loose from his leg and began to flop, now against the front of his shin and now against its back, as he continued to gallop insanely down the track articulating naked leg bone instead of metal-shod hoof against its grass. I could barely breathe from empathic pain as I watched the Club's vet rushing over to where he finally fell, and it seemed to take ages for the captive bolt of the vet's pistol to finally release him. For that to happen to a horse we knew and loved was so unthinkable that though we were loathe to do so we scratched Redstone's name from the list of runners for the Indian 2000 Guineas, the first of the season's Classic races.

We hoped that rest would enable him to resume form well before the deadline for acceptances for the Indian Derby, for soon a decision would need to be made on whether or not to run Redstone in that most prestigious of races. There is only one Derby in a horse's career and too few horses with Classic potential in an owner's lifetime, to turn down a chance however slim to tote home a Derby trophy. But as the Derby deadline neared Vimalananda seemed to relax into a more philosophical frame of mind. A morning or two before the die had to be cast I sat listening to him sing "*Avo Nagare More Hari*," a truly angelic song that invites Krishna to abide within the singer. At the tune's conclusion he put aside his harmonium and told me a story that I had heard many times before:

"Sudama was a Brahmana who had been Lord Krishna's *gurubhai* (fellow disiciple); both were disciples of Sandipani Rishi. One day when they were sent out to search for fuel for their guru's homa fire Sandipani's wife packed a lunch for them both, but Sudama became so hungry that he ate up both portions while Krishna got nothing. Krishna, who was *Purnatmaka Purushottama*—Perfection Personified—just laughed it off. But you cannot cheat God Incarnate and hope to escape unscathed. Sudama's fortunes took a nosedive from that day forward and he was soon cast into the direst poverty.

"Years passed for Sudama in a hand-to-mouth kind of existence until one day his wife heard talk of the glories of Dwaraka, where Krishna ruled as king. She immediately sat her husband down and told him to go straightway to Krishna and ask for financial help. Sudama was still embarrassed to see Krishna's face—a guilty conscience biting—and he could not even dream of asking a favor from someone he had cheated. He refused to go, but his wife had had it with being poor and would not take no for an answer. She said, 'If Krishna is all-knowing, as you say He is, He will know our plight without your having to say anything and of His own accord will offer you enough to tide us over.' When he realized that there was no escape Sudama told his wife that he could not go to his old friend empty-handed, like a beggar. He needed to carry a present with him. The cupboard was absolutely bare, so she went out and begged four handfuls of flattened rice, which she tied in a cloth. Taking this 'present' Sudama left for Dwaraka with a heavy heart, wondering all along the way what sort of face he could show to Krishna.

"When Sudama reached Dwaraka he introduced himself as a co-disciple of Sandipani Rishi and was immediately taken to Krishna's splendid palace. Seeing him coming Krishna jumped up and rushed out to embrace him. Krishna then seated him on his own cot, washed his feet, performed ritual worship of His guest, and fed him sumptuously. Then Krishna reminisced about life with Sandipani, and asked Sudama about all that had happened to him after he had finished his studies.

"All this time there was no mention of either Sudama's need for money. As the afternoon drew toward a close Sudama lost hope and decided to leave. As he was taking Krishna's leave Krishna asked him, 'Didn't your wife send some present for Me?' Sudama had been so embarassed at the meagerness of his gift that he had forgotten all about it. As Sudama drew the little cloth parcel from his clothing Krishna Himself grabbed hold of it and ate first one fistful, and then a second. By eating those two fistfuls of rice Krishna consumed all Sudama's evil karmas from his past births and from this present birth. As He raised the third fistful to His mouth, to remove all evil karmas from Sudama's births to come, His wife Rukmini, who was the incarnation of Lakshmi, the goddess of wealth, caught hold of His hand to prevent Him from taking even more. She asked Him, 'What are you thinking, Lord? If You eat that third handful You will be giving Me away to Sudama as his servant, and I am not prepared to agree to that.'

"Then Krishna laughed, released the third handful of rice, and said to Sudama, 'Now you can leave.' Sudama was so upset that Krishna had accepted his gift and offered nothing in return that he lost his temper, and said to Him, '*Kripana* (Miser)! I did not want to come to ask You for money; my wife put me up to it. At least You could have done something for her!' And he walked off. He conveniently forgot that he was in the wrong; that he was the thief, not Krishna.

"All along the road back to his house he rehearsed the excuses he would make to his wife for coming home emptyhanded—but when he reached his village he couldn't believe his eyes! His pathetic little hut was gone, and in its place was a fabulous mansion. When his wife came out to meet him he almost didn't recognize her, she was so well-dressed and looked so satisfied. Then he remembered the last thing he had said to his dear friend Krishna, the Krishna who had done all this for him; he remembered that his parting word to Krishna had been *kripana*. Now that Sudama was surrounded by luxury he lost all taste for the things of the world. He turned the mansion over to his wife for her to enjoy. He had a little hut built for himself nearby where he spent most of his time, his mind totally engrossed in Krishna.

"It's true, Robby," said Vimalananda in conclusion, "it is true that when

Krishna wants to bless someone He takes away that person's money, fame, pleasure, and other worldly joys. Eventually, when that man has lost everything, and everyone he knows has deserted him, he has no alternative but to remember Krishna and to get lost in His bewitching eyes."

Why he was then retelling me this story was not too clear to me, but as I watched Vimalananda stare at the illumined-from-behind transparency of Guru Maharaj that sat in front of his chair an ill-defined ominousness skittered like a cloud onto my mind's horizon. I knew that Vimalananda revered his Junior Guru Maharaj as Krishna incarnate; they used to wear saris and dance together for love of Krishna. I also knew that Guru Maharaj was quite capable of disrupting lives to guarantee spiritual development. At that moment a not-quite-formed thought flitted swiftly before my eyes, a thought that, had it been fully fledged, would have been, "I wonder if Guru Maharaj has something up his sleeve."

chapter nine

PRAKRITI SIDDHI

HAD I KNOWN THEN what I know now of Vimalananda's Junior Guru Maharaj I would have concluded that in the act of awarding him the transient felicity of Redstone's win Guru Maharaj had successfully stolen one of the few remaining joys from Vimalananda's life. Vimalananda, who must have suspected it all along, tried unsuccessfully to reveal this to me not long after the taxi-driver episode, during the course of an afternoon spent at Bhuleshwar. After offering our worship we sat resting inside the front passageway when Vimalananada looked me over in a unusually peculiar way and said, "I've told you before about Lord Krishna and His siddhi of *Kartum, Akartum, Anyathakartum.*"

"Yes, you have." I remembered his words well. *Kartum*: that which is difficult to do but is doable, which refers to Krishna's mastery over the mundane world. *Akartum*: that which is impossible for ordinary beings, which refers to His ascendancy in the spiritual world. *Anyathakartum*: that which, being beyond both the spiritual and the mundane, is inconceivable to humans. Anyathakartum refers to the astral world, the world of the mind, of subjective reality. These three siddhis gave Lord Krishna unlimited power in all three realms: mundane, spiritual and astral.

"*Prakriti Siddhi* is in the realm of Anyathakartum, that which is not only impossible but also unimaginable. Prakriti Siddhi is the ability to change the innate nature of any part of the Universal Prakriti, which means the ability to alter the consciousness of any being in the universe. When we talk about fate we are talking about Prakriti Siddhi. This is very deep; think about it very carefully. Fate is an ethereal being who knows and uses the highest of all the siddhis: Prakriti Siddhi. This is the only way he can do his work."

"So this is where Saturn comes in."

"Yes, this is where Saturn comes in. Saturn uses Prakriti Siddhi on his victims."

"You mean that Prakriti Siddhi is the means that Saturn uses to change your innate 'nature,' your prakriti, to force you to experience your karmas, good and bad alike, whether you want to or not."

"Correct."

"And Saturn—who represents the force of your karmas—can affect you so long as you have not completely conquered your prakriti, which is 'what comes naturally' to you."

"Yes."

"So if your fate comes from your karmas, and Saturn's influence comes from fate, and Prakriti Siddhi comes from Saturn, then everytime you perform a karma you basically perform Prakriti Siddhi on yourself!?"

"Almost. Everyone is the architect of his own destiny, in one way or another, via the amazing mechanism of the Law of Karma, which Nature created to coordinate these innumerable destinies. But Prakriti Siddhi goes beyond the constraints of destiny. Prakriti Siddhi permits you to become the architect of destiny, but only if—and this is a big *if*—you can understand prakriti. If you can know and understand your own prakriti you can change it. This is why they say the real heroes in life are those who change their own svabhava. To change someone else's prakriti you have to be able to know and understand that person's prakriti. If you want to be able to alter the consciousness of any being in the universe you must first know the Universal Prakriti, the universe's innate nature.

"It takes years and years of penance to achieve Prakriti Siddhi on even a limited scale. You begin by learning to change the prakriti of one person, which is much easier than changing the prakriti of a city, or a nation, or a planet. Our Earth is really a very small place. The real Prakriti Siddhi is the ability to change in a trice the character of an entire universe. When you can do that then you become the one who sends the prophets and avataras to the world.

"Prakriti Siddhi as practiced by the senior Rishis can change the behavior of whole nations and planets in the twinkling of an eye. To be able to do that you must be able to control the Adya Shakti, the first Shakti who emanates at the beginning of creation. She being the root of all universes, by controlling Her what cannot be controlled? The reason why only the Rishis possess the true Prakriti Siddhi is that you need to perform continuous penance for millions of births in order to control the Adya Shakti. Only the Rishis can even dream of being able to do something like that. Because Fate needs Prakriti Siddhi for his work they 'license' it him to use, but even with this license he can still only act when they direct him to act. Prakriti Siddhi is the means by which the Rishis control the universe. Fate performs all his work in accordance with the wishes of the *Rishi Mandala* (the 'Circle of Rishis')."

"The Rishi Mandala, then, is in control of everything that there is."

"Yes, it is. They are the real Bosses, of all the universes. But when they go too far even the Rishis can sometimes fall prey to Prakriti Siddhi. Why do you think Angiras Rishi got the idea to curse Anjani? There was no need to do so. And after cursing her, why did he promise to make her the mother of an immortal monkey god? It was the effect of Prakriti Siddhi. After blessing Anjani Angiras realized that he did not have enough shakti to fulfill the blessing on his own. Then he had acknowledge his misjudgment and request Nature to help to fulfill it.

"And what about the Rishi Yajnavalkya? Once, in the middle of a public philosophical debate, an ordinary young girl named Gargi asked him some questions that he could not answer."

"Like what?"

"Like, 'What is beyond the Absolute?' After a few of these questions Yajnavalkya lost his head with her and said, 'Woman, if you speak another word your head will not remain on your shoulders.' In that moment of losing control of his temper the fruits of ten thousand years of his penance were taken from him. When he realized what had happened—well, it was too late. He just had to start all over again. He married Gargi, too, in honor of her debating skill. But why should he have lost his temper? He lost it because his prakriti was affected. We have a proverb in Sanskrit: *aty ucche patanam*: 'That which is too high is bound to fall.' Yajnavalkya had too much pride in his penance, and someone taught him a good lesson. This is the beauty of Fate. Yajnavalkya's only thought when he went to that assembly was that he would win the debate and walk away with all the cows which were the prizes; instead he came away with a new wife, but minus ten thousand years of penance."

"Hmm."

"Parashara Rishi never knew he would marry Matsyagandha. Vasistha Rishi selected the moment for Ramachandra's crowning without realizing that the result would be that Ramachandra would have to go to the forest for fourteen years. And why should Durvasas Rishi, who loved Lallu (the Baby Krishna), have ever thought to insult King Ambarisha? Only because his intellect had become perverted. A clear case of Prakriti Siddhi, just to teach him not to be too arrogant. So long as they maintain their own independent existence even the Rishis are still subject to the Law of Karma, and when they err Nature creates for them situations in which they will have to admit that they have been wrong, just so their egos will not go out of control."

"Which means that even the Rishis are not the Biggest of the Bosses."

"At the center of the circle of the Rishi Mandala sits the Rishi who is running the whole show. He is the chief Rishi of the Rishi Mandala, the only Rishi who can fully control the Adya Shakti and the Universal Prakriti. All the other Rishis think they have independent existences, but even they are just his puppets. If the center disappears, can there be a circle? Whenever a Rishi starts to get a swelled head and tries to take over the Number One spot, Mr. Big—we can call him The Seniormost—uses Prakriti Siddhi to teach the offender a good lesson. The Seniormost plays about in his own way and no one can ever know him."

"Isn't this frustrating for the Rishis? They do penance for millenia and *still* they are subject to Prakriti Siddhi?"

"It is terribly frustrating; if you and I don't like to admit that we have been wrong the Rishis absolutely *hate* to have to admit that they were wrong. But that's just the way things are."

"Hmm. When you mentioned this sort of thing before, you attributed it to Saturn—OK, now I get it! So Shukracharya also used Prakriti Siddhi, to pervert the minds of Kacha and Devayani?"

"Something came over them, didn't it? Even the gods are not exempt. Krishna Himself never knew that Vishvamitra would curse his entire clan, and even though Krishna did His best to prevent it the curse had its full effect. Even the ocean participated in the curse, despite the fact that Krishna is of the lunar race whose progenitor, Moon, is lord of the ocean.

"Not even Mahakala was exempt from Prakriti Siddhi. He never knew He would have to take birth as Anjaneya."

"Mahakala never knew he would have to take birth as Anjaneya?"

"No. Do you remember that Shiva blessed Ravana that he would die when he stole another man's wife?"

"*Parastri haranam, Ravana maranam* (Ravana will die when he steals another man's wife.)."

"Precisely. Were it not for Shiva the events of the *Ramayana* need never have taken place, since without Shiva's blessing Ravana would never have needed to abduct Sita in order to die. This made Shiva the cause of the whole thing, which gave Him no choice but to take birth. He had to be available to assist Vishnu in His incarnation as Rama to ensure that Rama would successfully kill Ravana, to fulfill the terms of His blessing.

"And for that matter, Shiva would have never blessed Ravana had Ravana not decided to die, and Ravana would not have decided to relinquish his immortality had he not turned Saturn over, at the recommendation of Narada, when Ravana had the Nine Planets lying face down on the steps leading up to his throne. Something came over Ravana to make him agree with Narada's suggestion; what came over him was Prakriti Siddhi."

"Wow!" All these myths suddenly slipped into alignment with one another for me.

"Lord Shiva was also affected by Prakriti Siddhi on another occasion, when He saw Vishnu in His Mohini form as a gorgeous young tribal girl. When He saw Mohini's garment drop from Her perfect body Shiva was overwhelmed by Her nakedness. He ran after Her like a bull elephant pursues a cow, completely unashamed that His wife was watching Him make a spectacle of Himself. Only after He ejaculated did His mind clear sufficiently for Him to realize His predicament. Why should He have chased Mohini? When the very seeds of lust within Him had been fried, burned to ashes, how could they sprout again? Only Prakriti Siddhi could do it. Lord Shiva forgot Himself, just for a moment, and lust reappeared. And if this power can work against someone like Lord Shiva, who is the embodiment of permanent samadhi and has done the most terrible penances imaginable for eons upon eons, well, it must be something. This is the power of Prakriti Siddhi in the hands of an expert. What do you think happened to King Parikshit?'

"You mean the Parikshit who was the son of Abhimanyu, thanks to whom we have the *Shrimad Bhagavata*?"

"Yes, that Parikshit. When he was out hunting one day he came upon a Rishi sitting in samadhi, alone in his ashram. Parikshit was feeling terribly thirsty and called out for water. When the Rishi sitting in his trance did not offer him any the king became wild, and hung a dead snake around the Rishi's neck. Then he rode off.

"The Rishi's son returned to the ashram a few minutes later and saw the snake around his father's neck. Then he got wild, and spoke this curse: 'Seven days from now the snake which has been draped about my father's neck will come back to life. It will bite the perpetrator of this insult, and he will die.'

"The intense Tamas of this curse disturbed his father's concentration and brought him down from his samadhi. He divined the situation in a few moments and said, 'Child, child, what have you done? You have been overcome by Tamas. You must remain in Sattva.'

"The boy replied, 'Father, you don't know me. I am far beyond Sattva and all of that. I have deliberately cursed the king, and my curse will prove a blessing to him.'

"The father was goggle-eyed in amazement, realizing all at once that he knew nothing at all of the power of his son. He asked the boy, 'How is that?'

"His son said, 'Shukadeva, the young Rishi, will now meet the king and deliver to him the text of the *Shrimad Bhagavata*, which otherwise would never have come into the hands of mankind. And Parikshit will obtain moksha by hearing it.'

"And that is what happened. At the end of seven days of recitation, when the snake came to bite him Parikshit welcomed the serpent with these words:

'Go ahead, bite! Do you think that I am the body, that you can harm me?' And Parikshit merged his consciousness with the Universal Soul. An ordinary spirit, Dundubhi, who was sitting nearby listening, was freed as well. So it is all thanks to that young rishi that we have the *Shrimad Bhagavata*. What superb play! First he perverts Parikshit's mind, then he curses him for it, then the curse becomes a blessing."

"How could that young Rishi find any limitations left in King Parikshit's mind to pervert if he was so 'well tested'?"

"It was easy. So long as Kundalini identifies with your body you remain subject to time, space and causation. This means that your consciousness remains subject to the chemical patterns in your brain, patterns which can be tinkered with by anyone who knows Prakriti Siddhi. This is why Prakriti Siddhi is useful only for the living, because the chemical changes which occur in a corpse are destructive only. If a girl comes to a male corpse and jumps all over it and even climbs on top of it will its penis become erect? No. It is devoid of life, devoid of ahamkara. You can, if you like, change the prakriti of the dead spirit, but that change can take effect only after it has been born into another womb—unless you can bring it back temporarily.

"Eknath Maharaj did this when he called one woman's ancestors down to Earth so that she could feed them in person. Feeding them changed her prakriti entirely, which is why I always say that Pitri Tarpana is so important. You can really change things in your life if you can properly perform Pitri Tarpana. Obviously it would take too long to try to change the prakriti of a whole nation using Pitri Tarpana, so the Rishis use different methods. But for individuals it can be very effective. My Roshni is very clever. She tells me, 'If you don't want to teach me anything else, teach me Pitri Tarpana.' She knows that if proper Pitri Tarpana is ever done for her, her prakriti will change completely. All her bad tendencies will be wiped out.

"But does she realize what tremendous shakti it would take to wipe clean the karmic slate of even seven generations of her ancestors? If you are an ordinary human being it is really not feasible to eliminate all the evil, selfish personality traits of all your ancestors. Instead, you should use your sadhana to interdict and obliterate these traits before they have a chance to enter your mind and distort it. Sadhana is good because through it the gods and goddesses can perform a type of Prakriti Siddhi on you. It is a more limited sort of Prakriti Siddhi than the Rishis use, no doubt, but when a deity uses Prakriti Siddhi on a human being the effect is still permanent. That person's very genes and chromosomes are changed, and there is never a regression to the previous state.

"One day Rani Rasmani, who owned the temple in which Ramakrishna Paramahamsa was employed as a priest, had gone there to worship Ma. But instead of concentrating on her worship she was thinking about her business affairs. When Ramakrishna Paramahamsa noticed this he got up from where he was sitting and gave her a good slap. Then he told her, 'If you want to come to the temple come with an empty mind, and leave your worldly cares outside.'

"Most people interpret this story shallowly. They think that Ramakrishna Paramahamsa read her mind and then slapped her as a sort of shock treatment, so that she would not forget the lesson. But these people forget that at that moment Ramakrishna Paramahamsa was in *unmani*, a state in which he was not conscious of what he was doing. In real unmani there is not an iota of body consciousness, not even for a second. When you grope after the perception of Absolute Reality for too long it leads to madness, the divine madness of unmani. Your limited body consciousness is completely effaced, and something else plays within your body. In the case of Ramakrishna Paramahamsa it was the Divine Mother, in the form of the goddess Bhavatarini, Who played within him. It was She Who administered the slap to Rani Rasmani, using Ramakrishna Paramahamsa's hand as an instrument. That slap was a form of Prakriti Siddhi; after that slap Rani Rasmani's mind was always fixed on God.

"Any blessing or curse that you get from a saint or guru is actually one sort of Prakriti Siddhi. Why? Because by blessing or cursing you they are transmitting into you some of the power of their personal deities. For example, Eknath Maharaj had a son who was a bigoted Brahmana. He thought his father was soiling the family name by associating with outcastes and low-born people and he and his wife regularly harassed Eknath Maharaj. Then one day Eknath Maharaj asked the couple to appear before him in the clothes in which they had been married. He sat them down in front of him and said, 'The two of you make such a beautiful couple. Why can't your consciousnesses be as beautiful as you are?' In that second Prakriti Siddhi was performed on them, and their lives changed for good. This is the kind of guru to have: one who can force your mind to remain straight.

"In our world Prakriti Siddhi can be done in two ways: immediately, with a slap or whatever; and slowly, over a period of time. The fast way is much better, because there is an end to the thing. Unfortunately, unless the power of a deity is flowing through you at the proper moment you won't be able to do it the fast way. Then you will have to use the slow way, which makes everything linger on. But even if you have to use the slow way you can contrive to make the effect permanent. Take the recent case of a wastrel, an inveterate drunkard and debauchee. Even such punishments as being expelled from his home and getting a good beating from the police had failed to help improve him. But after his nature was affected he has apologized to his father, wife and family, and even worshipped their feet, as a sign of complete submission. He did all these things of his own free will, on his own initiative.

"This fellow will never know what is happening to him, because the process is entirely internal. He will never resist it, because all the changes in his personality come from within. The more egocentric a man is, the more he requires attention, the less likely he is to disagree with his own suggestions. It is only natural for such a man to be in the habit of believing that anything he says or does is right and desirable. He may even congratulate himself for doing such a fine thing, believing that he had thought of it himself. Could any external coercion ever provide motivation like that? No.

"This effect is temporary, to be sure. But even when the treatment is over and the old tendencies of mind return—as they must, since they are deeply embedded—they will have to compete with the new habits which have been formed. How long the effect will last will depend on the quality of material you are working with. A person who has a fundamentally good environment, like a good family, good teaching, and such, will be less likely to backslide than someone like Behram."

"Is this what happened the night that Behram changed his mind about going back to Iran and Anjaneya came through you? Did Anjaneya give him a dose of Prakriti Siddhi?"

"Yes, He did. I like to try to harmonize families, to improve people who have gone wrong, and Prakriti Siddhi can be very useful for this. Hasn't that family been materially benefitted because Behram went back?"

"It has."

"Though Prakriti Siddhi in the context of a family is almost always used for harmonization, there are times that it must be used for destruction as well. This problem is very uncommon, of course, because the truly harmonious family is very rare today. But if there is a family which is completely harmonious that family would go on being harmonious endlessly, which cannot be permitted to occur. So, the intellect of only one of the family members is perverted and the whole family falls apart. It sounds cruel, I know, and I know that it is hard to understand why it could be necessary. But only then can a new pattern form."

"Is this what happened to your own family? That after fifteen generations someone thought that it was time for a change and perverted Putlibai's mind so that she could pervert your father's brother's mind and have him bring the family crashing down?"

"Something like that."

At this a thin, dejected-looking pariah dog wandered up to us, tail between his legs, and we offered him a sugar cookie. After an brief conceptual struggle over whether accepting it might entail an eventual kick his hunger overcame his fear and he came up to my hand, accepted the cookie, and began to eat it weakly. I continued to feed him as Vimalananda talked.

"But these are not the only uses of Prakriti Siddhi. There is no end to its usefulness. For instance, long ago when I was a naked sadhu I was invited to Nepal by the Rana. He wanted to test me, so he lined the main staircase of his palace with beautiful young teenage girls, all of them naked to the waist. They had lovely, enticing breasts, but as I was deep in my sadhana I saw all of them as skeletons. I thought to myself, 'How can I have a romance with a skeleton?' And Nature was kind, because their prakritis changed, not mine, and instead of seeing me as a sexual object they saw me as a father or brother. Wasn't that better?"

"It was much better."

"And why go so far away? I used to play about with Chotu right here in Bombay. When I had a dairy in Borivali sometimes we would take the suburban train to the Churchgate Terminus. When I was in a certain peculiar mood I would tell him, 'Everyone will get down at Churchgate.' All of the people in our compartment would then get down at Churchgate, no matter what intervening station they had meant to alight at. They would walk out the door of the station and then realize, 'Oh, no, what have I done? I wanted to get down at such-and-such station, and here I am at Churchgate. I must have slept through it.' But they had not slept through it. Sometimes I would make everyone on the platform get on the train, even if it was the wrong train for them. Only later on would they figure it out. I used to enjoy playing about in this way. It was harmless fun, because there are plenty of trains for people to catch, and it gave me a chance to test my range, which is important for any siddhi.

"Now an example on a larger scale. Look at India, a poor country with rich enemies. But we have Prakriti Siddhi to protect us. America can send any number of planes, tanks and other armaments to Pakistan, and we don't bother about it. Why? Because planes, ships, tanks, cannon and everything else will not work without human beings. All that is necessary is to pervert the Pakistani soldiers' intelligence. Suppose a formation of warplanes is flying towards our country. What if all the pilots suddenly change course and go in the wrong direction at the wrong altitude, flying straight into our anti-aircraft guns? If they then forget to evade the anti-aircraft fire they will all be shot down. Just think: in the last war seventeen Sabre jets were shot down by one anti-aircraft gun. Seventeen! Is that at all possible? Only with Prakriti Siddhi.

"Or take the sinking of the submarine Ghazi in Vishakhpatnam harbor. We didn't even know it was there until the military police picked up two fishermen who were quarreling over the division of the money that the Pakistanis had given them to keep quiet about their presence. Then the Navy started dropping random depth charges. Random depth charges! They had absolutely no idea where the damned thing was and yet they sank it! Isn't that hard to believe? But it happened. Couldn't the Pakistani captain have thought to move his sub out of the harbor temporarily? He could have but he didn't, because his prakriti was perverted.

"A formation of Patton tanks crossed our borders. What to do? First, Nature was very kind to us; there was tremendous rain for twenty-four hours, quite out of season. The tanks were moving through sugarcane fields, where they got bogged down. Would any general ever think of attacking when the Pakistanis did, when crops are standing in the fields and the ground is still soggy from rain? Everyone knows that it is suicide to send out waves of tanks in these conditions. The Pakistani generals are not idiots, but they forgot what they knew at a crucial moment because their prakritis were changed. Then someone in our army got the bright idea of taking an iron bar and sticking it into the treads of the tanks. With the treads gone the tanks couldn't move, and were easily destroyed. You see, India cannot afford all sorts of premium weapons; we have to make do with what we have. An iron bar costs a few rupees, but it can stop a tank! Isn't the job done just as well? Nature is very kind to India."

"Prakriti Siddhi, then, could be used in any war."

"Why not? Think about the Second World War. Why did Hitler fail to pursue the English and French at Dunkirk? Why did he call off the Battle of Britain and the invasion of England, just when it might have succeeded? Why did he invade Russia two weeks too late? At crucial moments his mind was perverted, just a bit—but that was enough to sabotage all his plans. It was enough to dissolve his dream-edifice of conquest, his Thousand-Year Reich, after a mere dozen years."

"Who was it that perverted his mind? Some Rishi?"

"Maybe. And maybe not. But how does that matter? What matters is that the real use of siddhis, Robby, including Prakriti Siddhi, the ultimate siddhi, is not all this fancy stuff. The real use of siddhis is to make life a little easier for all the suffering beings in our wretched and thankless world. Look at what a gift we are giving to this poor little doggie! When we convinced him that we would not harm him he came near to us in trust, and we've been feeding him. Like all of us he has taken birth just to endure his karmas and is enduring them without even knowing why. We have satisfied his hunger, and loved him. Now we must make him go to sleep so he can get a good rest for once in his life of pain."

The dog did not want to snooze; he wanted to eat more. But we didn't want him to get sick. He sat down all of a sudden, as if pushed, and his head started to droop; though he made several valiant efforts to lift it, sleep overtook him inexorably. Soon he was peacefully snoozing, and Vimalananda and I shared a gentle grin over him. "When you love God," he said softly to me, "you see God in all His creations and cannot bear to see Him miserable. And then you offer everything you can to Him, spontaneously from the depths of your heart, even if that means using siddhis to tinker with fate."

"So don't feel bad," he concluded with a twinkle in his eye, "if you are exposed to Prakriti Siddhi someday. When even the Rishis and the gods have been affected by it why shouldn't you be?" Unexpectedly and unaccountably I had a vision of Vimalananda, his Junior Guru Maharaj and his Senior Guru Maharaj all aiming Prakriti Siddhi at one another, but I brushed it away as inspired by the gust of wind that had just ruffled our hair.

༄

On November 28, 1982 Redstone was nominated by the editor of our racing weekly as Champion Three-Year-Old Colt at Poona in honor of winning both the races in which he ran during the Poona season. His future looked bright, but as he was still not up to par by the time acceptances for the 1983 Indian Derby came due he was scratched from that race as well. We still had no reason to suspect any serious problem, nor had we any time for suspicion with the Auctions Sales impending. Thoroughbred breeding, which is one of the most speculative of businesses, attracts to it a smooth and sophisticated variety of operator. For a week before the sales begin these stud proprietors go on display along with their colts and fillies, and prospective owners buzz about them, Auction Catalogue in hand, evaluating and interrogating. The sellers calculate, cogitate, and deliberate; much tea is drunk and many comments are exchanged; and the vets do a brisk business in examinations for configuration and soundness.

About a third of the horseflesh brought to be vended is disposed of by private sale during these days. What is not purchased privately comes into the auction ring, where it fell in those days under a hammer brandished by Mr. B.K.F. Damania, an aged and crotchety Parsi sports writer known to all by his initials. BKFD's job was to extract the highest price for the lots he was assigned over the three days that the auctions continued, and he speckled his banter with temptations, threats, pleas and coaxings to spur recalcitrant buyers into commitments. There he sat on his little throne under an awning in the Paddock while the rest of us crowded into the seats surrounding him to hear his patter: "I want some more, I'm not a seller at that price"; "No more, then? All done? Sold, to … ."; or, when the reserve bid was not met, "Bought in."

Because this February we were just watching and not bidding, I sat there surveying the scene on this second of the three auction days. I was thinking of the fact that perhaps two out of every three of these two-year-olds might actually see the racecourse, that maybe half of those might win a race, and that with great luck one out of ten might be a fairly impressive racer. From this perspective Vimalananda was either exceptionally lucky or exceedingly perceptive. For, I had known him his horses's records had far surpassed these odds. An eye for talent, creative dietary supplementation, race manipulation, or Prakriti Siddhi: was there one principal instrumentality of his success, or did they all play their parts?

I mused on until BKFD's gavel fell for the last time that day, when Vimalananda and I progressed to another corral on the Club's grounds to enjoy the highlight of the Sales: the annual auction dinner. It was catered that year by a firm from Delhi, and was excellent. The Club's Stewards were apparently still reeling from the fiasco of two years before, when the Parsi Stewards had ordered Parsi food for everyone. The meat dishes were said to have been tasty that year, but the vegetarian menu was largely inedible. I personally was reduced to making a meal of Kersasp Kolah's Spicy Carrot Pickle with wheat rotis that a myopic eye and a lazy tongue might have misconstrued to be well-worn shoe soles. That dinner caused the Club's vegetarians to rise as one in rebellion. The next year's result was a happier meal, this year's even happier.

This year we sat enjoying drinks and tidbits as we compared notes over prices and purchasers with Tehmul and a few of his other owners, with Dr. Kulkarni, and with Mr. Tejwani, a refined man who built buildings to bank-roll his string of nearly a dozen horses. At our table also sat the jolly Barkat Ali Khan, a man Vimalananda much respected for his knowledge of horse-flesh and of music. Barkat Ali had become so disgusted with the discreditable ways and means of trainers that he had had himself declared a private trainer. Now he and his son took care of his horses himself, with some success. Vimalananda had talked of taking such a step himself, but his poor health now precluded him from doing it personally. Nor could his circle of confidants qualify: I being a foreigner would not be permitted to train and Roshni had a full-time job. Mamrabahen would have been overjoyed to nominate her pol-troon Jhendu Kumar for the post, but that would have been entirely like hiring a fox to supervise a henhouse. To call Jhendu Kumar feckless would be an insult to those who show some shreds of feck.

I sat at the table silently munching tri-corner samosas and spinach *pakodas*, uneasily watching the greasy Subhashbhai banter with Vimalananda in the hope of getting him to agree to purchasing a horse in partnership. That there was no chance of that happening I was sure; Vimalananda was neither so naive nor so drunk that he would consider even for a moment entering into a partnership with such a man as Subhashbhai, who left behind him when he walked a slime trail that would put a banana slug to shame. No, I was worried that Vimalananda might try to repeat a stunt of some years previous that he had recalled to mind that very morning. For some reason, back in the days when the British ruled India, he had wanted to get even with Admiral Eric Shipton, so when the Admiral hosted a party Vimalananda came equipped with a sausage. After several drinks he began to feign drunkenness and excused himself to visit the loo, where he inserted the dark red meaty cylinder into his open fly. When he emerged and people saw what they thought was his exposed state they began to cough in embarrassment, until Admiral Shipton himself felt it necessary to take him aside and point out his oversight.' "Whaaa?" said Vimalananda besottedly. "Oh, that bloody thing? Here, I'll take care of it… " Extracting a knife from his pocket he chopped that wurst in two.

Vimalananda claims that there were women who swooned on seeing this feat. Admiral Shipton was, I am sure, not in the least amused. At this auction dinner there were fortunately no sausages among the hors d'oeuvres, but I could not shake the feeling that Vimalananda was plotting something or other. Sure enough, after we finished eating Subhashbhai invited us to come with him to listen to music. Vimalananda accepted readily and asked the disgusted Barkat Ali, who being a good Muslim refused to drink, to accompany us. When he summarily declined, we departed. I drove, since I had done no more than sip at my whiskey. I knew that Vimalananda could drive perfectly well no matter how drunk he was, for drink did not affect him as it affected other people. Two years before he had safely driven me and Roshni home after the auction dinner after he had tippled an entire bottle of whisky. No, I was more worried that driving would just excite him more, as it had on that previous night when he sped up, gnarling, just to show he was still in control after Roshni gently chided him when once or twice he veered slightly onto the center line.

Via a number of ill-lit alleys, Subhashbhai took us to a location where he offered us paan, paan that we later discovered had been secretly laced with an illegal stimulant. Vimalananda was now beginning to become enthusiastic about the prospect of causing some sort of massive loss of face for Subhashbhai and the stimulant only heightened his mental clarity. When we pulled up in front of our destination I saw that we were within the purlieus of Bombay's sizable red-light district. As we made our way into the warren of rooms I was staggered by the wondrous sight of a mound of onions no less than four feet high, attended to by a human gnome who was swiftly peeling each one.

Two women who were evidently prostitutes seated us in a chamber in which sat a harmonium. Subhashbhai began to nod off as the women began their serenade. When they were finished Vimalananda told them, "That was very nice, but I would like to teach you something that I think your patrons will find most enjoyable. Could you please find me a *tabla* player?" Within five minutes a tabla player arrived and Vimalananda commenced his teaching concert. Soon all the ladies in the building who were not otherwise engaged had gathered in that small room, everyone appreciating and enjoying Vimalananda's thaumaturgy—everyone, that is, except Subhashbhai, who at one point tilted to his feet and headed for the door. When Vimalananda ran out of cigarettes some half an hour or more later and we bid the sorrowing cocottes adieu we found Subhashbhai lying in the gutter near our car, fast asleep, his driver eyeing him watchfully. As I drove us home Vimalananda said, "This will teach that debauchee a good lesson. Does he think that my mind can be led astray by intoxicants, by women, or by money? Ha!"

Subhashbhai gave both of us a wide berth from then on. By unspoken agreement we told no one but Tehmul of the humiliating performance he had put on. The distressing fact was, though, that he had somehow managed the effrontery to attempt to inveigle Vimalananda into participating in his schemes. This suggested that undersirable influences were beginning to accumulate in Vimalananda's environment, perhaps the curse that dogs Bombay was coming upon him. Another disconcerting reminder of Bombay's nature was provided to us shortly thereafter when Vimalananda pointed out to me a tall dreadlocked sadhu heatedly discussing the race book with a woman, standing on the grass in front of the First Enclosure at the Bombay racecourse just before a race.

"That's Shankargiriji," said Vimalananda.

"*The* Shankargiriji?" said I.

"The very one," replied Vimalananda. I peered down on the sadhu, as impressed by his appearance—he was said to be at least 125 years old—as I was distressed by his conduct back in 1949 during the Ranu episode. When Vimalananda, then in the jungle with Shankargiriji, saw a vision of the death of his nine-year-old son, Ranu, Shankargiriji repeatedly pooh-poohed it. Vimalananda insisted on rushing to Bombay anyway and arrived in time to meet Ranu alive once more but too late to save the boy from death. "Shankargiriji doesn't seem to do much except gamble nowadays," Vimalananda now murmured. "When his disciples come to see him he has them sit down and play cards. He's entitled to do as he pleases, but I don't like it when sadhus set bad examples for others who are not so advanced as they." The conversation ended there as I had to go downstairs to the Ring to bet, but that evening Vimalananda, as if from out of the blue, told me a story:

"There was once a woman who as a daily personal sadhana would cook a stack of rotis and feed them to her guru, who happened to be Durvasas Rishi. Every day she had to ford the river that separated her house from Durvasas' hut. One day during the monsoon the river rose so high after she had reached the Rishi with his lunch that she was unable to cross back over. She began to fret about the dinner she needed to cook for her husband until Durvasas said, 'What are you making such a big noise about? Go to the river and tell her, "Ma, if Durvasas has never eaten even one of my rotis please let me cross, but if he has eaten even one don't allow me to proceed."'

"The woman wanted to object, for Durvasas had been daily eating a big stack of rotis before her own eyes for weeks and weeks. But Durvasas said, 'Go!' Knowing his reputation as a curse-monger she kept her mouth shut, fearing for her destiny. She went back to the river, told the river what she had been told to say—and the water went down enough for her to cross.

"This really disturbed her mind. That evening while she was cooking her husband's dinner she could think of nothing but the afternoon's incident. It is never good to cook absent-mindedly, and because she was trying to use her limited brain to figure out what had happened she forgot to add any salt to the food. When her husband got home she served him absent-mindedly, which he noticed, and when he tasted the food he said to her, 'What is on your mind, goddess?'

"She replied defensively, 'Nothing; nothing at all!'

"He told her gently, 'Then why did you forget to add any salt to the food? You never forget such things.'

"Now she was abashed, and told him the whole story, ending with, 'But how could he do this?'

"Her husband said, 'Oh, this is truly a minor thing. Let's make an experiment. The river is still high, isn't it? Tomorrow, when you need to cross over to feed the Rishi, tell the river, "Ma, if my husband has never had sex with me, let me cross over; but if he has enjoyed intercourse with me even once don't let me pass."'

"Now the woman was really fed up. She was the mother of eight strapping sons! How could he claim he had never impregnated her? But her husband refused to listen to her complaints. Next morning when she reached the river it was in spate. When she told it what her husband had bidden her say it dropped enough for her to pass.

"When she reached Durvasas with her pile of rotis she waited watching while he ate them in peace. When he was done she described to him what had happened that morning. When he heard what her husband had said Durvasas told the woman, 'Don't come to me anymore. Your husband is advanced enough to take care of you himself.'"

Vimalananda fell silent. As I had read a similar story from a book of Indian parrot tales, and I thought he was simply recapitulating it for me. Then Roshni took me aside and said, "Whether or not this happened to Durvasas it did happen to Vimalananda; I was there. That woman with the rotis was Vimalananda's wife. The river she had to cross was actually Bombay harbor, which she used to cross by ferry to feed Shankargiriji, her guru who then lived in Alibag, on the coast. Both times it looked at first as if the ferry would not be able to go, but it did go—after she talked to the ocean as she had been told to do."

I had known Vimalananda's wife for some years by this time and got along with her well enough. But I knew that she had insisted on marrying Vimalananda—in spite of being frightened into illness after a trip to the smashan with him—and that after marriage she had continued to consider her husband quite the useless loafer for failing to focus his life on money-making. Now I found that even the words of the man she had taken as her guru had failed to shake this opinion. Was there any limit to the depth of rnanubandhana's influence in human life, I had to wonder, or to the pain that that influence could produce?

◌

Saturn had moved into Libra in October 1982 to sit atop my Moon (and Roshni's too), which accelerated the force of our Sade Satis. Events began to cumulate after Roshni's departure for East Asia on a Bank of America training tour. First Vimalananda, who had been complaining of shortness of breath for weeks, was diagnosed with congestive cardiac failure. I played the nurse, dosing him with potions and keeping him all but tied to the bed, and restricted him to one cigarette per day. But I saw that he was losing interest in his physical health and did little to complement this treatment with the well-nigh-miraculous powers of self-healing that I had seen him exercise before on so many occasions. The possibilities worried me, and solutions eluded me.

Then the grooms at the track again went out on strike, in continuation of a spell of labor unrest during the previous Poona season which had deteriorated into violence. The Poona police had had to fire some gunshots to control the crowd and of the three grooms who were injured one was literally gelded by a bullet. The police officer who was second in command of that operation was a friend of Tehmul's and had described the battle scenes for us from his perspective as a maintainer of the public order. He was a gung-ho young man, with an innuendo of a swagger in his stride, who seasoned his conversation with macho observations like, "The real danger, sir, and the real thrill, comes when you have to face an industrial mob. You don't know what they are like, sir, I tell you, an industrial mob is a real test of a man's mettle."

No violence marred this Bombay strike, but as there was a shortage of willing hands to care for the horses I had to go daily to the stables for a couple of weeks to help Tehmul handle them. I had previously watched some of the local *gymkhanas*, events in which amateur riders exhibited their skills, and anticipated being able to do my job at least as well as those teenagers could. Fortunately Fakruddin, the head groom, took pity on me and gave me the aged gelding Onslaught to lead on his walk around the stables. Then for the first time in my life I realized through personal experience what it was like to have control of nearly 1500 pounds of neurotic thoroughbred. Though Onslaught liked to nip at everyone he didn't rear up much, so I kept my distance from his mouth and was not bitten. Only once did Onslaught make as if to rear, just to show me who was boss, but Fakhruddin and Nakhodaji the farrier sped over to help me bring him under control.

"At least," said Vimalananda to me as I sat next to his bed delivering my report, "this strike is not the communists' doing."

"Would the communists be any worse than these people?" I griped.

"The communists? Oh my God! Once the communists in one of the unions at the racecourse decided that they had to have their way, even if it meant harming the horses. So they kept the horses hostage until their demands were negotiated. What did the horses ever do to them? Injure the owners if you want to, but why the horses? Those bastards knew that they had less to lose if they harmed the horses rather than the owners, so they went for the horses first. Such people do not deserve to be humans! I tell you, as soon as they die they will be born into appropriate wombs so that Nature can teach them some fine lessons. Human justice may slip up, but not divine justice."

"Why do you hate communism so much? Isn't it more appropriate to hate the people that the communists are fighting, the people who exploit the labor of others and pay them a miserly pittance?"

"One of the many reasons I hate communism is that communists believe that the end justifies the means—which is ridiculous. They believe this because they are frustrated and want to take their frustrations out on others instead of enduring them themselves. If you are miserable you must have performed some karma at some point to make you miserable. Should you not pay for that karma? Some kind-hearted person may assist you by showing you how to pay off the karma with less expenditure on your part. If he is *really* kind-hearted he might even take away some of your karmas from you and endure them himself. But you can't just grab hold of someone and force him to share your karmas; it just doesn't work that way. That way only creates new karmas."

"Does the end ever justify the means?"

"How can it? Is there an end? The end cannot possibly justify the means because the end *is* the means; the means determines the end. Cause is Effect concealed; Effect is Cause revealed. Only an absolutely desirable end could justify any means to attain it. But any end you can envision must be false, because a goal however noble is a limitation that you impose on Reality, which is unlimited. All limitations however slight are imperfect, which makes them only relatively, not absolutely, true. There is no end so absolute that it justifies any means, except maybe the end of getting yourself back to God. But if you don't understand the Law of Karma you will get into trouble even there. You always have to think of all the potential repercussions from what you do.

"One of Narsi Mehta's songs ends this way: 'People will beat you with their shoes when you sing these songs, but you will go to *Vaikuntha* (Vishnu's heaven).' *Gandhiji* (Mahahtma Gandhi) sang Narsi Mehta's songs, but he was never beaten with shoes. In fact he was worshipped. Why? Because first, he was devoted mainly to politics, not to God. Second, he had no faith in these songs. If he had had faith in them he would have left politics altogether. Third, and worst, he used Narsi's songs for political ends—to make people think he was a saint, a *mahatma*."

"He wasn't a mahatma?"

"What does *mahatma* mean? Atma is the soul, which is realized after many, many lifetimes. (*Maha + Atma = Mahatma* = "Great Soul.") That must be really something, mustn't it? Had Gandhi realized even the soul, much less the Great Soul? No, he had not. How can I say that? Well, for one thing, he relied on his intuition to tell him what to do. So many saints do that. But his intuition was always wrong, and what would happen? He would commit Himalayan blunders, confess them to everyone and then start all over again and repeat the process."

"Oh, but come on, you have to agree that he did achieve his goal; he did kick the British out of the country."

"Yes, Gandhi's aim was good. But he should not have claimed to be nonviolent when he was not nonviolent."

"What are you talking about?"

"He may have rejected physical violence, but what about his non-physical violence? What about all the time he spent coercing people to do what he wanted them to do by threatening to kill himself through fasting? Where's the non-violence in that? And don't ever forget the Law of Karma. You see what Gandhi did, and now look what has happened! Our politicians still use indefinite fasts and demonstrations and general strikes to manipulate people, but now they manipulate them into voting en masse for whichever candidate shares their caste or their religion. Gandhiji may have used his means for a noble end, but today his means has *become* the end. Today's politicians can think of nothing more than their own terms of offices, and they are willing to do anything in order to succeed. Why should I support them in inflaming religious and ethnic sentiments? Do you think I want to encourage bigotry of any sort? Never!

"Unfortunately, the vast majority of human beings are sheep. Long ago I too used to be in that flock of sheep. But then I ran away, and now that I have dedicated my life to staying away from that flock of sheep why would I want to return to it? Why do you think I refuse to vote?"

"Would participating in the democratic process ship you back to the flock?"

"*What* democratic process? If we had informed voters voting that would be one thing. But the majority of our voters are illiterate and, as in most democracies, they vote for whomever promises them the most. I'm sorry, but we got our independence very cheaply. If we had had to fight for it, like the Vietnamese did, I think we would value it much more.

"Do you mean that maybe it would be better for Nature *not* to continue to help India intercept enemy tanks, planes and submarines, just to teach your fellow countrymen to value their freedom?"

"No, not at all. Our brave soldiers and sailors and airmen fully deserve Nature's help. No, it will be better for the politicians to suffer. To be a politician you have to put your conscience on the shelf. Why should I support people who have no conscience, even if I only support them by stating my preference for them?

"I do try to support those politicians who are decent people, but decent politicians will never get very far, because they are not willing to stab their grandmothers in the back. And how many decent politicians are there, especially today? Look at our current crop of Indian politicians! All that they know how to do is to try to extort support from others by courting arrest. And where did they learn this tactic from? From Gandhi! By creating things like the 'Fill the Jail' agitation Gandhiji encouraged ambitious people to think that the only qualification to hold public office that they really require is to have been a jailbird."

"So what was Gandhiji's potentially justifiable means has become an unjustifiable political end," I reflected. "How well this supports your thesis."

"In my life I have found two touchstones. One was Ramakrishna Paramahamsa and the second was Gandhiji. Everyone who came in contact with Ramakrishna Paramahamsa became truly spiritual, and everyone who came in contact with Gandhiji became truly materialistic, greedy for fame or money or both. And still people worship Gandhiji as a saint! It's amazing. I once knew an old Muslim fakir who used to say, *Gandhi teri aandhi duniya ko paye mal, magar teri bhut pujayegi.*"

"I don't quite follow that." He was exaggerating for emphasis, as Indians tend to do, but the karmic implications intrigued me.

" 'Gandhi, your storm will wreak havoc on the world, but your statues will be worshipped.' And they are. India is a most unique country."

"You will at least admit that Gandhiji was brave."

"Yes, I'll grant you that. He stood up to the British and wouldn't give up until he got his way. But he was also very lucky that he was fighting the British, who at least showed some decency. If the Germans or the Japanese had been ruling India then how long do you think Gandhi would have lasted? Not very long! As soon as he stood up and made some noise they would have simply shot him dead."

"So India's independence is partly due to the British?"

"Think about this for a moment: Suppose the minds of some key Britishers became perverted and they decided that the best course of action was to give India its freedom without resisting much. Then Gandhi looks less like the man who caused it all and more like the instrument through which someone else caused it."

"Hmm."

"I tell you one thing today: this is exactly what will happen to communism. One of these days, and it will be sooner than you think, the minds of the top communists are going to be perverted. Without anyone else's help they themselves will destroy everything that their commissars have built atop all those mountains of corpses. And that will make me very, very happy."

I thought this prediction daft then, but of course it was merely prescient. Within a few short years of his death communism had begun its inevitable collapse.

Here Vimalananda stubbed out his cigarette and paused before continuing: "No matter how pure your motives are your ass can still be fired even if you keep your nose clean." While the Hindi phrase "to fire someone's ass" literally means to violate that person anally, in Bombay argot it suggests giving that someone a very hard time.

"You know, Chotu used to spend plenty of time with a sadhu named Chaitanyananda. Chaitanyananda was a good man, with a good knowledge of

Ayurveda. People would come to him all the time for treatment because he could cure many serious diseases, including the first stage of cancer. He would make whoever came to him stay for about a month. The first day he would tend to that person carefully to create a false sense of security. Then he would go out into the jungle and collect a certain plant. He would extract its juice, which he called *Ram-rasam* ('Rama's Juice'), and then administer it to the patient. Anyone who took Ram-rasam would purge and vomit. My God, *how* they would purge and vomit! Go on, purging and vomiting! Once the patient's insides were cleaned out Chaitanyananda would serve him *khichadi* (rice and split mung beans cooked together) into which a little *bhasma* (Ayurvedic metallic oxide medicine) had been added. Chaitanyananda would vary the type of bhasma according to the nature of the disease. The poor fellow would take this diet alone for two weeks or a month or whatever, and would leave cured."

"So he really fired their asses, literally, didn't he?"

"Yes, but it was for their own good. They were so ill that their bodies required that kind of severe discipline to be cured. Chaitanyananda was a very disciplined man. Every morning he would get up and tend to his patients. Then he would sit down in the lotus position and go into a samadhi during which he would not move all day long. This kind of samadhi is really not all that useful, though; it is just like being dead. Your mind is so concentrated on one object that it does not move, but it cannot go anywhere else either.

"Chaitanyananda had a good life, but when it came time for him to die Death told him, 'So, you have made so many people purge? Then you too will purge!' And he did purge, for days together, before getting release. And why? Because of the Law of Karma. Even though he cured many people his method of cure produced karma for him because he self-identified with it."

"Even his samadhi didn't save him from those karmas."

"Not at all! Some people to whom I tell this story complain to me that this does not seem fair. They say that the end that this old man was pursuing—the end of healing the sick—should justify the means he was using to obtain it. But I tell you again, there is no end so desirable that it will exempt you from enjoying the effects of the karmas you performed to achieve it. I am a perfect example of this. For years on end I have performed *basti* with hot water."

Basti, which means "enema," is performed by different means in Ayurveda and in Hatha Yoga. Vimalananda used the yogic method, using his abdominal muscles to suck water into his colon and swirl it around there before expelling it.

"One reason I do basti is to keep my insides clean. It is my internal bath, which helps to keep my awareness clear. Another reason I do basti is to prevent my food from going to form prostate fluid or sperms. Basti with hot water helps to send the food's juices to form ojas without any delay. The brain is a truly marvelous structure; it is a lake, a lake that is jellylike and full of ojas. In fact, the brain is your own personal Lake Manasarovara. Every brain cell is itself a lake of Amrita, with a mountain of knowledge—a Mount Kailash— contained within it."

"Right," I said. By combining basti with other spiritual practices he was able to obtain a maximum of ojas from a minimum of semen. Just as in the outer world Lord Shiva lives on Mount Kailash, which sits in Tibet just near Lake Manasarovara, even so in the inner world your personal Shiva—your consciousness—inhabits the mountain of knowledge within the lake of the brain's juices.

"I have done lots of basti," Vimalananda went on, "to keep my insides pure and to nourish my brain, and what is the result? The hot water has so thoroughly burned the lining of my intestine that it interferes with the assimilation of my food. So now when I really need good assimilation to regain my strength I find that my own purificatory practice is firing my ass."

"Hahaha," I responded—a good pun deserves a little compassionate laughter even when it hits close to home. I should have stayed silent, though, for it was my own ass which was next fired, thanks to my first interview on Indian TV. The interview, which was the outgrowth of a conference held in Bombay by the International Association for the Study of Traditional Asian Medicine, was held in *Marathi*, a language that I understand adequately but speak haltingly. I took the precaution, as I did for my second Marathi TV interview five years later, to have a script created and translated into grammatical Marathi. I then memorized it and delivered it with verve in a decent accent. The result was sufficiently successful that people still stop me on the street in Maharashtra to ask me if they have seen me on TV. When I admit that it was I they saw they then expect me to speak with them in fluent colloquial Marathi. There is no escape from the Law of Karma.

When the first interview was first screened I sat to watch it with Vimalananda and a couple of his 'children.' After the opening credits had rolled the interviewer asked me about the people who had most influenced my Ayurvedic studies. I responded by mentioning K. Narayana Baba of Hyderabad, who was instrumental in getting me admitted into the college; Dr. Vasant Lad, who helped me survive the college; and Vaidya B.P. Nanal, Poona's doyen of Ayurveda. When Vimalananda did not hear his name he asked me sharply, "Have you forgotten me?"

"Not at all," I shot back boldly. "But I don't want any new people coming to bother you with questions or ask for favors when you are not well."

"So what! Your acknowledgements were incomplete. This show does not deserve to be seen!" Then, without any warning, the TV's screen went blank. At first I thought he had vandalized our set, but the next day's *Times of India* reported that at the precise moment of Vimalananda's comment the power supply to Bombay TV's transmitter was mysteriously, inexplicably lost, interrupting broadcasts to the whole of Bombay for the rest of the evening. After Vimalananda read that story he exultantly had me read it myself, and taunted me with, "Now you see what happens when you fail to acknowledge your mentor!"

"All I wanted to do was to keep you from having any more trouble!" I retorted with cautious exasperation. "In the future I will always acknowledge you, if that's the way you want it, and you can go right ahead and live with the consequences. But there's nothing I can do about this interview. It's already in the can, and I don't quite know how I would explain to the producer that if he doesn't tape one more acknowledgement my mentor will continue to fire the ass of the TV station's power supply so that our program will never be seen!"

Vimalananda now began to laugh, and replied, "All right, my boy, all right, I won't interfere again—but don't forget the next time ..." One month later we watched the interview in its entirety. Since that day I have never neglected to give him credit where credit is due him.

One evening during the fortnight of my life as a groom I was walking slowly toward the ocean pondering a death under hooves when Param Singh drove by and offered me a lift as far as the Opera House. I thought that he must have some ulterior motive, but he only wanted to chat and to find out how Vimalananda was doing. I satisfied him by briefly outlining Vimalananda's physical condition. How could I explain to Param Singh, or to anyone else at the racecourse, that Vimalananda was growing more and more aloofly philosophical about life under the combined influences of two Sade Satis, multiple devotee shenanigans, and his Junior Guru Maharaj's whimsies?

Mamrabahen was also doing her best to make Vimalananda's life hell and it was beginning to show. "Mamrabahen is goading me to kill her," he would say, "but I'm not going to do so. She can kill me, if necessary, or be the cause of my death, but this curse is going to end this time around." When one day I cavilled about having to endure Mamrabahen's venom as well he retorted, "Don't you think you must be tangled up in this curse too, somehow? Otherwise why would she hate you so much? She hated you as soon as you two met."

"I keep asking you what I should do about this, and you never tell me to do anything."

"What you should do is to continue trying to remain calm. Eventually, if you are patient enough, your portion of the curse will dwindle. You may even be able to turn it into a blessing."

"What?"

"Why shouldn't it be possible to change a curse into a blessing? After all, both are forms of shakti. In fact, you can turn almost any curse into a blessing; the only question is how to do it."

"Well?"

"You can use one of the specific methods, if you know them. If you don't then the best thing to do is to find out who cursed you and patiently serve that individual. Do good service in a spirit of devotion. Don't even think about how long it might take. Just resolve to continue to serve for as long as necessary. There will come a time when the heart of your ill-wisher will be so overcome with love that it will melt. In that moment the change can be made."

"How am I going to find out who gave me this curse?"

"If you need to know you'll find it out."

In May of 1983 Vimalananda was feeling well enough to go to Poona to visit his horses. This time we carried with us Cawas Bilimoria, our long-time heart-patient friend from Bombay. After spending a couple of days at the stables Vimalananda and I drove out of Poona with Arzoo and Cawas to pay a social call on Mr. Chabbu Ranbuke, who had been Vimalananda's wrestling protegé toward the end of Vimalananda's career as a professional wrestler. Chabbu welcomed Vimalananda like a long-lost father and fed us the best mango juice that I have feasted on until today. After lunch we went on to a nearby town where lived an aged Muslim fakir whose skin had become so thin that the blood could be seen flowing through his vessels. Though the verbal conversation between Vimalananda and this holy man was unremarkable a diffuse sense of disturbance began to swirl within me as we departed. We drove past a favorite Ganesha shrine without stopping. When I turned to suggest that we halt there briefly Vimalananda pulled me up sharply and told me to keep my opinions to myself.

This was not like him at all, which further magnified my unrest. As we continued towards home my disquiet began to crystallize around the driving skills of the boy who sat behind the wheel of the car. Farokh, the 16-year-old son of Pesi and Fanny Sodabottliwala, was driving their car forward while turning his head backward to speak with Vimalananda. It was twilight. Forty-two kilometers from Poona, and five minutes after I reminded Farokh that most automobile accidents happen at twilight, he rammed us into the back end of a parked truck. So stunned that for a moment I could not speak, I pulled myself together sufficiently to turn and look at Vimalananda and Arzoo in the back seat. Great pain creased Vimalananda's face. Suddenly Cawas, who had been sitting next to me in the front seat, emerged from the wreck and lay down on the ground. Around him gathered a crowd of curious villagers, who started to shout, "He's dead! He's dead!"

"Go see if it's true!" commanded Vimalananda from behind me. "I promised his parents that I would take good care of him. What face will I have to show them if I have to tell them that he died because some young idiot was not watching the road in front of him?"

I would have loved to investigate Cawas's condition, but I was too firmly wedged into the front seat by the collapsed dashboard. I slowly dislodged myself, only to find that extensive bruises to my knees made it almost impossible to move. By the time I could could clamber out of the car Cawas was on his feet again and was shuffling back to see what had happened to the rest of us. We were all alive, though shaken and bruised. Vimalananda was worst off, with a couple of cracked bones and a severely strained heart, which, he said "felt as though it were about to explode." We flagged down a couple of cars to take us to Poona, and fell exhausted into bed on arrival.

Some days later when we were alone Vimalananda told me: "I was not too keen on going out that morning. Something just seemed wrong about the day. After Farokh showed up with the car, I realized that the force of our mutual karmas had gained too much momentum to easily stop. What to do? I decided that the best thing to do would be to go along with the ride that fate had prepared for us. Do you remember what I've always told you, Robby, about my attitude toward my fate?"

"You've always said that if you knew that you were fated to fall into a ditch one day and break your leg you would not wait for that day to come but would go out and find the ditch and jump into it straightaway to get the karma over with. Are you trying to tell me that you did that on this occasion, the only difference being that instead of jumping into a ditch you rammed a truck?"

"At first, when we met Chabbu, I thought that we'd be able to avoid trouble. But after we met that fakir I knew something bad was going to happen. I could tell that he had some shakti, and that he was going to interfere with our plans."

"Do you mean he cursed us? Or that his words or thoughts had the effect of a curse whether he wanted them to or not?"

Vimalananda shrugged his shoulders in assent. "What if he did? If he did it deliberately he'll have to pay for it, eventually. But how will that help us now?"

A meteor of annoyance flashed through the vault of my mind: "Did he do this to us because you challenged him somehow, like you usually do? Was that necessary?" I was all at once so agitated that I began to feel like relinquishing my power of speech.

"What did you expect me to do? Lie down and ask him to walk all over me?"

"But you didn't have to irritate him!" I sighed to myself, deeply. "Anyway, why did you refuse us a stop at the Ganesha temple?"

"By then I knew an accident was inevitable and didn't want poor Ganesha to be blamed. Have you forgotten that Arzoo, Cawas, and Farokh are all Parsis? Fine, all three of them have faith in our Indian deities. But what about their Parsi relatives? Few people are more bigoted than a bigoted Parsi. If we had had our accident just after we stopped at a temple some of these Parsi bigots would have been able to make a lot of noise about how impotent the Hindu gods are. They would have said that our gods couldn't even protect us after we asked them to. I didn't want that."

"So what was this whole drama? Was it just a matter of karmic abatement for all of us?"

"Let me be blunt: Farokh was destined to have died in an accident right about this time. When his parents have done so much for me shouldn't I do a little something for them? Do you have any idea of the pain of losing a child? I do; I've lost a son. For six months after my Ranu's death I was mad with grief, I tell you, off my head entirely. Farokh should have died, and I simply couldn't have that. I had been trying to whittle away at his karmas little by little so that the accident itself could be evaded. But his karmas were too strong and kept propelling him along. Then I decided to go along with his fate. By accompanying him I was able to manipulate some of his karmas, and some of yours too, and Cawas's and Arzoo's. It so happened that the fakir wanted to act as fate's instrument, which is fine with me. Let him deal with the majority of the karmas; why not? The main thing is that we were going to have the accident—and we did—but we all survived it. Isn't that good news for us all? The danger has passed for Farokh, for now, and he's been given such a good scare that he'll drive like a normal human being again for quite a while."

"But, dammit, you almost killed yourself!"

"I can't help that. What mother will not sacrifice herself for her children?"

The very next day came a phone call from Vimalananda's daughter announcing her impending marriage. After hanging up the phone Vimalananda turned to me and said, "I have seen this coming for months now. There is a peculiar astrological period going on right at the moment that I knew would make her fall in love and decide to marry. Look at her fate—she's only known this fellow for a week! She's going to get married; I can't avert it. But the marriage is not going to last." We made it back to Bombay in time for his daughter to call again to tell him it would be a closed wedding, for family only, and that I was not invited. I was happy not to go, but Vimalananda's physical condition would not permit him to travel alone in a taxi the twenty miles to the wedding's venue in North Bombay. He told her to either send a car for him or to have someone come down to South Bombay and bring him north in a taxi. It seemed to me an eminently reasonable request, but she hung up without comment. We did not hear from her again until the evening after the marriage, when she arrived unwillingly with her groom to request her father's blessings. After they left I asked Vimalananda suspiciously, "You didn't just create this accident to prevent yourself from being able to attend the ceremony, did you?"

He was silent for a moment before he said, "Well, not exactly, but it did give me a good excuse."

"Not exactly! Are you crazy!? I know you better than that. What was the big deal that made you break your bones just so you wouldn't have to attend her wedding?"

"I told you before, I saw this coming. We have just met this man for the first time and he looks very noble and refined, doesn't he?" I had to agree. "But I have known for a long time that my daughter is doomed to marry someone who will mistreat her. I want her to be able to escape that marriage whenever she needs to do so. When I go to weddings I always bring a coconut and have the bride and groom hold it together while I recite a mantra. After that procedure that marriage cannot be broken no matter how hard you may try to break it. What kind of father would I be if I did that for her and imprisoned her in an life of abuse? Would you have wanted that for her?"

No, certainly not; I recalled how effectively that mantra had worked for Shernaz and Behram. Indeed, Vimalananda's daughter left with her husband for his home on her wedding day. Eight months later—one month after Vimalananda's death—she hurried back home where she has remained ever since. Her husband, who had seemed so sweet on his surface, had begun to beat her almost as soon as the honeymoon ended and continued to beat her until she fled.

The combination of the physical trauma of the accident and the mental trauma of the wedding caused Vimalananda's health to take a pronounced downward turn, and in early June 1983 he was hospitalized for a month, to force him to rest. He was a great hit with doctors and fellow patients, all of whom were sorry to see him go when Roshni (now back from abroad) transported him back home.

By August he was healthy enough to make brief jaunts to Poona. In September 1983, as we stood near the northern end of the Poona racecourse in the brilliant afternoon sun, Vimalananda predicted his death by the end of the year. Facing southeast, toward the temple of Rama on the nearby Ramtekdi hill, he spoke clearly and firmly without any trace of dread or self-pity: "Immense changes are in store for the world. Lots of things that we take for granted will simply cease to exist and lots of things I have no interest in witnessing are heading our way. For example, now we have a new scourge in the world, the scourge of AIDS. Do you realize that AIDS has created thousands of Visha Kanyas, male and female, all over the world? Everyone who has AIDS is a Visha Kanya. Have unprotected sex with such a person, even once, and you may be doomed. Quite a strange fate, don't you think? Once only a few Visha Kanyas existed in the world, but now the world is going to be flooded with them.

"And this is just the beginning. Isn't it interesting that all religions have a time limit, and that the ending points of least three of these are approaching at about the same time, which happens to be now? Vallabhacharya said that his sect, which worships Lallu, the Baby Krishna, would last four hundred years; it is written that Islam will exist for only fourteen hundred years, which have just passed; and if Nostradamus' prophecies are to be believed, Christianity will be finished after two thousand years. And Buddhism and Jainism won't be spared this winnowing process either."

"Do you really pay that much attention to such prophecies?"

"No, and neither should you. In fact, you even have to be careful not to empower these prophecies when you repeat them, because that's a karma too. My point is that these prophecies agree that the world in general is deteriorating. Our job is to avoid deteriorating along with it, without making things worse in the world in general. All these people who fret about the end of the world are actually bringing the end nearer with their fretting! They would be do a lot better, for themselves and for the world, if they would spend their time remembering God instead. And they could best do that by focusing on the inevitable end of their own individual worlds: their own deaths.

"Everything has a natural time limit, including people. A human being is made of rnanubandhanas; they create our lives, and also bring them to a close. I have to be concerned about my own time limit because if I outlive my rnanubandhanas I will start creating new karmas, which will ruin me. Outliving my rnanubandhanas will force me to continue living in this body, which happens to be falling apart. I could do some rejuvenation on myself, but why? What do I have left here? One of the few things I used to look forward to was to spend some time each day with my little dog, and now she is gone."

I must have looked hurt, for he added, "I know that you love me sincerely; so does Roshni, and a few of the others. But no one has loved me like my animals have. I'm afraid that my two-legged friends have never been as loving and reliable as my four-legged friends have been. There is really nothing left for me here—and there are so many other places to play. It so happens that I already have another physical body, on this very planet; one that my mentors never wanted me to find. But I found it anyway, and I know that whenever I leave this one I will simply return to that one. It's that simple. I really have seen enough of this sort of life, and now that I am nearing the end of the set of karmas that I had to deal with when I was born it is time for me to die. I do not expect to see the beginning of 1984.

"I want you to remember one very, very important thing, Robby: Any time you try to impose your will on the universe you run the risk of creating a new karma whose repercussions may follow you for years, or for lifetimes. When you fail to live with reality, reality inevitably comes to live with you. I got back into racing just to indulge Mamrabahen. Little by little I became more involved in it. When I bred Redstone I thought that I had a Classic winner. I tried to help him along, and you saw the result. My mind was perverted when I asked that my Ranu die, and my mind was also perverted when I asked that my Redstone win."

He fell silent. I knew well that when Vimalananda's son Ranu lay dying of polio in Bombay Vimalananda had actually prayed that Ranu die, for he didn't want his sports-loving young son to live the cheerless life of a cripple. But this was the first time I was hearing that he had "helped" Redstone to win his Big Race. Now I really had no idea of what to say. When the wordlessness became too oppressive I threw out, "Maybe that race really is a hoodoo race."

"Maybe it is, and that is my point. If my mind had been perverted I would have believed that running my horse in a hoodoo race would be the best thing for him. It was just the slightest request—I'm telling you today, Robby—Redstone had just the slightest extra ethereal push, to guarantee his victory—and then everything went wrong with him because he had paid me back what he owed me before he was due to. I knew what could happen—had I not seen it with my buffaloes? But a tiny drop of preference just leaked out, and you saw the result. Let this be a lesson to you too: Never make the mistake of telling Nature what you want from Her. Let Her give you what is best from you, out of the endless bounty of Her unfathomable love."

"I will remember this. But I want to know if your mind was perverted on its own, or whether it had some help."

"All I can tell you is that Guru Maharaj doesn't want me in racing. He doesn't want me to be interested in anything except spirituality, which is as it should be, since he is my guru. But what he doesn't realize is that without something to attract my interest I am not going to be able to stay in this body.

I have other worlds to play about on, and I'll go there. But believe me, when I am gone, Guru Maharaj is going to regret it. He'll realize then what kind of toy he's lost. Mark my words, I'm going to make him cry."

On December 12, 1983, Vimalananda made us all cry.

EPILOGUE

THE FACTS OF VIMALANANDA'S dying are as easy to recount as they were tortuous to live through. Somehow I succeeded at cremating him at Bombay's Banganga Smashan, just as eight years and three months previously he had prophesied that I would. And, just as he had promised all those years ago, his wife and children did not come to watch the pyre, for their egos still smarted from his failure to attend his daughter's wedding. As the flames devoured him the mournful tones of his last request—"Precious Lord, Take My Hand," sung by Jim Reeves—ascended toward the heavens with the smoke. I kept rewinding the tape until when it finally snapped I concluded that he had had enough. Thereafter I sat silently, dreading the moment that the fire would die down and I would have to leave Vimalananda's hands behind me for good.

When Vimalananda decided to teach a lesson he was always prepared to suffer himself to drive his lesson home. His passage and its aftermath were the final lessons he could teach. They were delivered them with all the severity he could muster. Though Guru Maharaj shed no outer tears over his disciple's end I knew that Vimalananda's stiletto had indeed hit home. I visited Guru Maharaj in his southern eyrie at least once a year thereafter and on each occasion saw him shrinking further away from interest in external reality. Despite all the efforts of his well-meaning devotees he finally became totally fed up with physical existence and left his body on June 6, 1993.

Guru Maharaj's withdrawal from the world shocked but did not really surprise me, for Vimalananda was one of the few reasons he had for living. His departure did not blindside me, as Vimalananda's had. Though I had watched Vimalananda slowly deteriorate over the previous months I had also witnessed his sudden retreat from death's door on so many other occasions that I was certain that he would escape the noose again—or at the very least, rise again within a few hours of depature. When he did not I was thoroughly devastated, and passed the next several months in stupefied disengagement from life.

But life goes on. Though stunned I had to deal with that event's fallout. Soon it dawned on me that Vimalananda's death was not *his* death. He had been in such a hurry to go that he had elected to exit by suffering through the karmas of one Mr. Writer, a 99-year-old Parsi who wished to live to be a hundred. Mr. Writer was the uncle of Fanny Sodabottliwala who, with her husband Pesi, had served Vimalananda diligently on Mr. Writer's behalf that he might achieve his goal. Pesi and Fanny put on an excellent show, spending money freely on Vimalananda and on me without even an insinuation that they considered the sums they contributed to be loans instead of gifts. Less than a week after Vimalananda's cremation, however, Fanny shocked me with her sobbing over how much they had spent on him. Pesi, who had apparently itemized each expenditure, was moaning over how his business had not developed as speedily as Vimalananda had promised. Though a few months after Vimlananda's demise Mr. Writer did make it to 100 and then died, the Sodabottliwalas showed not the slightest thanks for Vimalananda's largesse toward either to her uncle or to her son Farokh, munificence which he had conferred at the expense of his own life.

Miss Bambhani also popped up to claim that she had paid Vimalananda more money than she was able to extract work from him. Bashermal, meanwhile, who Vimalananda used to call "my mature, mellow wine," who had been the most "senior" of Vimalananda's spiritual "children," underwent an inflation. Having concluded that Roshni and I should now obey him in the stead of our dear departed he attempted to impress us into submission by the unskillful means of imitating Vimalananda's evening talks. As neither of us could withstand the agonizing boredom of these well-meaning chats, we were overjoyed that the simple expedient of infuriating him caused him to give up on us as hopeless cases. His parting blessing was to direct his disciple Mundromal, the lawyer who was handling Vimalananda's will, to mishandle that document in such a way that Roshni, the executor and sole heir, ended up with nothing to inherit.

Kalubhai, Doshi, Harshbhai, and some of the others continued coming round to Roshni's place for a while to pay their respects to Vimalananda's photo until Mundromal's son began to claim that he was channeling Vimalananda's spirit. He set up one of the rooms in his flat to resemble Vimalananda's room, complete with an easy chair resembling the one into which Vimalananda had used to ease himself. Most of the "spiritual children" now shifted their focus to these channeling sessions. Roshni and I were also invited to attend, but both of us were certain that Vimalananda would never have deigned to tenant the body of such a mediocre individual. This certainty attained rock-like status when we learned that Mundromal's son had even kept a little dog, like Vimalananda's Lizoo, for the channeling sessions. But while Lizoo was a Pekinese, this canine was a Pomeranian. Vimalananda would never have sunk so low as to possess a Pom! I can hear his indignant bark now: "A Pom! What would I want with such a miserable breed of dog?"

Vimalananda's great hope, Redstone, died of equine cough in 1984. As executor Roshni then disposed of the remaining horses, keeping only Malika, Meherunnissa's daughter, racing in the name of Vimalananda's estate, for it was her desire to keep Vimalananda's colors active at the racecourse as long as she could. Ramakda went immediately to stud and produced two foals for the estate, both of which were sold. After winning a number of races, Malika was sold to a stud farm not long back, and then there were none.

Mamrabahen and Jhendu Kumar continue their interest in racing. In my capacity as Racing Agent for the Estate of the Late Mr. Vimalananda I began to accompany Roshni to the Paddock before races in which Malika was running, but I lost interest in the whole show on the afternoon that the disreputable Bapsi succeeded in rubbing suggestively against my leg as I strode through a crowd toward the Ring. Though Vimalananda had once declared that his cock would not get hard even if she jumped up and down on it, I had at one time thought she was rather cute, in a slatternly sort of way. On that day, though, I saw exactly what he meant, for when I looked into her eyes I saw naked, sticky lust, the kind of lust I had once seen in the "come hither" eyes of a debauched young male in Morocco. It was a clandestine, tawdry lust, one that smells of a rarely-aired room in which semen has been regularly and furtively ejaculated. Taking her frottage as a clear omen of what sort of circumstances lay in store for me if I continued my pilgrimages to the track I turned my energies elsewhere.

I continued for some years to make occasional tours of Bombay's stables to chew the fat with my friends there. Whenever I showed my face everyone who knew me invariably made me stop to reminisce about the days when it was a second home for me and "the old man." My visits ceased when the great doping scandal that rocked the Club to its very foundations closed those stables to casual visitors. It was a good time to escape; racing in today's India is growing hazardous to life and limb. In 1996 one famous jockey was threatened with death if he did not hook a horse and the daughter of another was kidnaped after he failed to boot home the favorite in a prestigious race. In 1997 two gunmen shot one bullet into the ground and two past the ear of Irish jockey Mark Gallagher outside the Bangalore Turf Club Gate. His ear required fifteen stitches to be made whole.

Like every individual I create my own universe among the many universes that coexist on this terrestrial globe. Like everyone else I continually find for myself the environment that my karmas require of me. The racecourse was a sizable slice of my universe for almost a decade, but when those karmas were done I left it to create a new cosmos for myself. Vimalananda remains a major part of this new universe and always will be, just as his Junior Guru Maharaj and Lord Shiva are ongoing residents therein. They are three of my constant companions on the long road of my life.

One of the daily practices Vimalananda suggested to me is contained in a verse from the *Shiva Manasa Puja* ("The Mental Worship of Shiva") that he used to recite each morning when he lived alone on Mount Girnar. In translation it goes something like this:

> You are the soul, O Lord of the Mountain-Born.
> The body's pranas are Your attendants, the body Your home;
> The sequence of enjoyment of sensory objects is
> Your worship, and sleep Your samadhi.
> All my movement is Your circumambulation,
> All praise is Your hymns;
> Whatever karmas I may perform, O Happiness-Bestower,
> I offer them all, without exception, to you as my worship.

Parvati, the "Mountain-Born," is the Kundalini Shakti, born from the range of mountains that the vertebrae form as they string together into the spine. Her Lord is Lord Shiva, the indwelling soul. Spiritual development occurs as Kundalini relinquishes her hold on the limited self and, turning her face toward her Lord, begins to act not from desire for personal gain but for the greater glory of That Which is Real. This creates true happiness. So long as I continue to realign my own Kundalini toward that soul I know that someone will correct every mistake I make and, dragging me out of whatever ditch in which I may have dropped, will return me to the path. This was the parting blessing of my friend-philosopher-guide, the token of his Aghori's love, the benediction he could bestow because he had so utterly devoted himself to offering himself to his Self. May the blessings of Shiva and Shakti attend everyone who seeks honestly to live up to the words of this verse, as Vimalananda did all the days of his extraordinary life.

And may those blessings fill them, as they filled Vimalananda, with the endless plenty of unconditional love.

GLOSSARY

Adya Shakti -lit. "first, original." Used as a synonym for the Adishakti, the first or original Shakti which manifests from the absolute and is the Mother of all the worlds.

Aghora - lit. "non-terrifying." Aghora is the most extreme of all Indian sects, concentrating on forcible conversion of a limited human personality into a divine personality.

Aghori - A practitioner of Aghora

Agni - "Fire"; the God Fire

Ahamkara - "I-maker"; the ego

Amrita - "Immortal"; nectar

Anjaneya - "Descendant of Anjani"; a name of Hanuman, the monkey king, because his mother was named Anjani

Apsaras - A class of semi-divine females who can change their shape at will; they move between water *(ap)* and clouds *(saras)*

Asura - "Demon, anti-god."

Atma(n) - The soul, the indwelling spirit which animates a living being. The Jivatma is the individual spirit which imagines itself trapped in a physical form and subject to the limitations of embodied existence. The Paramatma is the Universal Soul, the totality of spirit in the cosmos. All Jivas or Jivatmas belong to the Paramatma.

Avatara - "Descent, incarnation"; usually denoting one of the ten incarnations of Vishnu: Matsya (the fish), Kurma (the tortoise), Varaha (the boar), Narasimha (the man-lion), Vamana (the dwarf), Parashurama, Rama, Krishna, Buddha, and Kalki (the future incarnation)

Avishkara - Possession of one's body by an alien personality, especially that of a diety or saint

Bhakti - Religious or spiritual devotion

Brahmana - A member of the priestly class of society

Chillum - A pipe used to smoke marijuana or hashish mixed with tobacco. It is three or four inches long and is straight, tapering with a wide bowl to a thin mouth.

Darshana - The act of viewing a saint or diety; also, one of India's philosophical systems

Dattatreya - Name of a sage, son of Atri and Anasuya who was worshipped as a deity in the form of the triad Brahma, Vishnu, and Shiva

Deepaka - Name of a Raga (musical melody): the Kindling or Igniting Melody

Deva - "Deity, celestial being"

Dvapara Yuga - "Eon of one-half"; name of the third Yuga in the series of four, in which one-half of the dharma or righteousness of Satya Yuga remains. In Dvapara Yuga the primary sadhana and means of achieving desires is austerities *(tapas).*

Ganesha - The elephant-headed god, son of Shiva and Uma (*gana + isha*, lord of attendents)

Gati - "Gait, mode"; there are 108 gatis of sound *(nada)*. Numerologically 108 adds up to 9, the number of chakras in the body, according to Aghora. Which gati of nada one hears depends upon past karmas, present tendencies, ancestry, etc.

Gotra - 1) System of Vedic lineage ancestry, deriving from "protection of cows"; 2) "Protection for the senses"

Guna - lit. "qualities" or "attributes." The Three Gunas are the three fundamental attributes of conditional or limited existence: *Sattva* (equilibrium), *Rajas* (activity), and *Tamas* (inertia). In its purest state the mind is pure Sattva, and the two chief mental disturbances are Rajas (overactivity) and Tamas (inactivity).

Guru Droha - An offense or act of treachery against the guru

Guru Purnima - The full moon of the Indian month of Ashadha (usually in mid-July), during which the guru is worshipped

Halahala - The world-threatening poison drunk by Shiva that turned his throat blue

Hanuman - The mighty monkey of the *Ramayana* who is the archetype of the selfless devotee

Hiranyakashipu - A great demon king, father of Prahlada (q.v.), was eviscerated by Narasimha, the man-lion avatara of Vishnu

Hiranyaksha - A demon king, elder brother of Hiranyakashipu (q.v.), was killed by Varaha, the boar avatara of Vishnu

Homa - General term for any ritual in which offering into a consecrated fire is the primary action

Jiva - The individual personality which undergoes rebirth, because the karmas stored in the causal body need a physical body to permit their expression. (see *Atma*).

Jnana - Transcendent wisdom. Knowledge *(Vidya)* is an outward projection or objectivization of this innate, living wisdom

Jnani - One who has attained ordinary spiritual knowledge

Kali Yuga - The fourth of the four ages through which the cosmos passes in cycles of 4,320,000 years. Kali Yuga is supposed to last 432,000 years, and is characterized by lack of interest in spirituality among the populace, which leads to materialism, atheism, and the perpetuation of various cruelties by stronger beings onto weaker ones.

Kaula - Followers of Tantra who perform the practice of Rasa Vidya in order to turn Kundalini into Kula Kundalini (freed kundalini)

Kedara - Name of a Raga, the "Field Melody", sung to attract Krishna

Krida - "Play"; particularly unconscious play, such as *rati krida* ("love play"). Krida is controlled by someone or something other than the being who is playing. In love play, the glands and the genitals do the controlling, not the two people who romance each other.

Kshatriya - "Warrior"; a member of the warrior castes

Kundalini - Cosmic energy that manifests along the spine and within the chakras; the source and force of all experience

Lila - "Cosmic play"; distinct from Krida (q.v.). The divine play of Rishis and deities, especially Krishna and Rama, is called Lila, cosmic pastimes in which they are always in control.

Mahabharata - One of India's two great epic poems (the other being the *Ramayana)*

Mahakala - The God of Death

Mahalakshmi - The goddess of wealth and prosperity; the Bombay Racecourse is called "Mahalakshmi" in honor of a nearby temple of that goddess

Mahapurusha - "Great Soul"; refers to any being who has become immortal as a result of sadhana (q.v.). Rishis (q.v.), Munis (q.v.), Naths and Siddhas are all Mahapurushas.

Maharaj - "Great King"; also a common designation of a saint, who has achieved dominion over the spiritual world

Maha Shiva Ratri - "Great Night", otherwise called Maha Ratri, occurring on the night before the new moon during the lunar month of *Magha* (February or early March)

Maya - "Illusion"; usually indicates cosmic illusion

Megha - "Cloud"; name of a raga. If one wants rain, one plays Megha in a certain way and rain will come.

Moksha - Liberation

Mudra - A positioning of the hand or body in a particular way to channel and thus cultivate one's prana and consciousness

Muni - An advanced being (yet lower than a Rishi [q.v.]), who communicates telepathically or through the eyes

Nara Bali - Human *(nara)* sacrifice *(bali)*

Narasimha - "Man-lion", the name of this avatara of Vishnu

Narayana -A name of God, esp. of Vishnu

Nath - "Lord"; a highly advanced being, an Aghori

Niyama - The second limb of yoga, internal disciplilne

Ojas - That essence of physical energy which produces the aura as well as immunity (Ayurveda)

Paan -A common digestive consisting of areca nut and other ingredients wrapped in the highly astringent betel leaf

Para Vani - "Beyond"; the fourth and highest level of speech, purely telepathic. Only Rishis can access Para.

Parashurama - "Rama with the axe"; the sixth Avatara of Vishnu

Pitri Tarpana - A ritual performed for a deceased human, usually a father or mother or other progenitor, to satisfy any lingering cravings that individual might have had. Properly performed, this assures the individual an auspicious rebirth and enables him or her to maintain their spiritual progression.

Prahlada - Son of the demon king Hiranyakashipu (q.v.), was a devotee of Vishnu

Prakriti - Nature, the field in which manifestation arises. In the limited human sense prikriti is one's 'first action' *(pra + kriti)*, the choice of action which one naturally, instinctively makes when confronted by a situation that requires action.

Prana - "Breath life force." The five major breaths are: *prana* (the process of breathing as well as the breath that regulates the organs in the head), *apana* (the downward moving breath that regulates evacuation), *samana* (the evenly distributing breath that regulates digestion), *vyana* (the all-pervasive breath that provides movement of the limbs and joints), and *udana* (the upward moving breath through which the spirit departs at death).

Prasada - Any substance, usually food, which has been offered to a deity or saint, or to the image of a deity or saint, which is then partaken of by a disciple or devotee. Prasada is supposed to contain a tiny amount of the deity's or saint's *shakti*, which can exert a spiritualizing effect on the partaker.

Purusha - Absolute Reality

Rasa - "Flavor, emotion"

Rasa Vidya - "Knowledge of flavor"; Tantric alchemy

Ravana - Name of the demon king who abducted Rama's wife Sita, later killed by Rama

Rishi - lit. "Seer." Anything a Rishi sees or perceives becomes reality, because a Rishi is an ethereal being of the highest class, one who is almost totally unlimited, who can travel anywhere in the cosmos and can do anything. The Rishis "speak" the hymns of the Vedas, from which all the knowledge of ancient India is derived.

Rnanubandhana - The bondage of karmic debt

Roti - Generic name for Indian bread, usually indicating a chappati.

Rudra - lit. "the Crier," or "He Who makes others cry." Rudra is the ancient name for Shiva, the god of death, and is so called because he makes everyone cry who comes into contact with Him, because he separates them from their limited existence, to which they are tightly attached.

Sadhaka - One who practices a sadhana

Sadhana - Any spiritual practice. Aghora Sadhana is designed to replace the Aghori's personality with his deity's personality by creation of the deity's form in the Aghori's subtle body.

Sadhu - "A good person"; a wandering religious mendicant

Samadhi - A state of profound or one-pointed consciousness; trance

Samsara - The cycle of birth and death, ensnarement in the web of worldly existence

Samskara - Personality characteristic

Sannyasa - "Coma"; renunciation of the world

Shudra - "Laborer"; member of the hereditary castes of laborers

Siddha - An "accomplished one"; anyone who has obtained a Siddhi, or supernatural accomplishment is a Siddhi. Vimalananda restricted his use of the word Siddhi to indicate those beings who have achieved immortality.

Siddhi - "Perfection, accomplishment"; especially success at sadhana

Six Tastes - An Ayurvedic category: sweet, sour, salty, bitter, pungent or spicy, and astringent

Smashan - A charnal ground; an area in which dead bodies are burned or buried. This word is derived from "ashmashana," or "place where rocks lie," which suggests that burial was once more common in India than it now is.

Svabhava - One's innate nature, the thing that determines how one relates to one's surroundings. Roughly speaking, *prakriti* represents the root and *svabhava* the fruit of human awareness.

Vajroli - A yogic practice in which fluid is sucked into the penis or vagina by muscular force. During the sex act, Vajroli can be used to suck up the partner's secretions for both physical and spiritual benefit.

Vamana - The dwarf incarnation of Vishnu who rescued the world from the designs of the demon king Bali

Varaha - The boar Avatara of Vishnu

Vidya - "Knowledge"

Vijnana - Practical spiritual knowledge, higher than jnana. In vijnana one becomes a Siddha (q.v.), an immortal, because the ego has become absolutely purified.

Vijnani - One who possesses Vijnana

Vimalananda - "Stainless bliss"; a proper name

Visha - "Poison"

Visha Kanya - "poison damsel" (*visha* = poison); her touch means death

Wah - An exclamation of amazement, surprise or revelation

Yajna - Vedic fire ritual. In yajna, deities in ethereal worlds are invoked, then fed with the fragrance of smoke from the various burnt offerings.

Yantra - A diagram which acts as a receptacle for the power of a mantra. Tantra is the ritual by which the Yantra is empowered by the mantra. Any substance can be used for a Yantra, but Vimalananda averred that the best of all possible Yantras is the human body.

~ In The Series ~

AGHORA, At The Left Hand Of God
AGHORA II: Kundalini
AGHORA III: The Law Of Karma

for a complete list of titles
please write the respective publishers:

BROTHERHOOD OF LIFE, INC.
110 Dartmouth SE
Albuquerque, New Mexico 87106
Internet: www.brotherhoodoflife.com

SADHANA PUBLICATIONS
PO Box 365
Floresville, Texas